THE
BIG BOOK
OF
DASHBOARDS

THE
BIG BOOK
OF
DASHBOARDS

Visualizing Your Data
Using Real-World
Business Scenarios

STEVE WEXLER | JEFFREY SHAFFER | ANDY COTGREAVE

WILEY

Published by John Wiley & Sons, Inc., Hoboken, New Jersey.

Published simultaneously in Canada.

For general information on our other products and services or for technical support, please contact our Customer Care Department within the United States at (800) 762-2974, outside the United States at (317) 572-3993 or fax (317) 572-4002.

Wiley publishes in a variety of print and electronic formats and by print-on-demand. Some material included with standard print versions of this book may not be included in e-books or in print-on-demand. If this book refers to media such as a CD or DVD that is not included in the version you purchased, you may download this material at http://booksupport.wiley.com. For more information about Wiley products, visit www.wiley.com.

Library of Congress Cataloging-in-Publication Data

Names: Wexler, Steve, author. | Shaffer, Jeffrey, author. | Cotgreave, Andy, author.
Title: The big book of dashboards : visualizing your data using real-world
   business scenarios / Steve Wexler, Jeffrey Shaffer, Andy Cotgreave.
Description: Hoboken : Wiley, 2017. | Includes index.
Identifiers: LCCN 2016052146| ISBN 9781119282716 (paperback) | ISBN
   9781119282785 (Adobe PDF) | ISBN 9781119282730 (epub)
Subjects: LCSH: Dashboards (Management information systems) | Organizational
   effectiveness—Evaluation. | Management—Evaluation. | BISAC: BUSINESS &
   ECONOMICS / Business Communication / Meetings & Presentations.
Classification: LCC HD30.213 .W43 2017 | DDC 658.4/038011—dc23 LC record available at
https://lccn.loc.gov/2016052146

Printed in the United States of America.

10 9 8 7

Contents

Acknowledgments

From the three of us

Stephen Few, whose books have made a profound and lasting impression on us.

Alberto Cairo for his invaluable feedback and for his leadership in the data visualization community.

Our technical reviewers greatly improved our first drafts. Thanks to Troy Magennis, Andy Kirk, Jon Schwabish, Ariel Pohoryles, Trudy Weiss Craig, Michael Fry, Andy Kriebel, and a special thanks to Cole Nussbaumer Knaflic for introducing us to the Wiley team and who went far beyond our expectations with her detailed edits and comments.

All the contributors to this book gave significant time to tweak their dashboards according to our requests. We thank you for allowing us to include your work in the book.

Thanks, also, to Mark Boone, KK Molugu, Eric Duell, Chris DeMartini, and Bob Filbin for their efforts.

Our stellar team at Wiley: acquisitions editor Bill Falloon for fighting so hard on our behalf; editor Christina Verigan for her deft reworking and invaluable help optimizing flow; senior production editor Samantha Hartley for overseeing the daunting process of making this book a beautiful, tangible thing; copy editor Debra Manette for such detailed editing and insights; proofreader Hope Breeman for her meticulous proof check; the team at WordCo for a comprehensive index and marketing manager Heather Dunphy for her exceptional expertise in connecting author with audience.

From Steve

My wife, Laura, and my daughters, Janine and Diana, for the never-ending support and love.

Ira Handler and Brad Epstein, whose friendship, encouragement, and example have been a godsend for the past dozen years.

Joe Mako, who has always been willing to help me with "the difficult stuff" and provided much needed encouragement when I was starting out.

The Princeton University Triangle Club, where I learned how to bring talented people together to make wonderful things. Without my experiences there I don't know if I would have had the insight and ability to recruit my fellow authors.

Jeff and Andy, who not only made the book way better than it would have been had I tackled it on my own, but for providing me with one of the most rewarding and enriching experiences of my career. Your abilities, candor, humor, grit, patience, impatience, thoughtfulness, and leadership made for a remarkable ride.

From Andy

I would like to thank Steve and Jeff for approaching me to join this project. I'd been procrastinating on writing a book for many years, and the opportunity to work with two passionate, skilled leaders was the trigger I needed to get going. I would like to thank them both for many hours of constructive debate (argument?) over the rights and wrongs of all aspects of dashboards and data visualization. It has been an enriching experience.

Finally, to Liz, my wife, and my daughters, Beatrice and Lucy. Thank you for your support and the freedom to abandon you all on weekends, mornings, and evenings in order to compete this project. I could not have done it without you.

From Jeff

Thank you, Steve and Andy. It was a pleasure working with you guys. I will miss the collaboration, especially our many hours of discussion about data visualization and dashboard design.

A special thank you to Mary, my wife, and to Nina and Elle, my twin daughters, for sacrificing lots of family time over many long nights and weekends. I would not have been able to complete this project without your support.

About the Authors

Steve Wexler has worked with ADP, Gallup, Deloitte, Convergys, Consumer Reports, *The Economist*, ConEd, D&B, Marist, Tradeweb, Tiffany, McKinsey & Company, and many other organizations to help them understand and visualize their data. Steve is a Tableau Zen Master, Iron Viz Champion, and Tableau Training Partner.

His presentations and training classes combine an extraordinary level of product mastery with the real-world experience gained through developing thousands of visualizations for dozens of clients. In addition to his recognized expertise in data visualization and Tableau, Steve has decades of experience as a successful instructor in all areas of computer-based technology. Steve has taught thousands of people in both large and small organizations and is known for conducting his seminars with clarity, patience, and humor.

Website: DataRevelations.com

Jeffrey A. Shaffer is Vice President of Information Technology and Analytics at Recovery Decision Science and Unifund. He is also Adjunct Professor at the University of Cincinnati, where he teaches Data Visualization and was named the 2016 Outstanding Adjunct Professor of the Year.

He is a regular speaker on the topic of data visualization, data mining, and Tableau training at conferences, symposiums, workshops, universities, and corporate training programs. He is a Tableau Zen Master, and was the winner of the 2014 Tableau Quantified Self Visualization Contest, which led him to compete in the 2014 Tableau Iron Viz Contest. His data visualization blog was on the shortlist for the 2016 Kantar Information is Beautiful Awards for Data Visualization Websites.

Website: DataPlusScience.com

Andy Cotgreave is Technical Evangelist at Tableau Software. He has over 10 years' experience in data visualization and business intelligence, first honing his skills as an analyst at the University of Oxford. Since joining Tableau in 2011, he has helped and inspired thousands of people with technical advice and ideas on how to build a data-driven culture in a business.

In 2016 he ran the MakeoverMonday (http://www.makeovermonday.co.uk/) project with Andy Kriebel, a social data project which saw over 500 people make 3,000 visualizations in one year. The project received an honourable mention in the Dataviz

Project category of the 2016 Kantar Information is Beautiful Awards.

Andy has spoken at conferences around the world, including SXSW, Visualized, and Tableau's customer conferences. He writes a column for *Computerworld*, Living with Data (http://www.computerworld.com/blog/living-data/), as well as maintaining his own blog, GravyAnecdote.com.

Website: GravyAnecdote.com

Introduction

We wrote *The Big Book of Dashboards* for anyone tasked with building or overseeing the development of business dashboards. Over the past decade, countless people have approached us after training sessions, seminars, or consultations, shown us their data, and asked: *"What would be a really good way to show this?"*

These people faced a specific business predicament (what we call a "scenario") and wanted guidance on how to best address it with a dashboard. In reviewing dozens of books about data visualization, we were surprised that, while they contained wonderful examples showing why a line chart often works best for time-series data and why a bar chart is almost always better than a pie chart, none of them matched great dashboards with real-world business cases. After pooling our experience and enormous collection of dashboards, we decided to write our own book.

How This Book Is Different

This book is not about the fundamentals of data visualization. That has been done in depth by many amazing authors. We want to focus on proven, real-world examples and why they succeed.

However, if this is your first book about the topic of data visualization, we do provide a primer in Part I with everything you need to know to understand how the charts in the scenarios work. We also dearly hope it whets your appetite for more, which is why this section finishes with our recommended further reading.

How This Book Is Organized

The book is organized into three parts.

Part I: A Strong Foundation. This part covers the fundamentals of data visualization and provides our crash course on the foundational elements that give you the vocabulary you need to explore and understand the scenarios.

Part II: The Scenarios. This is the heart of the book, where we describe dozens of different business scenarios and then present a dashboard that "solves" the challenges presented in those scenarios.

Part III: Succeeding in the Real World. The chapters in this part address problems we've encountered and anticipate you may encounter as well. With these chapters—distilled from decades of real-world experience—we hope to make your journey quite a bit easier and a lot more enjoyable.

How to Use This Book

We encourage you to look through the book to find a scenario that most closely matches what you are tasked with visualizing. Although there might not be an exact match, our goal is to present enough scenarios that you can find something that will address your needs. The internal conversation in your head might go like this:

"Although my data isn't exactly the same as what's in this scenario, it's close enough, and this dashboard really does a great job of helping me and others see and understand that data. I think we should use this approach for our project as well."

For each scenario we present the entire dashboard at the beginning of the chapter, then explore how individual components work and contribute to the whole.

By organizing the book based on these scenarios and offering practical and effective visualization examples, we hope to make *The Big Book of Dashboards* a trusted resource that you open when you need to build an effective business dashboard. To ensure you get the most out of these examples, we have included a visual glossary at the back of this book. If you come across an unfamiliar term, such as "sparkline," you can look it up and see an illustration.

We also encourage you to spend time with *all* the scenarios and the proposed solutions as there may be some elements of a seemingly irrelevant scenario that may apply to your own needs.

For example, Chapter 11 shows a dashboard used by a team in the English Premier League to help players understand their performance. Your data might have nothing to do with sports, but the dashboard is a great example of showing current and historical performance. (See Figure I.1.) That might be something you have to do with your data. Plus, if you skip one scenario, you might miss a great example of the exact chart you need for your own solution.

We also encourage you to browse the book for motivation. Although a scenario may not be a perfect match, the thought process and chart choices may inspire you.

Succeeding in the Real World

In addition to the scenarios, an entire section of the book is devoted to addressing many practical and psychological factors you will encounter in your work. It's great to have theory- and evidenced-based research at your disposal, but what will you do when somebody asks you to make your dashboard "cooler" by adding packed bubbles and donut charts?

The three of us have a combined 30-plus years of hands-on experience helping people in hundreds of organizations build effective visualizations. We have fought (and sometimes lost) many "best practices" battles. But by having endured these struggles, we bring an uncommon empathy to the readers of this book.

We recognize that at times readers will be asked to create dashboards and charts that exemplify bad practice. For example, a client or a department head may stipulate using a particular combination of colors or demand a chart type that is against evidence-based data visualization best practices.

We hear you. We've been there.

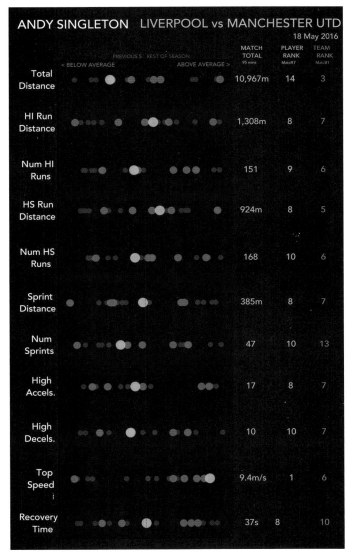

Although the dashboard in Figure I.1 pertains to sports, the techniques are universal. Here the latest event is in yellow, the five most recent events are in red, and older events are in a muted gray. Brilliant.

FIGURE I.1   A player summary from an English Premier League Club

(Note: Fake data is used.)

We've faced many of the hurdles you will encounter and the concepts you will grapple with in your attempt to build dashboards that are informative, enlightening, and engaging. The essays in this section will help smooth the way for you by offering suggestions and alternatives for these issues.

What to Do and What *Not* to Do

Although the book is an attempt to celebrate good examples, we'll also show plenty of *bad* examples. We guarantee you will see this kind of work out in the wild, and you may even be asked to emulate it. We mark these "bad" examples with the cat icon shown in Figure I.2 so that you don't have to read the surrounding text to determine if the chart is something you should emulate or something you should avoid.

FIGURE I.2 If you see this icon, it means don't make a chart like this one.

Illustration by Eric Kim

What Is a Dashboard?

Ask 10 people who build business dashboards to define a dashboard and you will probably get 10 different definitions. For the purpose of this book, our definition is as follows:

> A dashboard is a visual display of data used to monitor conditions and/or facilitate understanding.

This is a broad definition, and it means that we would consider all of the examples listed below to be dashboards:

- An interactive display that allows people to explore worker compensation claims by region, industry, and body part
- A PDF showing key measures that gets e-mailed to an executive every Monday morning
- A large wall-mounted screen that shows support center statistics in real time
- A mobile application that allows sales managers to review performance across different regions and compare year-to-date sales for the current year with the previous year

Even if you don't consider every example in this book a true dashboard, we think you will find the discussion and analysis around each of the scenarios helpful in building your solutions. Indeed, we can debate the definition until we are blue in the face, but that would be a horrible waste of effort as it simply isn't that important. What is important—make that *essential*—is understanding how to combine different elements (e.g., charts, text, legends, filters, etc.) into a cohesive and coordinated whole that allows people to see and understand their data.

Final Thought: There Are No Perfect Dashboards

You will not find any perfect dashboards in this book.

In our opinion, there is no such thing as a perfect dashboard. You will never find one perfect collection of charts that ideally suits every person who may encounter it. But, although they may not be perfect, the dashboards we showcase in the book successfully help people see and understand data in the real world.

The dashboards we chose all have this in common: Each one demonstrates some great ideas in a way that is relevant to the people who need to understand them. In short, they all serve the end users. Would we change some of the dashboards? Of course we would, and we weigh in on what we would change in the author commentary at the end of each scenario. Sometimes we think a chart choice isn't ideal; other times, the layout isn't quite right; and in some cases, the interactivity is clunky or difficult. What we recognize is that every set of eyes on a dashboard will judge the work differently, which is something you also should keep in mind. Where you see perfection, others might see room for improvement. The challenge all the dashboard designers in this book have faced is balancing a dashboard's presentation and objectives with time and efficiency. It's not an easy spot to hit, but with this book we hope to make it easier for you.

Steve Wexler

Jeffrey Shaffer

Andy Cotgreave

PART I

A STRONG
FOUNDATION

Chapter 1

Data Visualization:
A Primer

This book is about real-world dashboards and why they succeed. In many of the scenarios, we explain how the designers use visualization techniques to contribute to that success. For those new to the field, this chapter is a primer on data visualization. It provides enough information for you to understand why we picked many of the dashboards. If you are more experienced, this chapter recaps data visualization fundamentals.

Why Do We Visualize Data?

Let's see why it's vital to visualize numbers by beginning with Table 1.1. There are four groups of numbers, each with 11 pairs. In a moment, we will create a chart from them, but before we do, take a look at the numbers. What can you see? Are there any discernible differences in the patterns or trends among them?

Let me guess: You don't really see anything clearly. It's too hard.

Before we put the numbers in a chart, we might consider their statistical properties. Were we to do that, we'd find that the statistical properties of each group of numbers are very similar. If the table doesn't show anything and statistics don't reveal much, what happens when we *plot* the numbers? Take a look at Figure 1.1.

Now do you see the differences? *Seeing* the numbers in a chart shows you something that tables and some statistical measures cannot. We visualize data to harness the incredible power of our visual system to spot relationships and trends.

This brilliant example is the creation of Frank Anscombe, a British statistician. He created this set

TABLE 1.1   Table with four groups of numbers: What do they tell you?

Group A		Group B		Group C		Group D	
x	y	x	y	x	y	x	y
10.00	8.04	10.00	9.14	10.00	7.46	8.00	6.58
8.00	6.95	8.00	8.14	8.00	6.77	8.00	5.76
13.00	7.58	13.00	8.74	13.00	12.74	8.00	7.71
9.00	8.81	9.00	8.77	9.00	7.11	8.00	8.84
11.00	8.33	11.00	9.26	11.00	7.81	8.00	8.47
14.00	9.96	14.00	8.10	14.00	8.84	8.00	7.04
6.00	7.24	6.00	6.13	6.00	6.08	8.00	5.25
4.00	4.26	4.00	3.10	4.00	5.39	19.00	12.50
12.00	10.84	12.00	9.13	12.00	8.15	8.00	5.56
7.00	4.82	7.00	7.26	7.00	6.42	8.00	7.91
5.00	5.68	5.00	4.74	5.00	5.73	8.00	6.89

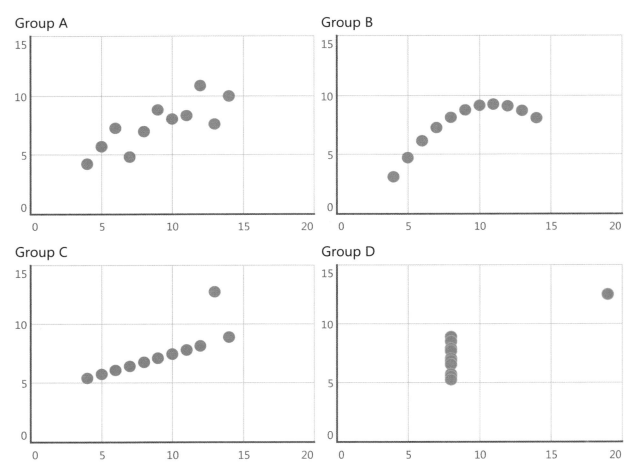

FIGURE 1.1   Now can you see a difference in the four groups?

of numbers—called "Anscombe's Quartet"—in his paper "Graphs in Statistical Analysis" in 1973. In the paper, he fought against the notion that "numerical calculations are exact, but graphs are rough."

Another reason to visualize numbers is to help our memory. Consider Table 1.2, which shows sales numbers for three categories, by quarter, over a four-year period. What trends can you see?

Identifying trends is as hard as it was with Anscombe's Quartet. To read the table, we need to look up every value, one at a time. Unfortunately, our short-term memories aren't designed to store many pieces of information. By the time we've reached the fourth or fifth number, we will have forgotten the first one we looked at.

Let's try a trend line, as shown in Figure 1.2.

TABLE 1.2   What are the trends in sales?

Category	2013 Q1	2013 Q2	2013 Q3	2013 Q4	2014 Q1	2014 Q2	2014 Q3	2014 Q4
Furniture	$463,988	$352,779	$338,169	$317,735	$320,875	$287,934	$319,537	$324,319
Office Supplies	$232,558	$290,055	$265,083	$246,946	$219,514	$202,412	$198,268	$279,679
Technology	$563,866	$244,045	$432,299	$461,616	$285,527	$353,237	$338,360	$420,018
Category	2015 Q1	2015 Q2	2015 Q3	2015 Q4	2016 Q1	2016 Q2	2016 Q3	2016 Q4
Furniture	$307,028	$273,836	$290,886	$397,912	$337,299	$245,445	$286,972	$313,878
Office Supplies	$207,363	$183,631	$191,405	$217,950	$241,281	$286,548	$217,198	$272,870
Technology	$333,002	$291,116	$356,243	$386,445	$386,387	$397,201	$359,656	$375,229

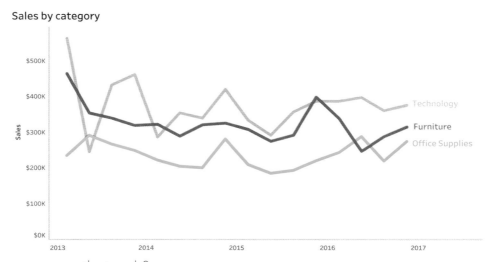

FIGURE 1.2   Now can you see the trends?

Now we have much better insight into the trends. Office supplies has been the lowest-selling product category in all but two quarters. Furniture trends have been dropping slowly over the time period, except for a bump in sales in 2015 Q4 and a rise in the last two quarters. Technology sales have mostly been the highest but were particularly volatile at the start of the time period.

The table and the line chart each visualized the same 48 data points, but only the line chart lets us see the trends. The line chart turned 48 data points into three chunks of data, each containing 16 data points. Visualizing the data hacks our short-term memory; it allows us to interpret large volumes of data instantly.

How Do We Visualize Data?

We've just looked at some examples of the power of visualizing data. Now we need to move on to how we build the visualizations. To do that, we first need to look at two things: preattentive attributes and types of data.

Preattentive Attributes

Visualizing data requires us to turn data into marks on a canvas. What kind of marks make the most sense? One answer lies in what are called "preattentive attributes." These are things our brains process in milliseconds, before we pay attention to everything else. There are many different types. Let's look at an example.

Look at the numbers in Figure 1.3. How many 9s are there?

How did you do? It's easy to answer the question—you just look at all the values and count the 9s—but it takes a long time. We can make one change to the grid and make it very easy for you. Have a look at Figure 1.4.

Now the task is easy. Why? Because we changed the color: 9s are red, and all the other numbers are light gray.

Color differences pop out. It's as easy to find one red 9 on a table of hundreds of digits as it is on a 10-by-10 grid. Think about that for a moment: Your brain registers the red 9s before you consciously addressed the grid to count them. Check out the grid of 2,500 numbers in Figure 1.5. Can you see the 9?

It's easy to spot the 9. Our eyes are amazing at spotting things like this.

```
2 2 5 6 7 1 1 6 9 1
9 1 7 5 5 5 6 2 5 9
4 5 2 9 6 9 7 6 4 6
8 1 5 7 8 5 6 6 6 7
7 2 3 6 8 9 1 7 9 1
3 8 6 8 4 5 6 9 4 5
4 9 9 2 3 7 1 9 1 2
3 7 8 1 6 1 5 6 1 6
5 6 6 8 6 6 9 1 2 6
3 2 4 2 6 9 4 2 7 1
```

FIGURE 1.3   How many 9s are there?

```
2 2 5 6 7 1 1 6 9 1
9 1 7 5 5 5 6 2 5 9
4 5 2 9 6 9 7 6 4 6
8 1 5 7 8 5 6 6 6 7
7 2 3 6 8 9 1 7 9 1
3 8 6 8 4 5 6 9 4 5
4 9 9 2 3 7 1 9 1 2
3 7 8 1 6 1 5 6 1 6
5 6 6 8 6 6 9 1 2 6
3 2 4 2 6 9 4 2 7 1
```

FIGURE 1.4   Now it's easy to count the 9s.

FIGURE 1.5 There is a single 9 in this grid of 2,500 numbers. We wager you saw it before you started reading any other numbers on this page.

```
2   2   5   6   7   1   1   6   9   1
9   1   7   5   5   5   6   2   5   9
4   5   2   9   6   9   7   6   4   6
8   1   5   7   8   5   6   6   6   7
7   2   3   6   8   9   1   7   9   1
3   8   6   8   4   5   6   9   4   5
4   9   9   2   3   7   1   9   1   2
3   7   8   1   6   1   5   6   1   6
5   6   6   8   6   6   9   1   2   6
3   2   4   2   6   9   4   2   7   1
```

FIGURE 1.6   Differences in size are easy to see too.

```
2   2   5   6   7   1   1   6   9   1
9   1   7   5   5   5   6   2   5   9
4   5   2   9   6   9   7   6   4   6
8   1   5   7   8   5   6   6   6   7
7   2   3   6   8   9   1   7   9   1
3   8   6   8   4   5   6   9   4   5
4   9   9   2   3   7   1   9   1   2
3   7   8   1   6   1   5   6   1   6
5   6   6   8   6   6   9   1   2   6
3   2   4   2   6   9   4   2   7   1
```

FIGURE 1.7   Coloring every digit is nearly as bad as having no color.

Color (in this case, hue) is one of several *preattentive attributes*. When we look at a scene in front of us, or a chart, we process these attributes in under 250 milliseconds. Let's try out a couple more preattentive features with our table of 9s. In Figure 1.6, we've made the 9s a different size from the rest of the figures.

Size and hue: Aren't they amazing? That's all very well when counting the 9s. What if our task is to count the frequency of *each* digit? That's a slightly more realistic task, but we can't just use a different color or size for each digit. That would defeat the preattentive nature of the single color. Look at the mess that is Figure 1.7.

It's not a complete disaster: If you're looking for the 6s, you just need to work out that they are red and then scan quickly for those. Using one color on a visualization is highly effective to make one category stand out. Using a few colors, as we did in Figure 1.2 to distinguish a small number of categories, is fine too. Once you're up to around eight to ten categories, however, there are too many colors to easily distinguish one from another.

To count each digit, we need to aggregate. Visualization is, at its core, about encoding aggregations, such as frequency, in order to gain insight. We need to move away from the table entirely and encode the frequency of each digit. The most effective way is to use length, which we can do in a bar chart. Figure 1.8 shows the frequency of each digit. We've also colored the bar showing the number 9.

Since the task is to count the 9s in the data source, the bar chart is one of the best ways to see the results. This is because length and position are best for quantitative comparisons. If we extend the example one final time and consider which numbers are most common, we could sort the bars, as shown in Figure 1.9.

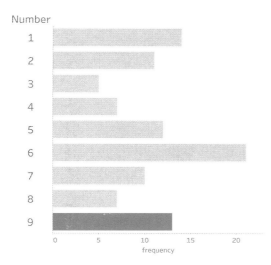

Number

FIGURE 1.8 There are 13 9s.

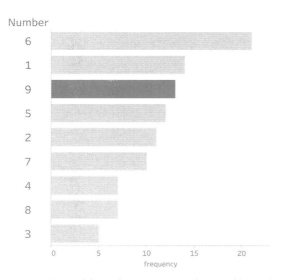

Number

FIGURE 1.9 Sorted bar chart using color and length to show how many 9s are in our table.

This series of examples with the 9s reemphasizes the importance of visualizing data. As with Anscombe's Quartet, we went from a difficult-to-read table of numbers to an easy-to-read bar chart. In the sorted bar chart, not only can we count the 9s (the original task), but we

also know that 9 was the third most common digit in the table. We can also see the frequency of every other digit.

The series of examples we just presented used color, size, and length to highlight the 9s. These are three of many preattentive attributes. Figure 1.10 shows 12 that are commonly used in data visualization.

Some of them will be familiar to you from charts you have already seen. Anscombe's Quartet (see Figure 1.1) used position and spatial grouping. The x- and y-coordinates are for position, while spatial grouping allows us to see the outliers and the patterns.

Preattentive attributes provide us with ways to encode our data in charts. We'll look into that in more detail in a moment, but not before we've talked about data.

To recap, we've seen how powerful the visual system is and looked at some visual features we can use to display data effectively. Now we need to look at the different types of data, in order to choose the best visual encoding for each type.

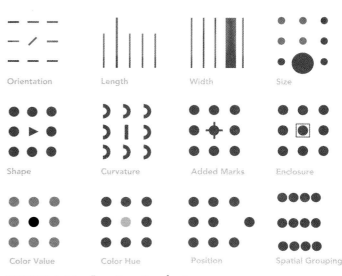

FIGURE 1.10 Preattentive features.

Types of Data

There are three types of data: categorical, ordinal, and quantitative. Let's use a photo to help us define each type.

Categorical Data

Categorical (or *nominal*) *data* represents *things*. These things are mutually exclusive labels without any numerical value. What nominal data can we use to describe the gentleman with me in the Figure 1.11?

- His *name* is Brent Spiner.
- By *profession* he is an actor.
- He played the *character* Data in the TV show *Star Trek: The Next Generation*.

FIGURE 1.11   One of your authors (Andy, on the right) with a celebrity.
Source: Author's photograph

Name, profession, character, and TV show are all categorical data types. Other examples include gender, product category, city, and customer segment.

Ordinal Data

Ordinal data is similar to categorical data, except it has a clear order. Referring to Brent Spiner:

- Brent Spiner's *date of birth* is Wednesday, February 2, 1949.
- He appeared in all seven *seasons* of *Star Trek: The Next Generation*.
- Data's *rank* was lieutenant commander.
- Data was the fifth of six *androids made* by Dr. Noonien Soong.

Other types of ordinal data include education experience, satisfaction level, and salary bands in an organization. Although ordinal values often have numbers associated with them, the interval between those values is arbitrary. For example, the difference in an organization between pay scales 1 and 2 might be very different from that between pay scales 4 and 6.

Quantitative Data

Quantitative data is the numbers. *Quantitative* (or *numerical*) data is data that can be measured and aggregated.

- Brent Spiner's *date of birth* is Wednesday, February 2, 1949.
- His *height* is 5 ft 9 in (180 cm) tall.
- He made 177 *appearances* in episodes of *Star Trek*.
- Data's positronic brain is capable of 60 trillion *operations per second*.

You'll have noticed that date of birth appears in both ordinal and quantitative data types. Time is unusual in that it can be both. In Chapter 31, we look in detail about how you treat time influences your choice of visualization types.

Other types of quantitative measures include sales, profit, exam scores, pageviews, and number of patients in a hospital.

Quantitative data can be expressed in two ways: as discrete or continuous data. Discrete data is presented at predefined, exact points—there's no "in between." For example, Brent Spiner appeared in 177 episodes of *Star Trek*; he couldn't have appeared in 177.5 episodes. Continuous data allows for the "in between," as there is an infinite number of possible intermediate values. For example, Brent Spiner grew to a height of 5 ft 9 in but at one point in his life he was 4 ft 7.5 in tall.

Encoding Data in Charts

We've now looked at preattentive attributes and the three types of data. It's time to see how to combine that knowledge into building charts. Let's look at some charts and see how they encode the different types of data. Sticking with *Star Trek*, Figure 1.12 shows the IMDB.com ratings of every episode of *Star Trek: The Next Generation*.

Table 1.3 shows the different types of data, what type it is, and how it's been encoded.

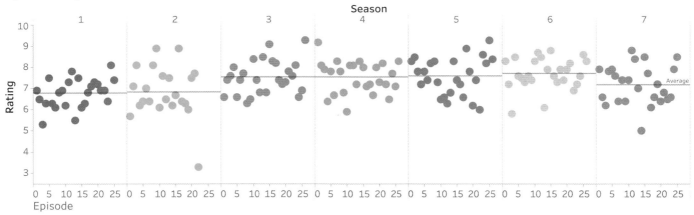

Star Trek: The Next Generation
Episode ratings from IMDB.com

FIGURE 1.12   Every episode of *Star Trek: The Next Generation* rated.

Source: IMDB.com

TABLE 1.3   Data used in Figure 1.12.

Data	Data Type	Encoding	Note
Episode	Categorical	Position	Each episode is represented by a dot. Each dot has its own position on the canvas.
Episode Number	Ordinal	Position	The x-axis shows the number of each episode in each season.
Season	Ordinal	Color Position	Each season is represented by a different color (hue). Each season also has its own section on the chart.
IMDB rating	Ordinal	Position	The better the episode, the higher it is on the y-axis.
Average season rating	Quantitative	Position	The horizontal bar in each pane shows the average rating of the episodes in each season. There is some controversy over whether you should average ordinal ratings. We believe that the practice is so common with ratings it is acceptable.

Let's look at a few more charts to see how preattentive features have been used. Figure 1.13 is from *The Economist*. Look at each chart and see if you can work out which types of data are being graphed and how they are being encoded.

Table 1.4 shows how each data type is encoded.

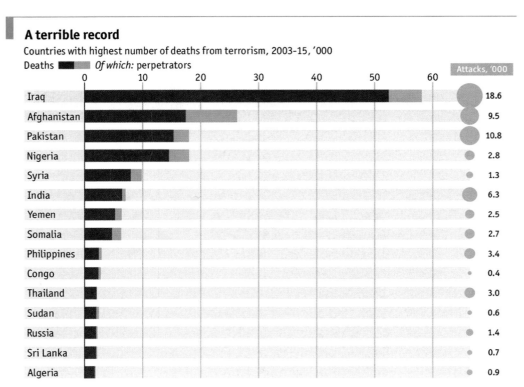

FIGURE 1.13   "A terrible record" from *The Economist*, July 2016.

Source: START, University of Maryland. *The Economist*, http://tabsoft.co/2agK3if

TABLE 1.4   Data used in the bar chart in Figure 1.13.

Data	Data Type	Encoding	Note
Country	Categorical	Position	Each country is on its own row (sorted by total deaths).
Deaths	Quantitative	Length	The length of the bar shows the number of deaths.
Death type	Categorical	Color	Dark blue shows deaths of victims, light blue shows deaths of the perpetrators.
Attacks	Quantitative	Size	Circles on the right are sized according to the number of attacks.

Let's look at another example. Figure 1.14 was part of the Makeover Monday project run by Andy Cotgreave and Andy Kriebel throughout 2016. This entry was by Dan Harrison. It takes data on malaria deaths from the World Health Organization. Table 1.5 describes the data used in the chart.

How did you do? As you progress through the book, stop and analyze some of the views in the scenarios: Think about which data types are being used and how they have been encoded.

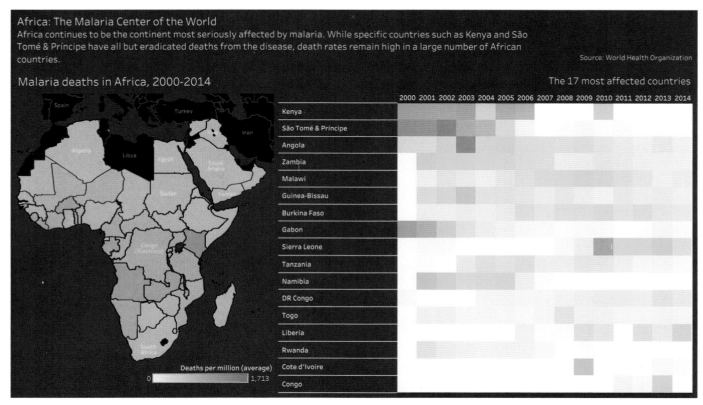

FIGURE 1.14   Deaths from malaria, 2000–2014.

Source: World Health Organization. Chart part of the Makeover Monday project

TABLE 1.5   Data used in the bar chart in Figure 1.14.

Data	Data Type	Encoding	Note
Country	Categorical	Position	The map shows the position of each country. In the highlight table, each country has its own row.
Deaths per million	Quantitative	Color	The map and table use the same color legend to show deaths per million people.
Year	Ordinal	Position	Each year is a discrete column in the table.

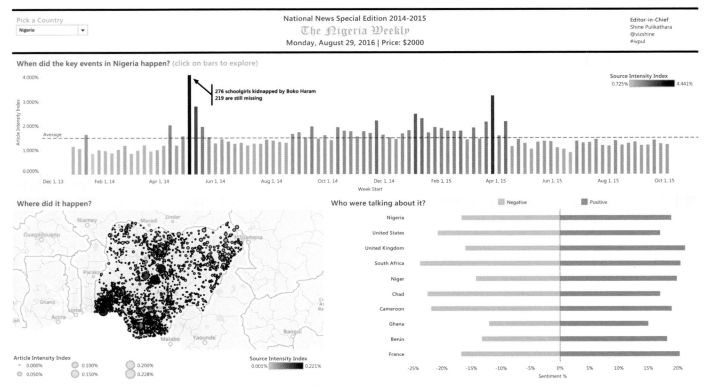

FIGURE 1.15   Winning visualization by Shine Pulikathara during the 2015 Tableau Iron Viz competition.
Source: Used with permission from Shine Pulikathara.

Color

Color is one of the most important things to understand in data visualization and frequently is misused. You should not use color just to spice up a boring visualization. In fact, many great data visualizations don't use color at all and are informative and beautiful.

In Figure 1.15, we see Shine Pulikathara's visualization that won the 2015 Tableau Iron Viz competition. Notice his simple use of color.

Color should be used purposefully. For example, color can be used to draw the attention of the reader, highlight a portion of data, or distinguish between different categories.

Use of Color

Color should be used in data visualization in three primary ways: *sequential*, *diverging*, and *categorical*.

In addition, there is often the need to *highlight* data or *alert* the reader of something important. Figure 1.16 offers an example of each of these color schemes.

Use of Color in Data Visualization

Sequential
color is ordered from low to high

Diverging
two sequential colors with a neutral midpoint

Categorical
contrasting colors for individual comparison

Highlight
color used to highlight something

Alert
color used to alert or warn reader

FIGURE 1.16   Use of color in data visualization.

Sequential color is the use of a single color from light to dark. An example is encoding the total amount of sales by state in blue, where the darker blue shows higher sales and a lighter blue shows lower sales. Figure 1.17 shows the unemployment rate by state using a sequential color scheme.

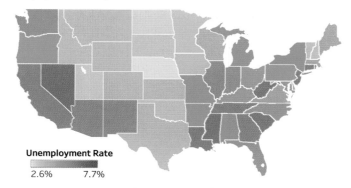

FIGURE 1.17 Unemployment rate by state using a sequential color scheme.

Diverging color is used to show a range diverging from a midpoint. This color can be used in the same manner as the sequential color scheme but can encode two different ranges of a measure (positive and negative) or a range of a measure between two categories. An example is the degree to which electorates may vote Democratic or Republican in each state, as shown in Figure 1.18.

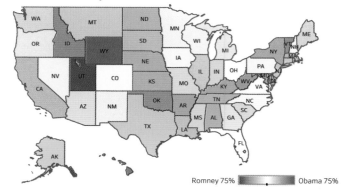

FIGURE 1.18 Degree of Democratic (blue) versus Republican (red) voter sentiment in each state.

Diverging color can also be used to show the weather, with blue showing the cooler temperatures and red showing the hotter temperatures. The midpoint can be the average, the target, or zero in cases where there are positive and negative numbers. Figure 1.19 shows an example with profit by state, where profit (positive number) is shown in blue and loss (negative number) is shown in orange.

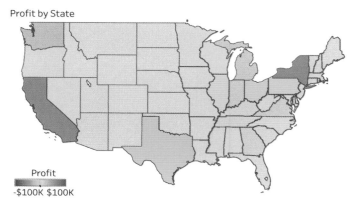

FIGURE 1.19 Profit by state using a diverging color scheme.

Categorical color uses different color hues to distinguish between different categories. For example, we can establish categories involving apparel (e.g., shoes, socks, shirts, hats, and coats) or vehicle types (e.g., cars, mini-vans, sport utility vehicles, and motorcycles). Figure 1.20 shows quantity of office supplies in three categories.

Highlight color is used when there is something that needs to stand out to the reader, but not alert or alarm them. Highlights can be used in a number of ways, as in highlighting a certain data point, text in a table, a certain line on a line chart, or a specific bar in a bar chart. Figure 1.21 shows a slopegraph with a single state highlighted in blue.

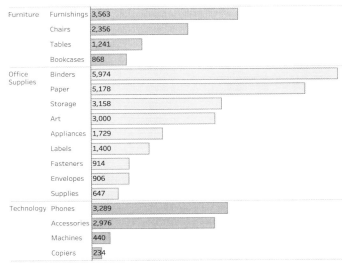

FIGURE 1.20 Quantity of office supplies in three categories using a categorical color scheme.

Alerting color is used when there is a need to draw attention to something for the reader. In this case, it's often best to use bright, alarming colors, which will quickly draw the reader's attention, as in Figure 1.22.

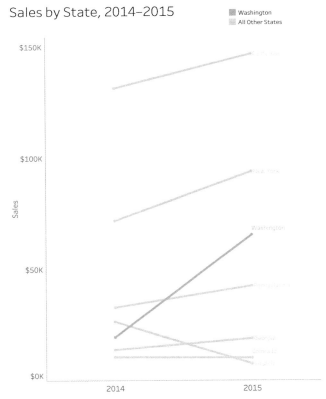

FIGURE 1.21 Slopegraph showing sales by state, 2014–2015, using a single color to highlight the state of Washington.

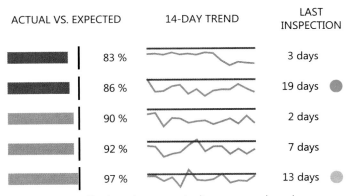

FIGURE 1.22 Red and orange indicators to alert the reader that something on the dashboard needs attention.

It is also possible to have a *categorical-sequential* color scheme. In this case, each category has a distinct hue that is darker or lighter depending on the measurement it is representing. Figure 1.23 shows an example of a four-region map using categorical colors (i.e., gray, blue, yellow, and brown) but at the same time encoding a measure in those regions using sequential color; let's assume that sales are higher in states with darker shading.

Color Vision Deficiency (Color Blindness)

Based on research (Birch 1993), approximately 8 percent of males have color vision deficiency (CVD) compared to only 0.4 percent of females. This deficiency is caused by a lack of one of three types of cones within the eye needed to see all color. The deficiency commonly is referred to as "color blindness", but that term isn't entirely accurate. People suffering from CVD can in fact see color, but they cannot distinguish colors in the same way as the rest of the population. The more accurate term is "color vision deficiency." Depending on which cone is lacking, it can be very difficult for people with CVD to distinguish between certain colors because of the way they see the color spectrum.

There are three types of CVD:

1. *Protanopia* is the lack of long-wave cones (red weak).

2. *Deuteranopia* is the lack of medium-wave cones (green weak).

3. *Tritanopia* is the lack of short-wave cones (blue). (This is very rare, affecting less than 0.5 percent of the population.)

Sales by Region

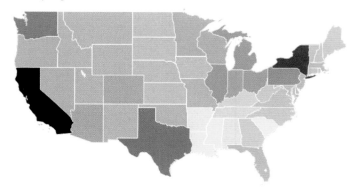

FIGURE 1.23   Sales by region using four categorical colors and the total sales shown with sequential color.

CVD is mostly hereditary, and, as you can see from the numbers, it primarily afflicts men. Eight percent of men may seem like a small number, but consider that in a group of nine men, there is more than a 50 percent chance that one of them has CVD. In a group of 25 men, there is an 88 percent chance that one of them has CVD. The rates also increase among Caucasian men, reaching as high as 11 percent. In larger companies or when a data visualization is presented to the general public, designers must understand CVD and design with it in mind.

The primary problem among people with CVD is with the colors red and green. This is why it is best to avoid using red and green together and, in general, to avoid the commonly used traffic light colors. We discuss this issue further in Chapter 33 and offer some solutions for using red and green together.

Seeing the Problem for Yourself

Let's look at some examples of how poor choice of color can create confusion for people with CVD.

In Figure 1.24, the chart on the left uses the traditional traffic light colors red, yellow, and green. The example on the right is a protanopia simulation for CVD.

One common solution among data visualization practitioners is to use blue and orange. Using blue instead of green for *good* and orange instead of red for *bad* works well because almost everyone (with very rare exceptions) can distinguish blue and orange from each other. This blue-orange palette is often referred to as being "color-blind friendly."

Using Figure 1.25, compare the blue/orange color scheme and a protanopia simulation of CVD again.

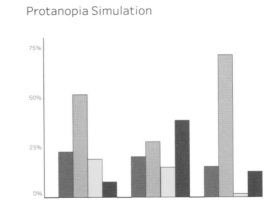

FIGURE 1.24 Bar chart using the traffic light colors and a protanopia simulation. Notice the red and green bars in the panel on the right are very difficult to differentiate from one another for a person with protanopia.

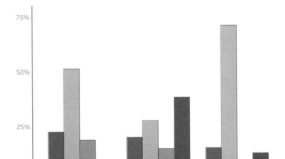

FIGURE 1.25 Bar chart using a color-blind-friendly blue and orange palette and a protanopia simulation.

The Problem Is Broader Than Just Red and Green

The use of red and green is discussed frequently in the field of data visualization, probably because the traffic light color palette is prevalent in many software programs and is commonly used in business today. It is common in Western culture to associate red with bad and green with good. However, it is important to understand that the problem in differentiating color for someone with CVD is much more complex than just red and green. Since red, green, and orange all appear to be brown for someone with strong CVD, it would be more accurate to say "Don't use red, green, brown, and orange together."

Figure 1.26 shows a scatterplot using brown, orange, and green together for three categories. When applying protanopia simulation, the dots in the scatterplot appear to be a very similar color.

One color combination that is frequently overlooked is blue and purple together. In a RGB (red-green-blue) color model, purple is achieved by using blue and red together. If someone with CVD has issues with red, then he or she may also have issues with purple, which would appear to look like blue. Other color combinations can be problematic as well. For example, people may have difficulty with pink or red used with gray or gray used together with brown.

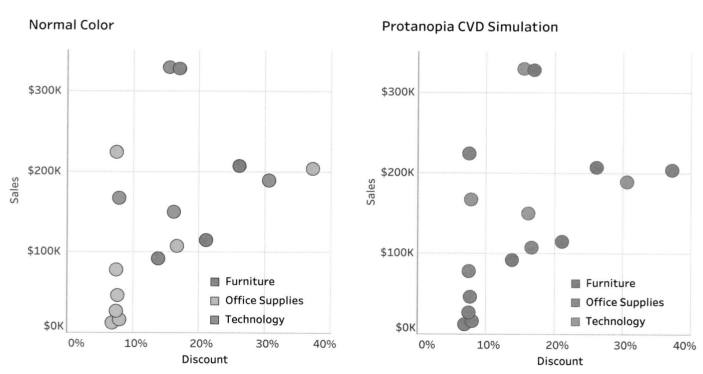

FIGURE 1.26   Scatterplot simulating color vision deficiency for someone with protanopia.

Figure 1.27 shows another scatterplot, this time using blue, purple, magenta, and gray. When applying deuteranopia simulation, the dots in the scatterplot appear to be a very similar color of gray.

It's important to understand these issues when designing visualizations. If color is used to encode data and it's necessary for readers to distinguish among colors to understand the visualization, then consider using color-blind-friendly palettes. Here are a few resources that you can use to simulate the various types of CVD for your own visualizations.

Adobe Illustrator CC. This program offers a built-in CVD simulation in the View menu under Proof Setup.

Chromatic Vision Simulator (free). Kazunori Asada's superb website allows users to upload images and simulate how they would appear to people with different form of CVD. See http://asada.tukusi.ne.jp/webCVS/

NoCoffee vision simulator (free). This free simulator for the Chrome browser allows users to simulate websites and images directly from the browser.

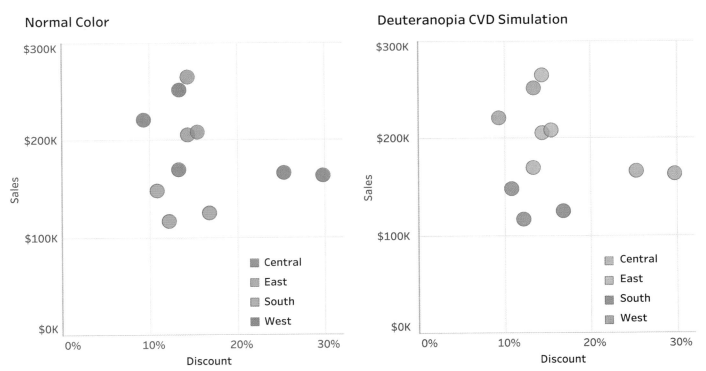

FIGURE 1.27 Scatterplot simulating color vision deficiency for someone with deuteranopia.

Common Chart Types

In this book, you will see many different types of charts. We explain in the scenarios why many of the charts were chosen to fulfill a particular task. In this section, we briefly outline the most common chart types. This list is intentionally short. Even if you use only the charts listed here, you would be able to cover the majority of needs when visualizing your data. More advanced chart types seen throughout the book are built from the same building blocks as these. For example, sparklines, which are shown in Chapters 6, 8, and 9, are a kind of line chart. Bullet charts, used in Chapter 17, are bar charts with reference lines and shading built in. Finally, waterfall charts, shown in Chapter 24, are bar charts where the bars don't have a common baseline.

Bar Chart

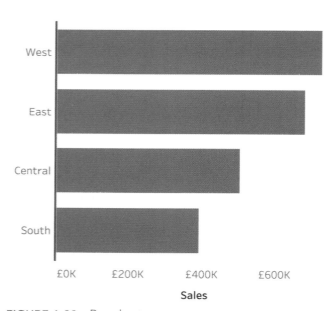

FIGURE 1.28   Bar chart.

Time-Series Line Chart

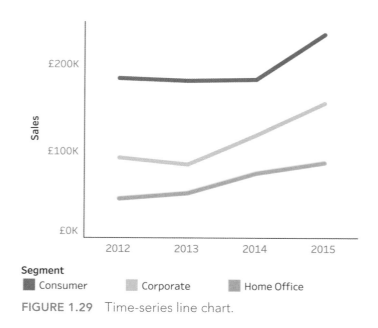

FIGURE 1.29   Time-series line chart.

A bar chart (see Figure 1.28) uses length to represent a measure. Human beings are extremely good at seeing even small differences in length from a common baseline. Bars are widely used in data visualization because they are often the most effective way to compare categories. Bars can be oriented horizontally or vertically. Sorting them can be very helpful because the most common task when bar charts are used is to spot the biggest/smallest items.

Line charts (see Figure 1.29) usually show change over time. Time is represented by position on the horizontal x-axis. The measures are shown on the vertical y-axis. The height and slopes of the line let us see trends.

Scatterplot

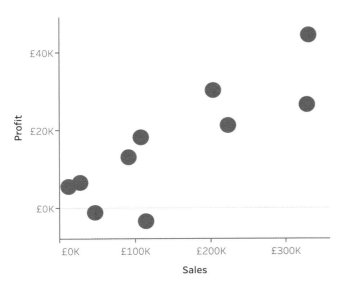

FIGURE 1.30   Scatterplot.

Dot Plot

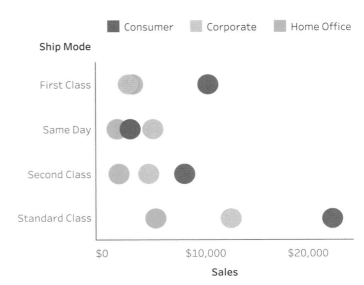

FIGURE 1.31   Dot plot.

A scatterplot (see Figure 1.30) lets you compare two different measures. Each measure is encoded using position on the horizontal and vertical axes. Scatterplots are useful when looking for relationships between two variables.

A dot plot (see Figure 1.31) allows you to compare values across two dimensions. In our example, each row shows sales by ship mode. The dots show sales for each ship mode, broken down by each segment. In the example, you can see that corporate sales are highest with standard class ship mode.

Choropleth Map

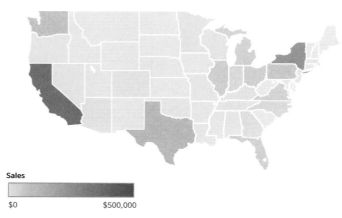

FIGURE 1.32   Choropleth map.

A choropleth (also known as a filled) map (see Figure 1.32) uses differences in shading or coloring within predefined areas to indicate the values or categories in those areas.

Symbol Map

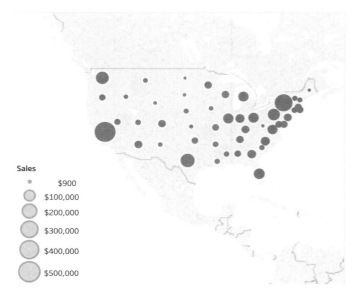

FIGURE 1.33   Symbol map.

A symbol map (see Figure 1.33) shows values in specific places. These could be the center points of large regions (e.g., the center of each U.S. state) or specific locations determined by an exact latitude/longitude measurement.

Avoid pie charts

Why isn't there a pie chart? Pie charts are common charts, but they are flawed. We don't recommend you use them. Check out the section titled "When Our Visual Processing System Betrays Us" for details.

Table

Sometimes you do need to be able to look up exact values. A table (see Figure 1.34) is an acceptable way to show data in that situation. On most dashboards, a table shows details alongside summary charts.

$111K	$131K	$138K	$154K
$132K	$117K	$157K	$215K
$77K	$68K	$79K	$106K

FIGURE 1.34   Table.

Highlight Table

Adding a color encoding to your tables can transform them into highly visual views that also enable exact lookup of any value. (see Figure 1.35.)

$111K	$131K	$138K	$154K
$132K	$117K	$157K	$215K
$77K	$68K	$79K	$106K

FIGURE 1.35   Highlight table.

Bullet Graph

A bullet graph (see Figure 1.36) is one of the best ways to show actual versus target comparisons. The blue bar represents the actual value, the black line shows the target value, and the areas of gray shading are performance bands.

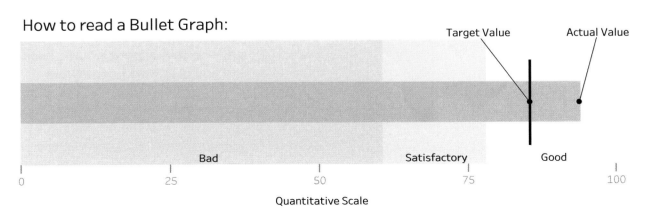

FIGURE 1.36   Bullet Graph.

When Our Visual Processing System Betrays Us

We have talked about how to use preattentive attributes to craft good data visualizations. By using those attributes, we can use the power of our visual system to our advantage. Unfortunately, our visual system also can be confused easily. In this section, we look at some common pitfalls.

Our eyes can be fooled in countless different ways. Figures 1.37 and 1.38 show two optical illusions.

In Figure 1.38, the top appears to be a well-lit gray surface and the bottom appears to be a poorly lit white surface that is in shadow. However, there is no shadow. Dr. Lotto added the gradient and shadows to the image. Our minds can't help but to see the shadow, making the top appear to be much darker than the bottom, but if you cover up the middle of

FIGURE 1.38   Does the top appear darker than the bottom? Put your thumb or finger over the center line and then try again.
Source: Image by R. Beau Lotto.

FIGURE 1.37   Is it a duck or a rabbit?
Source: Public domain. https://commons.wikimedia.org/w/index.php?curid=667017

the image, it becomes clear that the top and the bottom are exactly the same color.

Ambiguity in images makes for playful illusions, but this can be disastrous if your data visualizations confuse instead of clarify. In the previous section, we looked at the power of preattentive attributes. Now it's time to look into the problems with some preattentive attributes. Throughout the book, we discuss which preattentive attributes are being used in the scenarios and why they work in each case.

When we visualize data, we are, for the most part, trying to convey the value of the measure in a way that can be interpreted most accurately in the shortest time possible. Some preattentive attributes are better than others for this purpose.

Figure 1.39 shows the number of deaths each day from various diseases in Africa. Each circle is sized according to the number of deaths. We have removed all the labels except the one for malaria (552 deaths per day). How many deaths per day are there from diarrhea? How much bigger is the HIV/AIDS circle than the diarrhea circle?

How did you do? The actual answers are shown in Figure 1.40.

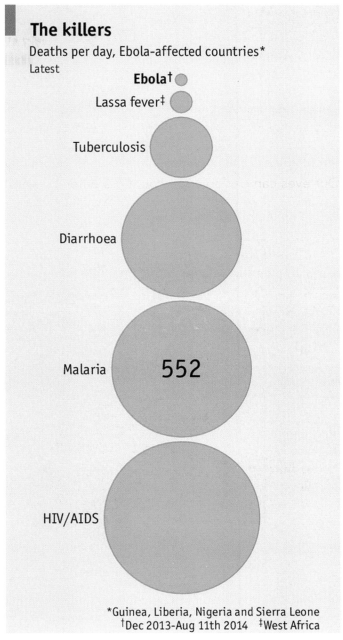

The killers

Deaths per day, Ebola-affected countries*
Latest

Ebola†

Lassa fever‡

Tuberculosis

Diarrhoea

Malaria 552

HIV/AIDS

*Guinea, Liberia, Nigeria and Sierra Leone
†Dec 2013–Aug 11th 2014   ‡West Africa

FIGURE 1.39   Deaths per day in Ebola-affected countries in 2014. We removed all labels except the one for malaria. Can you estimate the number of deaths from the other diseases?

Source: World Health Organization; U.S. Centers for Disease Control and Prevention; *The Economist*, http://tabsoft.co/1w1vwAc

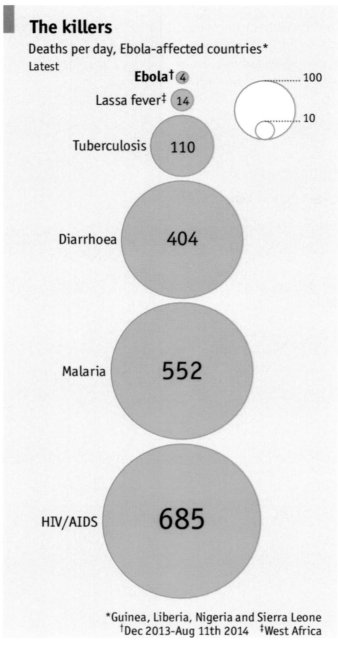

FIGURE 1.40 Deaths per day of various diseases in Ebola-affected countries, with labels added.

Source: World Health Organization; U.S. Centers for Disease Control and Prevention; *The Economist*, http://tabsoft.co/1w1vwAc

Most people underestimate the size of the bigger circles. The point is that while size is preattentive, we're not able to tell the differences with any accuracy. Consider the same data shown as a bar chart in Figure 1.41.

In the bar chart, we are encoding the quantitative variable, deaths per day, using length. Notice how accurately you can see the differences. This is why the bar chart is such a reliable chart to use: Length is one of the most efficient preattentive attributes for us to process.

Deaths per day, Ebola-affected countries

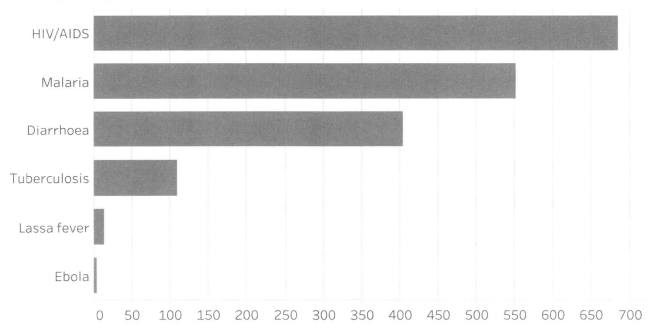

*Guinea, Liberia, Nigeria and Sierra Leone
Sources: World Health Organization; U.S. Centers for Disease Control and Prevention; *The Economist*

FIGURE 1.41   Bar chart version of the circle charts.

Yet using multiple preattentive attributes in one chart can lead to problems. Figure 1.42 shows a scatterplot of sales and profit for a fictional sales company. Position is used for sales (x-axis) and profit (y-axis). Color shows different segments, and shape shows the categories of products. Which category has, on average, the highest profits?

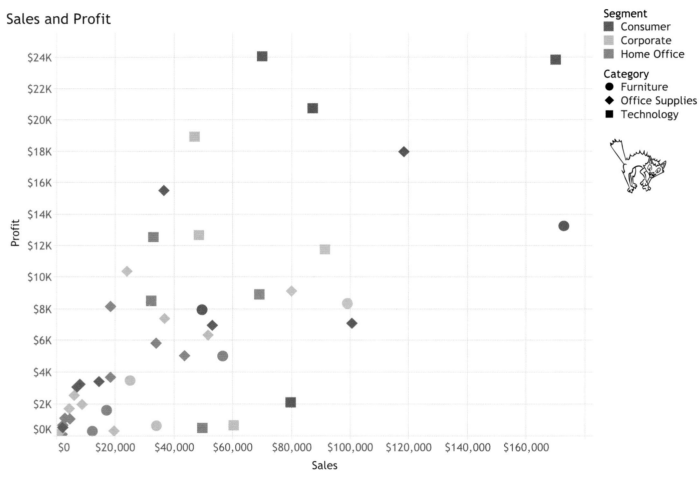

FIGURE 1.42   Scatterplot using shape and color. Which category has the highest profits?

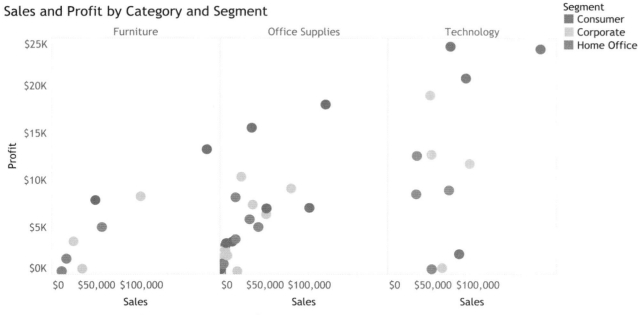

FIGURE 1.43   Sales and profit with one column for each category.

It's almost impossible to see anything, isn't it? Mixing position, color, and shape does not make for easy reading. What's a better solution? How about using position to represent category, breaking the single scatterplot into three panels? This is shown in Figure 1.43.

The result is much clearer. Now you can even see that technology sales, on average, have a higher range of profits than furniture and office supplies. That insight was certainly not apparent in the first scatterplot.

To close this section, let's look at some chart types you might be surprised *not* to see in our common chart types. The first is the pie chart. Sure, it is a common chart, but we do not recommend you use it. Let's see why pie charts don't play well with our visual system.

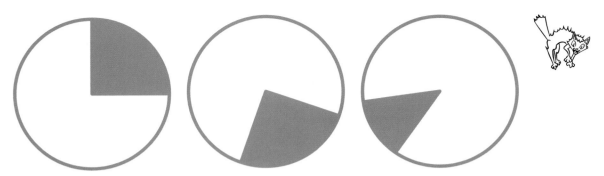

FIGURE 1.44   What percentage of each pie does the blue segment represent?

Look at Figure 1.44. What percentage of each circle is covered by the blue segment?

The one on the left is pretty easy: 25 percent. The middle? It's a little harder. It's also 25 percent, but because it's not aligned to a horizontal or vertical axis, it's harder to determine. And on the right? It's 13 percent. How did you do? We are simply not able to make accurate estimates of angle sizes, and if accurate estimates are the goal, it's a problem.

Let's look at another pie. The biggest slice in Figure 1.45 is easy to spot. But what about the second, third, and fourth biggest slices?

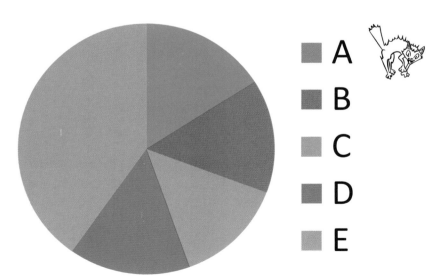

FIGURE 1.45   Can you order the slices from biggest to smallest?

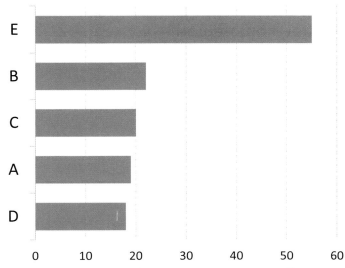

FIGURE 1.46   Bars make it very easy to see small differences in size.

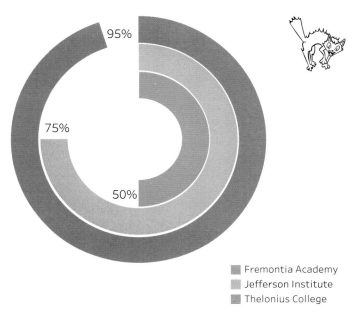

Fremontia Academy
Jefferson Institute
Thelonius College

FIGURE 1.47   A concentric donut chart (also called a radial bar chart).

That was really hard. Now look at the same data, shown in a bar chart, in Figure 1.46.

The sorted bar chart made it very easy to distinguish size differences: Length is such an effective visual attribute, we can see very small differences with ease.

To make effective dashboards, you must resist the temptation to use purely decorative chart types.

Let's look at one more example in order to keep you away from the lure of the circles. Sometimes people acknowledge the power of bars but then get

tempted to put them in a circle, fashioning what is known as a donut chart. Figure 1.47 shows an example.

"What's the problem?" you may ask. "The comparison seems easy."

Although you may be able to make the comparisons, you are in fact working considerably harder than you need to be. Really. Let us prove it to you.

Let's suppose you wanted to compare the heights of three famous buildings: One World Trade Center, the Empire State Building, and the Chrysler Building. (See Figure 1.48.)

Now, that's an easy comparison. With virtually no effort, we can see that One World Trade Center (blue) is almost twice as tall as the Chrysler Building (red).

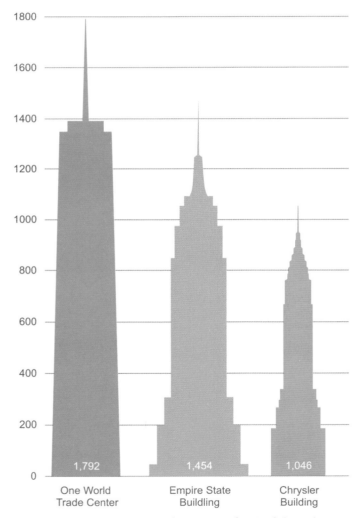

FIGURE 1.48 Comparing the size (in feet) of three large buildings.

Now let's see how easy the comparison is with donuts. (See Figure 1.49.)

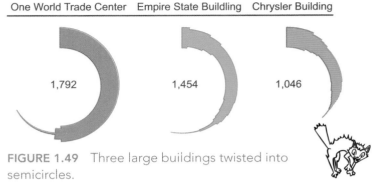

FIGURE 1.49 Three large buildings twisted into semicircles.

Figure 1.50 presents the same buildings rendered using a concentric donut chart. Can you tell the difference in heights of the buildings in this chart?

FIGURE 1.50 Three skyscrapers spooning.

Yikes!

So, with this somewhat contrived but hopefully memorable example, we took something that was simple to compare (the silhouettes of buildings) and contorted them into difficult-to-compare semicircles.

Every Decision Is a Compromise

However you choose to show your data, you will emphasize one feature over another. Let's have a look at an example. Table 1.6 shows a table of numbers. Let's imagine they are sales for two products, A and B, over 10 years.

Figure 1.51 shows eight different ways to visualize this data. Each uses a different mix of preattentive attributes.

Notice the compromises in the charts labeled 1 and 2. A standard line chart (1) showing each product lets us compare each product's sales very accurately. The area chart (2) lets us see total sales over time with ease, but now it is harder to compare the two products. You can't, in a single chart, answer every possible question or comparison. What you do need to do is assess whether the chart you do choose answers the question being asked.

TABLE 1.6   How would you visualize this data?

	2007	2008	2009	2010	2011	2012	2013	2014	2015	2016	Total
A	100	110	140	170	120	190	220	250	240	300	1,840
B	80	70	50	100	130	180	220	160	260	370	1,620

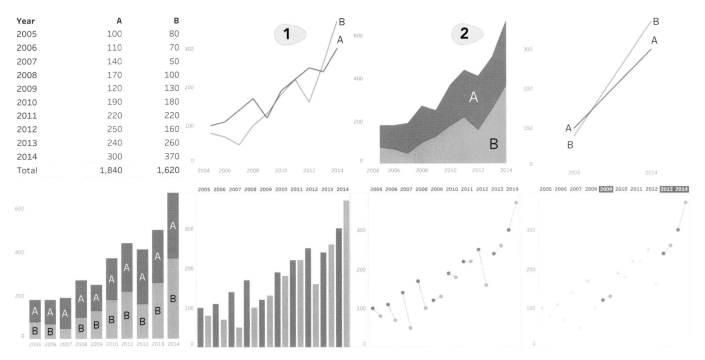

FIGURE 1.51   Eight different ways of visualizing the data.

Designing Dashboards That Are Functional and Beautiful

You now have a suitable vocabulary to interpret the charts in the scenarios in this book. Note that we have not offered a primer on graphic design. Instead, in each scenario, we point out where and how graphic design elements, such as white space, fonts, grid layout, and so on, contribute to the clarity of the dashboards.

We maintain that a dashboard must first be truthful and functional, but there are reasons you should go the extra mile to make dashboards that are elegant as well. We recommend considering the lessons from classic design books, such as *The Design of Everyday Things* by Donald A. Norman (Basic Books, 2013). In it, Norman says:

> Products [should] actually fulfill human needs while being understandable and usable. In the best of cases, the products should also be delightful and enjoyable, which means that not only must the requirements of engineering, manufacturing, and ergonomics be satisfied, but attention must be paid to the entire experience, which means the aesthetics of form and the quality of interaction. (p. 4)

Summary

This chapter has gone through the basics of data visualization. If you are new to visualization, you now have enough knowledge to interpret the charts in this book. You will be able to decode most of the charts you encounter. There is also a glossary of charts at the back of the book for further reference.

You might be inspired to find out more. There are many superb books on the theory and application of this science. Some of the examples in this chapter are based on examples first used in some of these books. Here are our recommendations:

Alberto Cairo's *The Functional Art* (New Riders, 2013). Alberto Cairo is an author who understands the need to balance functionality with beauty in charts. This book is an inspiring introduction to information graphics and visualization.

Stephen Few's *Now You See It* (Analytics Press, 2009). This is a practical and commonsense guide to table and graph design. It goes into great detail about each of the main chart types, explaining clearly when to use them and how to construct them well.

Cole Nussbaumer Knaflic's *Storytelling with Data* (Wiley, 2015). This is the data visualization guide for business professionals. It's an accessible look at not only the anatomy of charts but also at how to design charts to communicate messages effectively.

Colin Ware's *Information Visualization: Perception for Design* (Morgan Kauffman, 2013). This book has been called the bible of data visualization. In over 500 pages, it covers every aspect of the science of perception and its role in data visualization. It's an invaluable resource for anyone practicing data visualization.

Colin Ware's *Visual Thinking for Design* (Elsevier, 2008). Colin Ware presents a detailed analysis of the mechanics of visual cognition. The book teaches us how to see as designers by anticipating how others will see our designs. It's a fun book to read and makes detailed information about cognitive science a breeze to digest.

PART II

THE SCENARIOS

Chapter 2

Course Metrics Dashboard

Course metrics dashboard.
Dashboard Designer: Jeffrey A. Shaffer
Organization: University of Cincinnati

Course Metrics

Students

'12 '13 '14 '15 '16

52

1097
Total students in five years

Enrollments

'12 '13 '14 '15 '16

58 112 240 299 388

687
Total students in 2015-2016

Classes

'12 '13 '14 '15 '16

2 3 5 5 6

21
Total classes in five years

Ratings

'12 '13 '14 '15

8

4

0

7.7 of 8
Mean recent instructor rating (out of 8.0)

Semesters	Questions	● BANA ❘ College ● Shaffer	Ratings
2015 Fall Semester 001	I developed specific skills and competencies		6.9
	Overall, this was an excellent course		7.1
	The instructor communicated clearly		7.4
	The instructor graded fairly		7.5
	The instructor was well organized		7.3
	The instructor interacted well with students		7.3
	Overall, this instructor was excellent		7.3
2015 Fall Semester 002	I developed specific skills and competencies		7.2
	Overall, this was an excellent course		7.4
	The instructor communicated clearly		7.6
	The instructor graded fairly		7.6
	The instructor was well organized		7.5
	The instructor interacted well with students		7.7
	Overall, this instructor was excellent		7.7

5   6   7   Out of 8.0

Rating

Course Metrics Dashboard created by Jeffrey A. Shaffer. Data from University of Cincinnati Course Evaluations. **Blue indicates the 2 most recent rating periods.**

Scenario

Big Picture

You are a professor at a university or the head of an academic department. You want to know how a particular professor's course is rated compared to others in the department and the college. You want to know the overall course load, the number of students, and the overall growth or decline of a particular course. You also want to be able to see the rating comparing one specific course against all of the courses in the department and in the college.

Specifics

- You need to see how many courses an instructor has been teaching over time.

- You need to see how many students are registering for the classes.

- You want to see the trend over a specific period of time. This might be the entire span of the course (as shown in the overview dashboard), or it may be a rolling period of time, for example, the last five years.

- You would like to see the detailed ratings of the most recent course and instructor feedback.

- You need to be able to quickly compare this course and instructor to other courses in the department and the college.

Related Scenarios

- You conduct workshops or seminars and need to see ratings for these offerings.

- You conduct training programs at your company on various topics and need to track sign-ups and feedback for a particular topic or presenter.

- You want to track cohort size and performance over time and see the performance detail of the most recent cohort.

- You want to track reviews of your product or service, how many people have completed reviews, the ratings over time, and the details of the most recent reviews on, say, Amazon or Yelp.

- You want to see how sales in your department compare to sales in other departments or store averages.

How People Use the Dashboard

This dashboard shows the course history for the Data Visualization class at the University of Cincinnati. The course is taught by Jeffrey Shaffer in the Carl H. Lindner College of Business and is part of the operations, business analytics, and information systems department. Courses are registered under their discipline within the department.

- OM—Operations Management
- BANA—Business Analytics
- IS—Information Systems

The course number used in this dashboard is BANA6037, which is the same from semester to semester. A semester indicator and section ID are then used to distinguish the classes. 001 indicates the first section for Fall Semester 2016 and 002 is the second section.

The dashboard begins with a general overview of BANA6037. It shows the entire history of the course, which began in Spring Semester 2012. Figure 2.1 shows the number of students in each class over time.

Students

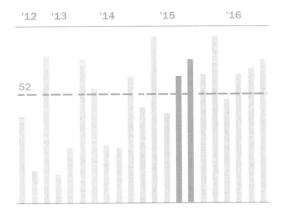

FIGURE 2.1 Number of students in each course by year with two recent rating periods highlighted in blue.

This chart indicates the class size for each individual class, which is very important for a number of reasons.

- Should the college keep offering the class? Success of a course can be measured by answering two questions:
  1. Are people signing up for the class?
  2. Are students rating the class well?
- This chart highlights the demand growth for the course. This particular class is an elective for the degree programs, so if no one were signing up for the course, then it wouldn't make sense to keep offering it.

- Each course has a registration capacity. If demand is growing, then there may be a need to offer additional courses in the future, which is the case in this example.
- Lecture halls have strict seating capacities based on fire code rules. Understanding course demand is critical in planning the course capacity and determining whether a course needs to be moved to a different lecture hall for additional seats to open.

A reference line is used to show the average class size. This line helps illustrate the growth of the classes in the most recent semesters versus the earlier classes from 2012 and 2013. A number of other alternatives could be used in this case, including:

- Comparing the average class size for the department to these classes.
- Comparing the average class size of the college to these classes.
- Using a bullet chart, with a target line on each bar chart, showing the course capacity. This would give an indication of how many open seats were available from semester to semester and could provide an indicator if a course was over capacity.

Figure 2.2 shows the enrollments by year. This is similar to the chart in Figure 2.1 but summarizes the enrollment by calendar year.

This particular example highlights the growth of the last two years. That is, there are 1,097 totals students in five years but 687 in 2015–2016. Figure 2.3 gives additional context as to why that is the case and shows the number of classes over time, which gives additional context to the large growth in the number of students.

Enrollments

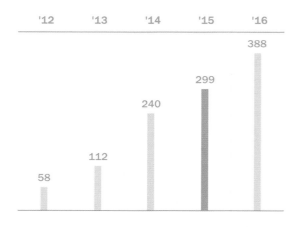

687

Total students in 2015-2016

FIGURE 2.2 Enrollments by year with the year of the two most recent rating periods in blue (2016 classes have been presented but have not yet been rated).

Classes

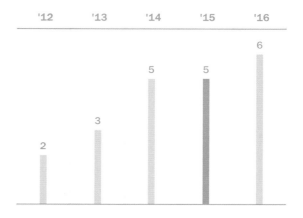

21

Total classes in five years

FIGURE 2.3 Number of classes by year. Only two classes were offered in 2012 compared to six in 2016. The year of the most two recent rating periods is highlighted in blue.

Figure 2.3 highlights an important part of the data: For example, do we simply have more students because the class size grew from a 25-person classroom to a 220-seat auditorium? In this case, the answer is no. Although the class size did grow some, it didn't grow that much. Rather, the biggest growth came from the number of classes, which grew from two classes in 2012 to six classes for 2016.

Figure 2.4 gives the overall course rating for each course semester by semester.

The course feedback is filled out by the students and is voluntary. A series of standard questions is asked

regarding every course using a rating on a scale of 1 to 8 and an opportunity for comments. These ratings and feedback are used by the department heads and college to monitor course performance. For example, if a course is rated excellent and also has at least a 50 percent response rate from students, the professor is named to the "Dean's List of Teaching Excellence" for the semester.

In some rating systems, there is a constant target set by an internal benchmark. In other rating systems, the target moves from rating period to rating period; for example, the benchmark may be set based on the average in the current period or the previous period.

Ratings

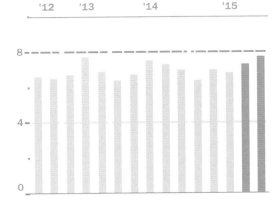

7.7 of 8

Most Recent Instructor Rating (out of 8.0)

FIGURE 2.4 Overall course ratings. Note that we only see rating through 2015 because ratings for courses presented in 2016 have not yet been tabulated.

Regardless of how it's calculated, a target line can add context to the data.

The dot plot on the bottom section of the dashboard, shown in Figure 2.5, provides a detailed comparison for each of the questions asked on the course evaluation survey.

The dark gray dot shows the rating for all courses in the department, listed as "BANA," and a light gray vertical line indicates the rating for all of the courses in the rating period for the entire college. The blue dot indicates the rating for BANA6037, the particular course selected for comparison. All of these ratings are on a scale of 1 to 8.

Notice that the axis for the rating does not start at zero. This makes sense because the values are within a small range of each other, and those differences within the small range matter.

FIGURE 2.5 Dot plot of course ratings comparing the Data Visualization course (blue) to the BANA courses (dark gray) and the college average (light gray line).

Why This Works

Easy-to-See Key Metrics

This dashboard provides a quick overview across the top of key metrics about this course. It shows the number of classes each semester and by year, the number of students, and the overall course rating. It provides quick information at a glance but also allows for a deeper analysis by comparing the metrics over time.

Simple Color Scheme

Only three colors are used in this dashboard: blue, light gray, and dark gray. Blue is used to highlight the two most recent rating periods. Since course feedback isn't available until weeks after a course is complete, registration for the next semester is already complete, and often a new course has begun. Therefore, blue highlights each portion of the chart that corresponds to the specified course rating period. In the first and last chart on the top row, the two specific courses are highlighted. In the second and third chart, the two courses are part of the five classes that are summarized in the year. In the dot plot, the blue represents those two courses versus the department and college averages.

Potential to Be Static or Interactive

This dashboard can work as a static dashboard that can be emailed as a PDF or printed, but it can also be interactive. The dashboard could connect to a database of all of the available courses. With a simple drop-down box with a list of courses, a department head or professor could easily select a course to generate this report.

Both Overview and Details Are Clear

This dashboard offers both an overview and details. The overview shows four key metrics across the top along with those details over time. The section on the bottom offers a very detailed look at each survey question. It provides a quick comparison for each survey question rating the course compared to the department and the entire college.

The Traditional Approach and Why You Should Avoid It

There are a number of problems with the current reports generated by the University of Cincinnati system illustrated in Figures 2.6 and 2.7.

Problems with Figure 2.6

- The current system requires a distinct report to be run for each individual semester. There's no easy way to compare one period with the previous period or to see trends over time.

- The reporting template lists each survey question on a separate page along with the feedback. This does not allow for a quick review of the scores or a comparison across questions.

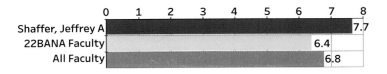

FIGURE 2.6   Example of the bar chart from the course evaluation report generated by the current system.

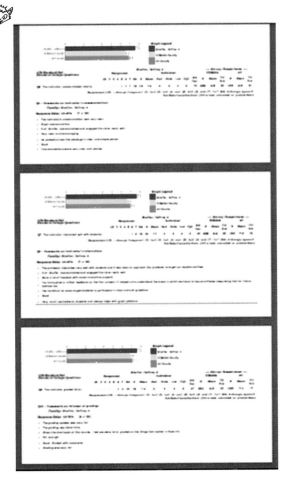

FIGURE 2.7   Three pages from the current evaluation report generated by the system.

Problems with Figure 2.7

- The graphical representation is a bar chart on a fixed axis. Although this encoding of the data works, it hides the small differences in the scale of the ratings. As an example, it's very hard to see the difference between 6.4 and 6.8 on the bar chart.
- The colors are bright and alerting. Bright yellow and bright red are being used to show a standard categorical color.

Author Commentary

JEFF: I chose to label the dot plot (see Figure 2.5.) with only the rating for the course. By doing this, I avoided over labeling the dot plot with every point. In an interactive version of the dashboard, a descriptive tool tip could be used that would provide detailed information about every point when the user hovers over them.

Labels could also be moved to the center of the dots. In this particular data set, the granularity of the data required one decimal place. Because of the extra decimal place, moving the labels inside the circles required a much smaller font size or a larger circle, so I chose to place them outside of the circles.

FIGURE 2.8   Example of the Course Metrics dashboard with less spacing between the bars on the bar charts.

One design choice I made was to keep the width of the bars on the bar charts similar from chart to chart (see Figures 2.1, 2.2, 2.3, 2.4). I typically set the width of bar charts to allow approximately 25 to 50 percent of the bar width as spacing between the bars on bar charts (and just a slight space between the bars on histograms).

Figure 2.8 shows what this might look like with wider bars. For me, this displays as a bar chart on the two inside charts and more of a lollipop-style chart on the two outside bar charts. Both styles encode the data using length and do not distort the data in any way so I used thinner bars as a style choice for the overall design.

Also, I chose the font very carefully in this dashboard. The large font for the title and key metric numbers is Leviathan, showing in a heavier style. The other dashboard text is Franklin Gothic Heavy and Medium, which are used together with Leviathan to achieve three distinct levels and weights of the fonts throughout the dashboard.

A special thanks to Darrin Hunter of Dish Design (http://www.dishdesign.com/) for reviewing this dashboard and offering design suggestions. Darrin is a former professor from the University of Cincinnati Design, Architecture, Art and Planning (DAAP) College and now runs his own graphic design company.

STEVE: Jeff's dot plot has become my go-to approach for comparing aggregated results from multiple sources (in this case an individual compared to a peer group compared to the college as a whole).

Chapter 3

Comparing Individual Performance with Peers

A jittered dot plot (aka jitterplot) showing a selected speaker's ratings in comparison to other speakers.
Author: Steve Wexler
Organization: Data Revelations

Speaker Ratings Comparison

Speaker 317 compared with all other speakers

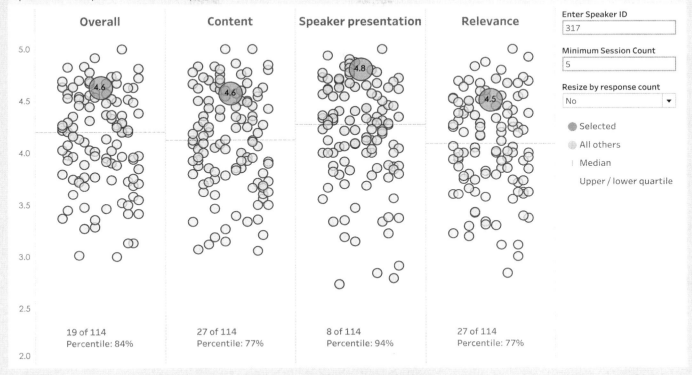

Overall	Content	Speaker presentation	Relevance
4.6	4.6	4.8	4.5
19 of 114	27 of 114	8 of 114	27 of 114
Percentile: 84%	Percentile: 77%	Percentile: 94%	Percentile: 77%

Enter Speaker ID

317

Minimum Session Count

5

Resize by response count

No

⬤ Selected

⬤ All others

│ Median

Upper / lower quartile

Scenario

Big Picture

Your company just had its annual three-day conference where hundreds of presenters educated, enlightened, and entertained over 10,000 participants. You know the conference was a big success, but you need to know which sessions were highly rated to begin planning for the next event.

This is not the first year the conference was offered. As in other years, the speakers themselves want to know if their sessions were well-received.

You create a dashboard that makes it easy for you, others in your organizations, and all the presenters to see how well or poorly their sessions were rated.

Specifics

- You hosted a conference and want to see how a certain speaker rated compared to the other speakers so you can plan for future events.
- You need to fashion a dashboard that allows individual presenters to see how they performed at the event.
- You need to make it easy to see how well or poorly a speaker performed compared to other presenters.
- You want to be able to see how many people rated a session—that is, did dozens of people rate a session or only a handful?

Related Scenarios

- You need to see how your store is doing across multiple categories compared with stores within a 50-mile radius.

- You need to show how an individual is performing across various benchmarks with respect to others within the department and others in the company.
- You need to show how an individual's salary compares with others who have similar experience and education and who work in the same industry.

Note to readers: At the end of this chapter, we present an alternative approach to this dashboard. (See Figure 3.14.) Although this alternative doesn't scale to thousands of dots and doesn't show quartiles, you may prefer it, in some situations, to this dashboard.

How People Use the Dashboard

The person interacting can type in a name (or in this case the speaker ID) and see ratings across various categories with the blue dot corresponding to the typed-in speaker ID and the gray dots corresponding to the other speakers. The individual can also filter to remove results for presenters that received very few reviews. (See Figure 3.1.)

Enter Speaker ID

323

Minimum Session Count

5

Resize by response count

No   ▾

FIGURE 3.1   The person interacting can type in a speaker ID and specify the minimum number or reviews. The person interacting can also resize the dots based on the number of people who rated the session.

The viewer can also hover over a mark to get more details about that mark, including how many people rated the presenter. (See Figure 3.2.)

To get a better sense of which speakers received many responses and which received few, the viewer can resize the dots based on number of survey responses by clicking "Yes" from the "Resize by response count" drop-down menu. (See Figure 3.3.)

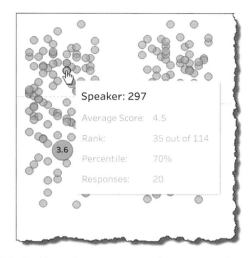

FIGURE 3.2   Hovering over a mark presents details about that mark.

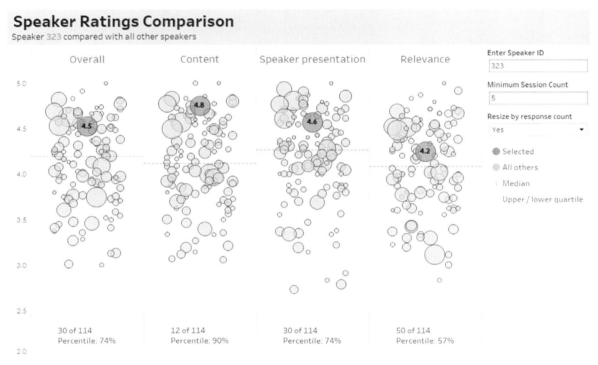

FIGURE 3.3   Champagne bubbles! Selecting "Yes" from the drop-down menu for "Resize by response count" resizes the dots based on the number of survey responses.

Why This Works

Clear Dot Color and Position

Although we could also use shape, it is the color more than anything else that makes the individual's ratings pop out from all the other ratings. The selected individual's dot is centered horizontally, but it is the different color that does the most to make the selected speaker stand out.

Number of Dots Tells a Compelling Story

We'll look at comparing an individual score versus the aggregate of all scores in a moment, but seeing all the dots allows presenters to see not just where they are relative to others but also just how many other people were rated. This immediately answers the question "Am I comparing performance with six other people or 600?" in a way just displaying a number of the count of respondents does not.

Quartile Bands and Median Line Show Clustering

By showing bands and a median line, presenters can immediately see if they are at or below the median and in which quartile they sit. (See Figure 3.4.)

> **Note**
>
> The dots are semitransparent so you can easily see how they overlap.

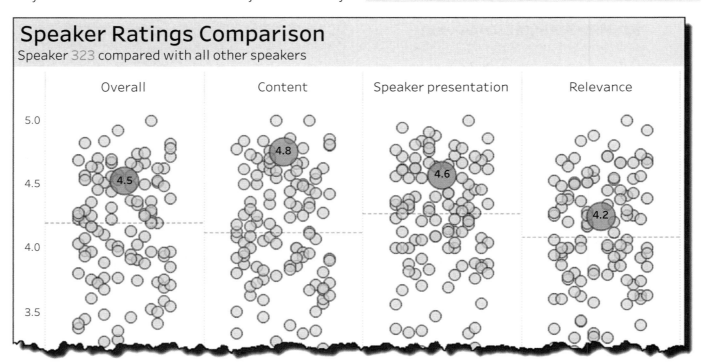

FIGURE 3.4   The jittered dot (jitterplot) plot shows at a glance that the selected speaker is above or near the top quartile for the first three categories and a little above the median for the last category.

| 21 of 114 | 25 of 114 | 25 of 114 | 14 of 114 |
| Percentile: 83% | Percentile: 79% | Percentile: 80% | Percentile: 90% |

FIGURE 3.5   Key performance indicator table at the bottom of the chart shows exact ranking and percentile.

Key Performance Indicators Present Exact Measures

A table along the bottom of the chart (see Figure 3.5) allows people to see their exact ranking and percentile.

Other Considerations

Why Not Resize the Dots Based on Response Count by Default?

Some speakers were rated by only a handful of people, and others received over 120 responses. Why not change the default so that the size of the dot is based on response count, as shown in Figure 3.3?

Most people who reviewed the dashboard found the different-size circles distracting. One commented that the marks looked like "champagne bubbles" so we elected to keep the size of the dots uniform for the default view. Resizing also compounds the difficulty in hovering over individual dots as a large dot may occlude several smaller dots.

> **Note**
>
> The alternative approach shown in Figure 3.14 avoids the champagne bubbles and occlusion problem.

If you still want to display session count without having people hover over a mark or creating champagne bubbles, you could always construct a second chart like the ones shown in Figures 3.6 and 3.7.

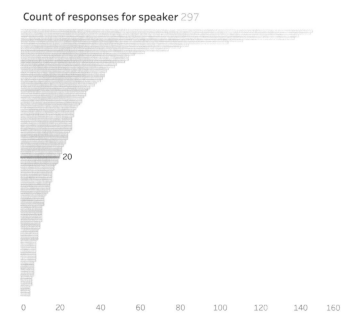

Count of responses for speaker 297

FIGURE 3.6   Bar chart showing number of responses for each speaker with the selected speaker colored blue.

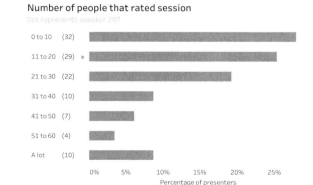

Number of people that rated session
Dot represents speaker 297

FIGURE 3.7   Histogram showing respondent count distribution.

What Is the x-Axis?

People not familiar with jittered marks may be wondering what is along the x-axis in this dashboard. The answer is there's nothing along the x-axis: there is nothing different about a dot that is toward the left than there is about a dot that is toward the right. We moved the dots left or right (jittering) so they did not overlap too much.

Consider the example in Figure 3.8, where we show the scores in a dot plot.

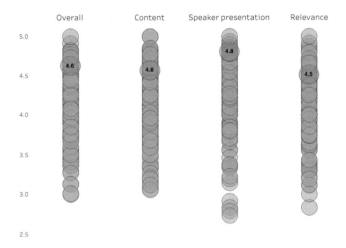

FIGURE 3.8   Dot plot with all ratings overlapping. By placing an "ugly cat" here we don't mean to suggest that a dot plot is a bad chart type. It's just a bad choice here because there are so many overlapping dots.

It's very hard to see how things cluster or whether there are 20 marks or 200 marks in each column. To address the first issue, we could show the distribution with a box and whisker plot, as in Figure 3.9.

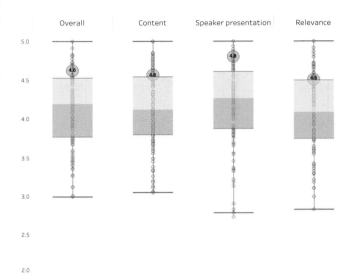

FIGURE 3.9   Box and whisker plot showing quartiles, median, and outliers.

The horizontal lines at the top and bottom of each strip (the whiskers) show the outlier range. The shaded rectangles (the boxes) show the two inner quartiles and the median.

Although Figure 3.9 is an improvement over Figure 3.8, the box and whisker view occludes the view of many marks and still doesn't adequately address the question of how many responses there were, as there are still a lot of overlapping dots.

Speaking about Axes, Why Doesn't the y-Axis Start at Zero?

In this case, the lowest speaker score was 2.7 on a scale of 1 through 5 (which is pretty impressive, no?). Although we could indeed present the y-axis starting at zero, doing so would just make it harder to distinguish the differences between a relatively poor speaker and a relatively good speaker as the dots will be packed closer together. (See Figure 3.10.)

Note

The box and whisker plot, in this author's opinion (Steve), is also ugly and clinical. But there are people who love box plots and may respond favorably to seeing a chart like the one in Figure 3.9. (See the Author Commentary from Andy at the end of this section.) My suggestion is to know as much about your audience as possible. If they will be able to decode the data more easily with a box plot, then use a box plot.

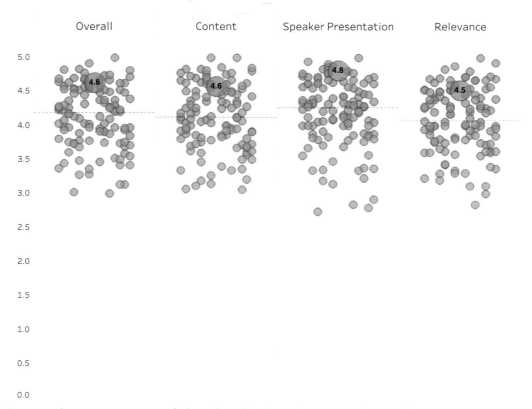

FIGURE 3.10   Starting the y-axis at zero only bunches the dots closer together, making it harder to compare and understand the spread of scores.

Why Not Just Compare the Selected Speaker with the Average of Everybody Else?

There will indeed be times when you don't have all of the scores and you will only be able to compare an individual score with an aggregate. But when you do have separate responses, showing the targeted score in context to other scores can be much more powerful.

Consider the scenario presented in Figure 3.11, where we want to show the performance of an individual employee (in this case, Louise) in comparison with her peers.

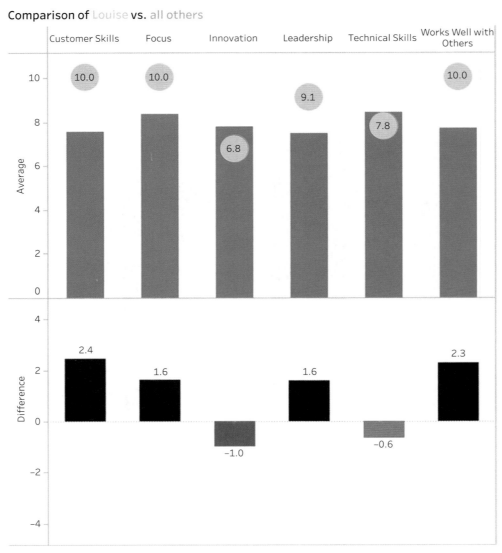

FIGURE 3.11   Combination bar chart and circle chart showing the performance of an individual compared with peers.

We can see that Louise got all 10s in customer skills, focus, and working well with others and that she is well above average in four of the six categories.

But how many other people got a 10 in these categories? And that bar for leadership—it looks like it's around 7.5—how was that score determined? Did half the group get a 10 and the other half get a 5, or were the scores more equally distributed?

Finally, just how many people were rated? Sure, we can have a label that reads "Louise's score compared to 19 others," but we still have to imagine what 19 looks like.

Compare this approach with the jitterplot in Figure 3.12.

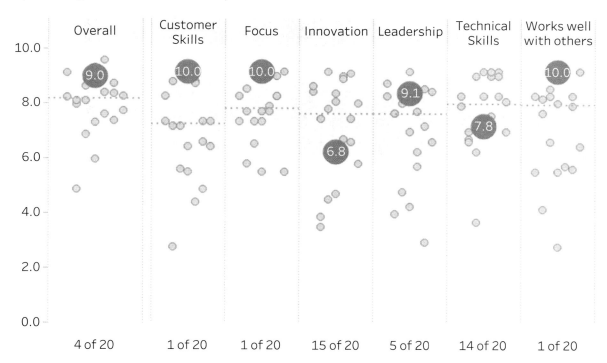

Comparerator
(Showing Louise and all others)

| 4 of 20 | 1 of 20 | 1 of 20 | 15 of 20 | 5 of 20 | 14 of 20 | 1 of 20 |

FIGURE 3.12   Comparing employee performance using a jitterplot.

It's the same data and the same scenario, but we can tell so much more from this figure than when we compare to the aggregate!

Aspect: leadership

Score: 5.2

Rank: 17 out of 20

FIGURE 3.13 An individual can see his or her score, but hovering over a mark should reveal only the score, not the person behind the score.

But what about anonymity? you may ask. For the people who did not perform well, isn't this a form of public pillorying?

Who says this information has to be public? Only the manager of the group should be able to see everybody's score. Otherwise, an individual should be able to see only his or her score with respect to peers. That is, when you hover over a dot, you should not be able to see which fellow employee is associated with that dot. (See Figure 3.13.)

Alternative Approach

In Figure 3.14, we present a different approach that may work better for you, depending on what you want to emphasize. Here it's easy to compare the size of the dots and explore individual marks.

The downside to the approach is that, unlike the jitterplot in Figure 3.1, the unit histogram will not scale to thousands of marks. In addition, with this approach, you cannot see in which quartile a dot sits.

What If There Are Millions of Dots?

The unit histogram works with hundreds of responses, the jitterplot with thousands, but suppose you have tens of thousands or even millions of responses?

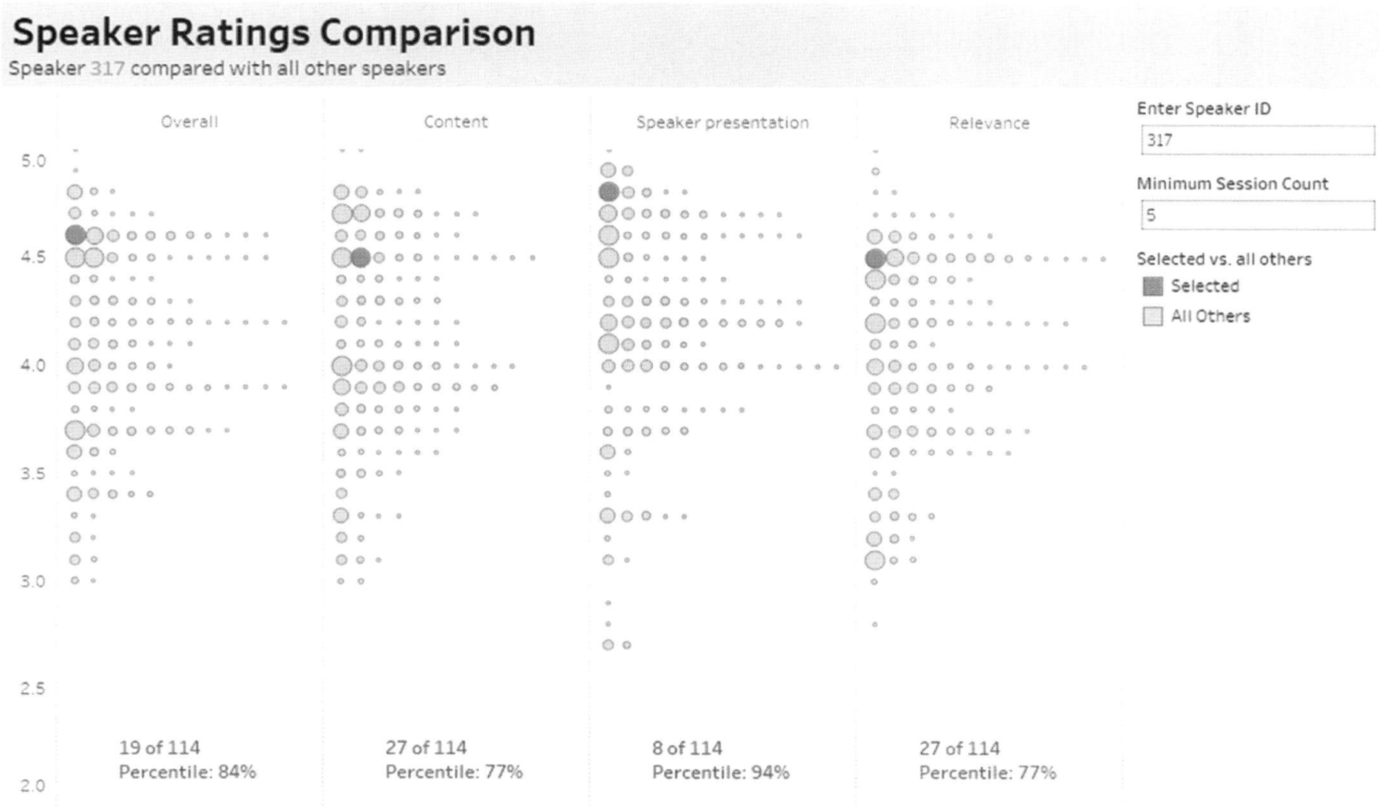

FIGURE 3.14 A unit histogram showing an individual's ratings compared to others.

In that case, the best approach may be a simple histogram (a bar chart showing a distribution) where the bar that is most like you is highlighted.

Consider the dashboard in Figure 3.15, where we see a bar chart showing age distributions of everyone living in the United States. Here you specify your age using the slider, and a bar corresponding to you (and several other million people) gets highlighted.

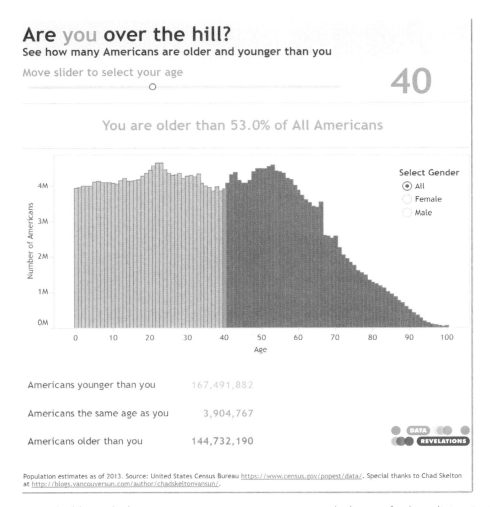

FIGURE 3.15   Histogram dashboard where you can compare your age with those of others living in the United States. (See http://tinyurl.com/h3w5ypw.)

Source: United States Census Bureau, https://www.census.gov/popest/data/. Special thanks to Chad Skelton at http://blogs.vancouversun.com/author/chadskeltonvansun/.

Author Commentary

JEFF: This dashboard has a very simple approach to visualize the data but, at the same time, has the complexity of having lots of data. It's easy to see the single session versus all of the others. It shows the scope of how many sessions there were in total, not in a precise way for comparison, but in a way that we can quickly determine the scope. The use of jitter is key here, because otherwise the dots would all be on top of each other.

STEVE: If you are working with aggregated data—that is, where you don't have access to individual responses—make sure you check out Jeffrey Shaffer's Course Metrics dashboard. (See Chapter 2.) Jeff has built what is my go-to way to compare an individual with a peer group and with the overall population. Even if you're not working with aggregated data, you should check it out as the dot plot technique is very valuable.

ANDY: While writing this book, we discovered that Steve doesn't like box plots! I agree with Steve's point that laypeople often don't know what they are. But, as with all charts, people can be trained to understand them. Consider the waterfall plot in Chapter 24. That's by no means a straightforward chart, but once you learn how to read it, it reveals a great deal of information. A box plot is the same.

Perhaps it's their appearance? We can make box plots look better, by narrowing the width/height of the box. (See Figure 3.16.)

Steve's also right that if you want to see every dot, the box plot prevents that. However, not all analytical questions need us to see all the dots.

Speaker rating comparison
Speaker 323 compared with all other speakers.

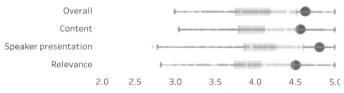

FIGURE 3.16   A more attractive box plot?

The box plot's very design is intended to overcome the issue of overlaid dots. The whiskers extend to 1.5 times the interquartile range. That sounds like scary statistical language, but it is just a way of describing how spread out the values are. What about the box? Its center point is the median, and its edges represent one quartile on either side of it. In other words, half of all the dots are within the box. Since the box, by definition, tells you where the quartiles and outliers are, do you still need to see all the dots when the primary question is just to see where your mark (the big blue dot in Figure 3.16) sits?

The box plot has additional strengths in that you can compare distributions very easily among different categories. In Figure 3.16, it's easy to see that the spread of values in each category is similar.

STEVE: What if there are a million dots?

ANDY: Steve presents a very nice way of showing the data in a histogram (in Figure 3.15). A box plot will work just as well with a million dots: As long as you learn to look primarily at the box, not the dots, a box plot is a great way to see a summary of the spread of data within a category.

Chapter 4

What-If Analysis: Wage Increase Ramifications

What-If dashboard that analyzes the impact of increasing the minimum wage within an organization.
Dashboard Designer: Matt Chambers

What-If Analysis: Impact of Minimum Wage

Proposed Minimum Wage
$15.00

Required Service
0

	Below	Above
	296 (32.1%)	625 (67.9%)

Dollar Impact of Minimum Wage: $1,788,805

Employees Below Minimum Wage: 296

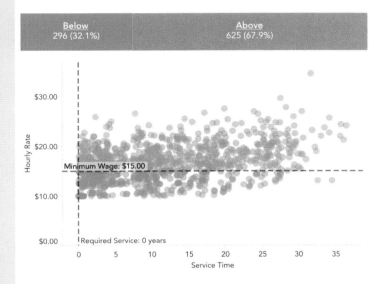

Minimum Wage: $15.00

Required Service: 0 years

Hourly Rate / Service Time

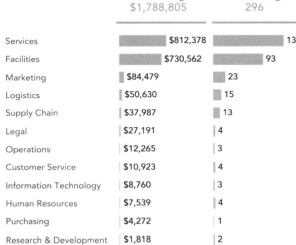

Department	Dollar Impact	Employees Below
Services	$812,378	131
Facilities	$730,562	93
Marketing	$84,479	23
Logistics	$50,630	15
Supply Chain	$37,987	13
Legal	$27,191	4
Operations	$12,265	3
Customer Service	$10,923	4
Information Technology	$8,760	3
Human Resources	$7,539	4
Purchasing	$4,272	1
Research & Development	$1,818	2

Current Distribution — Average Hourly Rate: $16.72

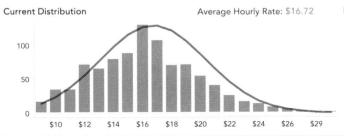

Distribution with Minimum Wage — Average Hourly Rate: $17.45

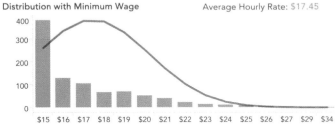

Scenario

Big Picture

For some time now, people within your company and throughout the country have been rumbling about raising the minimum wage. Because you have a lot of people on staff who are hourly wage earners, you need to address the ramifications of how a possible government-mandated increase will affect costs.

Although you suspect that the state and federal government won't approve such a wage increase for several years, your company is considering increasing the minimum wage before then as a way to attract more talent and generate employee loyalty. As any increase right now will be voluntary, you are considering tying the increase to the number of years someone has been an employee. For example, instead of raising the minimum wage across the board from $9 an hour to $15 an hour, you're considering an increase for people who have been with the company for at least three years.

Specifics

- You need to show the increase in wage expenses by department based on an anticipated increase in the government-mandated minimum wage.

- You need to see the distribution of wages and how minimum wage increases impact it.

- You want to see how many employees would benefit from an increase in minimum wage.

- Your company wants to know how many employees would be affected and how much it would cost to implement a voluntary "standard living wage" for

employees that have provided at least five years of service.

Related Scenarios

- What will be the impact on costs and productivity if your organization increases the number of months for maternity/paternity leave?

- What will be the impact if the national cap on Social Security is increased (i.e., how many employees will it affect, in which departments, and what will be the associated costs)?

- What will be the impact of cutting the tuition reimbursement program in your company by 25 percent?

How People Use the Dashboard

The controls in the upper-left corner of the dashboard allow users to experiment with changing the proposed minimum wage and years of required service. (See Figure 4.1.)

Adjusting these settings immediately shows the impact on individual employees, departments, the current wage distribution histogram, and the projected wage distribution histogram.

FIGURE 4.1   Sliders allow you to change the proposed minimum wage and the number of years of service required to receive the wage increase.

Why This Works

Easy-to-Adjust Controls

Adjusting the controls affects four charts on the dashboard, as shown on Figure 4.2.

Combination Chart to Show Which Workers Will Be Affected

Two charts comprise the first section of the dashboard. The first is a stacked bar chart showing the percentage of employees who are above and below

FIGURE 4.2   Moving the sliders changes four different charts. Compare the charts here with the ones on the dashboard shown at the beginning of this chapter.

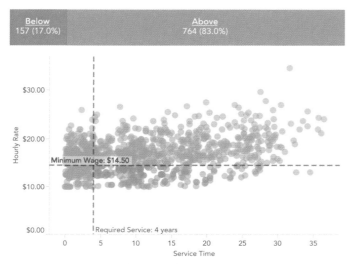

FIGURE 4.3   Stacked bar and scatterplot show overall and individual impact of wage increase and service requirement.

Bar Chart Shows Departmental Impact

The dual bar charts show both dollar and headcount impact broken down by department. (See Figure 4.4.)

Note that the bars are sorted in descending order by dollar amount. It's easy to see that Facilities and Services make up the lion's share of both wages and headcount.

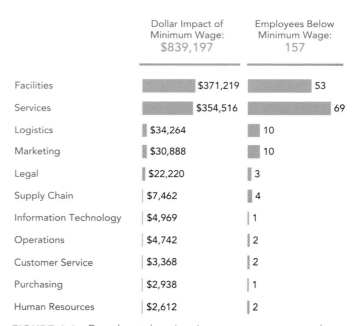

	Dollar Impact of Minimum Wage: $839,197	Employees Below Minimum Wage: 157
Facilities	$371,219	53
Services	$354,516	69
Logistics	$34,264	10
Marketing	$30,888	10
Legal	$22,220	3
Supply Chain	$7,462	4
Information Technology	$4,969	1
Operations	$4,742	2
Customer Service	$3,368	2
Purchasing	$2,938	1
Human Resources	$2,612	2

FIGURE 4.4   Bar chart showing impact on wages and headcount.

the parameters you set. The second is a scatterplot with one dot representing each individual worker. (See Figure 4.3.) The dots are positioned according to workers' length of service (on the x-axis) and their current wage (on the y-axis).

We can see that an increase in the minimum wage to $14.50 for people with at least four years at the company will impact a total of 157 people, or 17 percent of the hourly wage workforce.

These people are easy to see on the scatterplot. All the workers (blue dots) below the minimum wage line and to the right of the required service line will receive a wage increase to the amount set on the sliders.

Histogram and Normal Distribution Show Current and Projected Distributions

The histogram and associated normal distribution (also called a Gaussian curve) show the current distribution (see Figure 4.5) and projected distribution (see Figure 4.6).

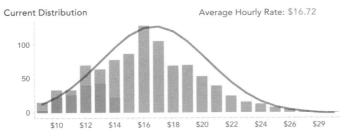

FIGURE 4.5 Current wage and headcount distribution. Blue bars indicate the group that would be affected by the wage increase.

The reason we see both blue and gray bars in the $9 through $14 range in Figure 4.5 is because not everyone will enjoy the wage increase as our what-if analysis stipulates a minimum of four years of service.

Figure 4.6 shows how the wages will be distributed after the increase. The $14 bar is now very tall. The blue section of this bar represents the people who will see a wage increase based on your parameter choices.

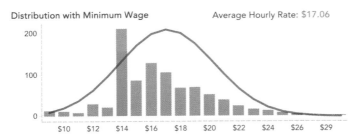

FIGURE 4.6 Projected wage and headcount distribution. On the tallest bar, the top, gray portion represents people who will earn between $14.00 and $14.49. The lower, turquoise portion represents people who will earn between $14.50 and $14.99.

Understanding the Normal Distribution

The superimposed bell curve helps people familiar with normal distribution curves get a better sense of how the wages are distributed, as shown in Figure 4.7.

The curve provides an easy read as to whether hourly wages are distributed evenly or if the data skews left or right. For example, if you change the number of required years to zero, the data skews strongly to the right, as the chart is dominated by the large bar at $14. (See Figure 4.8.)

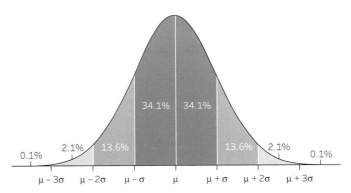

FIGURE 4.7 Symmetrical normal distribution curve. The data indicates that 68 percent is within 1 standard deviation and 95 percent is within 2 standard deviations

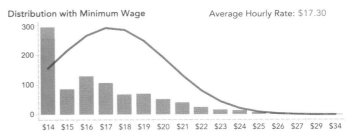

FIGURE 4.8 The distribution is right-skewed when the number of required years is set to zero.

Understanding distribution

A number of general types of data distribution exist. (See Figure 4.9.) "Skew" refers to the asymmetry of the distribution versus the even distribution of a normal distribution. Some people find skew labels confusing. Skew is easy to remember if you see skewed data as having a tail (i.e., gets thinner at one end). The direction of the skew matches the direction of the tail.

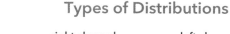

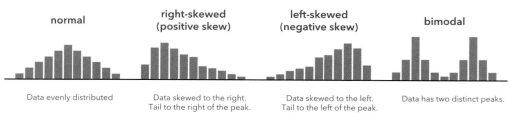

| normal | right-skewed (positive skew) | left-skewed (negative skew) | bimodal |
| Data evenly distributed | Data skewed to the right. Tail to the right of the peak. | Data skewed to the left. Tail to the left of the peak. | Data has two distinct peaks. |

FIGURE 4.9   A few examples of the types of distributions.

Great Use of Color

Color is used sparingly and consistently in the dashboard with the stacked bar chart at the top of Figure 4.4 acting as both a useful chart and a color legend. With these two colors established, it's easy to decode all the other charts on the dashboard. The same color is used on the scatter plot and the distributions as well as the key text throughout the dashboard.

Dashboard Designer Commentary

Matt Chambers: This dashboard showcases how visual design can make a difficult decision easy to understand. Tools such as this can show decision makers the exact outcome of decisions while allowing manipulation of the variables over which they have control. The ability to see the outcome of decisions in real time is what makes this tool so powerful.

Author Commentary

JEFF: I really liked this dashboard from the moment I saw it. Matt took great care in its design. I love the use of color, the dashboard layout, the chart types, and the font choice (Avenir), which has a clean appearance and is very readable. In addition, from a purely functional standpoint, the dashboard allows the user to interact in a way that allows scenario planning. It's a great example of functionality and beautiful design.

ANDY: I agree with Jeff. If we consider the response framework from Don Norman's *The Design of Everyday Things* (Basic Books, 2013), we see success in all three areas. The visceral response is positive: White space, simple colors, and plain fonts make for a positive first reaction. The behavioral response is great too. The affordances—the things that can be changed—are obvious. When we make a change to the parameters, we can immediately see the impact of our actions by the increase or decrease in the amount of blue on the dashboard. That leads us to the reflective phase: Did we like it? Yes. Did it work? Yes. Therefore, do I like this dashboard and want to use it again? Absolutely yes.

Chapter 5

Executive Sales Dashboard

Executive software license sales dashboard.

Dashboard Designer: The dashboard designer wishes to remain anonymous.
Note that product names and company names have been changed.

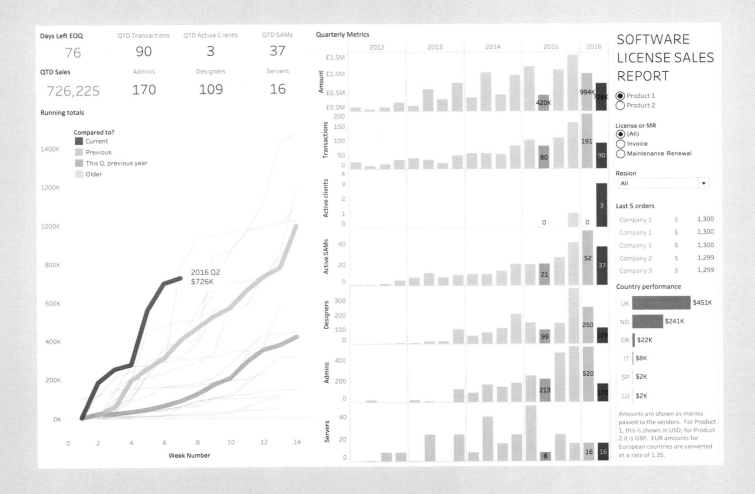

Scenario

Big Picture

You are a sales manager and want to know how you and the sales team have been performing this quarter. You want to be able to see, at any time during the quarter, exactly how total sales for that quarter compare to any previous quarter. You need to be able to see the overview for the whole business and also filter down to individual product lines or regions.

Specifics

- How are we doing this quarter?
- How is this quarter compared to last quarter and the same quarter last year?
- Are we on track to beat the previous quarter? Are we on track to beat the same quarter last year?
- What are the most recent transactions?

Related Scenarios

- Product managers would want to compare cumulative sales of different products launched at different times. Even though you launched Product X last year, did it sell quicker than Product Y, which you released this year?
- Social managers might want to measure how viral their campaigns were. Which campaigns got the most hits the most quickly? Which ones had the most longevity?
- Event organizers tracking registrations to recurring events would use a dashboard like this to see if their ticket sales are above or below target compared to previous events.

How People Use the Dashboard

This dashboard is designed to provide a complete overview of sales for two products. The company executives receive a copy of this email weekly. If they need more details, they can click on a link to go to the live, interactive version viewable in their browser.

Why This Works

Focus on Year-over-Year and Quarter-over-Quarter Growth Comparisons

In this organization, the most important things to know are: what's happening *now*, what happened last quarter, and what happened in this quarter last year. This is vital in a sales organization focusing on growth.

The index chart on this dashboard makes comparison to previous periods very easy. (See Figure 5.1.) The x-axis shows "Week of Quarter." Each quarter's sales begin in the same place: at zero on the x-axis. The line shows cumulative sales for each week of the quarter. There is a line for each quarter. The result, the index chart, allows you to see, at a glance, how progress in this quarter compares to previous ones.

Color and size help identify the most relevant quarters for comparison. Three lines are thicker than the others: current quarter, previous quarter, and same quarter last year. The current quarter is red, which stands out most clearly. The other two comparison quarters are different colors, making identification easy. All other quarters are shown as thin gray lines; they are there for context, but the gray allows them to sit in the background unless needed.

In the interactive version of the dashboard, the detail for any quarter can be seen quickly by hovering the mouse over the line: A tool tip reveals detail, and the relevant quarter is highlighted in the bar chart to the right.

In Figure 5.1, we can see that when this screen shot was taken (Q2 2016), sales are tracking very well. It is significantly better than the previous quarter and the same quarter last year. In fact, sales growth in this quarter has been exceptional.

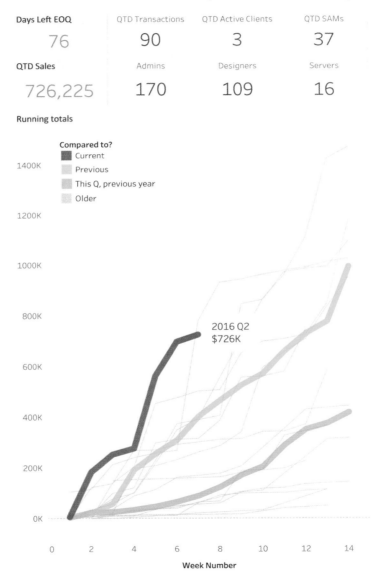

FIGURE 5.1 The index chart lets the executives see how sales this quarter are growing compared to other quarters. The previous quarter and same quarter last year are highlighted.

As discussed in Chapter 31: Visualizing Time, index charts are superb ways to track measures and compare them against different periods. This same company also has a simpler dashboard comparing only annual company growth. (See Figure 5.2.)

Although the index chart shows the growth rate comparison, the bar chart in Figure 5.3 shows the actual values for each quarter's sales. Each row of bars represents one of the seven metrics this business focuses on. Only the labels for the three important bars (this quarter, last quarter, same quarter last year) are shown. This reduces clutter on the dashboard while users retain the ability to look up the most important numbers without relying on interactivity.

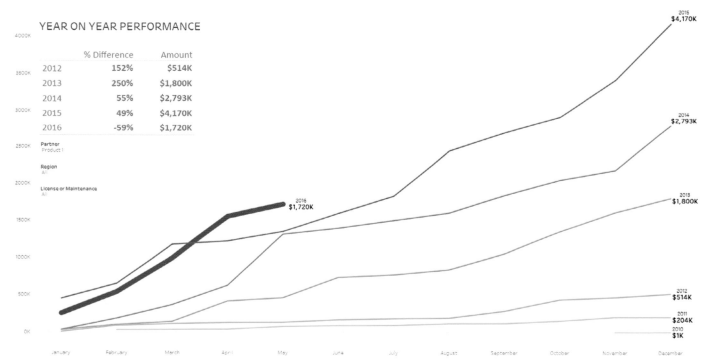

FIGURE 5.2   Year-over-year performance for a software company. As you can see, 2016 is tracking ahead of the previous year.

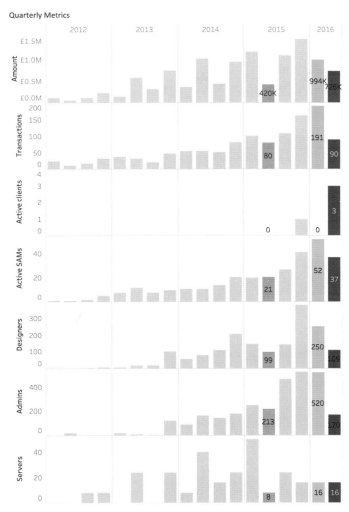

FIGURE 5.3   Growth over time is shown in detail in this bar chart. The labels allow the viewer to see the exact information in the most relevant quarters.

Key Metrics as Text

The top left of the dashboard is devoted to the table shown in Figure 5.4. At a glance, executives can look to the most prominent part of the dashboard and find exactly the numbers they need to see.

Days Left EOQ	QTD Transactions	QTD Active Clients	QTD SAMs
76	90	3	37
QTD Sales	**Admins**	**Designers**	**Servers**
726,225	170	109	16

FIGURE 5.4   It can be important to distill the information down to just a few key numbers. If that's the case, just show the numbers. You can show detailed charts elsewhere.

When looking at the dashboard at the start of a week or ahead of a meeting with a sales team, you can check just these numbers for the main takeaway.

Small Details Where Needed

This dashboard is dominated by the key metrics, the index chart and the detail bar chart. But the space below the filters is just enough to add extra information needed for a full business snapshot. In Figure 5.5, the last five orders are highlighted, as is a geographic snapshot of the countries this company sells to.

Color

As with so many dashboards in this book, it's the subtle use of color that makes this dashboard work, as shown in Figure 5.3. Red? Boom! That's this quarter, the most important thing to look at. Pink or salmon pink? That's important: this time last year and last quarter. Gray? Not as important. These small but significant color choices have a large impact on how easily people can identify the numbers they need the most.

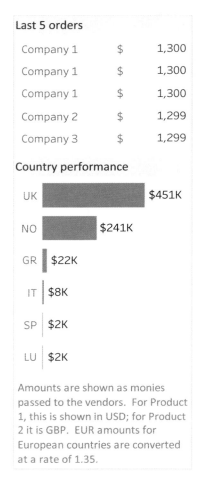

Last 5 orders		
Company 1	$	1,300
Company 1	$	1,300
Company 1	$	1,300
Company 2	$	1,299
Company 3	$	1,299

Country performance

UK	$451K
NO	$241K
GR	$22K
IT	$8K
SP	$2K
LU	$2K

Amounts are shown as monies passed to the vendors. For Product 1, this is shown in USD; for Product 2 it is GBP. EUR amounts for European countries are converted at a rate of 1.35.

FIGURE 5.5   Small charts fit perfectly into small places.

Author Commentary

ANDY: Where do you look first when you open a web page or dashboard? It's probably the left-hand side. That's where the most important information should go. Should that be where the filters are? Filters need to be discoverable for new users. Therefore, you could argue that they should be on the left. However, they also need to blend out of the way once you're familiar with the dashboard. Therefore, they could go on the right-hand side.

This dashboard is used by a team who know the data and the dashboard intimately. They don't need to discover the filters each time they use the dashboard; they already know they are there. For that reason, the filters are on the right.

If the dashboard is used by viewers who visit it only occasionally, it might be more important to put the filters on the left, as shown in Figure 5.6.

I always used to prefer putting filters on the right-hand side of a dashboard. As a dashboard designer, I knew the filters were on the right because I put them there. However, when user-testing these dashboards, I'd be in despair as I watched people use them: They'd click around, seemingly randomly, and most wouldn't use the filters.

"Why didn't you click on the filters?" I'd ask after the usability test. "What filters?" was a common answer. Much as you may love your dashboard, others will view it as new, and many won't cast their eyes to the right-hand side. Since they didn't put the filters on the dashboard, they don't think to look over on the right-hand side.

What's the solution? The dashboard in this chapter does put the filters to the right, because the company trains all users in how to use the dashboard. They are shown the filters and trained how they work.

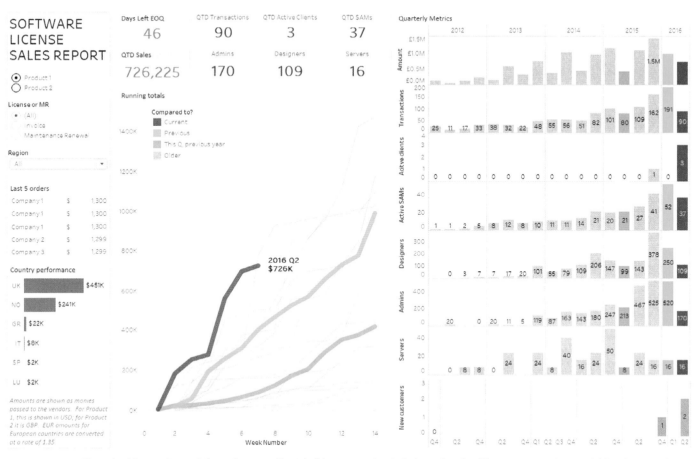

FIGURE 5.6   The dashboard would work as well with filters on the left-hand side. This approach would be better for people who use the dashboard infrequently.

JEFF: I like the chart types that were chosen for this dashboard: the key indicators at the top of the dashboard, the index chart, and the bar charts. The index really shows the trend against the prior period very well. This dashboard is packed with information. I think a few changes to the overall design would help its overall flow. I might compromise the placement of the filters to allow for things to be moved around a bit and give the components of the dashboard some breathing room.

Figure 5.7 shows an example redesign where I moved a few things around. I created a bit more space for things to fit. I also removed the data labels on the bars, since tool tips are available to get more detailed data. I avoided rotating text on the y-axis on the bar charts by moving the labels into the chart. Rotated text takes longer for users to read and can be difficult to read. As an example, there was a spelling mistake in this dashboard on "Active Clients." This dashboard had already gone through several reviews by a number of people, but until I rotated, the error was not caught.

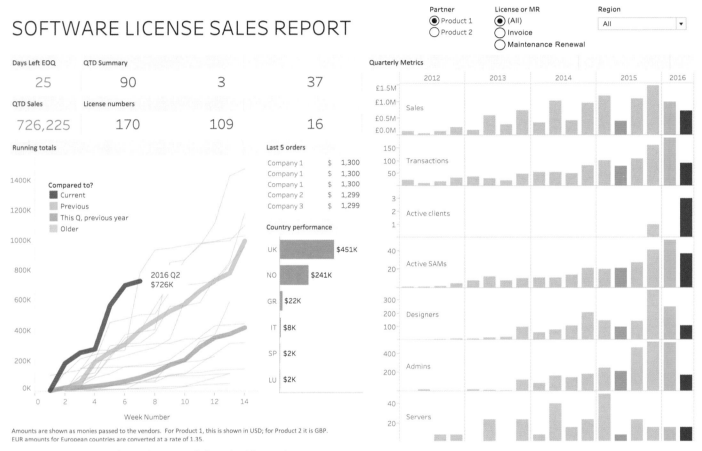

FIGURE 5.7 Sample redesign of the dashboard.

Chapter 6

Ranking by Now, Comparing with Then

Ranking by now, comparing with then dashboard for a single period.
Author: Steve Wexler
Organization: Data Revelations

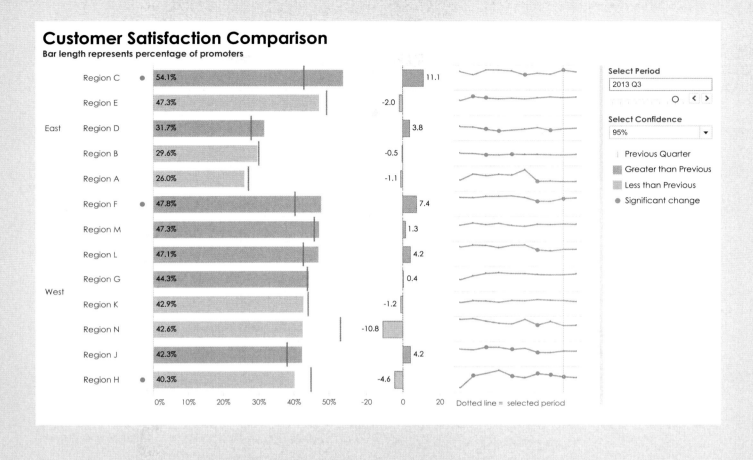

Customer Satisfaction Comparison

Bar length represents percentage of promoters

East	Region C	●	54.1%		11.1
	Region E		47.3%		-2.0
	Region D		31.7%		3.8
	Region B		29.6%		-0.5
	Region A		26.0%		-1.1
West	Region F	●	47.8%		7.4
	Region M		47.3%		1.3
	Region L		47.1%		4.2
	Region G		44.3%		0.4
	Region K		42.9%		-1.2
	Region N		42.6%		-10.8
	Region J		42.3%		4.2
	Region H	●	40.3%		-4.6

0% 10% 20% 30% 40% 50%   -20   0   20   Dotted line = selected period

Select Period

2013 Q3

○ ‹ ›

Select Confidence

95% ▼

| Previous Quarter
▨ Greater than Previous
▨ Less than Previous
● Significant change

> **Note**
>
> In this dashboard, we show the percentage of survey respondents who rated a product or service very highly ("Promoters"). For a discussion of how to visualize data that takes into account Promoters, Detractors, and people that don't care one way or another ("Neutrals"), see Chapter 17.

Scenario

Big Picture

Your company takes customer satisfaction very seriously. You monitor it on a monthly basis by major geographic areas (divisions) and subareas (regions) and need to see in which areas it's increasing, decreasing, or staying the same.

You want to be able to react to downturns quickly, but you don't want to panic unnecessarily so you need to see if changes from the previous time period are statistically significant. You also need to be able to look at changes over time to see if big swings are isolated to the particular period or indicative of a larger problem.

Specifics

- You are tasked with showing the percentage of customers who are very satisfied with your products and services ("Promoters"), broken down by division and region.

- You need to sort the data by region so it's easy to see in which divisions customers are most satisfied and in which they are least satisfied.
- You want to make it easy to see just how much more satisfied customers are in one region versus another.
- You need to compare performance by time period(s), for example, this quarter versus the previous quarter.
- You need to show whether changes from a previous period are significant using whatever litmus test the company uses to determine statistical significance.

Related Scenarios

- You need to rank sales for products and services, broken down by state, and compare them with a previous period or periods.
- You're reviewing your weekly email campaign and need to show the number or percentage of folks who opened emails and clicked, broken down by gender and age. You need to compare the current week with a previous period.

How People Use the Dashboard

In this dashboard, a viewer can select a region that interests him or her. In Figure 6.1, the viewer selects Region F, and the dashboard updates to show longitudinal information about that region.

Hovering over a bar will give you more information about a particular region, as shown in Figure 6.2.

Customer Satisfaction Comparison

Bar length represents percentage of promoters

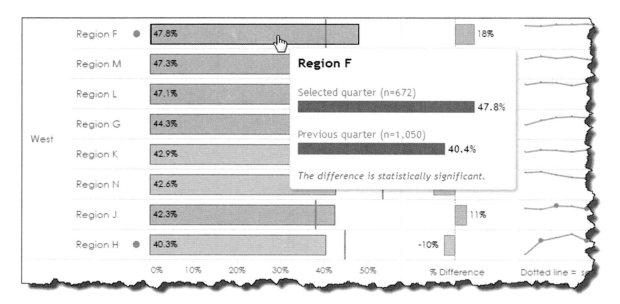

FIGURE 6.2   A pop-up window provides more information about a particular region.

Why This Works

The Bar Charts Make Comparison Easy

The bars make it very easy to see just how one region compares with another. Indeed, as shown in Figure 6.3, we can remove the labels inside the bars and still tell that Region C is doing roughly twice as well as Region A.

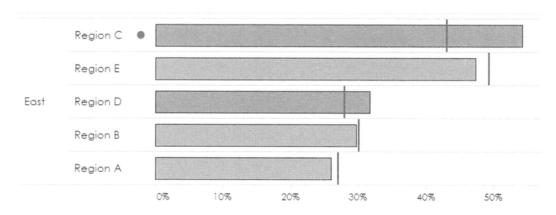

FIGURE 6.3   The bars make it easy to both sort and compare magnitude. Even without the labels, it's easy to see that the top bar is roughly twice the length of the bottom bar.

The Vertical Lines Make It Easy to See *How* Much Better or Worse

The vertical lines in Figure 6.4 allow us to see that Region C did quite a bit better in the current period compared with the previous period and that Region E just did a little bit worse.

The Bar Colors Make It Easy to See Better or Worse

Although the vertical lines may make the color coding and color legend unnecessary, by using color, we can very quickly see in Figure 6.5 that two regions in the East division performed better than in the previous

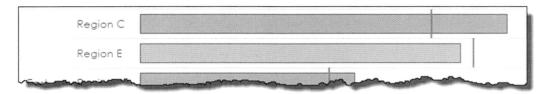

FIGURE 6.4   The vertical reference lines make for easy comparison.

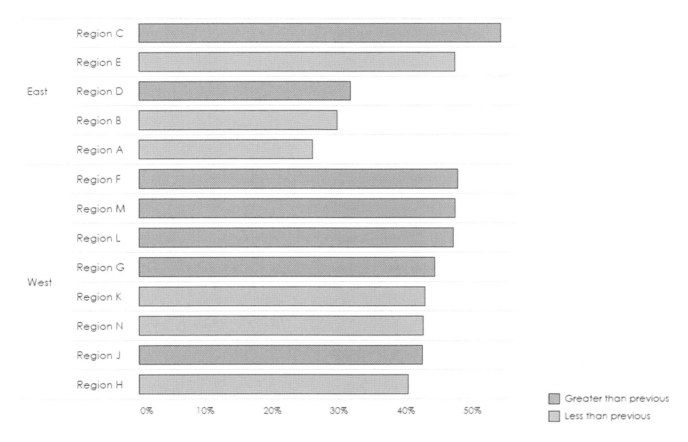

FIGURE 6.5   Color coding prominently contrasts regions' performance in current periods against performance in previous periods, allowing clear visualization of whether performance declined or improved.

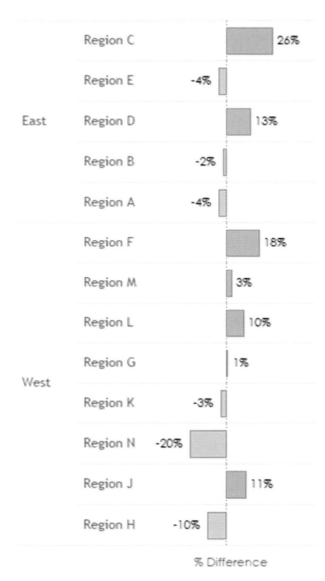

% Difference

FIGURE 6.6   Bar length and direction correspond to percentage difference from the previous period.

period and five regions in the West division performed better than in the previous period.

Percentage Change from the Previous Period

Although it is not essential, it can be very useful to show the percentage difference from the previous period. (See Figure 6.6.)

Note that some people prefer seeing the point difference rather than the percentage difference, so you may want to add a dashboard widget that allows people to switch between the two ways of displaying the difference.

The Red Dots Make It Easy to See Which Differences Warrant Further Investigation

A quick glance at Figure 6.7 makes it easy to see that something is special about Regions C, F, and H, and it's not that the differences are particularly large. For example, there's a big gap between current and previous values for Region N, but there's no red dot. The legend (above left) indicates that the difference between the current and previous period is *significant*, using whatever test for significance is deemed appropriate for this situation.

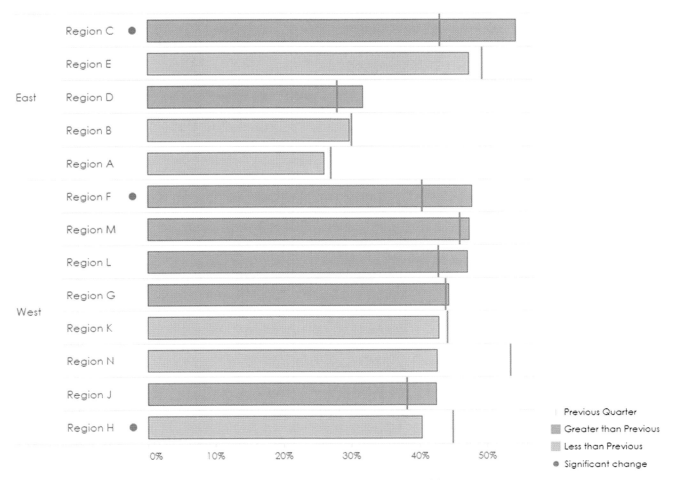

FIGURE 6.7   Red dots make it easy to identify possible opportunities/problem areas.

The Sparklines Make It Easy to See How Values Have Changed over Time

Sparklines show us, at a glance, how each region is performing over time and any significant variations (i.e., whether there are none, some, or many). In Figure 6.8, we can see that there is a lot of volatility in Region H in particular. Note that many factors go into whether an increase or decrease is significant, including the number of people who responded to a survey during the period. This is why we don't see a red dot for Region A at its peak. Although the increase was indeed very large, it was not statistically significant based on the applied test for statistical significance.

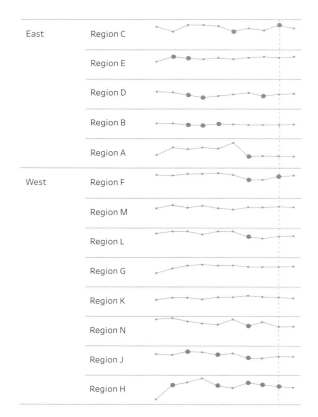

FIGURE 6.8   Sparklines give us a quick read of performance over time. A red dot indicates that a change from the previous value was significant.

Other Features of the Dashboard

Notice that there is a "Select Period" parameter control on the dashboard. (See Figure 6.9.)

Select Period

2013 Q3

FIGURE 6.9   "Select Period" widget allows viewers to focus on any period and not just the current period.

The parameter allows viewers to compare any period with a prior period versus only the current period with the prior period.

Why is this useful?

Suppose it is February 27, and somebody wants to compare January figures with December figures. After a long weekend, the person comes into the office to finish the analysis, only to discover the dashboard now shows February versus January figures because it's March 2. This parameter allows people to focus on whichever period interests them.

The Traditional Approach, and Why You Should Avoid It

Many organizations deal with this scenario using a traditional type of scorecard, as shown in Figure 6.10.

Given this chart type's popularity, why shouldn't you use it?

There are at least five shortcomings with this approach:

1. The uniform size of the cells makes it difficult to see how much better or worse one region is performing when compared to another region. Without the numbers in each cell, we would not be able to tell that the percentage of promoters in Region C is more than twice the percentage of promoters in Region A.

2. The traffic light colors will alienate people who suffer from a color vision deficiency (about 8 percent of the male population).

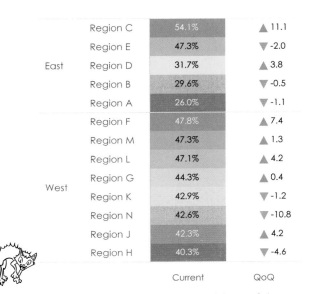

		Current	QoQ
East	Region C	54.1%	▲ 11.1
	Region E	47.3%	▼ -2.0
	Region D	31.7%	▲ 3.8
	Region B	29.6%	▼ -0.5
	Region A	26.0%	▼ -1.1
West	Region F	47.8%	▲ 7.4
	Region M	47.3%	▲ 1.3
	Region L	47.1%	▲ 4.2
	Region G	44.3%	▲ 0.4
	Region K	42.9%	▼ -1.2
	Region N	42.6%	▼ -10.8
	Region J	42.3%	▲ 4.2
	Region H	40.3%	▼ -4.6

FIGURE 6.10 A typical and not terribly useful scorecard.

3. The colors are based on rank and not performance, which could present a problem. Most people equate red with bad, but in this case it indicates last. Indeed, all the scores within a division may be very good, but the *least* very good score still would be red. Consider Region H with 40.3 percent. It's red because it is ranked last, but if it were in the East division, it would be light green or yellow.

4. The key performance indicators (the up- and down-pointing triangles) show only increase and decrease, not the *degree* of increase and decrease. There's no easy way for readers to see where there are big differences.

5. The colors for the key performance indicators conflict with the color-coded cells. That is, green indicates the top rank in one case but a simple increase in another.

Other Approaches

There are other ways to show change between two periods across different categories.

One approach is the distributed slope chart, shown in Figure 6.11, as it makes sorting by performance across divisions and seeing the degree of change between periods easy.

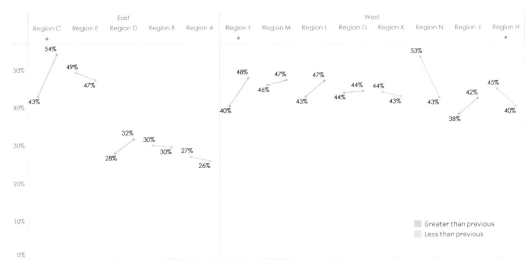

FIGURE 6.11 Distributed slope chart.

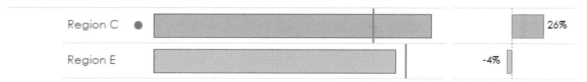

FIGURE 6.12   The distance from the reference line to the end of the left-hand bars shows the same information as the percentage difference bars on the right.

Why use a sorted bar chart instead of a slope chart? The sorted bar chart worked better with the other elements of the dashboard. Specifically, the sparklines, which provide an at-a-glance longitudinal view, would not complement the slope chart.

Author Commentary

ANDY: You could argue that the bars showing the percentage difference are not necessary, since the bar and the reference line let you see that too. (See Figure 6.12.)

Sure, you could remove the percentage difference bar and let the reference line do all the work, but it would be much harder to parse multiple questions when viewing this dashboard. On one day your primary question might be on the highest and lowest satisfaction rates. If that's the case, focus on the bars on the left. The reference lines give you some information of secondary importance.

On another day, you might want to know about the percentage difference. In which case, you're not left trying to gauge the length of the gaps on all the bars. Try working out which had the highest percentage change based on the bars alone in Figure 6.13.

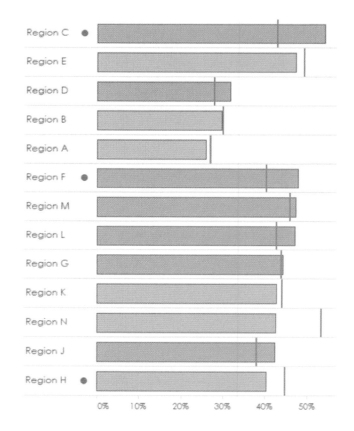

FIGURE 6.13   Which region had the highest change from the previous period (i.e., which bar end is farthest away from the reference line?)

The percentage bar makes it easy to switch from one question to the other and compare either set of values against a common baseline.

You do need to consult with your audience as to which is the most important question and make that one most prominent. In the dashboard in this chapter, it's "What is the level of customer satisfaction?" The percentage question is of secondary importance.

If you find the percentage question is the most important, then it's just a matter of switching the layout and bringing one into a more prominent focus, as shown in Figure 6.14.

Customer Satisfaction Comparison
Bar length represents percentage of promoters

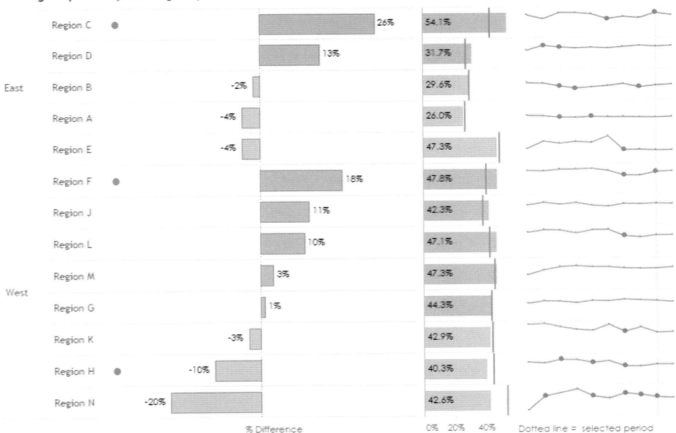

FIGURE 6.14 Give the most prominence to the most important question. If percentage difference is more important than actual values, make it the bigger chart.

Chapter 7

Are We on Pace to Reach Our Goals?

Measures that are on pace to achieve goals, along with key metrics for TV and social media for the current month.
Author: Ryan Sleeper
Organization: Evolytics LLC

KEY INSIGHTS

- Consumer Sales is 5% ahead of pace; this is most likely driven by our M 18-34 demographic.
- Corporate Sales is well-behind pace as expected due to our advertising budget cutbacks in Q3.
- Merchandise is 6% off pace; consider re-allocating spend so we can hit 5 of 7 revenue goals.

REVENUE KPIs

ON PACE NEAR PACE BEHIND PACE

	Pace to Goal	Goal
Consumer Sales	$3,465,979	
Corporate Sales	$1,343,448	
Concessions	$800,277	
Television Revenue	$3,117,965	
Merchandise	$2,236,364	
Advertising Revenue	$2,798,632	
Sponsorship Revenue	$600,442	

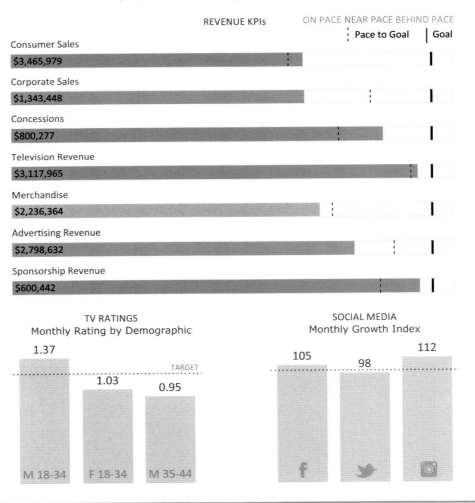

TV RATINGS — Monthly Rating by Demographic

M 18-34	F 18-34	M 35-44
1.37	1.03	0.95

TARGET

SOCIAL MEDIA — Monthly Growth Index

f	twitter	instagram
105	98	112

Scenario

Big Picture

Despite valiant efforts to get everyone in your organization to rely on interactive dashboards, certain executives insist on receiving a weekly one-page summary of key revenue, TV ratings, and social media measures. Although your organization tracks hundreds of measures, each executive asks for a custom report that contains only certain measures.

The executive using this dashboard doesn't want to spend more than two minutes reviewing the findings and is particularly concerned with seeing if revenue key performance indicators are on pace to reach the company's goals.

Specifics

- You need to provide an at-a-glance executive summary of key measures to executives via email.
- You need to show how the organization is performing at the moment but also in the context of how the organization is performing for the entire year.
- You need to normalize different measures so that performance is easy to compare even though scales for the various measures are different.
- Executives need to see progress toward a goal for various revenue measures as well as period-specific TV and social media ratings.

How People Use the Dashboard

This is a terrific example of a personalized, explanatory dashboard. The dashboard is personalized in that measures presented are of specific interest to the executive receiving the dashboard. The dashboard is explanatory in that is gets delivered via email to the executive's inbox. There's no interactivity or exploration in this case, just the key metrics presented very clearly.

The goal is to make it as easy as possible for the executive to see, at a glance, which key measures are performing well and which are performing poorly.

Notice that the dashboard author also telegraphs the key findings with bullet points at the top. (See Figure 7.1.) These are likely the three questions that come into the executive's head when he or she reviews the dashboard, and the bullets provide the context to better understand the numbers.

Why This Works

The Pace Chart Clearly Illustrates Progress

The pace chart is a variation of Stephen Few's bullet chart in that it shows progress toward a goal (the heavy black line) as well as whether the organization

KEY INSIGHTS

- Consumer Sales is 5% ahead of pace; this is most likely driven by our M 18-34 demographic.
- Corporate Sales is well-behind pace as expected due to our advertising budget cutbacks in Q3.
- Merchandise is 6% off pace; consider re-allocating spend so we can hit 5 of 7 revenue goals.

FIGURE 7.1   Bullet points at top of dashboard present key findings.

FIGURE 7.2 Pace chart shows current performance (the bar chart), whether we are on pace to reach our goal (dotted line), and our goal (solid vertical line).

is on pace to achieve that goal (the dotted line). (See Figure 7.2.)

Note that the revenue measures have been normalized based on the goal, not on the actual revenue amounts. That is, bar length is based on what percentage of the goal has been achieved. This explains why the corporate sales revenue bar, at $1.3M, is shorter than the concessions revenue bar, at $800K.

Note also the color coding. It's very easy to see that consumer sales, concessions, television revenue, and sponsorship revenue are ahead of pace (blue); merchandise is near pace (gray); and corporate sales and advertising revenue are behind pace (orange).

The Reference Line Clarifies Ratings

In Figure 7.3, we can see immediately that TV ratings for males between the ages of 18 and 34 are above target while ratings for the other key demographics are below target.

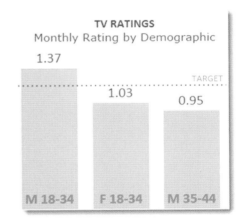

FIGURE 7.3 TV ratings for key demographics with target reference line.

Monthly Growth Index Offers an Easy Comparison

Here's a case where the dashboard author assumes that the dashboard recipient understands the index. In Figure 7.4, a value of 100 indicates that the growth for the current month is the same as the previous month.

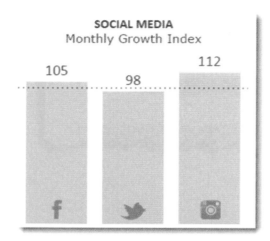

FIGURE 7.4 Comparison of growth among Facebook, Twitter, and Instagram.

The value of 105 for Facebook indicates that there was a 5 percent increase in new likes from the previous month. For example, in the previous month, there might have been 1,000 likes, but in the current month, there were 1,050 likes.

As with the revenue comparison, the growth index normalizes the raw counts, as the number of Instagram users is likely to be considerably smaller than the number of Facebook users. By using a common index, it's easy to compare growth rates and see that Twitter growth is down compared to the previous month while Instagram growth is up by 12 percent.

Author Commentary

STEVE: Even without any advance understanding of the nature of the business, we were able to figure out almost all of what was going on with the dashboard without any explanation from the author. The only place where we needed help was in understanding the Social Media Monthly Growth Index.

Although we may have needed some handholding, we're confident that the target executives of this dashboard would not need any explanation. Indeed, the cherry-picked measures and their associated presentation demonstrate a deep and thorough understanding of what the consumers of the report want to see.

Notice that we used the word "report." Although this endeavor definitely fits our definition of a dashboard, the key findings, commentary, layout, and brevity suggest this is something that should take no more than two minutes for the target audience to consume, most likely via email.

We particularly liked the pace chart, which takes seasonality into account. Also noteworthy is the clean and uncluttered design as well as the simple and instantly recognizable icons for Facebook, Twitter, and Instagram, all embedded within the bars.

One thing I do question is why the bars along the bottom are not color coded based on being ahead of or behind target. Although color coding is not necessary because it's easy to see which bars are above and below the reference line, coding based on color might be a welcome addition.

ANDY: This dashboard could be condensed in order to take up less space. However, in this instance, the requirement was very clearly to create a printable dashboard with just these key pieces of information. If we managed to convince our executives to switch to looking at these on their cellphones, then we could create something much denser to fit into a small space.

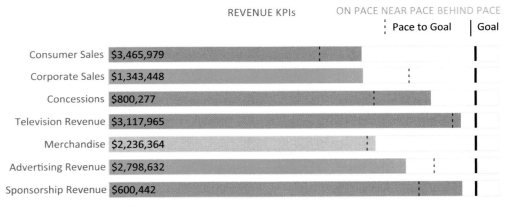

FIGURE 7.5   Labels aligned to the left.

The first thing I would change is to move the labels on the bars to the left of the bars rather than above them. (See Figure 7.5.)

This improves the readability of the chart. Now, with a single sweep of my eye, I can read down the categories and identify the one I want to look at. I can quickly read down the numbers too with a single sweep of the eye. With the labels positioned above the bars, I have to work harder to cast my eye over the categories or values. (See Figure 7.6.)

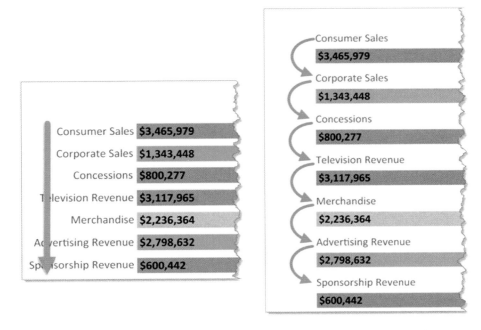

FIGURE 7.6   How your eyes read two versions of the chart. The red lines represent how your eyes have to move around the page to consume the information.

Chapter 8

Multiple Key Performance Metrics

Key performance indicators with multiple measurement types.
Author: Robert Rouse
Organization: InterWorks, Inc.

KPI Executive Overview

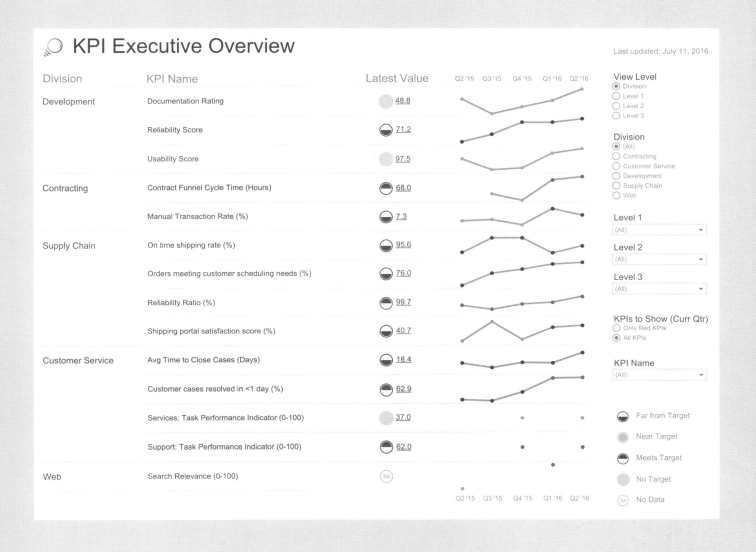

Division	KPI Name	Latest Value	Q2 '15	Q3 '15	Q4 '15	Q1 '16	Q2 '16
Development	Documentation Rating	48.8					
	Reliability Score	71.2					
	Usability Score	97.5					
Contracting	Contract Funnel Cycle Time (Hours)	68.0					
	Manual Transaction Rate (%)	7.3					
Supply Chain	On time shipping rate (%)	95.6					
	Orders meeting customer scheduling needs (%)	76.0					
	Reliability Ratio (%)	99.7					
	Shipping portal satisfaction score (%)	40.7					
Customer Service	Avg Time to Close Cases (Days)	18.4					
	Customer cases resolved in <1 day (%)	62.9					
	Services: Task Performance Indicator (0-100)	37.0					
	Support: Task Performance Indicator (0-100)	62.0					
Web	Search Relevance (0-100)	NA					

Q2 '15   Q3 '15   Q4 '15   Q1 '16   Q2 '16

View Level
- ● Division
- ○ Level 1
- ○ Level 2
- ○ Level 3

Division
- ● (All)
- ○ Contracting
- ○ Customer Service
- ○ Development
- ○ Supply Chain
- ○ Web

Level 1
(All) ▼

Level 2
(All) ▼

Level 3
(All) ▼

KPIs to Show (Curr Qtr)
- ○ Only Red KPIs
- ● All KPIs

KPI Name
(All) ▼

- Far from Target
- Near Target
- Meets Target
- No Target
- NA No Data

Scenario

Big Picture

You are tired of trying to maintain dozens of different dashboards that address various aspects of your business, so you decide to build a single master dashboard with hundreds of key performance indicators (KPIs) that monitor the health of the entire organization. The dashboard needs to be compact and allow stakeholders to easily focus on the items that are pertinent to them and also see how things fit within the big picture.

The dashboard must show, at a glance, if you've met your targets for the current period as well as if you are consistently making or missing your targets. You also need to allow people to zoom in and see details about a particular KPI.

Specifics

- You need to show actual values versus targets for all areas of the business with many different ways of measuring performance.
- You want to make it easy to show only the areas of the business that are underperforming.
- Your company does quarterly reviews and needs to see the current quarter along with trends from preceding ones.
- Your company has set thresholds and requires measured values to stay within a given percentage above or below that goal.

Related Scenarios and Additional Functionality

- You need to navigate all levels of an organizational hierarchy to serve managers at those levels.
- You need to provide easy access to measurement definitions and goal values for a particular KPI.

- You want to show the numbers behind calculations like ratios or percentages in a detail view.
- You need a means of getting to more specialized views unique to a business unit or KPI.

How People Use the Dashboard

The dashboard shows KPIs for many levels of hierarchy within an organization. Using filters along the right side of the dashboard (See Figure 8.1), the user can select a division and related business levels for his or her reporting needs.

The left portion of the dashboard then shows totals for each business level and details based on the view-level selection. (See Figure 8.2.)

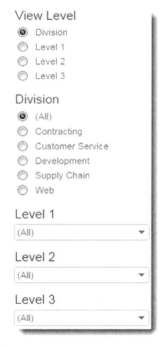

FIGURE 8.1 Filter and parameter controls allow the user to focus on the KPIs associated with a particular division and level within that division.

FIGURE 8.2   Divisions and KPIs associated with the filter and parameter settings.

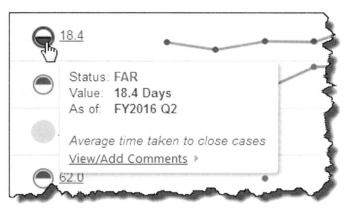

FIGURE 8.3   A tool tip appears on hover to give details and link to a commenting system.

Hovering over a shape shows a tool tip with a definition and link to a system where users can annotate facts relevant to the selected KPI. (See Figure 8.3.)

When a user clicks a KPI name, a pane appears with pertinent details about that KPI. (See Figure 8.4.)

FIGURE 8.4   Selecting a KPI (in this example customer cases resolved in under one day) shows details about that KPI.

In Figure 8.4, we see the following details:

- Specifics about the goal and whether the values are above or below a threshold.
- Details related to the current period's calculations. This particular example shows the cases resolved in one day (numerator) and the total cases handled (denominator).
- A larger trend view with the goal value as a dotted line.
- Definition of the selected KPI, which may include how it is measured or any exceptions involved.
- A link to view more details on a separate dashboard designed specifically for this business unit and KPI.

Why This Works

Shapes Add Context for KPI Values versus Target

Circles with filled areas above or below the center show how the current value relates to the target. (See Figure 8.5.) The different shapes and the color make it easy for users to find underperforming

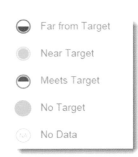

Far from Target

Near Target

Meets Target

No Target

No Data

FIGURE 8.5 Shapes indicate performance versus target.

business units. Gray-colored circles show where no target is defined or where data is unavailable for the current period.

Sparklines Indicate Performance Improvement or Decline

This dashboard shows several KPIs with no set target. For these KPIs, the goal is simply to continue improving each period. Trend lines easily show improvement (or lack thereof) in those areas.

Where there is a set target, the trend shows the number of successive periods that the business did or did not meet its goals. This gives important background to find out if a certain area is an ongoing concern or a one-time problem.

Business Hierarchy Navigation Serves Multiple Needs in One View

Showing values for the sublevels in the same view as higher business levels helps users diagnose points of interest without switching back and forth among dashboards. (See Figure 8.6.) These filter and parameter controls allow a single dashboard to serve a wide range of business needs, reducing the dashboard development effort needed when users request changes.

Filters Allow Users to Focus on KPIs that Are below Threshold

With literally hundreds of KPIs, the filter shown in Figure 8.7 allows users to focus just on KPIs that are below target for the current period.

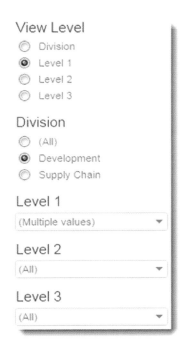

FIGURE 8.6   Filters and parameters allow users to focus on certain levels of business hierarchy.

Alternative Approaches

How do you visualize the progress toward a goal? In this dashboard, Robert Rouse chose a variety of circle icons. To make identification easy, viewers must learn the color and shape of each icon. That's a small disadvantage, although it's not much of a burden for anyone using the dashboard regularly. Since it is a KPI dashboard, it should be used regularly. The circles also take up very little space, which is a big advantage.

In Figure 8.8, we present an alternative approach on a similar KPI tracking dashboard.

Jonathan Drummey's dashboard tracks occurrence of infection issues and nursing issues, such as the number of falls, number of cases of *Clostridium difficile*, and so on. There are major similarities between the first dashboard in the chapter and the dashboard shown in Figure 8.8: one row per KPI, a colored sparkline showing trends, and exact numbers allowing lookup of exact values.

FIGURE 8.7   Filter allows users to focus on only those KPIs that are below target for the current period.

SMHC Unit Dashboard for SMHC
Showing Rolling Quarterly Results
for Nursing and IP Measures

Bundle	Measure	Most Recent Quarterly Results		Days Since Last	Last 13 Months of Quarterly Results	Filters
Infection Prevention	C. difficile per 10K Patient Days	8/16	6.40			Choose Group
	CAUTI per 1K Device Days	8/16	0.00	280		Nursing and IP ▼
	CL Insertion Bundle	6/16	100.0%	52		Choose Unit
	CLABSI per 1K Device Days	8/16	3.17	81		SMHC ▼
	Hand Hygiene	9/16	95.8%			Choose Rolling Period
	VAE per 1K Device Days	8/16	0.00	44		Quarterly ▼
	Ventilator Bundle	8/16	100.0%	426		
Nursing Indicators	Falls w/Injury: SMHC Rate	8/16	1.2	34		Show Targets
	Falls w/Injury: Reported Rate	8/16	1.1	68		No ▼
	Falls: All Falls	8/16	4.2	9		✓ Click for NRCPicker HCAHPS Results
	HA PU - Stage 1 or higher	8/16	2%			

FIGURE 8.8   Health care KPI-tracking dashboard.

Source: Jonathan Drummey of Southern Maine Healthcare

The big difference is the lollipop in the center, which we think is an interesting and useful approach to tracking progress. (See Figure 8.9.)

Here's how the lollipop components work:

- The vertical blue line marks the target. A circle to the right is meeting the target; to the left is underperforming.
- Blue circles show targets that are performing above target.
- Red circles indicate low-performing, high-priority measures compared to target.
- Pink circles represent low-performing, lower-priority measures.
- The lollipop stick shows comparison to the prior period (usually a month, sometimes a quarter). The

stick runs from the previous period's performance level to the current period's circle. If there is no stick, performance hasn't changed.

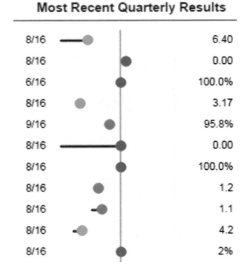

Most Recent Quarterly Results

8/16	6.40
8/16	0.00
6/16	100.0%
8/16	3.17
9/16	95.8%
8/16	0.00
8/16	100.0%
8/16	1.2
8/16	1.1
8/16	4.2
8/16	2%

FIGURE 8.9   Lollipop shows progress toward a goal.

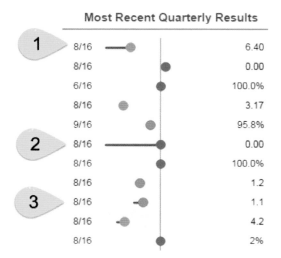

FIGURE 8.10   Lollipop chart shows progress toward a goal.

Let's take a look at Figure 8.10 to see how the lollipop chart works.

The circle marked 1 is pink, indicating that it is not high priority for the group selected in this dashboard. It is underperforming, but the lollipop stick indicates that it is improving.

The circle marked 2 is blue. It is on target, *just*. The lollipop stick shows that there has been a very large improvement over the last period.

The circle marked 3 is red. It's a high-priority target that is underperforming but has improved a little since the last period.

Showing progress toward a goal can be done in many ways. See also Chapter 7, the pace chart by Ryan Sleeper. Bullet charts are also good ways to show progress toward a goal.

Author Commentary

STEVE: This dashboard presents a great approach to the "how am I doing right now" question that we've seen in several other dashboards. Here the focus is on how the organization is performing versus the target for the period, and it also shows trends over the past five periods.

A lot of attributes to this dashboard won us over with the most compelling being that we are able to figure out the KPIs and associated details without needing any instructions. We also liked the designer's icons for whether the KPIs were below, near, or above target.

One of the more impressive features of the dashboard that is difficult to present in a book is just how many levels of KPI are embedded in the dashboard. The designer went to great lengths to allow a stakeholder to find levels and the associated KPIs without having to develop multiple dashboards.

ANDY: This dashboard solves a major challenge: How do you visualize hundreds of KPIs? One way is by extensive filtering. Another way might be to pack all the KPIs in tiny sparklines on a huge screen. Although they are valid design solutions, it might be worth asking a more fundamental business problem: Why does the business have so many KPIs?

When designing dashboards, it is always worthwhile to challenge the design brief. In this case, how will you measure whether the KPIs get looked at? I would recommend this business monitors which KPIs are actually looked at. If many of the hundreds of KPIs are never looked at, I would recommend the business reassesses how it measures success.

Chapter 9

Power Plant Operations Monitoring

Wind and solar (GTA Power) dashboard.
Source: Images courtesy of Dundas Data Visualization, Inc. (www.dundas.com)
Dashboard Designer: Stas Kashepava
Organization: Dundas Data Visualization
Link: https://samples.dundas.com/Dashboard/fa1ee851-8049-457d-92a1-2e2e0c311991?vo=viewonly

GTAPOWER
Empowering the Nation

Power Plant Monitor
—— Trend

TOTAL CAPACITY	SPINNING RESERVE	WATER PRODUCTION	TOTAL LOAD	STANDBY RESERVE	WATER EXPORT
10,858 MW	758 MW	394 MIGD	6,646 MW	1,847 MW	356 MIGD

Local Metrics (Real-Time)
—— Target

SYSTEM FREQUENCY	AMBIENT TEMP	RELATIVE HUMIDITY
51.88 HZ	33.3°C	36.0%

NG TOTAL FLOW
- 2K
- 1K
- 0K

GD HEAT RATE
- 2K
- 1K
- 0K

REAL-TIME DATA FEED — Disabled

Details (All Locations)

LOCATION	CURRENT OUTPUT (kW)	EXPECTED OUTPUT (kW)			14-DAY TREND	LAST INSPECTION
1833 Appleby Line	350,370	420,453		83 %		3 days
1833 Highway 4	3,374	3,917		86 %		●
48 Davis Dr	5,058	5,602		90 %		
144 Howard Cavasos	655,698	714,991		92 %		
2 Jack Hanoka Dr	5,342	5,521		97 %		●
22 Daybreak Dr	3,053	3,148		97 %		
1 Whitestone Rd	4,579	4,711		97 %		
1552 Flintrock Rd	5,342	5,488		97 %		●
1335 County Line	5,087	5,210		98 %		
1 Jack Hanoka Dr	3,307	3,338		99 %		●
1525 West Line	946,311	954,645		99 %		
1335 Omoo Rd	847,260	854,289		99 %		
18819 Guelph St	1,060,307	1,068,858		99 %		●
1 Adam West Rd	652,373	650,426		100 %		
11820 Dover Tr	900,606	884,292		102 %		
15 Rural Rd	1,200,261	1,174,570		102 %		

Scenario

Big Picture

You are the manager of a power plant, and part of your job is to monitor consumption and output. You need to know if the output today is different from the last few days and how the output is trending. Certain things impact your production level, so you also follow real-time metrics for those variables.

You need to monitor different locations to determine if they are producing the expected output and if their production is changing over time. You also manage the routine inspections of these locations, so you need to know when the last inspection occurred and flag locations that were not inspected recently.

Specifics

- Your job is to create an overview dashboard to provide all of the listed information to the operational management team. The dashboard should be interactive to provide additional details and allow the users to drill down to the location level and see historical data.

- You need to show the data by the location of the installation. You need to show current output versus the expected output so that it is easy to see which locations aren't producing as needed.

- You want to see which locations consistently miss or exceed expected output over time.

- You need to sort data by each location's last inspection time so it is easy to identify the locations in which you need to spend more time during your next trip.

- You need to provide a real-time data feed for the operation center to stay up to date.

- You need to provide a detailed level of data about specific locations that are not yielding expected output and view that data and additional operational service-level data by location.

Related Scenarios

- You need to track the output/performance of any distributed part of a manufacturing process, which is spread across multiple locations.

- You need to get a quick real-time summary of capacity metrics compared against the recent past (e.g., last 14 days), which allows for analysis across longer historical terms (last 90 days/last X years).

- You need to display real-time results within an operation center on a mounted display with no manual interaction (e.g., online service support center, manufacturing service center, telecom network operations center).

How People Use the Dashboard

The top section of the dashboard is used to quickly review the current consumption and output of the power plant. Area charts show the recent period trend; a red dot is used to show the most current value. (See Figure 9.1.) The reader can review the current value against the trend and quickly gauge if the current value goes above or below the linear regression line for the data.

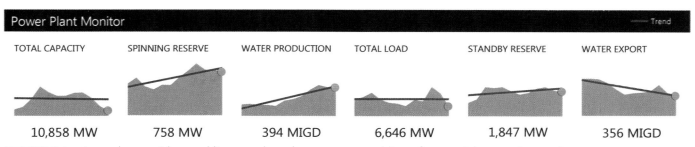

TOTAL CAPACITY	SPINNING RESERVE	WATER PRODUCTION	TOTAL LOAD	STANDBY RESERVE	WATER EXPORT
10,858 MW	758 MW	394 MIGD	6,646 MW	1,847 MW	356 MIGD

FIGURE 9.1   Area charts with trend lines and markers act as sparklines for a quick at-a-glance view.

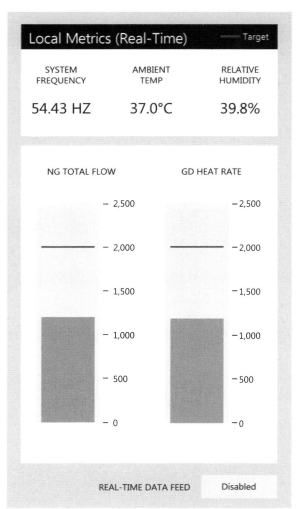

FIGURE 9.2   Real-time metrics are shown, and the real-time data feed can be turned on or off as needed.

Field managers can turn on real-time data feeds to constantly monitor condition metrics (like temperature and humidity) that affect the field operations. A simplified bullet chart is used to show the actual versus target data. (See Figure 9.2.)

Location (installation) managers and overall management use location details to quickly identify locations where output fails to meet expectations. (See Figure 9.3.) They can see if particular locations consistently fail to meet expectations or if shortfalls are isolated incidents. They can also focus on inspections and track which locations need inspection (more than 15 days since the previous one) and which ones are getting close to needing inspection. (The indication starts after 10 days.)

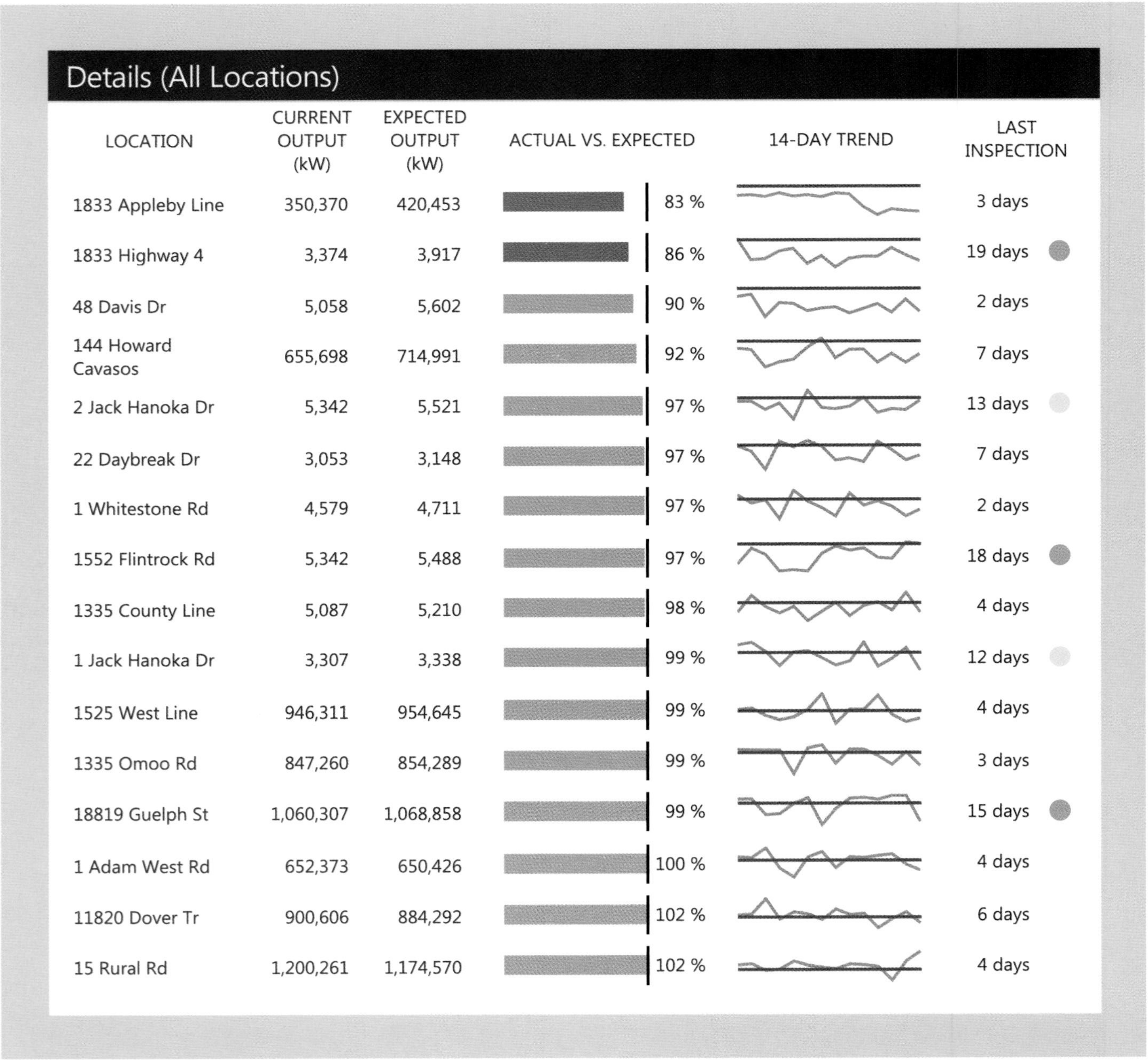

Details (All Locations)

LOCATION	CURRENT OUTPUT (kW)	EXPECTED OUTPUT (kW)	ACTUAL VS. EXPECTED	14-DAY TREND	LAST INSPECTION
1833 Appleby Line	350,370	420,453	83 %		3 days
1833 Highway 4	3,374	3,917	86 %		19 days ●
48 Davis Dr	5,058	5,602	90 %		2 days
144 Howard Cavasos	655,698	714,991	92 %		7 days
2 Jack Hanoka Dr	5,342	5,521	97 %		13 days ○
22 Daybreak Dr	3,053	3,148	97 %		7 days
1 Whitestone Rd	4,579	4,711	97 %		2 days
1552 Flintrock Rd	5,342	5,488	97 %		18 days ●
1335 County Line	5,087	5,210	98 %		4 days
1 Jack Hanoka Dr	3,307	3,338	99 %		12 days ○
1525 West Line	946,311	954,645	99 %		4 days
1335 Omoo Rd	847,260	854,289	99 %		3 days
18819 Guelph St	1,060,307	1,068,858	99 %		15 days ●
1 Adam West Rd	652,373	650,426	100 %		4 days
11820 Dover Tr	900,606	884,292	102 %		6 days
15 Rural Rd	1,200,261	1,174,570	102 %		4 days

FIGURE 9.3   Details provide key metrics for each location.

Clicking on any location opens a new dashboard showing details about a particular location, including the location model breakdown and service-level data required by the global support team. (See Figure 9.4.)

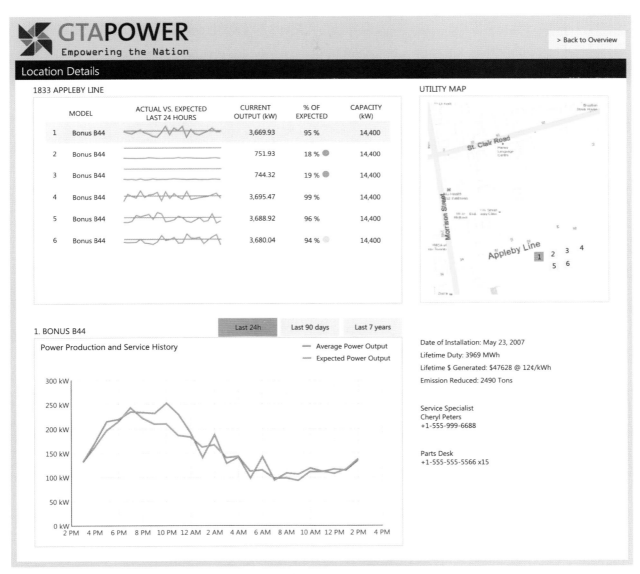

FIGURE 9.4   User-selected details-on-demand view of each location.

Why This Works

Focus on Up-to-Date Data

Highlighting the current value in the area charts allows the user to focus on that value and compare it to the overall trend. (See Figure 9.5.) This helps the reader to shift attention to the current value rather than to the highest and lowest values, which are no longer relevant.

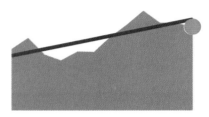

SPINNING RESERVE

758 MW

FIGURE 9.5   The simple design is easy to understand, provides a quick at-a-glance view, and highlights important points.

Serving All Levels of Users

The dashboard provides a summary across aggregated metrics and all of the locations involved, allowing higher-level management to get a quick overview of performance by location. The dashboards also answer questions for the field manager and support personnel in real time.

A user can click any location on the dashboard. A second dashboard appears showing plant details and key statistics for the location. (See Figure 9.6.) Clicking each model provides an even more detailed view, filtering the line chart, which can show the last 24 hours, 90 days, or 7 years. There is also a map showing the location of each selected model.

Ben Shneiderman's mantra

Consider Ben Shneiderman's mantra when designing dashboards: *Overview first, followed by zoom and filter, and then details-on-demand.* This example clearly follows this recommendation.

The line chart allows the user to analyze location output across a specific time range instead of a single point in time. It also enables the user to cross-match data with inspection dates. This allows for a quick drill-down on key locations to get all of the operational data needed for a selected location's maintenance. A service person can then compare the location layout on a street-level map via Google Maps and can see the install date and the service history.

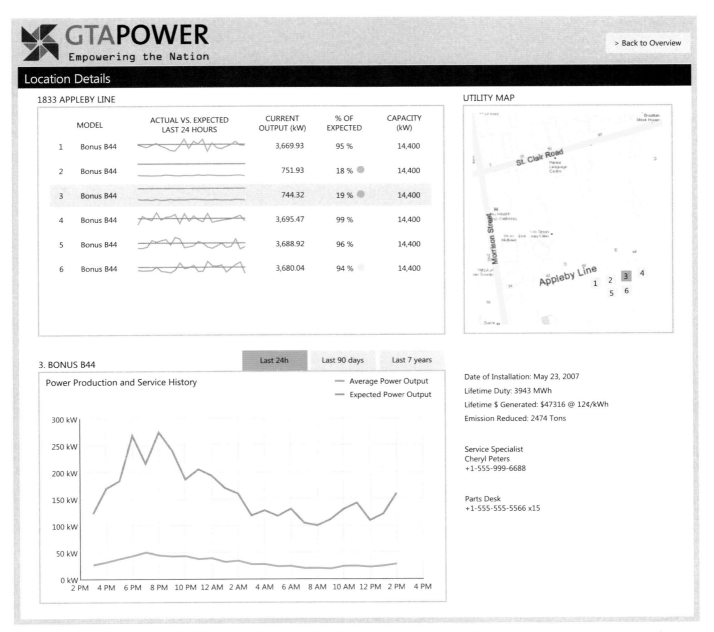

GTAPOWER
Empowering the Nation

> Back to Overview

Location Details

1833 APPLEBY LINE

	MODEL	ACTUAL VS. EXPECTED LAST 24 HOURS	CURRENT OUTPUT (kW)	% OF EXPECTED	CAPACITY (kW)
1	Bonus B44		3,669.93	95 %	14,400
2	Bonus B44		751.93	18 %	14,400
3	Bonus B44		744.32	19 %	14,400
4	Bonus B44		3,695.47	99 %	14,400
5	Bonus B44		3,688.92	96 %	14,400
6	Bonus B44		3,680.04	94 %	14,400

UTILITY MAP

St. Clair Road

Morrison Street

Appleby Line 1 2 **3** 4 5 6

3. BONUS B44

| Last 24h | Last 90 days | Last 7 years |

Power Production and Service History

— Average Power Output
— Expected Power Output

300 kW
250 kW
200 kW
150 kW
100 kW
50 kW
0 kW

2 PM 4 PM 6 PM 8 PM 10 PM 12 AM 2 AM 4 AM 6 AM 8 AM 10 AM 12 PM 2 PM 4 PM

Date of Installation: May 23, 2007

Lifetime Duty: 3943 MWh

Lifetime $ Generated: $47316 @ 12¢/kWh

Emission Reduced: 2474 Tons

Service Specialist
Cheryl Peters
+1-555-999-6688

Parts Desk
+1-555-555-5566 x15

FIGURE 9.6 Selecting a model filters the line chart for the selected period of time and shows the location on the map.

Simple Use of Bullet Graphs, Sparklines, and Performance Indicators

Figure 9.7 contains simple, well-designed bullet graphs and sparklines. They show a target line that allows the reader to put the data in context. For example, in some locations, the trend is constantly below the target. When sparklines are used, they often show only the trend of the data. Adding the target line helps put the trend of the data in context to where it should be.

A blue dot is used to indicate when a certain length of time has elapsed since the date of the last inspection at that location. The light blue dot is shown for 13 days since inspection and a dark blue dot for 19 days since inspection.

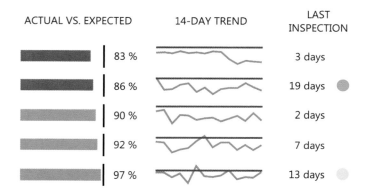

ACTUAL VS. EXPECTED   14-DAY TREND   LAST INSPECTION

83 %		3 days
86 %		19 days
90 %		2 days
92 %		7 days
97 %		13 days

FIGURE 9.7 Simple bullet graphs show actuals versus targets, and sparklines show the 14-day trend.

Author Commentary

JEFF: I really like the design of this dashboard. I especially like the design and layout of the bullet graphs and sparklines in the data table. This is almost identical to the look and layout of the Executive Dashboard we use at my company. We don't have a range for the target, so we don't use performance bands with our bullet charts, just as in this example. When teaching data visualization, I often find there is some confusion in understanding bullet graphs. If performance bands are not needed, then I recommend dropping them and using a design like this. It is simple to understand—an actual bar with a target line, although typically shown with a quantitative scale.

The one design choice I question on this dashboard is the use of blue, sequentially from light to dark, to show the severity of the time elapsed since inspection. If I want the reader to interpret the dot as a bad thing, then I might choose a different color, something bright and alerting, such as a red or orange, and change the marker used on the area chart to blue. Using an alerting color will help draw the reader's attention to the locations where too much time has passed since the last inspection. (See Figure 9.8.)

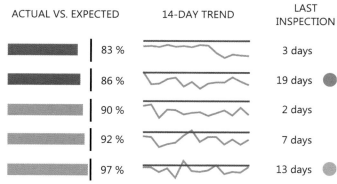

ACTUAL VS. EXPECTED   14-DAY TREND   LAST INSPECTION

83 %		3 days
86 %		19 days
90 %		2 days
92 %		7 days
97 %		13 days

FIGURE 9.8 Using red and orange to alert readers that something needs their attention.

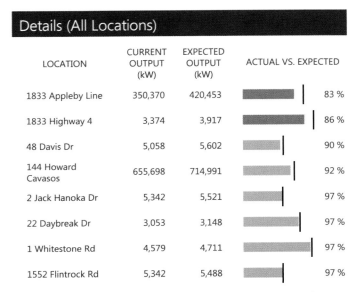

LOCATION	CURRENT OUTPUT (kW)	EXPECTED OUTPUT (kW)	ACTUAL VS. EXPECTED	
1833 Appleby Line	350,370	420,453		83 %
1833 Highway 4	3,374	3,917		86 %
48 Davis Dr	5,058	5,602		90 %
144 Howard Cavasos	655,698	714,991		92 %
2 Jack Hanoka Dr	5,342	5,521		97 %
22 Daybreak Dr	3,053	3,148		97 %
1 Whitestone Rd	4,579	4,711		97 %
1552 Flintrock Rd	5,342	5,488		97 %

FIGURE 9.9   Bar charts on an independent axis scale.

Details (All Locations)

LOCATION	CURRENT OUTPUT (kW)	EXPECTED OUTPUT (kW)		
1833 Appleby Line	350,370	420,453		83 %
1833 Highway 4	3,374	3,917		86 %
48 Davis Dr	5,058	5,602		90 %
144 Howard Cavasos	655,698	714,991		92 %
2 Jack Hanoka Dr	5,342	5,521		97 %
22 Daybreak Dr	3,053	3,148		97 %
1 Whitestone Rd	4,579	4,711		97 %
1552 Flintrock Rd	5,342	5,488		97 %

FIGURE 9.10   Bar charts on a common scale of kW output.

In the original version of this dashboard, the designer used an independent scale for each bar in the bar chart (see Figure 9.9). This was done to show the ratio of the actual output to the expected output. One of our reviewers pointed out that this was very confusing. He asked, "why is the bar longer for the 1 Whitestone Rd location vs. 1552 Flintrock?" And we agree, Figure 9.9 is very confusing.

The designers also considered showing the bars using a common scale of kW output (see Figure 9.10.). The dilemma here is that if the bars are shown on the same quantitative scale based on kW output, then all of the smaller power stations will always show target lines near zero and no visible bar.

Another alternative is to show the bars on a common scale of 0% to 100%, so that the target lines match for each location (see Figure 9.11). This is a good approach, but notice, in this case, that it is difficult to see the small gaps as the actual value approaches 100% and it does not show the impact of the gap in kW output.

Details (All Locations)

LOCATION	CURRENT OUTPUT (kW)	EXPECTED OUTPUT (kW)	ACTUAL VS. EXPECTED	
1833 Appleby Line	350,370	420,453		83 %
1833 Highway 4	3,374	3,917		86 %
48 Davis Dr	5,058	5,602		90 %
144 Howard Cavasos	655,698	714,991		92 %
2 Jack Hanoka Dr	5,342	5,521		97 %
22 Daybreak Dr	3,053	3,148		97 %
1 Whitestone Rd	4,579	4,711		97 %
1552 Flintrock Rd	5,342	5,488		97 %

FIGURE 9.11   Bar charts on a common scale of 0% to 100%.

This is a great example of why it is important to understand the question being answered by the visualization. If you are the location manager for the 48 Davis Drive location, then it would be important for you to know that output at your location is only 90% of expected output, which is clear in Figure 9.11. However, if you are the regional manager for all of these locations, then it might be more important to know that 1833 Appleby Line and 144 Howard Cavasos are responsible for the largest gaps in expected output, nearly 130,000 kW gap combined.

One alternative in this case might be to plot the difference from 100% instead of the actual values. That can be done with a dot plot. In Figure 9.12, the actual output vs. the expected output is shown as a percent using the position of the dot from the 100% target line. This allows the reader to see small differences that may be very important. In addition, the size of the gap (measured in the absolute number of kW between the current output and the expected output), is encoded using the size of the dots. This shows the impact of the kW difference relative to the size of the facility rather than simply expressing it as a percent. This is very important, because in this example, the facility at 92% of expected output actually had a larger negative impact on output than the facilities that were a lower percent, at 86% and 90% of expected output.

Details (All Locations)

Location	Current Output (kW)	Expected Output (kW)	Actuals vs. Expected
1833 Apple Line	350,370	420,453	83%
1833 Highway 4	3,374	3,917	86%
48 Davis Dr	5,058	5,602	90%
144 Howard Cavasos	655,698	714,991	92%
1 Whitestone Rd	4,579	4,711	97%
2 Jack Hanoka Dr	5,342	5,521	97%
22 Daybreak Dr	3,053	3,148	97%
1552 Flintrock Rd	5,342	5,488	97%
1335 County Line	5,087	5,210	98%
1 Jack Hanoka Dr	3,307	3,338	99%
1335 Omoo Rd	847,260	854,289	99%
1525 West Line	946,311	954,645	99%
18819 Guelph St	1,060,307	1,068,858	99%
1 Adam West Rd	652,373	650,425	100%
11820 Dover Tr	900,606	884,292	102%
15 Rural Rd	1,200,261	1,174,570	102%

100%

FIGURE 9.12   A dot pot showing the actual output vs. the expected output with the size of the dots representing the difference in the output measured in kW units.

Chapter 10

Showing Year-to-Date and Year-over-Year at the Same Time

Year-to-date/Year-over-year dashboard optimized for mobile devices.
Author: Steve Wexler
Organization: Data Revelations

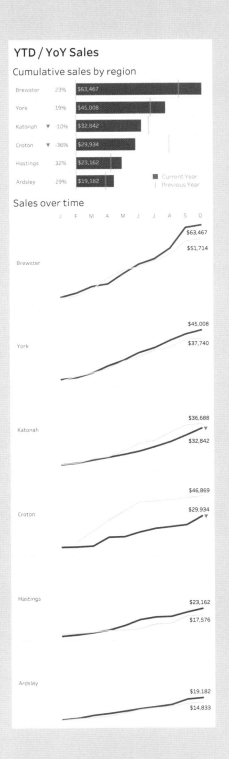

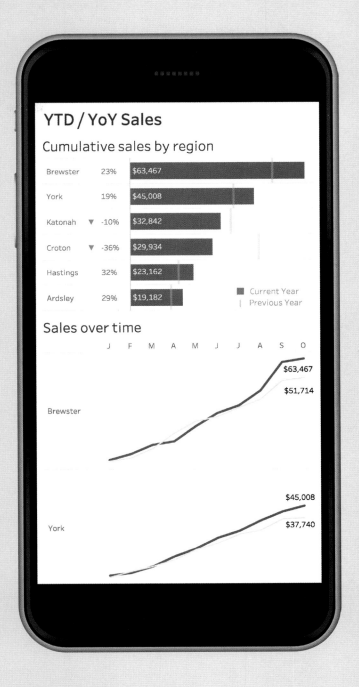

> **Note**
>
> Depending on your needs, you may want to go with the alternative approach suggested by Andy Cotgreave at the end of this chapter.

Scenario

Big Picture

You received a promotion in June of this year that involves managing sales for six different regions. Your number-one goal is to make sure that by the end of the year, the sales for each region will be greater than they were for the previous year.

You came into the new job knowing that two of the regions were way behind where they needed to be. In your discussions with upper management, you made the argument that a reasonable goal would be to exceed sales in four regions and improve the trend in the other two regions that were tanking.

As you are often out of the office visiting individual stores, you want to have a collection of mobile-friendly dashboards that allow you to monitor current performance, trends, and near-real-time details on demand. Back at the office, you have a single dashboard that combines all these elements into one view.

Here we'll look at how to fashion a dashboard that makes it easy to compare performance across regions and years and also detect trends.

Specifics

- You need to rank year-to-date (YTD) sales performance for six regions and compare with sales for the previous year (i.e., year-over-year [YoY]).
- You need to see, at a glance, how much better or worse the regions are performing.
- You need to see trends to know whether you are on track to hit your goals.
- You need a way to view sales activities for a particular region and for a particular time period.

Related Scenarios

- You need to monitor first-call resolution rates for several different products and compare them with rates from the previous year.
- You are the head of annual giving for a university and need to rank and compare donations for 10 different regions for this year and for the previous year.
- You monitor attendance for theatrical productions and need to compare current YTD ticket sales with the previous year's sales.
- In this book, check out these chapters: Chapter 5, which uses an index chart to compare quarter-to-date performance; Chapter 6, which compares one quarter to another; Chapter 7, which shows if you are ahead of or behind where you need to be to reach your goals; and Chapter 8, which compares current performance against goals.

How People Use the Dashboard

Opening the dashboard shows a summary of the six regions as of today. (See Figure 10.1.)

The key performance indicator (KPI) icons show there are problems in Katonah and Croton, so the user can scroll down and look at trends for those two regions. (See Figure 10.2.)

YTD / YoY Sales

Cumulative sales by region

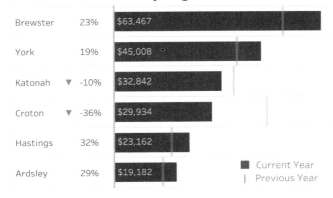

		Current Year / Previous Year
Brewster	23%	$63,467
York	19%	$45,008
Katonah	▼ -10%	$32,842
Croton	▼ -36%	$29,934
Hastings	32%	$23,162
Ardsley	29%	$19,182

■ Current Year
| Previous Year

Sales over time

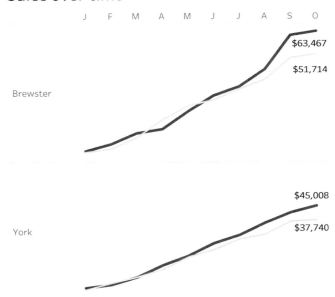

J F M A M J J A S O

Brewster — $63,467 / $51,714

York — $45,008 / $37,740

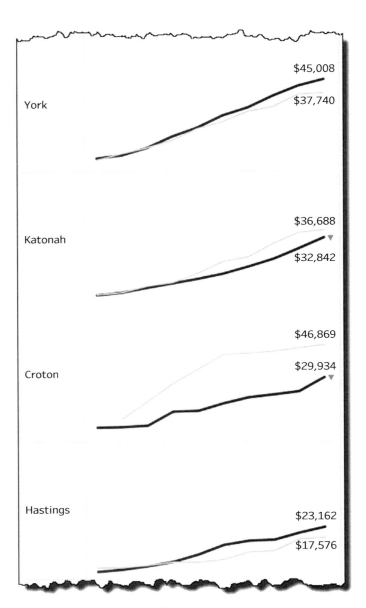

York $45,008 / $37,740

Katonah $36,688 / $32,842

Croton $46,869 / $29,934

Hastings $23,162 / $17,576

FIGURE 10.1 Initial dashboard view showing summary and trends for first two regions.

FIGURE 10.2 Scrolling allows the user to look at the regions that are underperforming.

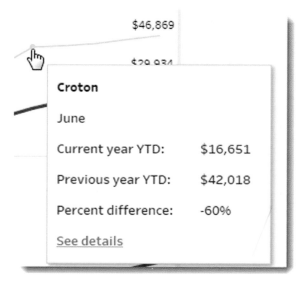

$46,869

Croton

June

Current year YTD:	$16,651
Previous year YTD:	$42,018
Percent difference:	-60%

See details

FIGURE 10.3   Pressing a point shows details about activity for that month.

The good news here is that while YTD sales are down as of today, things are much better now than they were a few months ago when you took the job. You can place your finger over a data point and see information about that time period. (See Figure 10.3.)

If you want to see sales details for the region and period in question, you can press the "See details" link. Examples of what you might see would be sales by day of the week and for individual items.

Why This Works

Bars Allow for Easy Comparison

The bar chart makes it very easy to see just how much greater one region's sales are compared with another's. (See Figure 10.4.)

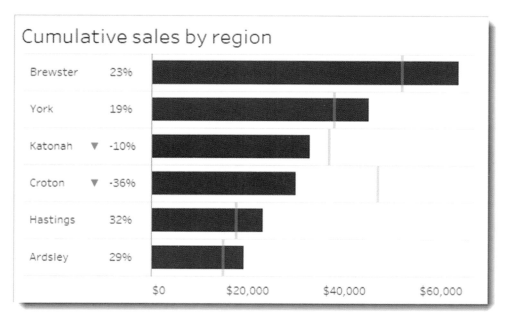

FIGURE 10.4   Bars make it easy to see how much larger one region's sales are compared with another's.

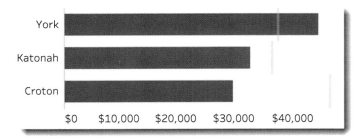

FIGURE 10.5 Reference lines make it easy to see how far ahead or behind we are.

Indeed, we could leave the labels that are inside the bars off the visualization, and it would still be easy to tell that sales for Brewster are about twice those of Katonah.

Reference Lines Make It Easy to See How Far Ahead or Behind We Are

Again, we can remove the numbers and the KPI icons but still see that Croton is significantly behind the

previous year while Katonah is only a little behind and York is quite a bit ahead. (See Figure 10.5.)

Good Use of Color and Good Placement of Color Legend

We show the current year in a dark green and the previous year in light gray, as the current year is our primary concern. (See Figure 10.6.) The color and shape legend (which users don't even need at this point because they've looked at this dashboard hundreds of times) is tucked inside the chart and does not take up any additional screen space.

Although the KPI icon is red, the very existence of the icon and the fact that it is pointed down alerts all users (even those with color vision deficiency) that there is a problem in Katonah and Croton.

Number Placement Optimizes Space

Given that the target device is a smartphone, there's not a lot of room for the bars. Placing the numbers

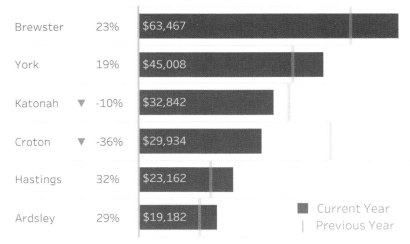

FIGURE 10.6   Colors, icons, and legend placement make it easy to decode the chart.

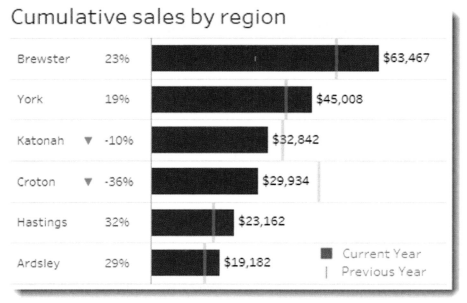

FIGURE 10.7   Numbers placed outside the bars cramp the chart and conflict with the reference lines.

inside the bars gives the chart more space and avoids a conflict with the reference lines.

Figure 10.7 shows what the chart would look like if the numbers were placed outside the bars.

Line Charts Make It Easy to Glean Trends

Although it's great to have a quick summary view, it's important to know how things are trending. For example, Katonah is down 10 percent from the previous year. Did that gap happen recently, or has there been a problem from the beginning of the year? The trend line in Figure 10.8 makes it easy to see

that the gap was much larger earlier in the year and that the sales for the region have made up a lot of ground from the previous year.

FIGURE 10.8   Trend lines show that the gap is narrowing.

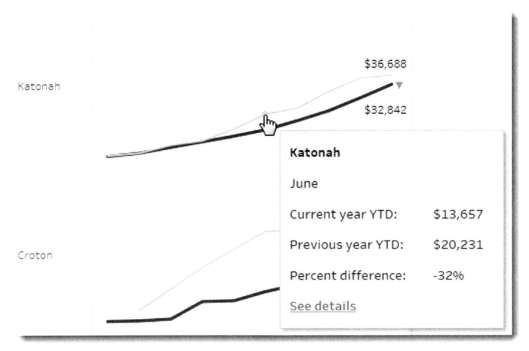

FIGURE 10.9   Back in June, current YTD sales trailed the previous year by 32 percent.

Selection Allows Easy Exploration of Different Time Periods and Details on Demand

The user can press any point and get additional information about that point. In Figure 10.9, we see that the sales gap in June was quite a bit larger than it is now.

The "See details" hyperlink allows users to see sales details about the selected period. The link could jump to the actual sales system or to a dashboard with details about the month and region in question.

The Traditional Approach, and Why You Should Avoid It

Figure 10.10 exemplifies the tabular scorecard approach to displaying YTD and YoY data.

Cumulative sales by region

		Current Sales	Previous Sales	% Difference
Brewster		$63,467	$51,714	23%
York		$45,008	$37,740	19%
Katonah	▼	$32,842	$36,688	-10%
Croton	▼	$29,934	$46,869	-36%
Hastings		$23,162	$17,576	32%
Ardsley		$19,182	$14,833	29%

FIGURE 10.10   A typical scorecard approach to displaying YTD and YoY data.

The table with the KPI icons is not aesthetically unpleasing; it just makes us work very hard to understand the magnitude and differences in the numbers. For example, Brewster has sales of $63,467 and Ardsley is at $19,182. What are users to make of this? Users have to do mental math to understand that the region with the most sales is more than three times as much as the region with the least sales.

The same goes with the percent difference column. Users must do mental math and imagine bars of different lengths. Compare this with Figure 10.5, where users don't have to work nearly has hard to really understand the difference in magnitude.

Dashboard Designer Commentary

Steve: The reason I wanted to include this example was that I have seen so many companies struggle to show YoY performance. The chart in Figure 10.10 typifies their efforts.

I admit that I may have left some important considerations out of the scenario. For example, if this were a desktop dashboard, I would almost certainly show the sales details on it.

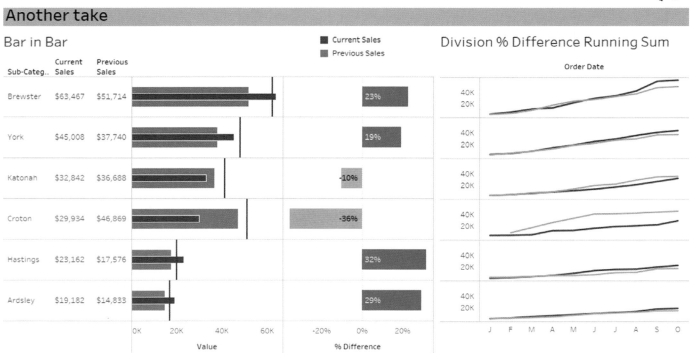

FIGURE 10.11   An early attempt to compare current-year YTD sales and prior-year YTD sales along with progress toward a goal.

And suppose, in addition to showing performance this year versus performance last year, I wanted to also show a goal for each region. Sure, we want to have better sales this year than last year, but we don't just want it to be better; we want it to be at least 20 percent better in each region. How can we show that too?

Figure 10.11 is a very early iteration of such a dashboard where I present a bar-in-bar chart showing current-year versus prior-year sales and a reference line showing a goal.

Although it is a good first effort, this chart is nowhere near ready to go into production. Between the bar-in-bar chart and the reference line, there's a lot for the user to parse. And I can't tell if the blue and orange bars showing percentage difference compare current progress with last year or with the goal.

I also placed the trend lines to the right of the bar chart in an attempt to make it easy to see trends for each region. The problem here is that the height for each row restricts the ability to see all but the most obvious gaps.

If I had a client who needed all this functionality, I would revisit this approach, but for the particular scenario I established, I think the simpler, mobile-friendly dashboard does the job.

Author Commentary

Which Chart to Choose?

ANDY: When tracking YoY performance, you often have to consider two options:

Do you visualize both years' actual sales on top of each other?

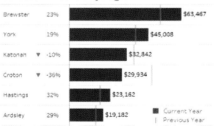

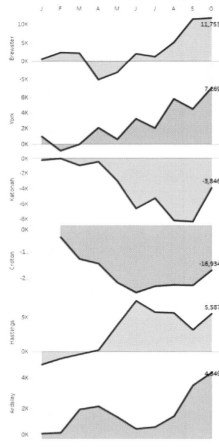

FIGURE 10.12   A version of the dashboard showing the YoY difference rather than cumulative sales. Note that each axis in the area chart is independent.

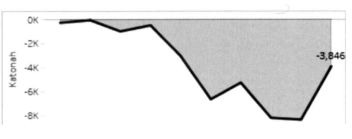

FIGURE 10.13   Two approaches to showing YoY sales for Katonah.

Do you visualize the actual difference itself?

Both methods have pros and cons. In this case, Steve chose the former. In his example, you see the actual number represented on the line. You can see whether the gap is large or small between the years, but it's not easy to visually measure the gap precisely.

That got me thinking: What does this look like if we visualize the actual difference itself? (See Figure 10.12.)

Now we see the difference with absolute clarity. Remember that problem we have in Katonah and Croton? You can see just how bad that is. The YoY differences have gotten worse in almost all months this year. The most recent month has seen an improvement, but there is still some way to go to achieve the goal.

In Figure 10.13, you can compare the different approaches. If knowing the exact YoY difference is most important, I recommend using the approach on the left. The downside of this approach is that you can no longer see the *actual* cumulative sales. That's a reason to go with the approach on the right.

Could you also build a dashboard that visualizes both actuals and the difference? You could, but then you begin to complicate the dashboard, which could mean the insight is lost and, ultimately, people don't use it, because it's not simple enough. One compromise would be to have a switch that allows the person interacting to toggle back and forth between the two views. (See Figure 10.14.)

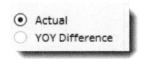

FIGURE 10.14   A simple switch at the top of the dashboard allows users to toggle back and forth between the two views.

Bars or Tables

Steve rightly compares the efficiency of bar charts and tables in Figures 10.5 and 10.10. Bar charts with reference lines are without doubt a more efficient way to accurately compare values in different categories. However, I will put forward a defense of tables, lest you think we're advocating you never put a table on your dashboard.

If the purpose is to compare many values at a glance then a chart trumps a table all the time.

However, *if* you need to look up exact values *and* fast comparison is not the primary task, then a table or highlight table might be best. Our visual system is amazing, which is why we visualize data, but do be mindful that there are circumstances where it is more important to know the exact number than anything else.

Chapter 11

Premier League Player Performance Metrics

A player summary from an English Premier League Club.

Dashboard Designer: Andy Kirk (visualisingdata.com)

Organization: An English Premier League club

Note the data in this example is genuine game data for an anonymous player in the English Premier League in the 2015–2016 season. Andy Singleton is not a real player name, and this data is not from a Liverpool v. Manchester United game.

ANDY SINGLETON

LIVERPOOL vs MANCHESTER UTD
18 May 2016

	MATCH TOTAL 95 mins	PLAYER RANK Match 17	TEAM RANK Match 21
Total Distance	10,967m	14	3
HI Run Distance	1,308m	8	7
Num HI Runs	151	9	6
HS Run Distance	924m	8	5
Num HS Runs	168	10	6
Sprint Distance	385m	8	7
Num Sprints	47	10	13
High Accels.	17	8	7
High Decels.	10	10	7
Top Speed	9.4m/s	1	6
Recovery Time	37s	8	10

< BELOW AVERAGE   PREVIOUS 5   REST OF SEASON   ABOVE AVERAGE >

Scenario

Big Picture

You play on an English Premier League soccer team. You played a game on Saturday and spent Sunday in recovery. It's now Monday, and you're due at the training field at 10 a.m. for a team debrief on the match. How did you do? Just as you arrive, you receive your personal player dashboard via email to your iPhone. It shows your physical performance metrics for the match:

- How did you perform in the most recent game?
- How did your performance compare to that of the most recent games and to the rest of the season?
- Did your performance match the rest of the team's?
- How was the team's performance relative to that of the rest of the season?

Specifics

- Players need to understand their match-day physical performance and see several key metrics, including total distance run, number of sprints, and top speed.
- Players need to know if their performance was above or below average. This helps them relate their performance to the coach's desired tactics for the specific match.
- To add context, players need to know how their individual match performance compared to their performance in the most recent games (especially, e.g., if they are recovering from injury). For deeper context, the entire season's games are shown too.

- Finally, each player needs to know how his performance, good or bad, was related to the team's performance on match day.
- Everyone receives the dashboard in time for arrival at training, encouraging data-driven conversations and even a little friendly rivalry.

Related Scenarios

- Any key performance indicator scenario could be applied here. The yellow dot would show the current state of the key performance indicator, the red ones could show recent periods, and the gray ones could show all time.
- You want to compare current and previous values for any discrete item (e.g., employees, products, countries, etc.).
- You need to track performance of individuals: How do their performance metrics compare to those of previous periods?
- You are in information technology, tracking the speed of your key overnight processes, and want an overview of most recent performances.

How People Use the Dashboard

In the first training session following a match for this English Premier League team, all players are required to arrive for breakfast at a given time. Just before arriving, they receive, on their phones, their personal copy of this dashboard. They look at the dashboard before they sit and chat with their teammates. As well as being a personal reference for their own performance, the dashboard also generates conversation at the right moment in the team's training cycle: when they are ready to review the most recent match. The timing of delivery is also engineered to be when the players get together: Management encourages competitive comparisons.

All players who played 70 minutes or more (in a 90-minute soccer match) receive the dashboard. If they didn't play the full 90 minutes, the metrics are normalized to a 90-minute scale. Metrics for players who played fewer than 70 minutes cannot be reliably scaled to 90 minutes; thus, they do not receive a dashboard for the match.

The dashboard shows each player how he performed across 11 key game metrics. The 11 metrics relate to running distances and speeds. Figure 11.1 shows the detail for the first metric, total distance run.

Great attention has been applied to the scales for the measures. They all display varying measures, with very different magnitudes. For example, total distance is typically many kilometers, but high-intensity run distance is less than one kilometer. All scales are drawn to a normal distribution, not a linear scale. A dot on the extreme right or left is a truly exceptional

performance. Players have been taught to understand that the absolute position isn't the most important. Using a normal distribution means all the metrics can be compared with each other.

Data is only one part of an organization's decision-making structure, especially in professional sports. Players talk through the dashboards with their coaches. Coaches and players work to add context to the data. For example, a player might be recovering from injury. If that's the case, he can look at this match and the previous five to see if he is progressing as expected. Another example is if a player has a specific tactical objective in a given game. Perhaps he was tasked with marking a particularly fast and agile opponent. In that case, some of the player's statistics might be skewed above or below average, but in a way that was expected.

Why This Works

Good Use of Color

Color is used very cleverly in the dashboard, as shown in Figure 11.2. Yellow represents the most recent game and is used in the game name, date, dots representing

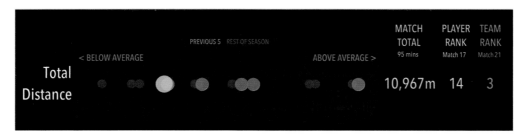

FIGURE 11.1   Detail showing the total distance metric for the player dashboard. The yellow dot represents the player's performance in the match. Red dots show the five previous matches. Gray dots show all other matches during the season. Match Total shows the sum for that metric. Player Rank: This was the player's 14th highest distance out of 17 matches he played this season. Team Rank: The whole team distance was also the third highest for the 21 matches played so far this season.

FIGURE 11.2   Each color is bold and clear. Text also explains what each color represents.

most recent performance, and relevant stats on the right. Red represents the previous five matches and is deliberately slightly less vibrant than the yellow. The gray dots are visible but relegated somewhat into the background to reflect their relative role in this display. Green represents the team performance. The color palette is very basic but strong.

The dashboard does use red and green, which can be a problem for readers with color vision deficiency. On this dashboard, this problem is solved by double encoding all information as follows:

• The latest match is represented by a larger circle than the others.

• The previous five matches are midsize circles.

• The green "Team Rank" is differentiated by the column header and position.

Over time, as the dashboards become familiar, the colors enable fast recognition of the salient facts.

Scale Orientation

All measures are oriented so that dots on the right represent higher-than-average performance. As an example, Figure 11.3 shows top speed and recovery time. Top speed should be as high as possible, whereas recovery time should be as low as possible. In order to maintain consistency, all measures are oriented so that marks on the right are better.

Normalized Scales

The scales don't show a linear numerical scale. If they did, it would not be easy to compare relative performance of top speed and total distance, as one is a speed and the other is a distance. Once the scales are normalized, it is possible to compare the metrics in terms of their difference from an average performance. (See also Chapter 7.)

Minimal Use of Numbers

The only numbers shown are those for the most recent match. Other than that, the information is kept to a minimum so as not to overload players and coaches. Showing fewer numbers helps focus on the key goal for the dashboard: How did you perform in the last match, and how did that compare to other matches?

Social Interaction Promoted

Introducing data into soccer players' lives is a modern trend. The data is delivered directly to their smartphones at a time when all players come together for training. In

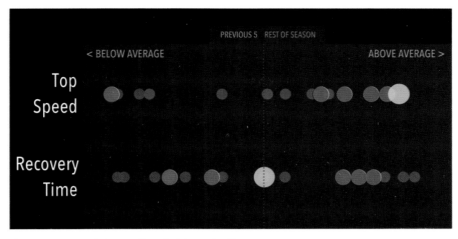

FIGURE 11.3   For both measures, dots on the right are better.

this way, coaches know players have the dashboards, and the dashboards fit into a regular training schedule. This helps improve acceptance and usage.

The potential for players to compare their performances with others is deliberate. Competitive people love to have proof points showing where they did well. The timing and manner of the delivery of the dashboards to players is designed to encourage this.

Mobile Friendly

This dashboard is delivered to mobile devices and designed to be consumed on them. Its dimensions are optimized to a cellphone. It is not interactive. By having a static dashboard without interactivity, it does reduce the amount of information the dashboard can contain, but this is intentional. In a culture where data is being introduced slowly, a static, mobile, simple dashboard is a more prudent choice.

Quick Comparisons to Individual and Team

The prime purpose of the dashboard is to compare the player to his own recent performances. Figure 11.4 shows how this player's sprint statistics were below average in the recent match. However, what happens if it was a really bad match? What if the whole team played badly? Wouldn't that affect the player's results?

FIGURE 11.4   The numbers to the right of the dot plot show that this match was the player's tenth best performance out of 17 matches played. That was better than the team overall, for whom the match was the thirteenth best out of 21.

For this reason, the team rank, in green, on the right side of each metric, helps put a good or bad result into context. If both the player *and* team ranks are low, it indicates that the entire team had a bad week, suggesting that the result isn't as bad for the player as first thought.

The comparison to the player's other performances is the key objective of this dashboard. You might think that the comparison to the rest of the team is as important. Maybe that's right for some dashboards, but in this one, the objective is to benchmark the player against himself. The team rank is there not to let him see if he outperformed his teammates but if his personal performance might have been affected by overall team performance.

In soccer, comparing oneself too much to other players is not informative. Players in different positions have different roles and face different physical challenges and expectations. Additionally, perhaps a player had different tactical objectives that week.

Author Commentary

ANDY: A dashboard like this is not just about the data. It's about culture change. Many organizations choose to bring data into their culture slowly. Coaches' opinions about data in professional sports are divided. Some coaches think that sports such as soccer are so fluid it is not possible to quantify performances accurately. Harry Redknapp, one of the most successful English Premier League managers of all time, was famously antistatistics. After a losing game, he once said to his analyst, "I'll tell you what, next week, why don't we get your computer to play against their computer and see who wins?" ("How Computer Analysts Took Over at the Britain's Top Football Clubs," *The Guardian*, March 9, 2014. https://www.theguardian.com/football/2014/mar/09/premier-league-football-clubs-computer-analysts-managers-data-winning)

Other clubs use data much more deeply, but nobody claims data should replace intuition and experience. The club is carefully introducing this example dashboard to help data inform players and coaches. It is a coaching aid, designed to inform discussion between players and coaching staff. Its simplicity, mobile-friendly design, and delivery timing all foster sharing and discussion of the data.

The simplicity of the design is intentional. One thing the analysts wanted to avoid was alienating players and coaches by providing too much too soon. Many extra things could have been added to this dashboard, such as:

- Interactivity, with tool tips for each dot, adding more context.
- Labeled dots showing actual values, not just position on a normalized scale.
- Buttons to switch from normalized to actual scale values to allow players to see more about their data.
- The result of the match.

Had the team introduced too much too soon, there was every chance the players and coaches would be overwhelmed with the volume of data. Instead, it's possible to educate players and coaches slowly and steadily, letting each new piece of information embed gradually.

Any organization bringing data into its culture for the first time could adopt this approach. Analysts often get excited about all the data they have and throw everything into their output in one go. Their unsuspecting colleagues in other parts of the business can become overwhelmed and, instead of embracing the new data-informed culture, retreat back into their Excel spreadsheets.

Remember: All dashboards have to compromise somewhere, often by omission. If you're starting off, it's better to start slowly and introduce complexity very gradually.

Jeff: We discuss the use of the traffic light colors in Part III: Succeeding in the Real World, and this is a good example of that color palette in action. This dashboard shows well in simulation for color vision deficiency because the dots in the dot plot are not red and green. The bright yellow dots show up very well in most cases, making it easy to tell the yellow dots from the red. Also, the dots are sized differently: The red dots are a little bit bigger than the gray dots, and the yellow are just a bit bigger than red. As seen in Figure 11.5, this helps distinguish the dots from each other. (For more on traffic light colors, see Chapter 33.)

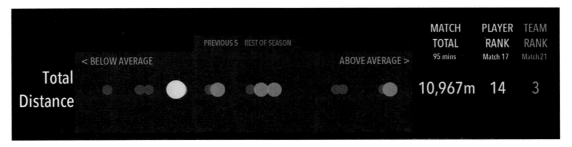

FIGURE 11.5   Portion of the dashboard as seen by people with color vision deficiency.

Source: Made using the Chromatic Vision Simulator at http://asada.tukusi.ne.jp/webCVS/

Chapter 12

RBS 6 Nations Championship Match Performance Analysis

Match summary for France versus Italy in the 2016 RBS 6 Nations Championship.
Dashboard Designer: Charlie Archer
Organization: Javelin Group & Accenture. Data provided by Opta.

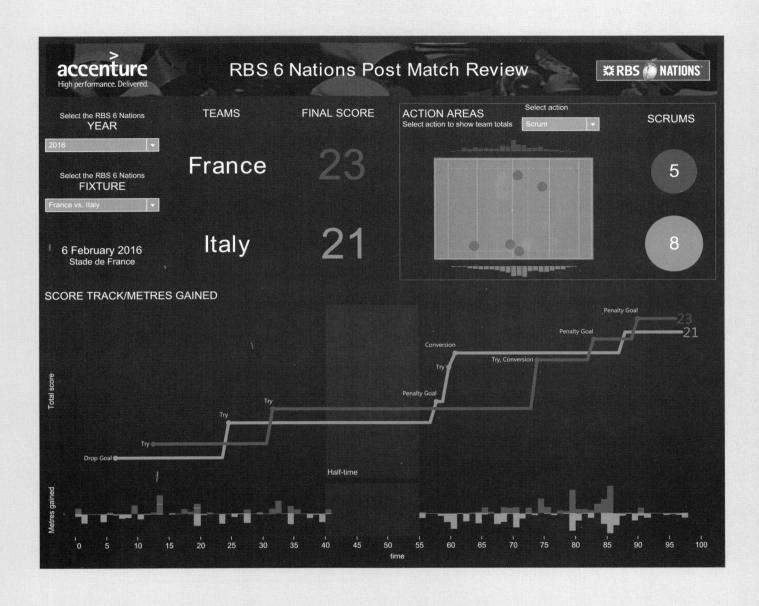

Scenario

Big Picture

The RBS 6 Nations Championship is an annual international rugby union competition among six European nations—England, Wales, Scotland, Ireland, France, and Italy—battling to be crowned champion. Data can reveal the story of the game, and this dashboard enables you to do this by looking back at the 16 years of the 6 Nations Championship. The score tracker shows how close the game was and how many times the lead changed hands. The action areas section lets you choose an event category, such as tackles, and see where such events took place on the pitch. In essence, if you like rugby and data, this is a dashboard you will enjoy exploring.

Specifics

- What was the final score in any given RBS 6 Nations game?
- How did the scoring progress?
- Where did most of the action take place on the pitch?

Related Scenarios

- You want to create a sports match tracker for any sport with two teams and frequent scoring opportunities. For example, basketball and football are great candidates, whereas soccer has too few goals to build an effective tracker.
- You need to create a political dashboard where there is a need to track, say, delegate counts or seats won in order to identify government majorities.

- You need to create a sales dashboard where the cumulative quarterly sales are important. (See Chapter 5.)

How People Use the Dashboard

During the championship, each of the six nations plays each other once. This dashboard, created by Accenture, Official Technology Partner of the RBS 6 Nations, has play-by-play data for all games since 2000. Users choose the game they want to see using the filters on the left. The match details (i.e., score, date, and venue) are shown next the filters. Let's look at the dramatic France versus Italy game from 2016 shown in Figure 12.1.

The line and bar charts are where the dashboard really reveals the story. (See Figure 12.2.) The x-axis shows minutes played in the match. The line shows the score for each team throughout the match. Each score is labeled to show how the points were scored. (In rugby, that's by a try, conversion, kick, or penalty.) Every time the two lines cross represents a time the lead switched.

FIGURE 12.1   Game selection and details.

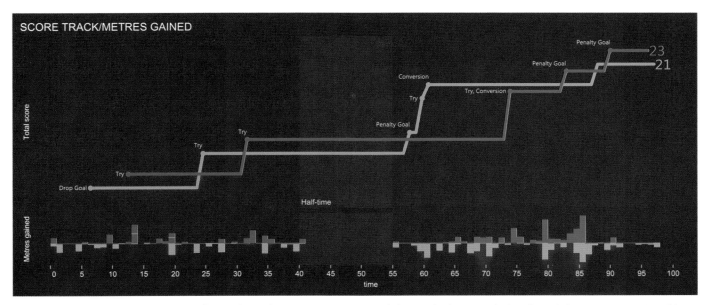

FIGURE 12.2   The main section shows how the score progressed through the match (top) and the meters gained by each team during each minute of the match (bottom).

As you can see, the 2016 France versus Italy match was a dramatic encounter. The lead changed eight times, with France, the prematch favorite, just beating Italy at the end.

The final section allows the user to explore the details of the game. In Figure 12.3, turnovers conceded has been selected. The user could also select tackles, scrums, passes, and others. The pitch map shows where each action took place. Play direction is from left to right for both teams; their defensive end zone is at the left side of the pitch map.

The histograms above and below the pitch map show the amount of time each team had possession in that part of the pitch. In this game, you can see that Italy spent most of the time just ahead of the halfway line (the lower, lighter blue, histogram in Figure 12.3).

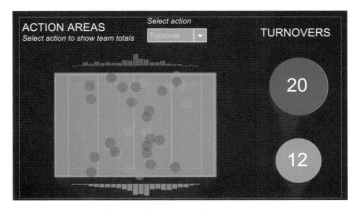

FIGURE 12.3   The third section shows game action details.

Why This Works

Running Totals Create an Engaging Story

In the previous section, we looked at one of the exciting RBS 6 Nation 2016 matches. The running total scores tell the thrilling story of that dramatic match. These lines work well for other types of matches, such as when one team dominates another or when one team stages a dramatic comeback.

Figures 12.4 and 12.5 illustrate very different games with clear stories revealed by the cumulative totals. Imagine the drama, joy, or dismay felt by fans of these games as they unfolded.

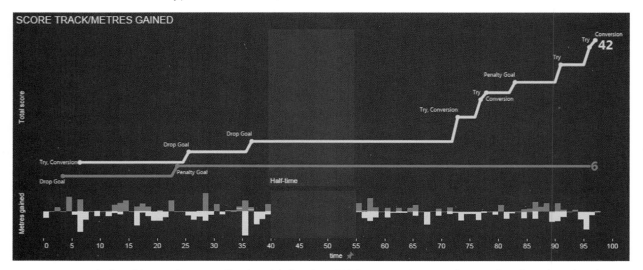

FIGURE 12.4   Ireland (green) versus England (white) in 2003 was a 42–6 win for England, with Ireland not scoring after minute 25.

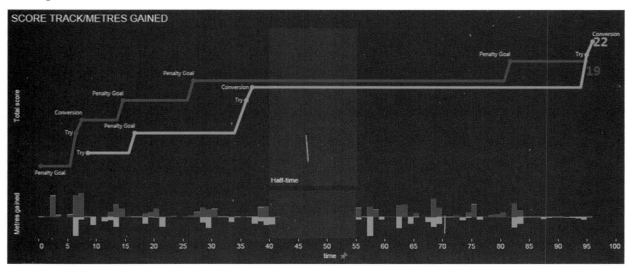

FIGURE 12.5   Scotland (dark blue) versus Italy (light blue) in 2015. Scotland led the entire game until Italy crept back and won the match with a last-minute try and conversion.

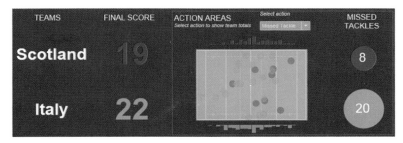

FIGURE 12.6   Missed tackles during the 2015 Scotland versus Italy match.

Pitch Map Shows Details on Demand

The pitch map is a good way to show spatial details in a data-driven way. Using a background image, each action is mapped onto the pitch. In Figure 12.6, we're seeing missed tackles during the 2015 Scotland versus Italy game. The large circles to the right of the pitch map clearly show that Italy missed the most. The labels give us the values. (Italy missed 20 and Scotland only 8.)

The histograms above and below the maps show where each team had possession position are powerful too. Let's look at the 2008 Ireland versus Wales game, which Wales won. The results are shown in Figure 12.7. In this case, the passes by each team are shown on the pitch map and histograms. Wales' data (the red circles and bars) clearly show that they spent most of the match in Ireland's half.

Appropriate Use of Fonts

Many different sizes of fonts are used, which helps guide readers where they need to look. The biggest font is the team name and score. That draws readers' eyes in to what is, ultimately, the most important pair of numbers in the data.

In contrast, the cumulative score lines are annotated with the score type (e.g., try, conversion, penalty, etc.) but in a much smaller font. In this case, the font doesn't draw much attention to itself. It is there if readers want to see it, but if users just want to follow the lines, the font doesn't get in the way.

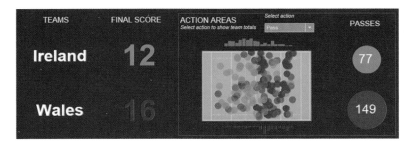

FIGURE 12.7   Ireland versus Wales, 2008: a close match with Wales in near-constant attack.

Author Commentary

ANDY: Lots of people enjoy sports, and we happily digest pages and pages of newspapers and blogs reading up on analysis of the games. Showing the story of a game through dashboards is very powerful. You can easily see comebacks, huge victories, or games where the lead changes multiple times. This is surely just as powerful as reading a report about the match.

One aspect of this dashboard that is interesting is the choice of color. The colors were chosen to represent each team's national color or uniform color. The background color of the dashboard was chosen to match the corporate colors of RBS, the championship sponsors. Independently, both of these choices make sense, but there are two major issues.

The first is the potential to confuse viewers with color vision deficiency. In Figure 12.7, we compared scores and possession of Ireland (green) and Wales (red). In this case, the color choices are not friendly for those with color vision deficiency.

The second issue is that dark colors against a dark background are harder to read because of the low contrast. Figure 12.6 is an example where the dark blue of Scotland's score is hard to read against the dark blue background.

A dashboard such as this is a marketing tool as well as an analytics tool, and thus it's understandable why these decisions were made. In a business environment, our goal is maximum understanding in minimal time. For that reason, you should always choose background colors that are in high contrast to the data. It's why the vast majority of dashboards in this book have white or off-white backgrounds.

Chapter 13

Web Analytics

Web Analytics dashboard.
Dashboard Designer: Jeffrey Shaffer
Organization: Data Plus Science, LLC

Website Analytics

All data from August 1, 2015 through July 15, 2016

data + science
= transforming data to insight

DATAPLUSSCIENCE.COM

174,828
pageviews

81,938
users

32
blog posts

Daily pageviews

M T W T F S S

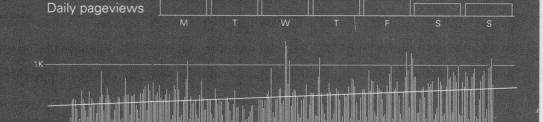

1K

Aug 1, 15   Oct 1, 15   Dec 1, 15   Feb 1, 16   Apr 1, 16   Jun 1, 16   Aug 1, 16

Most Visited Topics
(pageviews)

Topic	Pageviews
Sankey	32,977
Tableau Reference Guide	19,240
Tableau with Reveal.js and Deck.js	11,381
Node Link Tree Diagram	5,529
Geocoding in Tableau Using R	4,601
Venn Diagram	4,072
Tableau Jitter	4,050
Tableau Tips	3,809
iframe for Tableau maps	3,303
Tableau Converter	2,588
Tableau Voice Recognition and Response	1,086

Location of Visitors

Scenario

Big Picture

You host a blog or website, and you need a dashboard to track various metrics. The dashboard will connect to Google Analytics or another database that updates the data on the dashboard.

Specifics

- You need to track visitors to your blog or website. You need to see these visitors over some period of time.
- You want to see total pageviews (a common website metric), total visitors, and number of blog posts during the period.
- You want to see the blog posts or webpages that have the highest number of pageviews.
- You want to see visitors' geographic location.
- You want to see the distribution of the visitors by weekday.

Related Scenarios

- You are a publisher tracking book sales, the number of books sold, the top books being sold, and the locations of the sales.
- You need to track customer acquisitions for various product lines, showing total acquisitions over time and the top product line categories.
- You need to track subscribers to your service.

  You need to track something over time, on an aggregated basis, showing the top *n* and the geographic location.

How People Use the Dashboard

The user will review this dashboard at some regular interval, such as monthly, quarterly, or as needed on demand. The dashboard gives an overview of the key statistics that the user tracks. In the field of website analytics, pageviews is a common metric. This is the number of times a web page is viewed. The dashboard shows pageviews in a number of ways as well as a few additional metrics.

At the top of the dashboard in Figure 13.1, three high-level metrics are shown: the total pageviews for the time period, which is noted at the top of the dashboard, the total number of visitors, and the number of blog posts. A bar chart shows the daily pageviews over time along with a trend line to help visualize the trend for that period. A histogram is used to show the pageviews by the day of week.

The histogram in Figure 13.2 does not have an axis label or data labels. It's used in a similar manner as a sparkbar, simply to visualize the overall distribution for the days of the week. Data labels could easily be added, but in this case there is no need to see that one day is 31,966 compared to another day. Also, there are tool tips built in, so users can hover over any point, including the histogram, and see the data if they choose to. (See Figure 13.2.) The big takeaway: There are far more pageviews during the workweek with Tuesdays and Thursdays getting the most views.

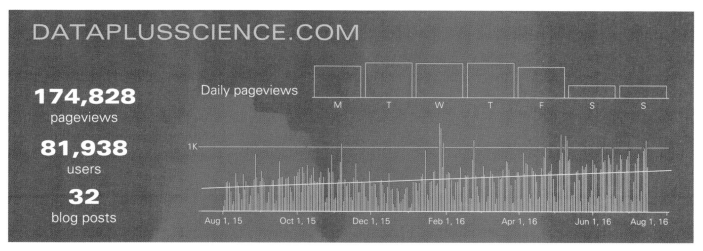

FIGURE 13.1 Key metrics are displayed on the left side. A bar chart shows the daily pageviews over time along with a histogram to show the pageviews by week day.

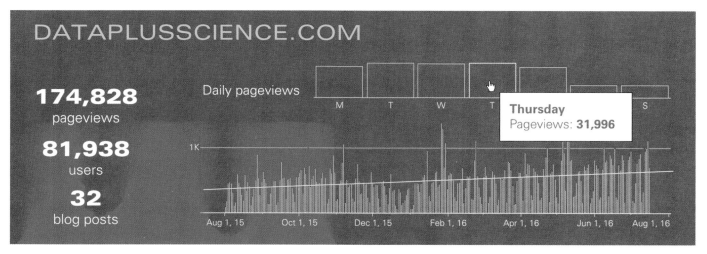

FIGURE 13.2 Tool tips are used throughout the visualization to show the details of the data for any point selected or highlighted.

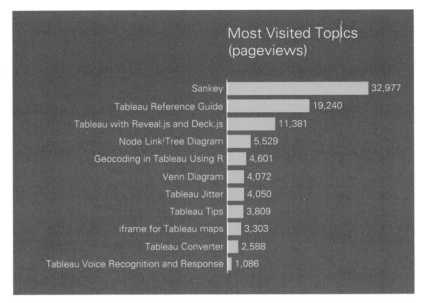

FIGURE 13.3   Bar chart showing total pageviews for each blog post.

The bar chart in Figure 13.3 is used to show the top blog posts by pageviews. Depending on what users would like see, this could show the top 5 or top 10 or even be interactive to allow users to specify the top *n* in the view. You could also add a dashboard action that allows users to click a bar and see a list of all blog posts and/or web pages associated with the bar. Clicking an item from that list would then jump to an individual blog post or web page.

Rank the bars

Ranking bar charts in descending or ascending order provides additional context to the data and makes it easier to compare values.

The map in Figure 13.4 shows the location of the users across the world. The styling of the map is very simple. There are no country or city labels, only points on the world map. The mapping controls allow users to zoom, pan, and even search for cities.

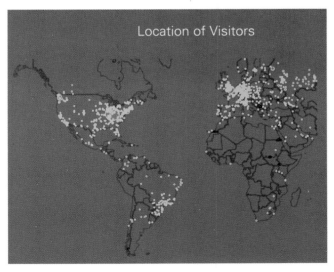

FIGURE 13.4   Map of visitors to the website zoomed in on a portion of the world.

Why This Works

A Few Key Metrics Tracked in a Simple Way

This dashboard has only a few key metrics, pageviews being the primary metric. The line chart, histogram, and bar chart all show variations of this metric; the bar chart with trendline shows pageviews over time, the histogram shows pageviews by day, and the bar chart shows pageviews by top blog posts. The number of users and number of blog posts are added in text. The only other item on the dashboard is the location of the users on the map.

Simple Use of Color

Other than white text, a single color is used on this dashboard for all of the charts. The color is not used to encode data in any way. Any color combination could work—for example, using corporate colors or team colors. This dashboard would work equally well if all color were removed, such as using a white background with gray or black as shown in Figure 13.5.

Good Chart Types for the Various Comparisons

The primary method of encoding data on this dashboard is the preattentive attribute of length (i.e., the length or height of the bars). Except for the trend line and map (where position is used), the length/height of the bar is used to encode all of the data on this dashboard. This makes the comparisons very easy and precise. In Figure 13.6, users can quickly see that there are far fewer pageviews on weekends than there are during the workweek. In fact, even when the values are close, the small differences can

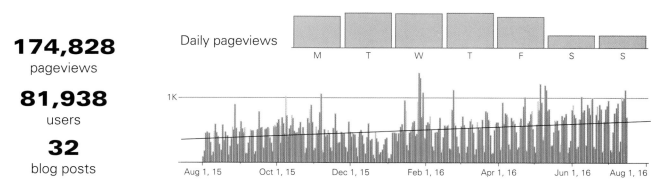

FIGURE 13.5   An example of what this dashboard might look like without using color.

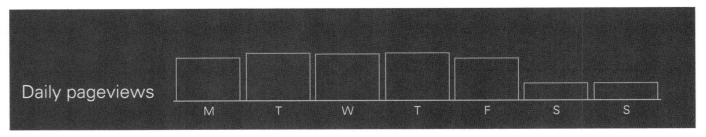

FIGURE 13.6   Histogram of pageviews by week. Notice the small differences between weekdays.

still be seen; for example, pageviews on Monday are slightly lower than pageviews on Tuesday, Wednesday, and Thursday.

Clean, Uncluttered Design

As mentioned previously, only a few charts are displayed. If you examine those charts closely, you will see that they are not heavily labeled. The histogram in Figure 13.6 does not have a y-axis, and there are no data labels. The bar chart, as shown in Figure 13.1, does not have axis labels, only data labels, and pageviews over time has a single label on the y-axis indicating a gridline for 1,000 pageviews. Additional data is available via the tool tips, but these choices give the dashboard a very clean and simple design.

Author Commentary

Steve: I loved exploring this dashboard and found it clean, clear, and intuitive. And while I tend to prefer light backgrounds, I had no trouble reading text and decoding the charts.

The dashboard was so inviting that I found myself wanting to know more about the site's traffic. The maps made me want to see how much traffic came from inside the United States versus outside. I would have liked to see the addition of a bar chart like the one shown in Figure 13.7.

This also piqued my curiosity to see pageviews by city. Although the treemap in Figure 13.8 is a bit of overkill, it reveals that the most views come from London and not inside the United States.

In addition, the bar chart in Figure 13.3 made me curious about the content that was driving those pageviews. In a future version of the dashboard, I would like a way to see all the posts related to the topic that interested me and have a way to jump directly to those posts.

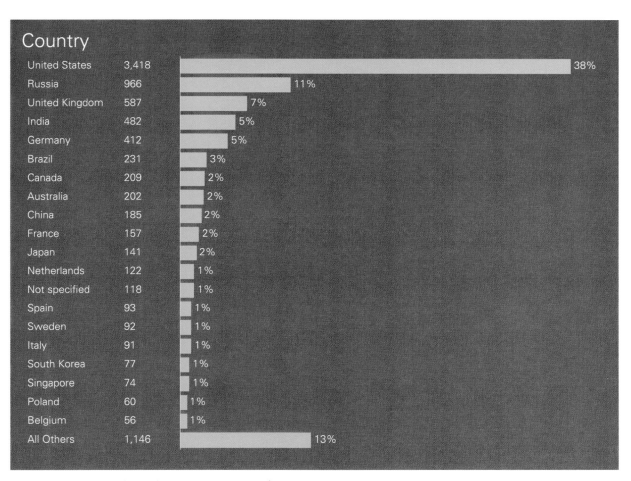

FIGURE 13.7 Bar chart showing pageviews by country.

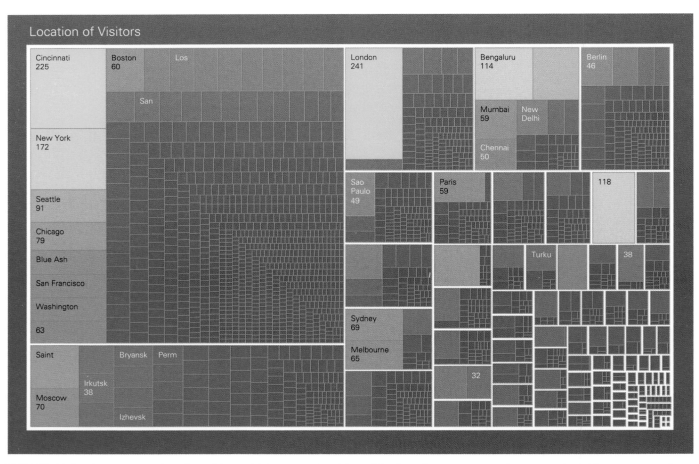

FIGURE 13.8 A treemap showing cities within countries (the white borders separate the countries). Here we see that London was responsible for more pageviews than any other city.

Chapter 14

Patient History Analysis of Recent Hospital Admissions

Planning tool for unscheduled day care at the NHS Southern Health Trust.

Dashboard designer: Simon Beaumont

Organization: Southern Health NHS Foundation Trust, England

ICT unscheduled care daily planning tool - Known to the ICT

Southern Health **NHS**
NHS Foundation Trust

Select an Area	Select your Team	Select a Practice	Select the inpatient provider	Days you wish to view the most recent admissions for
NHS WEST HA.. ▼	All ▼	All ▼	All ▼	1 ▼

Patients known to the ICT (receiving care in the last 30 days); admitted 1 day(s) ago

14

LOS	Pseudo Patient Name	Current service
1	Patient 19	Admission - Acute Hospital
	Patient 95	Admission - Acute Hospital
	Patient 64	Admission - Acute Hospital
	Patient 205	Admission - Acute Hospital
	Patient 103	Admission - Acute Hospital
	Patient 193	Admission - Acute Hospital
	Patient 191	Admission - Acute Hospital
	Patient 180	Admission - Acute Hospital

Apr 16   May 16   Jun 16   Jul 16

Patients known to the ICT (receiving care in the last 30 days) currently in hospital (admitted earlier than 1 day(s) ago)

124

LOS	Pseudo Patient Name	Current service
29	Patient 181	Admission - Acute Hospital
28	Patient 139	Admission - Acute Hospital
	Patient 63	Admission - Acute Hospital
	Patient 25	Admission - Acute Hospital
27	Patient 82	Admission - Acute Hospital
26	Patient 152	Admission - Acute Hospital
	Patient 228	Admission - Acute Hospital
	Patient 245	Admission - Acute Hospital
	Patient 27	Admission - Acute Hospital
	Patient 48	Admission - Acute Hospital
25	Patient 24	Admission - Acute Hospital
	Patient 190	Admission - Acute Hospital

Apr 16   May 16   Jun 16   Jul 16

Clinical intervention type colours explained

■ Admission   ■ Discharge   ■ Adults Physical Health   ■ Older Persons Mental Health

Created and maintained by the Southern Health Information Department
Version control (number, last amended date, author) : 2.0, 20/03/2016, Simon Beaumont

Scenario

Big Picture

You are a clinician working at a health trust with many hospitals. Your role is to provide individualized health care to patients in your region. One aspect of this is responding to patients' hospital admissions. Your job is to help clinicians understand patient histories and use that information to create a plan to get the patient home as quickly as possible.

This dashboard shows the activity of individuals admitted to the hospital in the last 24 hours. Patients' recent medical histories help explain the reasons for their admission to the hospital. Along with personal knowledge of the patients, this information allows you to plan a successful intervention.

Specifics

You want to know which patients were admitted to the hospital in the last day and in the last month. Of those who have been admitted, what health care visits have they had in the last five months?

Related Scenarios

The presentation used in this scenario can translate to any other scenario in which it's important to see patterns in individual events rather than aggregated data. Such scenarios include, for example:

- Schools that want to track truancy for individual students.
- Sales organizations that want to track customer activity on their websites in order to adapt their sales strategy to the individual.
- Database administrators who need to understand bottlenecks and downtime in company infrastructure.

How People Use the Dashboard

Each day, clinicians meet to plan their work. The dashboard is opened and filtered to patients relevant to the group. The same dashboard is used across the health trust, covering multiple areas, hospitals, and teams.

As shown in Figure 14.1, there are two main areas on the dashboard.

FIGURE 14.1   The first section shows admissions in the last day. In this example, there were 14.

The top area shows data about patients admitted to hospital in the last 24 hours. The number of patients is displayed in the green callout on the left. In this example, 14 patients were admitted. Eight are shown on the screen, and the rest can be seen by scrolling. Each dot represents a visit with a health care worker, a hospital admission, or a discharge. The patterns of the dots tell a rich story about each patient, which we detail later.

Clinicians can look at the recent pattern for each patient, along with their personal knowledge of each case, to work out a suitable plan for each patient. Each dot has a hyperlink directly to the detailed record for that intervention.

Each row in the figure tells a detailed history about a real person. Over time, this story becomes easier and faster to read as clincians learn to decode the dots and the colors. Let's look at three different patient stories our dashboard tells us.

1. Patient 64 has had almost continuous visits from Adults Physical Health (orange/peach dots) services for the duration of the time shown on this view. The only gap was a period spent in the hospital (the time between the first red dot and the blue dot showing admission and discharge). What this shows is that intensive home care has largely succeeded in giving this patient time at home, providing him or her with valuable independence. Despite these interventions, this patient still has been admitted to the hospital.

2. Patient 103 has had fewer interventions, but the recent admission is the fourth time in the hospital in the past five months. (Each red dot represents a hospital admission.) The visits by the

Adults Physical Health care team haven't been as frequent as for Patient 64, but they have helped the patient stay at home for significant amounts of time.

3. Patient 191 has just been readmitted after a recent discharge. Prior to the first visit, there had been regular visits by the Adults Physical Health service, and during the time Patient 191 was in the hospital, there was also a need for the Older Persons Mental Health team to spend time with him or her (the gray dots).

The lower section, as seen in Figure 14.2, shows patients who have been in the hospital and were admitted more than 24 hours ago.

Clinicians use this dashboard to discuss the history of each patient in their daily meetings.

Why This Works

Complete Data, Not Aggregated Data

A lot of the dashboards in this book focus on key performance indicators and aggregated metrics. This is good when looking at the higher levels of a business, but consider what the data in health care is all about: each record is a patient, a patient who might be struggling. Working out the average symptoms for all patients might provide a picture for those governing the health care provider, but the overall average is of no use to the provider trying to help an individual patient. Each patient is different, and each needs individualized plans.

This doesn't mean a single dashboard view is needed for every single patient. Instead, this dashboard provides a holistic view of the history of all the patients under

Patients known to the ICT (receiving care in the last 30 days) currently in hospital (admitted earlier than 1 day(s) ago)

LOS	Pseudo Patient Name	Current service
29	Patient 181	Admission - Acute Hospital
28	Patient 139	Admission - Acute Hospital
	Patient 63	Admission - Acute Hospital
	Patient 25	Admission - Acute Hospital
27	Patient 82	Admission - Acute Hospital
26	Patient 152	Admission - Acute Hospital
	Patient 228	Admission - Acute Hospital
	Patient 245	Admission - Acute Hospital
	Patient 27	Admission - Acute Hospital
	Patient 48	Admission - Acute Hospital
25	Patient 24	Admission - Acute Hospital
	Patient 190	Admission - Acute Hospital

124

Apr 16   May 16   Jun 16   Jul 16

Clinical intervention type colours explained

■ Admission   ■ Discharge   ■ Adults Physical Health   ■ Older Persons Mental Health

FIGURE 14.2   Patients admitted more than one day ago.

the care of the team. With one screen all the patients' details can been seen and discussed.

Stories about Real People Told Linearly

These are real patients. Their stories cannot be aggregated into averages. Looking after their health requires being able to see the complete narrative, which this dot plot enables. The dot plot in Figure 14.2 showing each interaction along a horizontal line makes it easy to follow this history visually.

Single-Number Callouts

How many new patients were admitted in the last 24 hours? How many patients who have been admitted in the last 30 days are still in the hospital? Both of these questions are important to answer. The answers are the biggest and most obvious features of the dashboard, as seen in Figure 14.3. The answers are 14 and 124, respectively, shown in large numbers on the left-hand side of each section's dot plot.

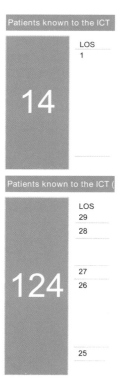

FIGURE 14.3   Key numbers are made as large and visible as possible.

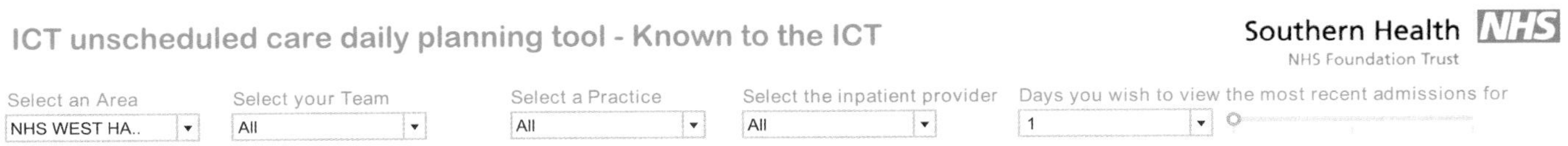

ICT unscheduled care daily planning tool - Known to the ICT

Southern Health NHS
NHS Foundation Trust

Select an Area	Select your Team	Select a Practice	Select the inpatient provider	Days you wish to view the most recent admissions for
NHS WEST HA.. ▼	All ▼	All ▼	All ▼	1 ▼

FIGURE 14.4 The filters need to be reset each time the dashboard is opened. Therefore, they are positioned at the top of the dashboard.

Filters at the Top

This single dashboard is used by multiple teams, so they need filters to get to the right data quickly. Therefore, for this dashboard the filters are at the top, where people are most likely to look first (see Figure 14.4.). In an ideal situation, the filters should be retained so that each time the viewer opens the dashboard, the filters are already set. If that's the case, and the filters no longer need to be reset on each view, it would be possible to move them to a less prominent position, such as the right-hand side.

We discuss the positioning of filters at length in the Author Commentary in Chapter 5.

Dashboard Designer Commentary

SIMON BEAUMONT: In the health care field, data is often used only to support and measure targets and to facilitate conversations around only the targets. This data normally is summarized using the traditional red, amber, green rating. The problem with this approach is that it misses the purpose of health care: to support individual patients to lead healthy, independent, and fulfilling lives. By aggregating numbers, we lose this connection with the people we are here to serve, our patients. That is not to say that we do not measure the success of

initiatives: We do that on other, higher-level dashboards. But our health care providers, for their day-to-day work, looking after patients, need detail, not aggregates.

Prior to this dashboard being implemented, there was simply no way for clinicians to see all patient history data. When a patient was admitted, the clinicians would receive a text message on their phone. In order to see the case history, clinicians had to click a link in the text message or copy it into a browser. There was no way to see the entire history in one view; instead, clinicians needed to click through every past appointment. This was inconvenient and disruptive. The end result was that it was simply too cumbersome a process for clinicians to follow.

This dashboard has been revolutionary. Its purpose is the number-one priority of all clinicians: to maximize the effectiveness of the care they provide to their patients. The data directly supports clinicians in their working day. It complements their clinical knowledge with automated, timely information from across the health economy. Instead of data being seen as an aggregated hindrance, it is seen as an asset that directly supports the delivery of personalized care.

Author Commentary

ANDY: So many dashboards are about aggregating an organization's activity into a small set of numbers. When those numbers represent people, we get into uncomfortable areas. There is no such thing as an "average" person, whether they are patients, students, or employees; someone in a class at school might have an average IQ but they won't be average in other categories. This is not to say that hospitals such as Simon's shouldn't also look at aggregated data; they should. The lesson from this dashboard is that data should be viewed at different levels of detail.

Chapter 15

Hospitality Dashboard for Hotel Management

Hospitality dashboard.

Source: Images courtesy of Dundas Data Visualization, Inc. (www.dundas.com)

Author: David Voung

Organization: Dundas Data Visualization

Link: https://samples.dundas.com/Dashboard/9a7c2299-e20b-4e78-b257-0a69396996b9?e=false&vo=viewonly

THE | WEXFORT HOTEL

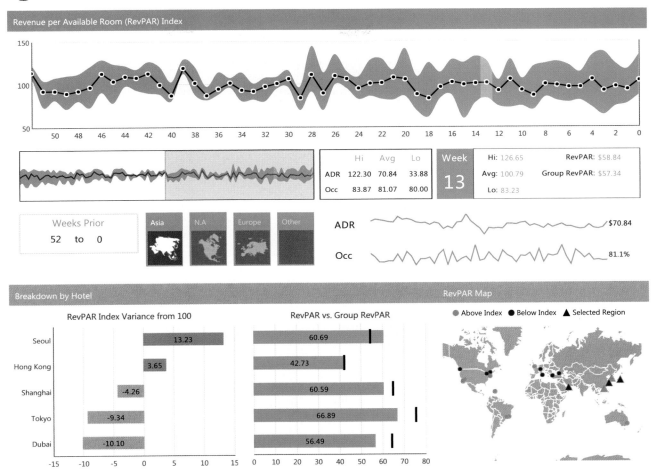

Revenue per Available Room (RevPAR) Index

	Hi	Avg	Lo
ADR	122.30	70.84	33.88
Occ	83.87	81.07	80.00

Week 13

Hi: 126.65	RevPAR: $58.84
Avg: 100.79	Group RevPAR: $57.34
Lo: 83.23	

Weeks Prior: 52 to 0

Asia | N.A | Europe | Other

ADR — $70.84
Occ — 81.1%

Breakdown by Hotel

RevPAR Index Variance from 100

Seoul	13.23
Hong Kong	3.65
Shanghai	-4.26
Tokyo	-9.34
Dubai	-10.10

RevPAR vs. Group RevPAR

Seoul	60.69
Hong Kong	42.73
Shanghai	60.59
Tokyo	66.89
Dubai	56.49

RevPAR Map

● Above Index　● Below Index　▲ Selected Region

Scenario

Big Picture

You are a manager for a large chain of hotels. You need a dashboard to monitor some key metrics, including how revenue did last week in comparison to previous weeks. You need to see if the revenue is being influenced by the current daily rate promotions and if the promotions are aligned to occupancy. There are multiple locations around the world, so you also need to know which hotels are the best and worst performers within their respective region. You also need the ability to drill further into the details for any specific weeks as necessary.

Specifics

- You are tasked with showing the revenue per available room (RevPAR) for your hotels and in comparison to a peer group.
- You need to organize hotels by regions and compare those to hotels within the same region.
- You need to show data over time, showing a selected number of weeks in the past.
- You want to see the spread for available rooms from the lowest-priced room and the highest-priced room.
- You need to understand how quickly the business is reacting to these prices and how much alignment exists between the different locations.
- You need to provide an on-demand (interactive) breakdown to the daily rate by segment and channel.

- You need to provide on-demand (interactive) access to a specific hotel.

Related Scenarios

- You manage airline reservations and need to gauge the impact of changing ticket prices on occupancy.
- You need to analyze movie theater occupancy over time and in different locations.
- You need to analyze retail customer rate and revenue for a retail store and compare it with all other stores and with stores in certain regions.

How People Use the Dashboard

The primary view of this dashboard focuses on the current time period and looking back in weeks for some selected period of time. In the top chart (see Figure 15.1), the x-axis of the line chart shows the range of weeks that has been selected. This allows the user to gauge the overall trend as well as the spread of revenue per room within that week.

The spread of revenue per available room (the blue band) shows the lowest-priced and highest-priced rooms for that week, and the black line in the middle is the average. (See Figure 15.2.)

The user can hover over the RevPAR trend and see the highlighted week's statistics; for example, Week 13 is highlighted, as indicated by the light blue color on the line chart in Figure 15.3.

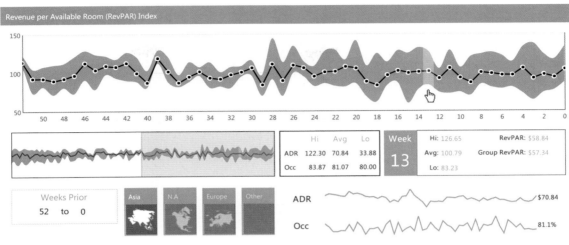

FIGURE 15.1 Highlighting week 13 in the top chart updates the key metrics on the other charts.

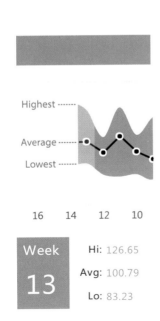

FIGURE 15.2 The spread from the lowest-priced to the highest-priced available room is shown by the blue band. The black line shows the average.

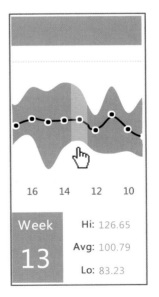

FIGURE 15.3 The highlighted week is shown as a light blue band. The data in the text boxes will update showing the details for the highlighted week.

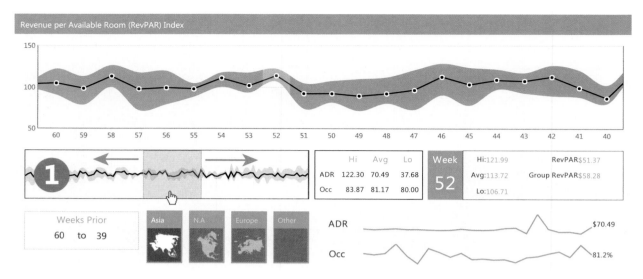

FIGURE 15.4 The slider control (1) for the top graph.

The blue-shaded window can be resized to select a shorter or longer time range. It can also be panned from the left to right (marked with red arrows) to move the time range from older weeks to more recent weeks. (See Figure 15.4.)

RevPAR values are indexed so all locations within a region can be compared to each other regardless of the different countries' currencies and standard rates. Regions can be selected easily by clicking on one of the four regional map icons in Figure 15.5.

Once a region is selected, the dashboard updates with that region's metrics. The map shows color dots

for hotels that are above the index and below the index. The hotels in the selected region use the same color scheme but use triangles to show them as selected. (See Figure 15.6.)

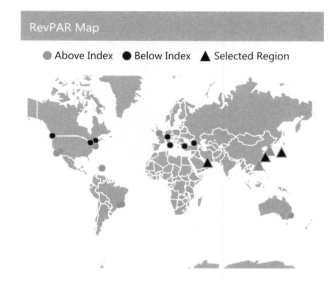

FIGURE 15.6 Map showing the selected region with triangles. All points are colored as above or below index.

FIGURE 15.5 Region selector showing Asia selected.

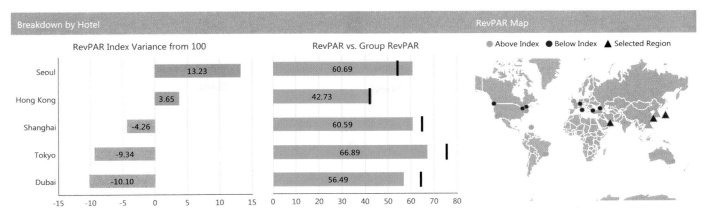

FIGURE 15.7   Bar charts on the bottom of the dashboard display a breakdown by hotel. The blue bars show the RevPAR per hotel. The black line is the Group RevPAR.

At the bottom of the dashboard, a diverging bar chart is used to show RevPAR variance from an index of 100. There is also a bar chart with reference lines showing the hotel location's RevPAR compared to the Group RevPAR. (See Figure 15.7.)

The map in Figure 15.6 uses the preattentive attribute of color to distinguish between the hotels above and below the index. Another preattentive attribute, shape, is used to distinguish the selected regions (triangle) from the nonselected regions (dots). Notice the clean design of the map and bar charts and the simple use of color.

Why This Works

Interactivity That Preserves Context

The dashboard is highly interactive. Nearly every object on the dashboard acts as a highlight or a filter or presents details on demand. When drilling down into more detailed data, the visualizations remain connected to the main dashboard. The portions of the dashboard that are used as selectors are still in view and actionable. This allows the user to immediately change the selection to update those details while still in the details window.

For example, in Figure 15.8, when the user selects a city (in this case, Seoul) (1), details for Seoul will show in a new window (2). If the user clicks a different bar on the bar chart in the main dashboard—for example, Hong Kong—then the details window will update to reflect this new selection (and update using animated transitions). Because all these choices can be made without closing the details window, fast selections can be made from one hotel to another, providing quick and easy comparisons.

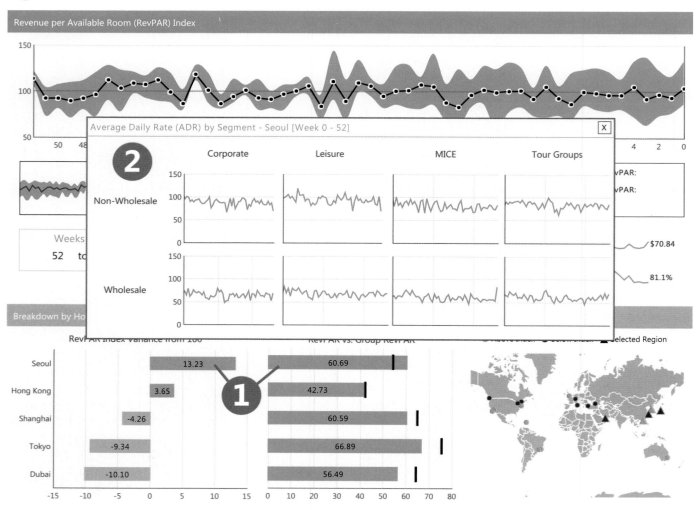

FIGURE 15.8 Clicking on the bar charts in the breakdown section (1) gives a detailed view of Wholesale versus Non-Wholesale in a small multiple-line chart (2).

Likewise, the user can select a hotel on the map and immediately see the details on demand for that location. Without closing that window, the user can select another city, and those details will update. This allows the user to compare these metrics by location without having to close and open the window or navigate between different pages. (See Figure 15.9.)

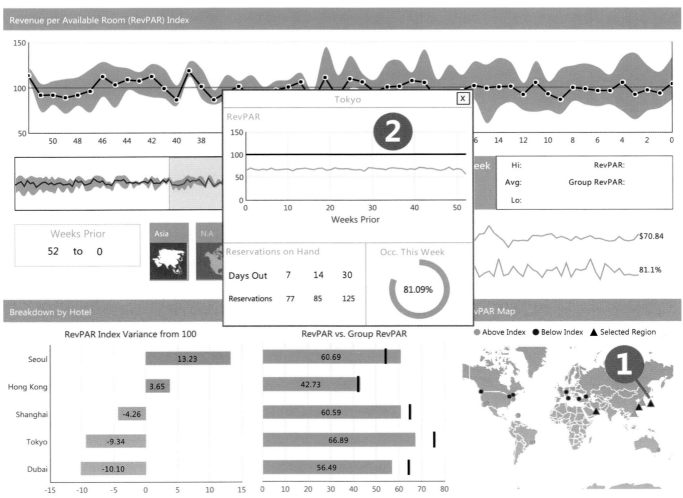

FIGURE 15.9 Clicking on the Tokyo hotel on the map (1) opens a detailed window for that location (2). Without closing the detail window, another city can be selected to update the view.

As the user adjusts the size of the slider or moves the slider to adjust the time range, the dashboard is updating immediately, letting the user quickly see the different patterns in the data. When the user adjusts the slider and the dashboard updatess, key metrics are updated, showing the average daily rate (ADR) and the occupancy rate for the time period selected from the slider control. The user can then move the mouse to hover over any week in the top chart, and the data for that week will update in the other box.

For example, in Figure 15.10, Weeks 60 to 39 are selected using the slider control (1). The dashboard updates, showing an average daily rate of $70.49 for that time period (2). These weeks then can be compared to Week 52, which is highlighted using the mouse (3). This updates the Week 52 window, showing the average for the week of $113.72 (4), which is the highest average in the selected time period and which also has a very narrow range (3) when compared to the overall ADR.

Clear Focus on Key Measures and Dimensions

The dashboard shows only three measures—RevPAR, daily rate, and occupancy—and provides the measures across three dimensions—week, region, and hotel. More dimensions and details are available as details on demand, but the clear focus on these metrics helps the user analyze and understand the data without complication.

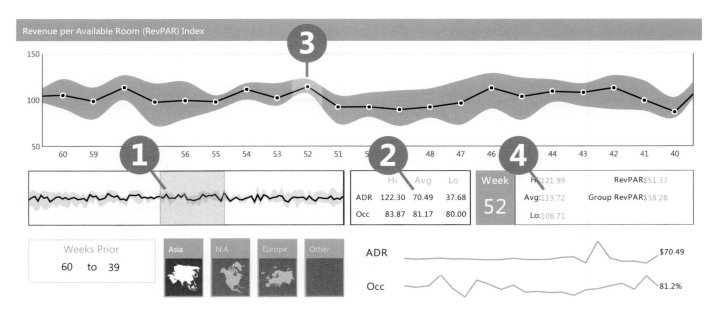

FIGURE 15.10 Moving the slider from the left to right or resizing immediately adjusts the dashboard in a responsive way and allows for exploration of the data and immediate analysis.

Author Commentary

JEFF: This dashboard is so interactive and fluid that it reminds me of music editing software. The selection of the time range is very similar to how one would select a portion of music in a sound file to edit it. It allows the user to dynamically select a time band in the window, and the rest of the visualization then updates. Combined with the other interactive features and the details on demand, it makes this dashboard very powerful. It's fun to play with.

I love the use of color in this dashboard as well. I might have kept the "below index" color on the map (dark red) the same on the bar chart (light gray) for consistency of color. Also, axis labels aren't really needed on the bar charts since there are data labels, but in this case, they do help the reader see that one axis goes below zero and the other starts at zero. I typically add a zero line on bar charts, especially diverging bar charts, so that the common baseline is clearly marked.

You won't find too many pie charts or donut charts in this book. In general, there are better ways to visualize data (see Figure 15.9). This topic is discussed in depth in Chapter 34. It's important to note in this particular donut chart that it is not used for any type of comparison. It is simply used as an occupancy indicator. Occupancy is bounded in this case, meaning it's not possible to go over 100 percent occupancy. The donut chart simply shows a single number approaching 100 percent.

Chapter 16

Sentiment Analysis: Showing Overall Distribution

Sentiment Analysis.
Dashboard Designer: Jeffrey Shaffer
Organization: Data Plus Science, LLC

Sentiment Analysis

Distribution of Sentiment for All Banks
Scoring 421 Bank Tweets (filtering out unrelated)

<--- low   high --->

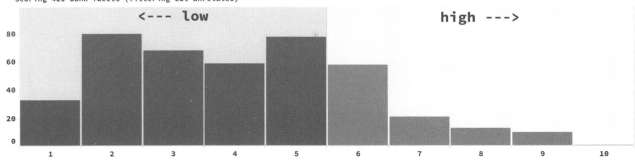

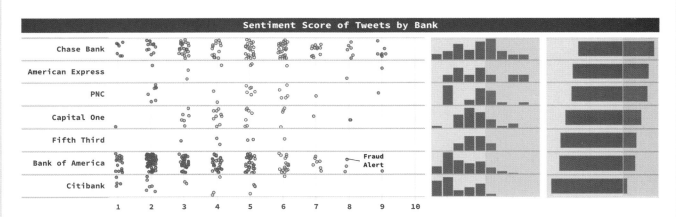

Sentiment Score of Tweets by Bank

Chase Bank
American Express
PNC
Capital One
Fifth Third
Bank of America — Fraud Alert
Citibank

1 2 3 4 5 6 7 8 9 10

  Account Alerts are a hot topic:

"Chase, stop emailing me daily bank account updates with numbers. a
sad face will suffice at this point."

"I couldn't tell you how many times a day I get low bank account
alerts from Chase."

Note:

Sentiment analysis is not always accurate.
The best algorithms are often only 70% accurate.

Data from: twitter

Dashboard created by Jeffrey A. Shaffer

Scenario

Big Picture

You are a social media manager, brand manager, or business analyst studying consumer sentiment for a specific brand/company and its competitors. You download tweets from Twitter and examine the sentiment around them, rating them using a tool such as Amazon's Mechanical Turk.

Specifics

- You have text comments from consumers for some period of time. This could be tweets from Twitter, customer service notes, consumer review websites, or texts or emails from consumers.
- You have cleaned the text and had the comments rated, either manually reviewed or using computer algorithms.
- This sentiment is on a scale of 1 to 10, with 10 being the best (most positive) and 1 being the worst (negative).
- You want to see how this sentiment compares to the sentiment of your other brands or your competitor's brands or as a company over all.
- You have a large number of data points: hundreds, thousands, or even more.

Related Scenarios

- You need to show reviews of product on websites, such as those on Amazon, Yelp, or *Consumer Reports*.
- You need to show results of satisfaction surveys.

- You need to show the results of customer feedback forms.
- You need to show movie reviews, such as the reviews on IMDB or Rotten Tomatoes.
- You are a manager and need to show the results from performance reviews.
- You are a professor or a teacher and you need to show grades for a class.

How People Use the Dashboard

This dashboard uses a similar technique to the dashboard in Chapter 3. However, in that scenario, your company or you specifically are one of the dots, and you are comparing yourself to all of the other dots. In this scenario, all of the dots are customers giving feedback about you, your brand, or your company. The comparison to other brands or companies comes from comparing the distribution of the dots across the rows or columns rather than from comparing the position of one dot versus the position of another dot.

The top portion (see Figure 16.1) shows the overall distribution of the tweets. In this case, the data is a collection of tweets about different banking institutions.

This histogram shows the sentiment of the tweets using a scale of 1 to 10. By visualizing the sentiment as a histogram, the reader can quickly see the distribution of that sentiment. For example, in this case, the data is right-skewed. There is clearly more negative sentiment about the banks than positive sentiment.

Sentiment Analysis

Distribution of Sentiment for All Banks
Scoring 421 Bank Tweets (filtering out unrelated)

<--- low   high --->

FIGURE 16.1   A histogram showing the distribution of sentiment from tweets about banks on Twitter.

Understanding distribution

A number of general types of data distribution exist. (See Figure 16.2.) "Skew" refers to the asymmetry of the distribution versus the even distribution of a normal distribution. Some people find skew labels confusing. Skew is easy to remember if you see skewed data as having a tail (i.e., gets thinner at one end). The direction of the skew matches the direction of the tail.

Types of Distributions

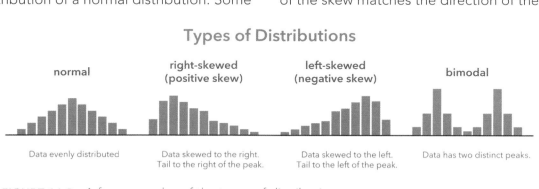

normal	right-skewed (positive skew)	left-skewed (negative skew)	bimodal
Data evenly distributed	Data skewed to the right. Tail to the right of the peak.	Data skewed to the left. Tail to the left of the peak.	Data has two distinct peaks.

FIGURE 16.2   A few examples of the types of distributions.

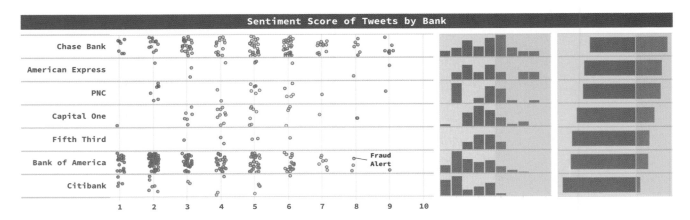

FIGURE 16.3   A dot plot, histogram, and diverging bar chart showing the distribution of sentiment by bank.

The reader can see each bank and compare the distribution of the sentiment. (See Figure 16.3.) The dots give the reader a sense of how many tweets a particular bank has. The data can be explored point by point to see the individual tweets, and overall comparisons among banks can be made using the distribution of the dots in the dot plot, the histograms, and the diverging bar chart. In this particular data set (only 421 tweets after filtering), the user can see that Bank of America and Citibank, at the bottom of the list, are much more right-skewed than Chase Bank.

Why This Works

The Double Jitter Shows Distribution of the Discrete Points

The dot plot shows each individual data point. In this case, each individual tweet by a consumer is plotted by the sentiment score. Since the rating is a discrete number, from 1 to 10, when the dots are plotted, they would all be on top of each other,

completely hiding the visualization of the individual points. As we did with the dot plot in Chapter 3, we apply jitter to separate the points from each other. However, in this dot plot, jitter is used on both the x-axis and the y-axis; in other words, the plot is double jittered.

On the y-axis, jitter is a random number separating the points across the row from the top of the row to the bottom of the row. However, even when using the jitter on the y-axis, the points still would be on top of each other. Since the x-axis shows the sentiment score, it is critical that we don't distort the data. Therefore, on the x-axis, a jitter is applied carefully, moving the points just above or below the actual data point so that they group together around the true data point. In other words, a score of 3 is plotted as 2.9 for one dot and as 3.1 for another. (See Figure 16.4.)

The amount of jitter depends on the number of points in the data set. The more points you have, the more overlap occurs in the dot plot.

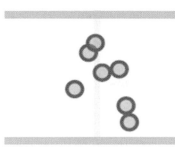

FIGURE 16.4   The dots in the dot plot are randomly distributed between the top and bottom but also to the left and right of the data line.

How much jitter?

Determining the right amount to jitter can be tricky. (See Figure 16.5.) If you use too little jitter, the points will overlap too much. If you use too much, you can skew the appearance of the data. Like the temperature of Goldilocks' porridge, the amount to jitter has to be just right.

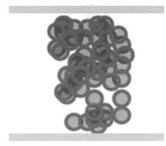

FIGURE 16.5   This data has so many points with the same value that the dots are on top of each other. This graph could be jittered more, but care must be taken not to jitter too much and skew the data.

Easy Exploration of Multiple Data Points

Dot plots allow for easy exploration of the data. Because these plots use individual data points, the user can hover over any point and see the tweet. The user thus can explore the data and, when doing so, sometimes discover interesting things. For example, by exploring this data, an instance of fraud was found and annotated, as shown in Figure 16.6.

FIGURE 16.6   Hovering over the tweets uncovered one that appears to be fraud (annotated as Fraud Alert).

This customer of Bank of America tweeted:

> All about lying to Bank of America about y u over-drafted so u can get the money refunded back into ur account #3itmes #$$straightoalochol

The Histogram Makes It Easy to See the Distribution for Each Bank

The histogram on the right side of the dashboard is really a sparkbar: there are no axis labels or data labels. Sparkbars aren't used to give precise numbers but rather to see a quick view of the distribution of sentiment for one bank versus another. The user can quickly scan the right side and see that one institution has more negative sentiment when compared to another. Rather than counting dots or trying to make estimates of one bank versus another, the histogram gives a simple summary in a small space.

Other Approaches

Box plots could be used to show the distribution of the points. Figure 16.7 shows the same data using a dot plot with a box plot.

Although the box plot does a great job showing the distribution of the points, it may not be universally understood by readers whereas the histogram showing the distribution will likely be understood by a broader audience.

Dot plots or strip plots can be used without jitter, but when plotting many points, there is too much overlap of the points to be useful. Figure 16.8 shows test scores of a particular course. Notice the overlapping dots in the regular dot plot compared to the dot plot using jitter and performance bands.

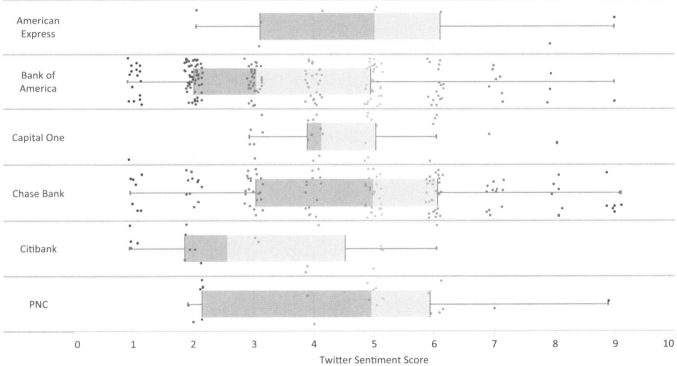

FIGURE 16.7   A dot plot and box plot showing the distribution of sentiment.

Data Visualization Class Test Grades

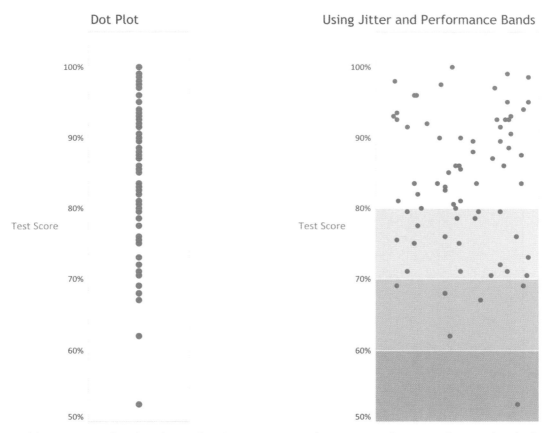

FIGURE 16.8 Adding jitter to the dot plot makes it easier to see the points without overlap, and including performance bands can add additional context for those points.

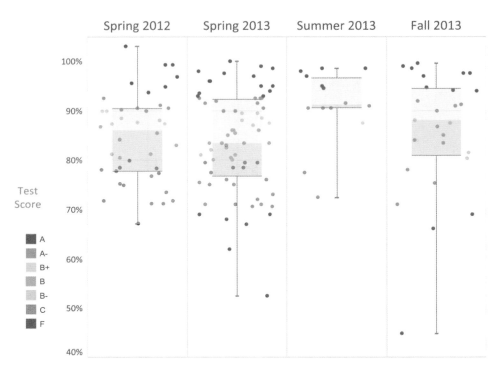

FIGURE 16.9   Using a dot with jitter and color to encode grades and adding a box plot allows a quick comparison across classes.

Figure 16.9 shows that same data using a dot plot with jitter and a box plot. Instead of performance bands, the grades are encoded with color in a similar manner as the sentiment dashboard.

Sometimes sentiment is categorized on a different scale; for example, it might simply be positive, negative, and neutral or a Likert scale. In this case, refer to Chapter 17 to see alternative ways in which you can visualize this data.

Author Commentary

STEVE: I wish people reading the book could see just how many iterations we go through with

these dashboards. This one in particular generated a lot of lively discussions as Jeff and I discussed the merits of using a histogram versus a divergent stacked bar chart to show how sentiment skews.

Part of the issue for me is I'm accustomed to seeing a divergent stacked bar for these situations, and I argued in favor of the approach shown in Figure 16.10.

Jeff still maintained that the common baseline in the histogram was important for comparing

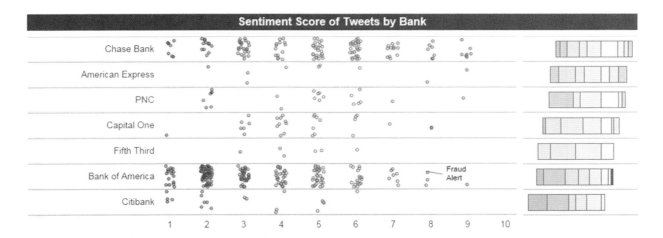

FIGURE 16.10   Using a divergent stacked bar chart to show and rank sentiment for different banks.

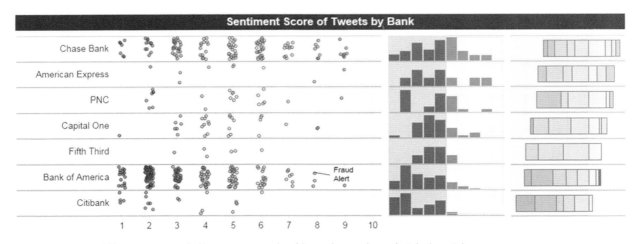

FIGURE 16.11   Histogram and divergent stacked bar chart placed side by side.

values, so we tried using both charts, as shown in Figure 16.11.

Jeff then pointed out that we didn't need so much detail in the divergent stacked bar approach, as the histogram already contained that detail. He suggested the approach that made it into the final dashboard. (See Figure 16.3.) I think it works very well.

This particular scenario has me rethinking how to show Net Promoter Score (NPS). Figure 16.12 is an alternative approach to the dashboard we present in Chapter 17.

ANDY: I'm very fond of jitterplots and like their use on this dashboard. I would caution readers not to think jitterplots should be used every time you are considering using a dot plot. Box plots were specifically created to solve some of the problems of overplotting. Jitterplots also introduce the risk that untrained viewers will interpret the position as an indication of a measure, even though one doesn't exist. I discussed this further, with examples, in Chapter 3.

NPS Experiment

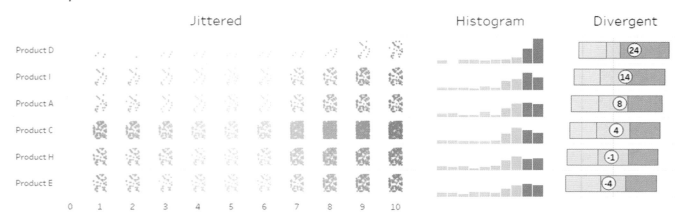

FIGURE 16.12   Combining several approaches to presenting Net Promoter Score data.

Chapter 17

Showing Sentiment with Net Promoter Score

Net Promoter Score dashboard.
Author: Steve Wexler
Organization: Data Revelations

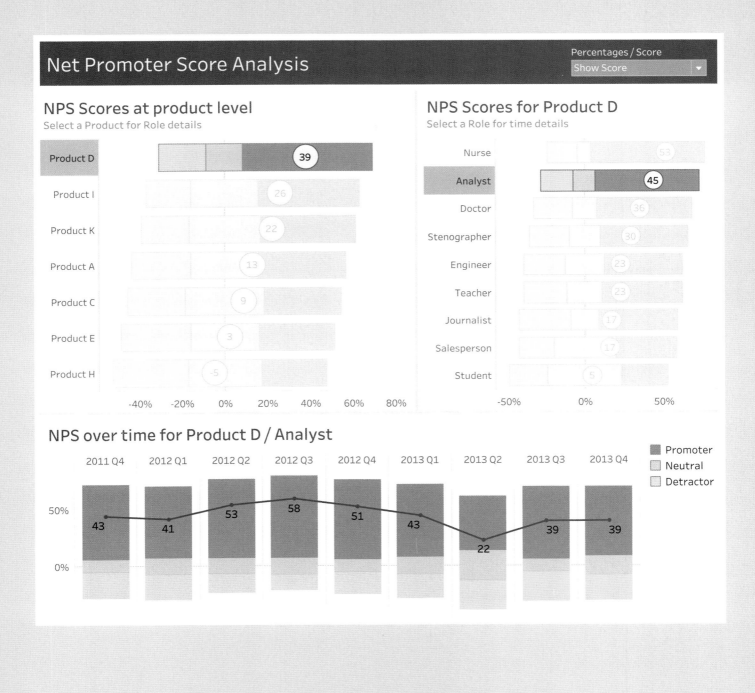

Scenario

Big Picture

You are a market researcher and need to track consumer preferences for several brands. You need to be able to see how different respondents feel about each brand and how opinions have changed over time.

Although you will consider asking your survey panel many different questions, you know for sure that you will present the classic Net Promoter Score (NPS) question—"Would you recommend this product or service to a friend or colleague? Please specify a rating from 0 to 10"—as your company has standardized on NPS as a measure of customer sentiment.

Specifics

- You need to show the NPS for a variety of products to see which ones people would recommend and which ones they would not.
- You need to see if people in different roles would recommend or not recommend a product.
- You need to see how NPS has changed over time for a particular product, both overall and for people in different roles.

Related Scenarios

- You need to see results for a series of Likert-scale questions asking survey respondents to indicate the degree to which they agree or disagree with a series of statements.

Likert scale

The Likert scale (pronounced "Lick-ert") is named after Rensis Likert, the founder of the Human Resources Institute. Likert came up with the idea of applying a quantitative scale (usually 1 through 5) to qualitative measures. For example, "On a scale of 1 to 5, where 1 means strongly disagree and 5 means strongly agree, please give your opinions about the following statements."

- You need to see how favorably or unfavorably people rate different candidates running for office.
- You want to know how often survey respondents use different social media outlets and how this usage differs based on age and gender.

Understanding NPS

In an NPS survey, respondents are presented with the question "Using a scale from 0 to 10, would you recommend this product/service to a friend or colleague?"

- Anyone who responds with a 0 through 6 is considered a detractor.
- Anyone who responds with a 7 or 8 is considered a passive (or neutral).
- Anyone who responds with a 9 or 10 is considered a promoter.

FIGURE 17.1   How to compute NPS.

The NPS is computed by taking the percentage of people who are promoters, subtracting the percentage of people who are detractors, and multiplying that number by 100. (See Figure 17.1.)

How People Use the Dashboard

In its initial state, the dashboard shows only ratings/rankings for several different products. (See Figure 17.2.)

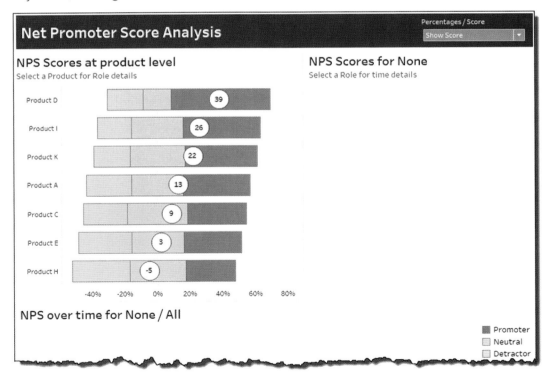

FIGURE 17.2   Initial state of the dashboard shows only ratings/rankings for the seven products being studied.

After a product is selected, you can see both how people in different job roles feel about the selected product and how NPS for the product has changed over time. (See Figure 17.3.)

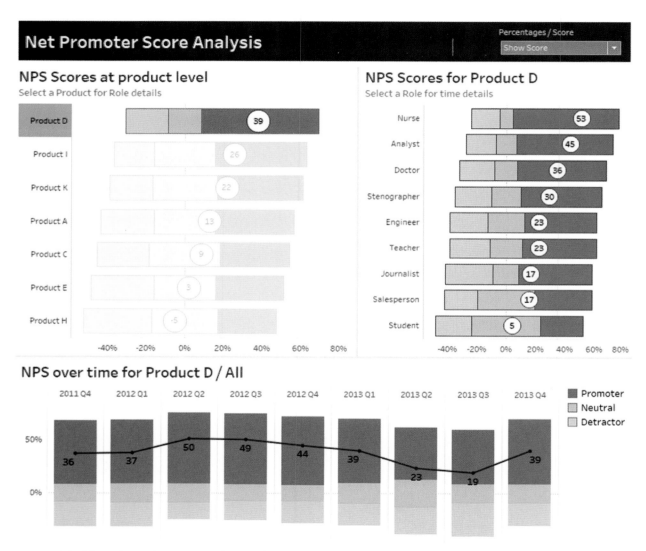

FIGURE 17.3   NPS by role and over time for Product D.

After a particular role is selected, you can see how NPS for the selected product has changed over time for that role, in this case analysts. (See Figure 17.4.)

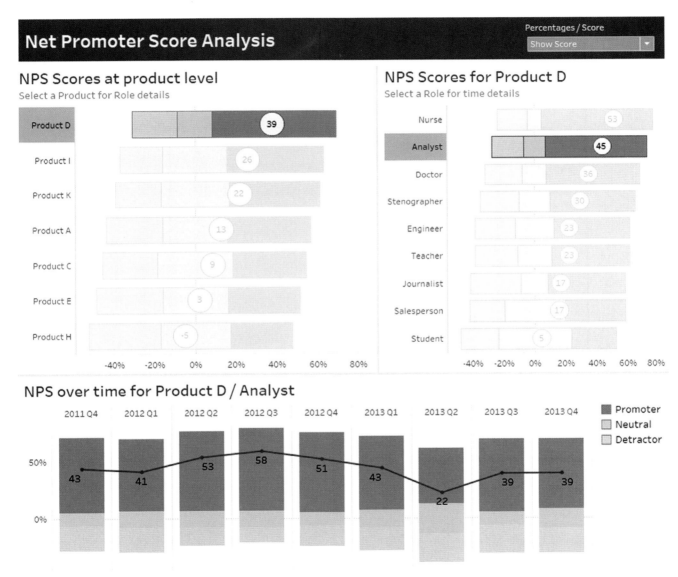

FIGURE 17.4 What analysts think about Product D over time.

Parameters drop-down toggle

When "Show Percentages" is selected, the view is changed so that you can see the percentage of promoters, neutrals, and detractors. (See Figures 17.5 and 17.6.)

FIGURE 17.5   Drop-down toggle.

Note that at any point, people interacting with the dashboard can change the view to instead show the percentage of promoters, neutrals, and detractors rather than the NPS. (See Figure 17.6.)

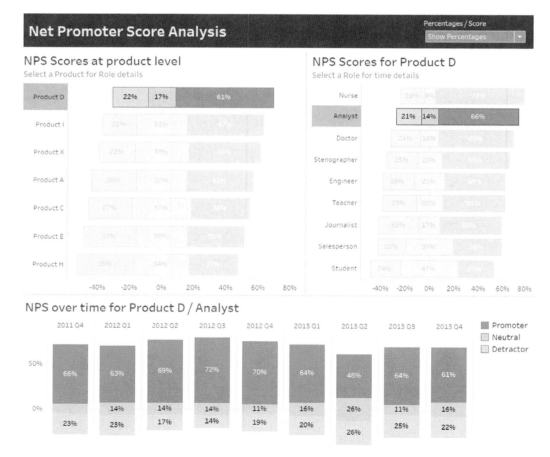

FIGURE 17.6   Showing percentages instead of NPS.

Why This Works

The Easy-to-Understand Combination Chart

The main visualization (see Figure 17.2) is a combination chart that combines divergent stacked bar charts with an overall score (the circles).

The divergent stacked bar makes it very easy to see how sentiment skews either positive or negative. (See Figure 17.7.) That is, the entire bar moves either left or right to show which products have a more favorable rating.

Note that, in this case, half of the neutral respondents are on the positive side and half are on the negative side, as we want to show these responses and how they center around zero. (For an alternative approach to dealing with neutrals, see Figure 17.19 later in the chapter.)

The Neutrals Tell Us a Lot

A typical NPS chart shows just the scores, not the distribution of positive, negative, and neutral responses. (See Figure 17.10 later in this chapter.) Neutrals represent the big tipping point with NPS because folks who selected a 7 or 8 are just one point away from being either promoters or detractors. A product with a large percentage of neutrals presents a great opportunity to turn respondents into promoters.

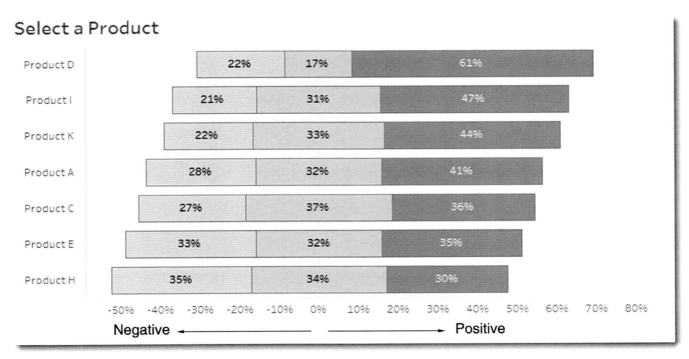

Select a Product

FIGURE 17.7   Sorted divergent stacked bars make it easy to see which products are more favorably rated.

Breakdown by Role Provides Additional Insight

The ability to select a product and see its performance by a particular demographic (in this case, role) enables users to see how sentiment differs based on that demographic.

In Figure 17.8, we can see that the NPS for Product A among doctors is 35 but is –2 among students.

Avoiding the Traditional Approach to NPS

Consider the snippet of NPS survey data shown in Figure 17.9 with responses about different companies from people in different roles.

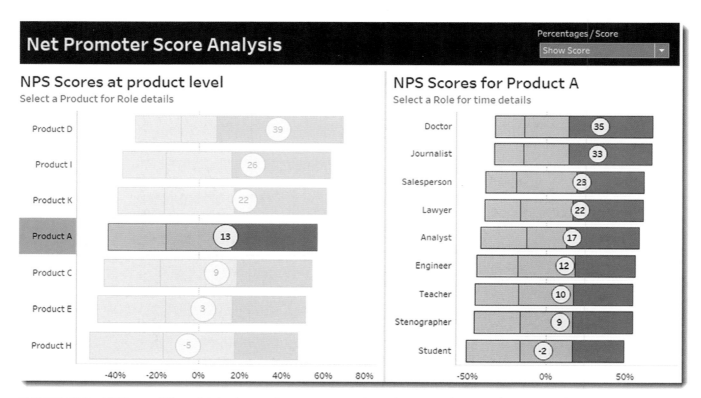

FIGURE 17.8   NPS can differ widely depending on respondent demographics, in this case, role.

ID	Company	Role	Response
1004fu85p1apxwys2w	H	Other	3
1005snzpcjxh5uuplc	H	Architect	9
1005t40dugzy8lmkga	B	Student	9
10074yq2iivnze1j9g	B	Student	5
100f4sp6ll3absivr8	A	Student	10
100fp9su1bqoa6tlxg	H	Student	8
100lrtua6er94cgyhr	B	Student	9
100ne7wa8w5dug2g1	F	Student	5
100nlg01cfn0msxpur	H	Other	8
100y25xxs0nv0il9p0	H	Student	8
100y2h4bkc2p0srgcl	B	Student	8
100ys9lpwygoyfsmtk	A	Student	10
10129h0ue2g5rka41p	I	Teacher	7
10134x62b8h5xra3uv	A	Student	5
10136cd35tap0qg4ea	H	Doctor	3
10187wtl372sf48ayo	B	Architect	7
101c9em3yv4b10p1jt	B	Retiree	10
101eumtd2d0x8ry0rd	A	Student	3
101h3owvofp46e9t6y	I	Teacher	9
101hbvthsqx03oi2jb	J	Student	5
101ln7j98hvmwycrve	B	Employee	9
101nohawdhwo1v9b:	B	Student	8
101op61th1xw17o86a	A	Teacher	8
101rph2x8niiaen9k8	B	Student	9
101rr82z0otkrika4	B	Architect	8
101wt6qmvdbvjs1uej	G	Salesperson	8
1022hef1uafdabzbh7	C	Student	7
1024d28z3pac8brhc2	I	Student	8
1026xy49c3k9k9r3k	A	Student	8

FIGURE 17.9 Raw NPS data about different companies from people with different occupations.

If we just focus on the NPS and not the components that comprise it, we can produce an easy-to-sort bar chart like the one shown in Figure 17.10.

Yes, it's easy to see that Company D has a much higher NPS than Company H, but by not showing the individual components, we're missing an important part of the story. In particular, the neutrals/passives are

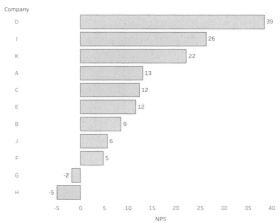

FIGURE 17.10 The traditional way to show NPS.

right on the cusp of becoming promoters, so their sentiment is vitally important.

For example, an NPS of 40 can come from:

- 70 percent promoters and 30 percent detractors or
- 45 percent promoters, 50 percent neutrals, 5 percent detractors.

Same score, big difference in makeup. (See Figure 17.11.)

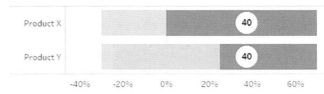

FIGURE 17.11 Here we see the problem when you just show the results of an aggregation. The Net Promoter Scores for both product X and Y are the same, but they are derived from very different responses.

More Thoughts on Visualizing Sentiment

We looked at why the traditional approach to showing NPS often falls short. What about Likert scale survey data, survey data that asks people to indicate the degree to which they agree or disagree with a series of statements? Let's look at different approaches and see what we should avoid and what we should employ.

Why Default Charts Don't Work Well

Consider Figure 17.12, which shows the results from a fictitious poll on the use of various learning modalities.

It's hard to glean anything meaningful from this figure. What about a bar chart? (See Figure 17.13.)

How often do you use the following learning modalities?

	Never	Rarely	Sometimes	Often
Chat rooms	1%	49%	30%	20%
Classroom instruction	0%	7%	12%	81%
Learning Games	12%	20%	14%	54%
Mobile Learning	6%	25%	31%	38%
Podcasts	4%	21%	26%	49%
Simulations	7%	25%	28%	39%
Social Networking	3%	21%	21%	55%
Virtual classrooms	2%	9%	24%	64%
Wikis	11%	46%	21%	22%

FIGURE 17.12 Table with survey results.

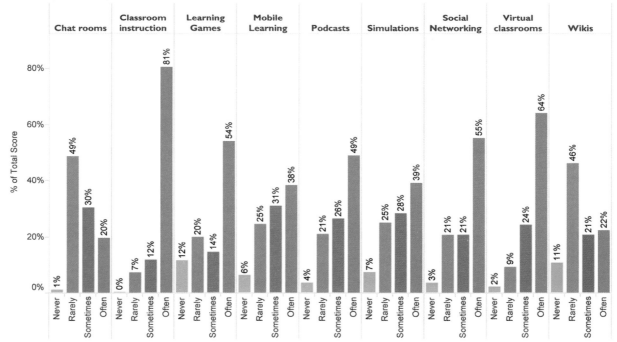

FIGURE 17.13 Likert scale questions using a bar chart.

Wow, that's really bad. What about a 100 percent stacked bar chart instead? (See Figure 17.14.)

Okay, that's better, but it's still pretty bad as the default colors do nothing to help us see tendencies that are

adjacent. That is, *often* and *sometimes* should have similar colors, as should *rarely* and *never*.

So, let's try using better colors. (See Figure 17.15.)

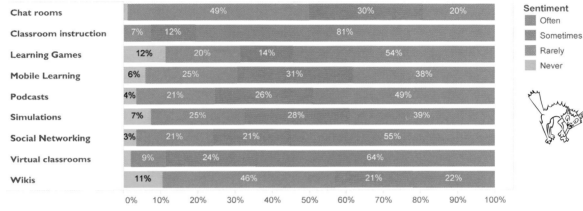

FIGURE 17.14   100 percent stacked bar chart using default colors.

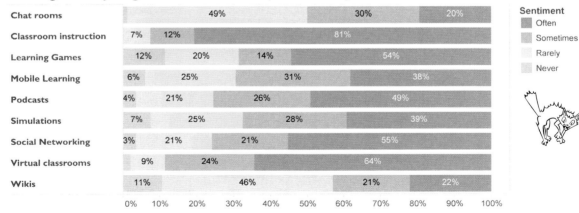

FIGURE 17.15   100 percent stacked.

Figure 17.15 is certainly an improvement, but the modalities are listed alphabetically, not by how often they're used. Let's see what happens when we sort the bars. (See Figure 17.16.)

It's taken us several tries, but it's now easier to see which modalities are more popular. But we can do better. Figure 17.17 shows the same data rendered as a divergent stacked bar chart.

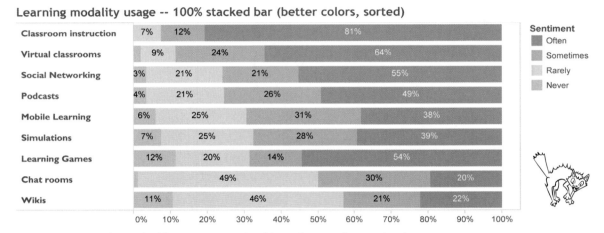

Learning modality usage -- 100% stacked bar (better colors, sorted)

				Sentiment
Classroom instruction	7%	12%	81%	■ Often
Virtual classrooms	9%	24%	64%	■ Sometimes
Social Networking	3%	21%	21%	55%	□ Rarely
Podcasts	4%	21%	26%	49%	■ Never
Mobile Learning	6%	25%	31%	38%	
Simulations	7%	25%	28%	39%	
Learning Games	12%	20%	14%	54%	
Chat rooms	49%	30%	20%	
Wikis	11%	46%	21%	22%	

0% 10% 20% 30% 40% 50% 60% 70% 80% 90% 100%

FIGURE 17.16   Sorted 100 percent stacked bar chart with good colors.

Learning modality usage -- Divergent stacked bar (sorted)

				Sentiment
Classroom instruction	13%	14%	72%	■ Never
Virtual classrooms	7%	15%	26%	52%	□ Rarely
Social Networking	10%	30%	20%	40%	■ Sometimes
Podcasts	10%	30%	25%	35%	■ Often
Mobile Learning	16%	32%	27%	25%	
Simulations	19%	32%	24%	25%	
Learning Games	29%	25%	12%	34%	
Chat rooms	60%	25%	12%	
Wikis	23%	50%	15%	12%	

-80% -60% -40% -20% 0% 20% 40% 60% 80%

<< Never / Rarely   Sometimes / Often >>

FIGURE 17.17   Sorted divergent stacked bar chart with good colors.

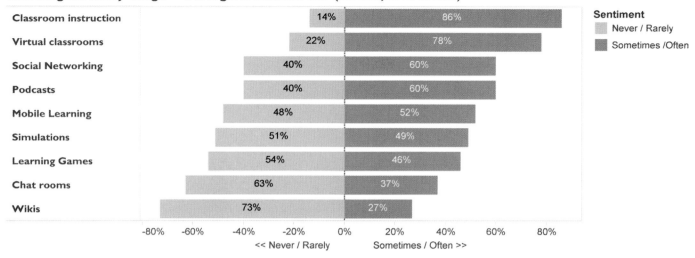

Learning modality usage -- Divergent stacked bar (sorted, two levels)

FIGURE 17.18 Divergent stacked bar chart with only two levels of sentiment.

Of course, we can also look take a coarser view and just compare sometimes/often with rarely/never, as shown in Figure 17.18.

Author Commentary

Steve: I find that the divergent approach speaks to me, and it resonates with my colleagues and clients.

I don't have a problem comparing the magnitude of the neutral percentages that we saw in Figure 17.7,

but some of my colleagues suggest that you may want to isolate the neutrals in a separate chart, as shown in Figure 17.19.

Here we have a common baseline to compare the positives, the negatives, and the neutrals as opposed to Figure 17.7, where the neutrals center at zero.

Select a Product

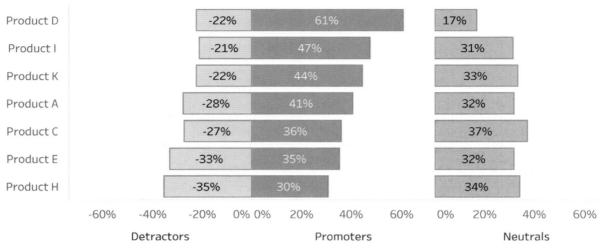

FIGURE 17.19   Alternative approach to dealing with neutrals in a divergent stacked bar chart.

Chapter 18

Server Process Monitoring

A server-monitoring dashboard highlighting delayed and failed processes for any given day.
Dashboard Designer: Mark Jackson (http://ugamarkj.blogspot.com)
Organization: Piedmont Healthcare

Tableau Server Data Status

Search: All ▼   Select Type: Datasource ▼

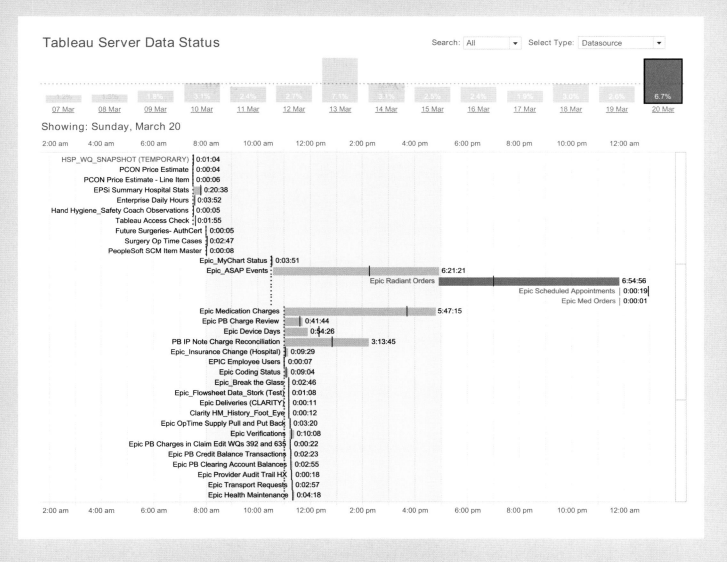

1.2%	1.3%	1.8%	3.1%	2.4%	2.7%	7.1%	3.1%	2.5%	2.4%	1.9%	3.0%	2.6%	6.7%
07 Mar	08 Mar	09 Mar	10 Mar	11 Mar	12 Mar	13 Mar	14 Mar	15 Mar	16 Mar	17 Mar	18 Mar	19 Mar	20 Mar

Showing: Sunday, March 20

	Time
HSP_WQ_SNAPSHOT (TEMPORARY)	0:01:04
PCON Price Estimate	0:00:04
PCON Price Estimate - Line Item	0:00:06
EPSi Summary Hospital Stats	0:20:38
Enterprise Daily Hours	0:03:52
Hand Hygiene_Safety Coach Observations	0:00:05
Tableau Access Check	0:01:55
Future Surgeries- AuthCert	0:00:05
Surgery Op Time Cases	0:02:47
PeopleSoft SCM Item Master	0:00:08
Epic_MyChart Status	0:03:51
Epic_ASAP Events	6:21:21
Epic Radiant Orders	6:54:56
Epic Scheduled Appointments	0:00:19
Epic Med Orders	0:00:01
Epic Medication Charges	5:47:15
Epic PB Charge Review	0:41:44
Epic Device Days	0:54:26
PB IP Note Charge Reconciliation	3:13:45
Epic_Insurance Change (Hospital)	0:09:29
EPIC Employee Users	0:00:07
Epic Coding Status	0:09:04
Epic_Break the Glass	0:02:46
Epic_Flowsheet Data_Stork (Test)	0:01:08
Epic Deliveries (CLARITY)	0:00:11
Clarity HM_History_Foot_Eye	0:00:12
Epic OpTime Supply Pull and Put Back	0:03:20
Epic Verifications	0:10:08
Epic PB Charges in Claim Edit WQs 392 and 635	0:00:22
Epic PB Credit Balance Transactions	0:02:23
Epic PB Clearing Account Balances	0:02:55
Epic Provider Audit Trail HX	0:00:18
Epic Transport Requests	0:02:57
Epic Health Maintenance	0:04:18

2:00 am 4:00 am 6:00 am 8:00 am 10:00 am 12:00 pm 2:00 pm 4:00 pm 6:00 pm 8:00 pm 10:00 pm 12:00 am

Scenario

Big Picture

You are a business intelligence manager. Your employees rely on your business intelligence service being online with the latest data when they arrive at work in the morning. You need to know if something went wrong with the overnight processes—before everyone gets to work. What you need is a dashboard you can look at each morning that shows you what, if anything, is holding up your server. If anything's going wrong, you can jump directly to that process and take corrective action. Also, you can delve into that process's recent history to see if it's been consistently problematic. If it has, you need to do more research and decide on a course of action to fix the process. To determine what to do next, you might ask the following questions:

- Did our server processes succeed today?
- Which processes failed?
- Are the failing processes repeatedly failing?
- Which processes are taking longer than usual?

Specifics

- You manage a server and need to respond quickly if processes fail. If these processes are going to cause problems for the users, those problems need to be identified and addressed quickly.

- You need an email each morning with a summary report of overnight processes. If a high number fail or if some key processes fail, you need to click the email to go to the live dashboard and drill into the details.

- For any given failed process, you need extra contextual details to help you diagnose and fix the problem. Was this failure caused by a problem earlier in the process chain? Is this process consistently failing?

Related Scenarios

- You are a manufacturer and need to track the production schedule's progress towards completion.
- You are an event manager and need to track that tasks begin correctly and run to time.

How People Use the Dashboard

As an administrator responsible for keeping your enterprise's systems up and running, you need to know if things are going wrong. A static image of the dashboard is emailed to Mark Jackson, the dashboard designer, each morning. The bar chart at the top shows percentage of failures for each of the last 14 days. The most recent is at the far right (the highlighted bar in the overview dashboard). Comparing last night to the last two weeks allows Mark to easily see if last night was normal or an outlier. The average failure rate is shown as a dotted line.

Mark can see that 6.7 percent of processes failed overnight. That's a real problem, and significantly above the average failures for the previous 14 days. Some investigation is needed.

Mark can see all the processes that took place that day. Gray ones succeeded, and red ones failed. Reference lines on each Gantt bar show the scheduled start time (dotted line) and the average time the task has taken (solid line). The Epic Radiant Orders task is the clear problem on this day.

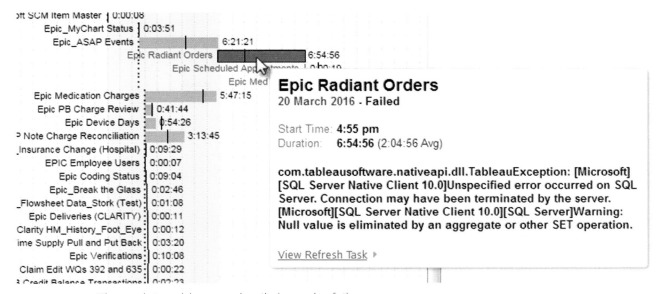

FIGURE 18.1   The tool tip adds extra detail about the failure.

If Mark wants to investigate any task in detail, he can hover over it to see a tool tip for extra contextual information. (See Figure 18.1.)

Now Mark can see details about the Epic Radiant Orders task. Not only did the task fail, it took nearly seven hours to fail. On average, it takes around two hours to complete.

From here, he has two options. The tool tip has a URL link in it: He can click the link in the tool tip to go and see the task on the server itself. His other option is to click on the Gantt bar, which reveals a new view at the bottom of the dashboard showing detail for the task.

In Figure 18.2, Mark can see that the Epic Radiant Orders task has been failing consistently recently.

Whatever preventive medicine he has been applying has not yet succeeded.

The detail view shows the performance of a single task over the previous month. Clearly the Epic Radiant Orders task needs some investigation. It's failed seven times in the last month.

Throughout this process, Mark has gone from receiving an email with a daily alert to being able to see the overview for the day. From there, he can drill down into detail where he needs to explore further and finally go straight to any server processes that need investigation.

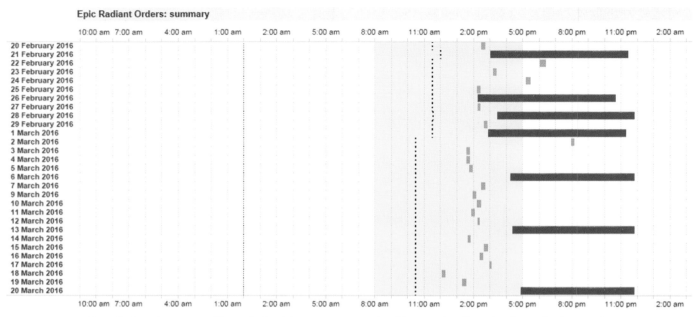

FIGURE 18.2   Detail view for a specific task. In this case, we are looking at the Epic Radiant Orders task.

Why This Works

Labels on the Gantt bar

Mark could have put the header labeling each task at the left-hand edge of the chart, in a header area. Instead, he chose to label the Gantt bar itself. On first glance, this makes the view look busy: there's an awful lot of text butting up against the bar. When you look at Figure 18.3, though, you can see why he did it. When he sees a red, failing task, its name is right there, where his eyes are. He doesn't need to do a careful look up to the left to find the name of the task.

Reference Lines

In addition to finding the failing processes quickly, Mark needs an indication of which other processes might be contributing to the failures. In this case, he uses reference lines to show schedules and durations.

In the example in Figure 18.4, Mark can see that the Epic Radiant Orders task failed. (It's red.) The dotted vertical lines for each task show him when each task was due to start. We can see in this case that Epic Radiant Orders was significantly delayed. It should start around 10:30 a.m. but didn't start until around 5 p.m.

The solid vertical lines show the average duration of each task. In this case, Mark can see that the previous task, Epic ASAP Events, also finished later than normal. Did one delay cause the other? Mark knows he'll have to investigate both of these.

URL Actions

The tool tip contains a URL (see Figure 18.1). Mark can find which details need further investigation and, with a single click, can go straight to the relevant information. This speed and directness is important to any

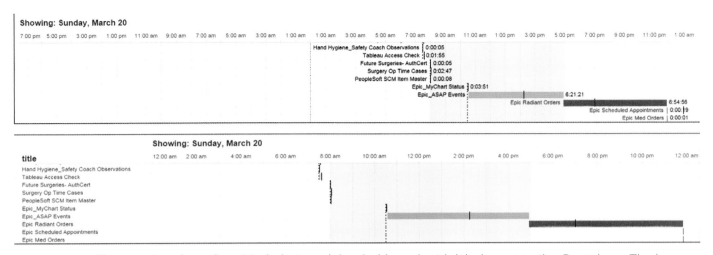

FIGURE 18.3   The top view shows how Mark designed the dashboard: with labels next to the Gantt bars. The lower view shows the labels on the left.

FIGURE 18.4   Each scheduled task is shown by a Gantt bar. The dotted lines indicate scheduled start time and the solid lines indicate average task duration.

dashboard as it puts users in the flow. Mark doesn't have to waste time finding the relevant next dashboard; the URL takes him there directly.

Overview, Zoom and Filter, Details on Demand

As we know, one aspect of successful dashboards is to create an exploratory path through the data. Ben Shneiderman, Distinguished Professor in the Department of Computer Science at the University of Maryland and a pioneer of information visualization study, described his mantra of data visualization:

- Overview
- Zoom and filter
- Details on demand

The dashboard in Figure 18.5 demonstrates this flow. Starting at the top, Mark has an overview of the server performance for recent days (1). Clicking on a day allows him to filter down to a single-day view (2). He can then get details on demand by clicking on a task (3), to open the details on task summary view (4), or use the URL to go directly to the task on the server itself (5). The flow is top down and easy to follow.

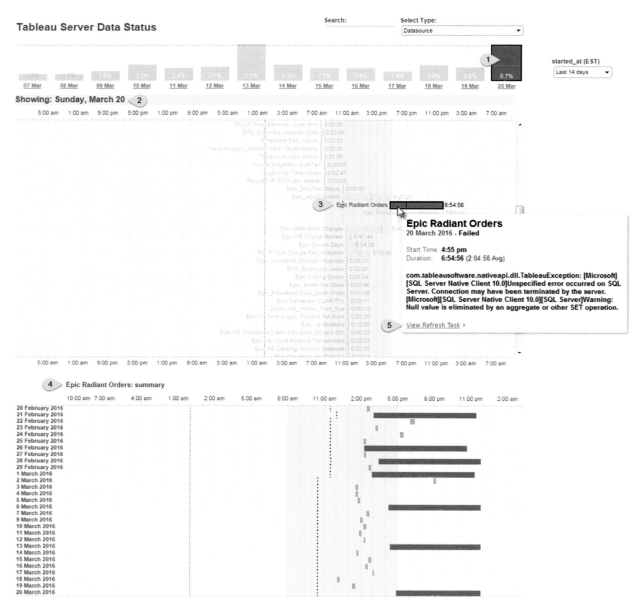

FIGURE 18.5 A dashboard with a great top-down flow.

The task summary view is not visible in the emailed report or when the report is first opened. That view appears only when it is clicked. This dashboard is a nice way of showing as much detail as possible in the initial view and bringing in contextual information only when it is needed.

Author Commentary

ANDY: This is a simple dashboard. I think that works in its favor. Mark designed it to answer the three most important questions he has each day:

1. How many tasks failed?
2. Which ones were they?
3. Are the failures a trend or a one-off?

Bar chart. Gantt chart. Gantt chart. That's all it took and the dashboard needed no other adornment

In anticipation that follow-up questions will arise, the URL link lets Mark get to the next set of questions he might need to ask. The strategy of linking dashboards together allows you to keep each one from becoming cluttered. Attempting to answer too many questions in one dashboard reduces clarity.

There are several issues with text overlapping the vertical reference lines in the Gantt bar. That might have earned a few "ugly cats" but this dashboard got an exemption for an important reason: It is for his eyes only. Because the destined audience is himself, he has built something that works for him.

When designing a dashboard, how much spit and polish should you put on it? If it's just for you, then, really, what you put on your dashboard is between you and the computer screen. If it works for you, that's fine. However, if it's for consumption by an entire organization, you have to make the experience as smooth as possible. If Mark's dashboard was to be used by the entire organization, we might suggest workarounds to avoid the overlapping text.

Chapter 19

Big Mac Index

The Economist Big Mac Index.
Dashboard Designer: Donald Hounam (developer), Roxana Willis (data), and Pam Woodall (index originator)
Organization: *The Economist* (http://www.economist.com/content/big-mac-index)

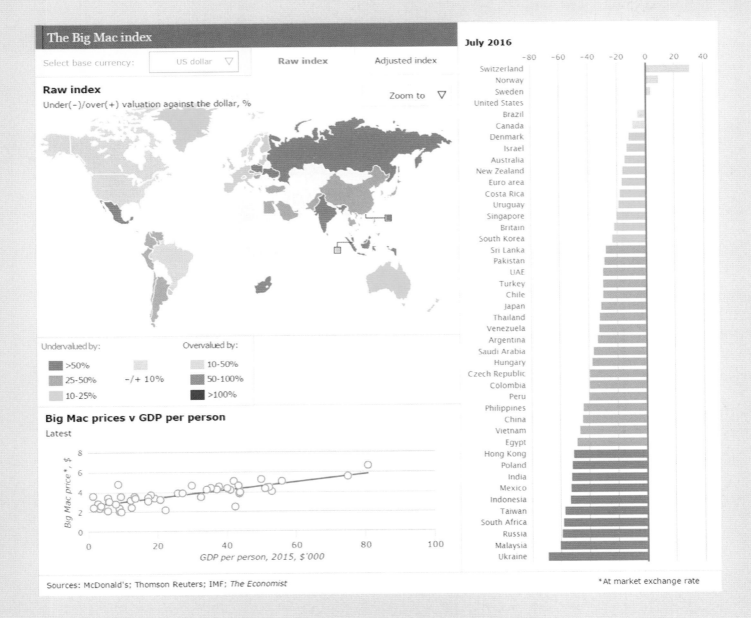

The Big Mac index

Select base currency: US dollar ▽   Raw index   Adjusted index

Raw index

Under(−)/over(+) valuation against the dollar, %

Zoom to ▽

Undervalued by:
>50%
25-50%
10-25%

−/+ 10%

Overvalued by:
10-50%
50-100%
>100%

Big Mac prices v GDP per person

Latest

Big Mac price*, $ (y-axis: 0, 2, 4, 6, 8)

GDP per person, 2015, $'000 (x-axis: 0, 20, 40, 60, 80, 100)

Sources: McDonald's; Thomson Reuters; IMF; *The Economist*

July 2016

(−80, −60, −40, −20, 0, 20, 40)

Switzerland
Norway
Sweden
United States
Brazil
Canada
Denmark
Israel
Australia
New Zealand
Euro area
Costa Rica
Uruguay
Singapore
Britain
South Korea
Sri Lanka
Pakistan
UAE
Turkey
Chile
Japan
Thailand
Venezuela
Argentina
Saudi Arabia
Hungary
Czech Republic
Colombia
Peru
Philippines
China
Vietnam
Egypt
Hong Kong
Poland
India
Mexico
Indonesia
Taiwan
South Africa
Russia
Malaysia
Ukraine

*At market exchange rate

Scenario

Big Picture

You are an economist, or someone interested in economics, and want to compare the levels of one currency against another. You could do this using complex models based on large shopping baskets of diverse goods. Or you could compare the price of one product that is the same across the world: a Big Mac. How much does one cost in countries around the world relative to the major currencies? For example, is a Big Mac in China over- or undervalued compared to the U.S. dollar? That measure is the Big Mac Index (BMI).

Specifics

- You want to see the worldwide variation in currency valuations.
- You want to compare gross domestic product (GDP) to the BMI price.
- You want to be able to see how the index has changed over time.
- You want to see a ranking of all currencies balanced against one base currency (dollar, pound, euro, or yen).

Related Scenarios

- Compare unemployment rates in different countries or in different states in the same country.
- Compare currencies with the price of gold.

How People Use the Dashboard

In 1986, *The Economist* developed the BMI as a fun currency valuation tool. Since then, it has become wildly popular with economists, academics, and students of exchange-rate theory. The purpose of the BMI is to determine currency misalignment, and it's based on the concept of purchasing-power parity (PPP), which states that identical goods should be priced equally across countries, when GDP and exchange rates are accounted for. As *The Economist* describes it, "[T]he average price of a Big Mac in America in July 2016 was $5.04; in China it was only $2.79 at market exchange rates. So the raw BMI says that the yuan was undervalued by 45 percent at that time." (Source: http://www.economist.com/content/big-mac-index.)

PPP is an indicator of future exchange rates over the long term, but it cannot bring clarity to current currency equilibrium. The BMI corrects for this by looking at the relationship between GDP per citizen and Big Mac prices.

The scatterplot on the lower-left panel of the dashboard illustrates the GDP per person for the measured countries. The red line illustrates the best fit of the adjusted index. Currency valuation is determined by calculating the difference between the country dots and the red line. If they intersect perfectly, the currency for that country is accurately valued. A dot above the line indicates an overvalued currency, while one below the line indicates an undervalued currency. These values are displayed from highest to lowest in the panel on the right.

Users can choose the base currency to compare all the others with, as shown in Figure 19.1. In this example, we're going to compare to the U.S. dollar. Users can also choose sterling, the euro, or yen and to use the raw or adjusted index. The raw index takes the raw cost of the Big Mac in each country; the adjusted index adjusts it for that country's GDP per person.

The map in Figure 19.2 shows all the countries, with a color scheme showing how over- or undervalued

FIGURE 19.1   Selectors.

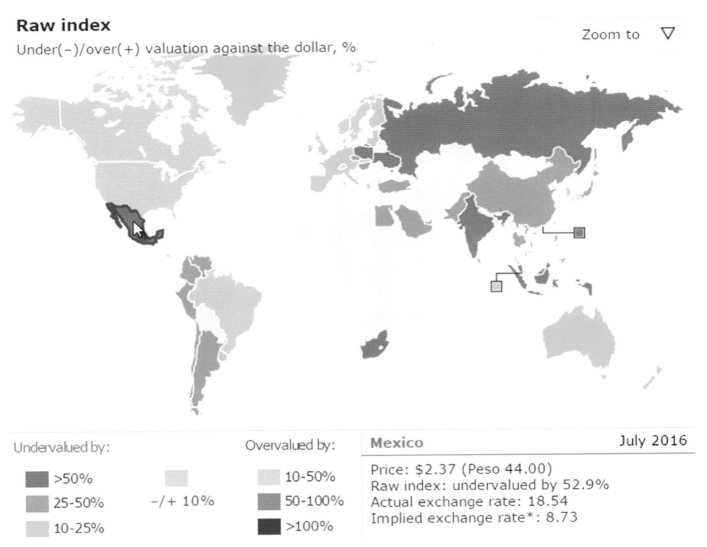

Raw index

Under(–)/over(+) valuation against the dollar, %

Zoom to ▽

Undervalued by:

■ >50%
■ 25-50%
■ 10-25%
□ –/+ 10%

Overvalued by:

□ 10-50%
■ 50-100%
■ >100%

Mexico   July 2016

Price: $2.37 (Peso 44.00)
Raw index: undervalued by 52.9%
Actual exchange rate: 18.54
Implied exchange rate*: 8.73

FIGURE 19.2   Map shows the BMI relative to the United States. Mexico is highlighted.

a Big Mac is compared to the base currency. (In this case, we selected dollars.)

Mexico has been highlighted. It is bright red, indicating that it is highly undervalued (>50 percent). The details are shown in the text panel to the right of the color legend. The Big Mac is only $2.37 in Mexico compared to $5.04 in the United States (not shown in Figure 19.2). Big Macs are relatively cheap in Mexico.

On the right of the dashboard, the same data is shown in an ordered bar chart. (See Figure 19.3.) We can see that the Big Mac is overvalued relative to the dollar in only three countries: Switzerland, Norway, and Sweden. In fact, the Big Mac in Switzerland is priced 30.8 percent higher than in the United States, at $6.59.

When a country is selected, the scatterplot on the bottom left of the dashboard is replaced with a timeline showing the BMI for the selected country. Figure 19.4 shows the dashboard after the user has clicked on Switzerland.

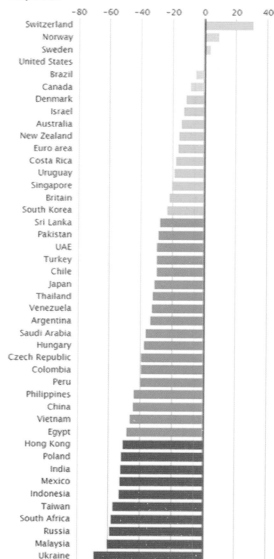

July 2016

FIGURE 19.3   The bar chart shows the details of each currency, sorted by valuation.

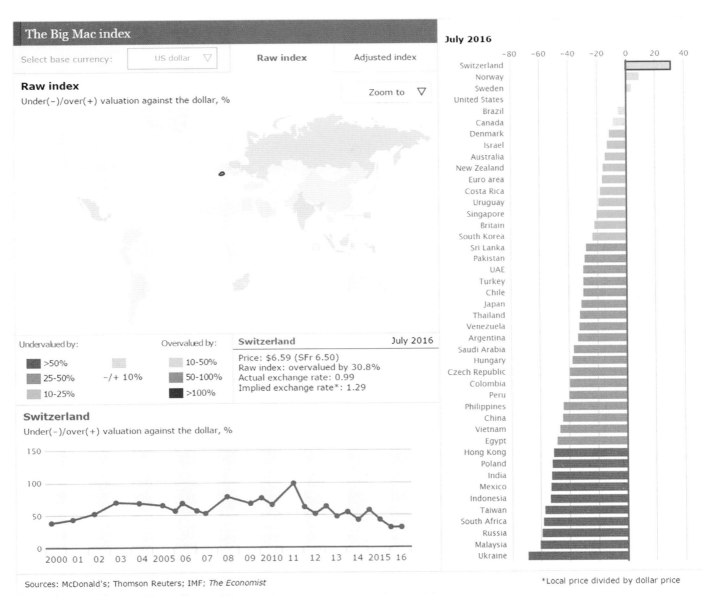

FIGURE 19.4 Once a country is selected (in the case, Switzerland), a BMI timeline for that country replaces the scatter plot in the bottom left.

We can see in Figure 19.4 that in 2011, the Big Mac in Switzerland was overvalued by almost 100 percent against the dollar. In 2016, the BMI was at its lowest since 2000. Contrast that with the changing BMI for Britain, relative to the dollar, shown in Figure 19.5.

The British Big Mac was overvalued against the dollar from 2000 through 2009. Since then, it has been undervalued except for a short period in 2014. Since 2014, the Big Mac has been getting more and more undervalued relative to the dollar. Those Big Macs are feeling cheaper for the British.

If no country is selected, the lower portion of the dashboard shows a scatterplot comparing GDP with the BMI. The line of best fit shows how, generally, Big Macs are cheaper in poorer countries where labor costs are low. It's easy to spot the outliers, such as Brazil, where the Big Macs are expensive relative to GDP. (See Figure 19.6.)

Why This Works

Multiple Views of the Same Data

There's no rule saying one should pack as many dimensions and measures as possible onto a dashboard. This dashboard really only shows one metric: the BMI. It shows the BMI as a map, allowing us to see spatial distributions of countries with similar valuations. It shows the BMI as a sorted bar chart, which allows us to easily compare countries. And it shows the BMI over time for a country. The dashboard is simple but effective.

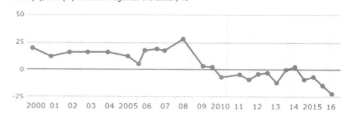

Britain
Under(–)/over(+) valuation against the dollar, %

FIGURE 19.5   The Big Mac in Britain.

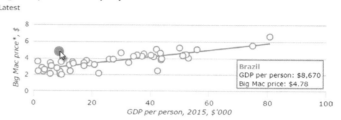

Big Mac prices v GDP per person
Latest

FIGURE 19.6   The Big Mac in Brazil.

Filters on the Top Left

Users will generally not be using this dashboard every day. Therefore, it's useful to put the filters and selectors where the users will look: beneath the title on the top left. If the filters are placed on the right or at the bottom, there is a high chance users will not see them.

Sorted Bar Charts Make Comparisons Easy

The sorted bar chart (see Figure 19.3) makes it easy to see how the countries rank against each other. The baseline (the U.S. dollar) is clearly shown as a vertical red line. Because length and position are preattentive features, it's extremely easy to decode which countries are over- and undervalued relative to the dollar.

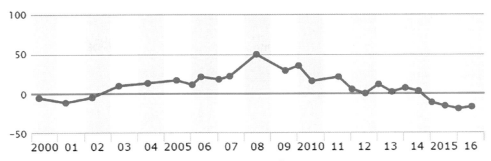

Euro area

Under(−)/over(+) valuation against the dollar, %

FIGURE 19.7   BMI timeline showing the euro against the U.S. dollar.

Reference Line on Timeline and Bar Chart

When comparing one measure against another, it's nice to have a clear reference line. *The Economist* chose a simple but very effective red line for the line charts and bar charts. The red line makes it very easy to see where the BMI moved from negative to positive. Figure 19.7 shows the BMI for the euro against the U.S. dollar. The preattentive features of color and position make it easy to see exactly when the BMI was over- or undervalued to the dollar.

Add context with reference lines

Reference lines add context to numbers, providing information about a target or an average.

Details on Demand

Whenever users hover over a country, the text panel shows the details for that country. This allows users to move a mouse around the map and see the details quickly. Figure 19.8 shows the details for the Euro, undervalued against the dollar.

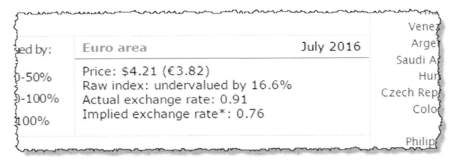

FIGURE 19.8   In July 2016, the euro was undervalued against the U.S. dollar.

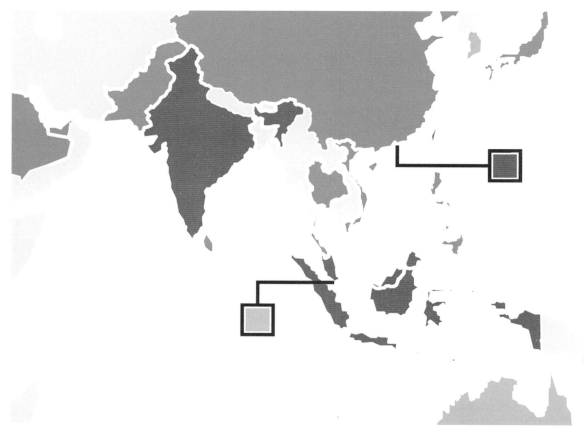

FIGURE 19.9   Small countries are visible through callouts

Callouts for Small Countries

Hong Kong and Singapore are tiny countries and are barely more than a pixel on this dashboard. The designers created a callout so users can see the values of these two countries. (See Figure 19.9.)

Author Commentary

ANDY: This dashboard was published in 2012, which is ancient history in terms of Internet technology. At time of writing, a major overhaul is being planned to make the dashboard responsive on different browsing platforms and to use newer display technologies, such as d3. We included the dashboard in this book because it is a great example of showing a single index in a variety of different ways.

The original designs for this dashboard are also fascinating. *The Economist* was kind enough to share its original wireframes for the project, which ran from July 2011 to May 2012. These are shown, with the designers' comments, in Figures 19.10 to 19.13.

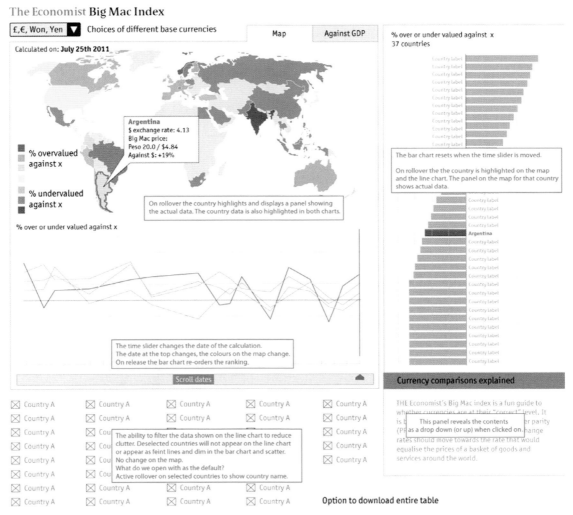

FIGURE 19.10   July 2011.

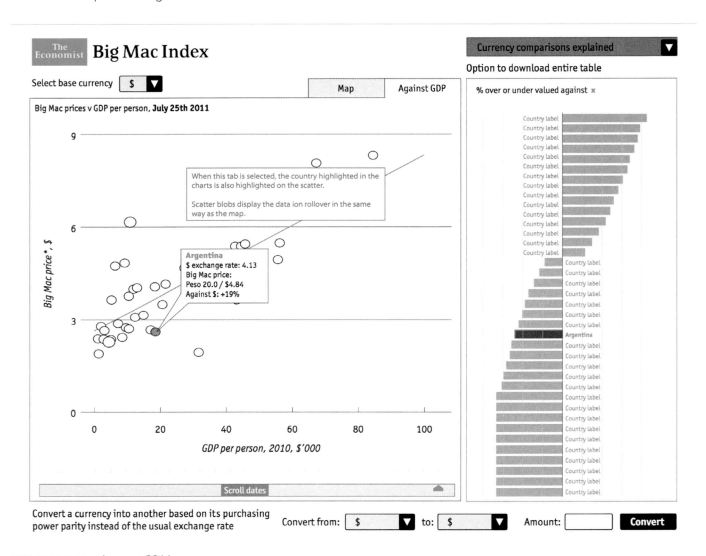

FIGURE 19.11   August 2011.

Iteration of dashboards is vital, both before and after publication. Designers need to review with users whether the dashboards work or not and then evolve them over time in order to keep them relevant. What I like with *The Economist*'s wireframes is the progression around a similar theme. It's clear the sorted bar chart was liked, and it stayed in the same position throughout, but everything else changed. In one iteration, the map disappeared behind a tab but then reappeared.

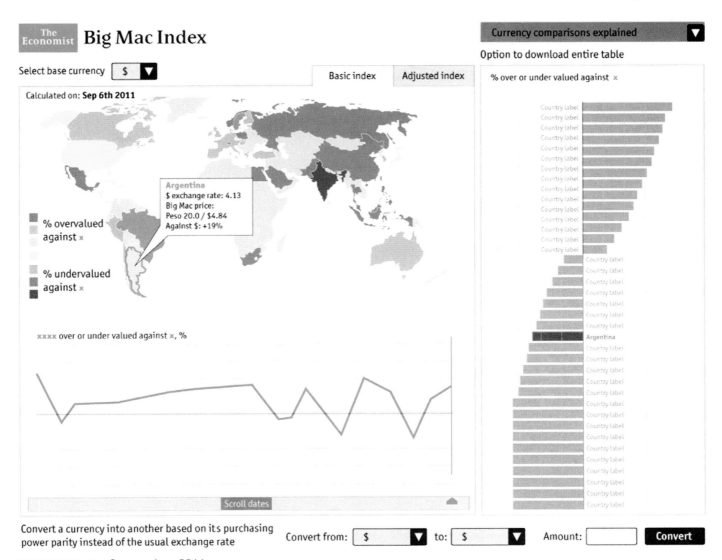

FIGURE 19.12   September 2011.

There was a lot of experimentation in how to show the timeline. (As we see in Chapter 31, there are many different ways of showing time.) In the final iteration, the designers were experimenting with Big Mac icons (see Figure 19.13). The progression

from July 2011 to May 2012 was slow by today's standards. Today, it would be preferable to sit in a room with stakeholders and iterate quickly with some options. The four-month wireframe process could easily be reduced to days.

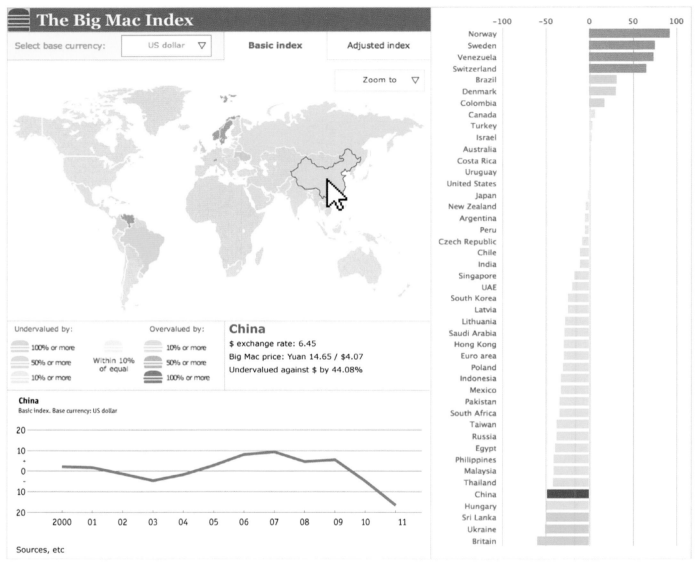

FIGURE 19.13 May 2012.

Chapter 20

Complaints Dashboard

Complaints dashboard.
Dashboard Designer: Jeffrey Shaffer
Organization: Unifund

Complaints Dashboard

Total Complaints:

	Closed	Open	Total
	288	39	327

Complaints by Month

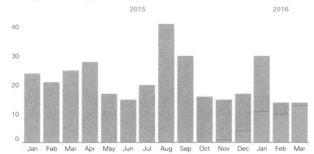

2015   2016

Open Complaints by State *(click to filter)*

Complaints by Reason

Closed | Open

- Taking/threatening an illegal action
- Communication tactics
- Disclosure verification of debt
- Cont'd attempts to collect debt not owed
- Other Complaint
- FDCPA Violation
- Balance Dispute
- False statements or representation
- Inquiry through Complaint Portal
- FCRA Violation
- Fraud Claim
- Improper contact or sharing of info
- Paid Prior
- ID Theft

Complaints by Party *(click to filter)*

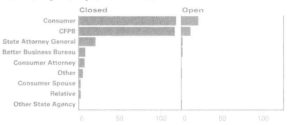

Closed | Open

- Consumer
- CFPB
- State Attorney General
- Better Business Bureau
- Consumer Attorney
- Other
- Consumer Spouse
- Relative
- Other State Agency

Scenario

Big Picture

You work for a bank or credit card company. You receive complaints on a regular basis. These complaints must be handled appropriately and swiftly. Complaints can come directly from consumers, or they can be channeled through regulators, such as federal or state agencies. Once the complaints are handled appropriately, they are then marked as closed.

Specifics

- You need to see the number of consumer complaints for a specific time period.
- You need to see how many complaints are open and closed.
- You need to see the volume of complaints by reason.
- You need to see the volume of complaints by the party making the complaint.
- You need to see the number of complaints by state, and you need to be able to filter the dashboard by state.
- You need to be able to change the date range to see the complaints for different periods of time.

Related Scenarios

- You need to monitor consumer complaints for financial products. Examples include:
  - Banks and credit unions
  - Credit card issuers
  - Collection agencies
  - Attorneys
  - Account receivable management companies
  - Student loan issuers or servicers
  - Auto loan companies
  - Credit counseling companies
  - Payday loan companies
  - Online financial service companies
- You need to monitor customer complaints for any product or service. Examples include:
  - Online retailers
  - Food service providers
- You need to monitor complaints in the workplace. Examples include:
  - Harassment
  - Working conditions
  - Diversity
  - Protected classes
  - Injuries
  - Misconduct

How People Use the Dashboard

Compliance is a key issue in many industries. In financial services, any company that is regulated by the Consumer Financial Protection Bureau (CFPB) is expected to handle consumer complaints appropriately and timely. Companies are also expected to have a complaint management system, along with policies and procedures to handle complaints, regardless of their nature or origin.

Complaints are received though a number of channels. Some complaints are received directly from the consumer, while others come directly from the CFPB, state agencies, or other entities. Each complaint is logged with the reason for the complaint and the channel through which the complaint was received.

The chief compliance officer or members of the compliance team use this dashboard on a regular basis to help monitor the compliance with the complaint management system. Actions can be taken as needed—for example, following up on or investigating a complaint that has been open for a long period of time. Figure 20.1 shows the total complaints over time.

The default time range is the past 12 months, but the user can adjust the slider control to change the time period. (See Figure 20.2.)

A state map using hexagons displays the open complaints by state. Open complaints, indicated by darker coloring, are especially important to monitor to make

FIGURE 20.2   Slider control to adjust the time period and to select the source type or open/closed status.

sure the necessary action is taken and response is timely. Clicking on a state filters the rest of the dashboard by state. (See Figure 20.3.)

The reason for the complaint is logged when it is received. These reasons are shown on the dashboard for both closed and open complaints. (See Figure 20.4.)

The party filing the complaint is shown in the bar charts in Figure 20.5. Selecting a party from this chart will filter the rest of the dashboard by that party.

Combining filters allows the user to narrow the focus quickly. For example, the user can click California on

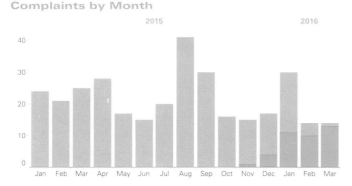

FIGURE 20.1   Totals are displayed at the top and a stacked bar chart shows the open and closed complaints over the selected time period.

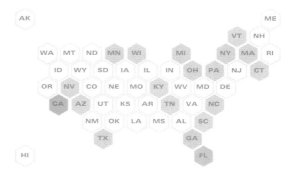

FIGURE 20.3   Hex map showing the open complaints by state. The user clicks any state to filter the dashboard.

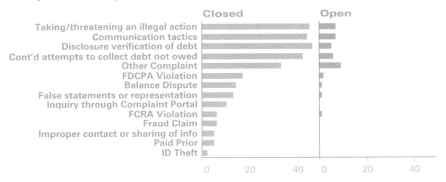

FIGURE 20.4   Closed and open complaints are shown by reason.

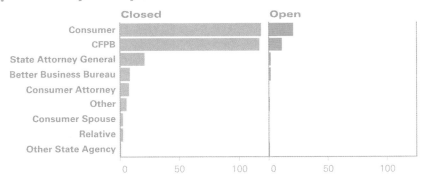

FIGURE 20.5   Closed and open complaints are shown by the party sending the complaint.

the hex map and then click State Attorney General in the Complaints by Party bar chart. This will cause the entire dashboard to update immediately to show the complaint history for the California Attorney General's office.

Why This Works

Simple Use of Color

Two categorical colors are used in this dashboard, medium sky blue for closed complaints and a reddish peach color for open complaints. Color is consistent throughout the dashboard. For the map, the color for open complaints is used as a sequential color scheme, shading from white to the reddish peach color. Some states may not have any complaints for the selected period. Rather than filtering them out of the view, the states with zero complaints are shown in white with the hexagonal border. This shows a complete hex map with all of the states regardless of the time period or other filters that may be applied.

Good Chart Types for the Various Comparisons

Most of this dashboard is made up of bar charts, which are great for making accurate quantitative comparisons. A stacked bar is used to show the total number of complaints over time and displays the number of open complaints versus the closed complaints. (See Figure 20.6.)

Notice in Figure 20.6 that the open complaints are on the bottom of the stacked bar. The open complaints are the most important because they represent work that needs to be done and monitored on this dashboard. By putting them on the bottom of the stacked bar, the user is able to make a very accurate comparison of the bar heights. For example, even without

providing data labels, it's very easy to see in this figure that there is one more open complaint in January than in February. This is because the bars are fixed to a common baseline, the x-axis, allowing an accurate comparison of bar heights. It's also really easy to spot the oldest open complaint, the one open complaint from November 2015.

Using Figure 20.6, try comparing the closed complaints (the blue bars) for November and December. Which one has more complaints, and how many more?

This determination is much more difficult because there isn't a common baseline. The difference between open and closed complaints is actually the same as in Figure 20.7. There is exactly one more closed complaint

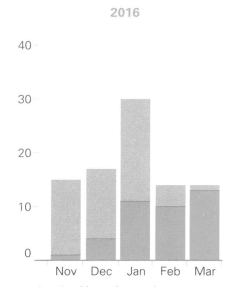

FIGURE 20.6 Stacked bar charts showing open and closed complaints.

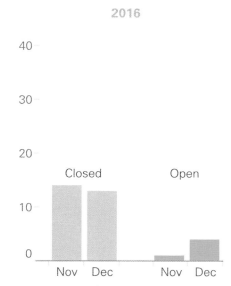

FIGURE 20.7 Unstacked bar chart comparing the same number of closed and open complaints as Figure 20.6 for November and December.

in November than in December. Thankfully, the user doesn't need this level of precision for the closed complaints, although they have the option from the drop-down box to filter for them should the need arise.

Comparing stacked bars

Stacked bars make precise comparisons difficult for any segment other than the first segment. Put the most important piece of information on the first segment, and be careful not to slice bars into too many segments.

Be very careful when using stacked bars. They are helpful for two reasons: (1) for showing a part-to-whole relationship where the whole is important and (2) for comparing one segment to the whole. In this case, the user wants to see the total complaints over time. Since open complaints are also very important, we can see them compared to each other. This is because they are the bottom segment of the stacked bar. We can also see the open complaints in relation to all of the complaints, the part-to-whole comparison. Stacked bar charts are not useful to accurately compare one segment to another segment within the same bar.

The other bar charts on the dashboard are divided up between open and closed. This allows for a quick and easy comparison of open and closed complaints both by Reason and by Party (the channel through which the complaint came in).

Dashboard Designed to a Grid

The dashboard is separated into four quadrants. There is clear horizontal and vertical alignment between all four sections, and there is space between each section of the dashboard. This reduces clutter on the dashboard so that it doesn't look busy. Good organization of your dashboards can help users see the information clearly and quickly.

A Hex Map Where All States Are Equal

Complaints are considered equally important, regardless of channel or volume. The hex map allows the user to see every state equally. When using a traditional choropleth (or filled) map, it can be hard to see very small states. For example, Delaware, Maryland, Rhode Island, and Vermont can be hard to see, and especially hard to click, compared to larger states, such as California and Texas. Also, Alaska and Hawaii often require special handling and sometimes are placed on the map out of position. The hex map solves these problem. It visualizes the states equally regardless of their land size.

Figure 20.8 demonstrates the difficulty seeing smaller states in the Northeast. Rhode Island, Connecticut, Vermont, New Hampshire, Delaware, and Maryland all are very difficult to see on a full map of the United States. If the map is used as a filter, which it is in this dashboard, then it would be very difficult for the user to select the small areas on the map to filter.

Notice the equal treatment of the states with the hex map in Figure 20.8. Data analysts can also benefit from the straightforward presentation of a hex map. On a related dashboard, there was a coding problem behind the scenes, and Connecticut was not appearing in the data. It was immediately apparent on the hex map, but it would not have been caught so quickly on a choropleth map.

States shown as a choropleth map

States shown as a hex map

FIGURE 20.8   A comparison of the northeastern states demonstrating how difficult it is to see smaller states on a choropleth map.

Hex maps have their disadvantages, though. Most important, the position of the states isn't exact because compromises have to be made for their placement. Figure 20.9 shows the locations of states in the southeast on a common choropleth map versus a hex map. Examine the placement of the states on the hex map. Georgia isn't south of Alabama and South Carolina. Because states are not in their usual location, it is essential to provide a two-letter state code so that the user can quickly find the states.

Another issue with using a hex map is that it may not work well for different countries or regions. There are a number of different templates for the United States, but creating a hex map of the countries in the United Kingdom would be more difficult. In the United Kingdom, where the countries are closer in size, a choropleth map would likely be a better approach.

Other Approaches

Visualizing data on a map can be challenging. Many compromises have to be made. On the hex map, the decision was made to show only the open complaints. In this case, the data could be shown on a choropleth map, as described earlier. (See Figure 20.10.)

However, Figure 20.10 demonstrates again the difficulty of seeing the smaller states, especially when the map is a full U.S., map and it is placed in a small area of a dashboard.

Showing part-to-whole relationships on a map can be especially challenging. In this case, a filled map won't

States shown as a choropleth map

States shown as a hex map

FIGURE 20.9 A comparison of a choropleth map versus a hex map showing the position of the states.

Complaints by State *(click to filter)*

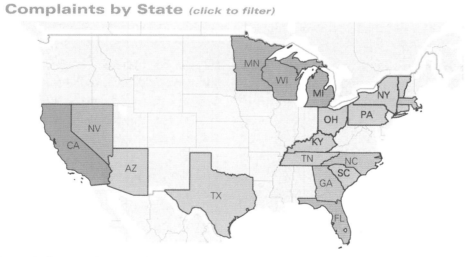

FIGURE 20.10 A choropleth map showing the open complaints by state.

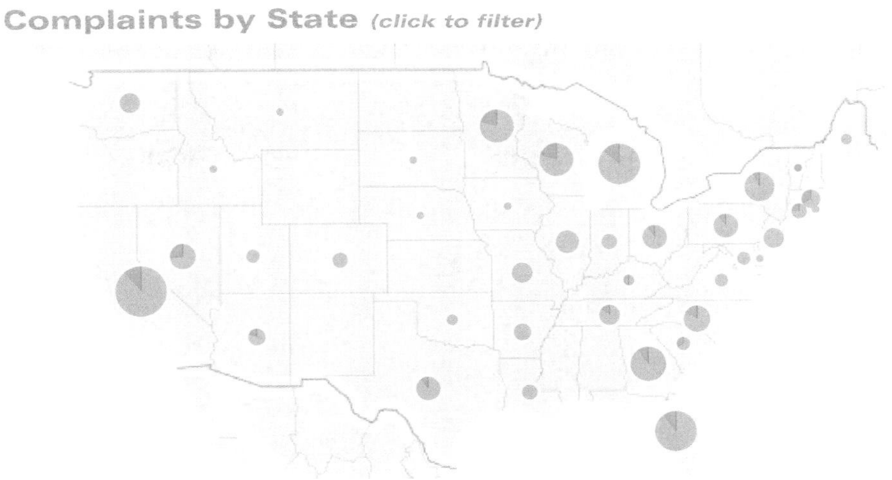

Complaints by State *(click to filter)*

FIGURE 20.11   Open and closed complaints shown on a map using pie charts.

work. Although pie charts generally are not the best choice for visualizing data, they can be useful in this case to show a part-to-whole relationship on a map. (See Figure 20.11.)

This solution suffers from some of the same issues that a filled map does. Smaller volumes have smaller pie chart sizes, which makes the comparisons very hard to see and difficult for a user to hover over or select.

Another alternative is to avoid a map altogether. Just because data is geographic in nature does not mean that it has to be plotted on a map. Figure 20.12 shows a treemap. The treemap was designed to visualize hierarchical data, but it can also be used when there are many categories to show—in this case, 50 states.

The advantage to this solution is the data is now ordered by the most complaints. It's easy to see that Florida has the second highest number of total complaints and Michigan the third, something that can't

be easily discerned from the other maps. The treemap also shows us the part-to-whole relationship between open and closed complaints in each state.

The problem with this solution is that it can be hard to find states if the user needs to select them to drill down into the data. The smallest states aren't visible either, as some are missing the state labels. These issues could be solved with a drop-down menu and tool tips, but that still would require a user to find very small areas of the treemap to select, much like the choropleth map, but without the aid of a known geographical location.

Another option would be using ranked bar charts, but when dealing with 50 states or 196 countries, bar charts will quickly become impractical. If you don't need to list all of the categories, then a bar chart of the top 10 could be a great solution. However, in this dashboard, it was important to see every state, treat them with equal importance, and allow the user to filter them easily.

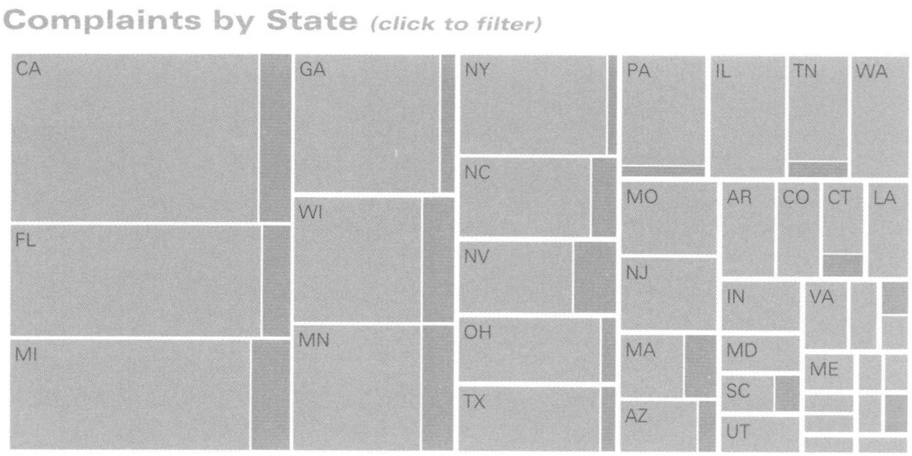

Complaints by State *(click to filter)*

FIGURE 20.12   A treemap showing open and closed complaints by state.

In the end, the designer felt that the hex map was the best compromise to show the open complaints on the dashboard.

Author Commentary

Steve: There are three things that I thought were particularly clever in this dashboard.

1. **The key performance indicators are also a color legend.** (See Figure 20.13.) Notice that there isn't a color legend. Instead, the summary numbers at the top of the dashboard are color coded. Not only do I know that there are

Complaints Dashboard

Total Complaints:	Closed	Open	Total
	288	39	327

FIGURE 20.13   The key performance indicators also serve as the color legend.

288 closed cases and 39 open cases; I also know that blue means closed and red means open.

2. **The hex map is a value-added filter.** Whenever I see a hex map or tile map, I get suspicious and think that the dashboard designer may be succumbing to the temptation to add something cool at the expense of something that is analytically sound. That is not the case here. The hex map is in fact a filter that also provides additional insight into the data. The dashboard designer knows that users need to be able to filter by state and could have deployed a simple multiselect list box from which the user could select a state or states. The hex map provides that same functionality and adds really useful insights into the data.

3. **Perfect use of a stacked bar chart**. The stacked bar chart in this dashboard (shown in Figure 20.1) is a great choice as we can easily compare both the overall number of complaints per month and the number of open complaints per month.

Chapter 21

Hospital Operating Room Utilization

Dashboard showing how efficiently hospital operating rooms are being scheduled and utilized.
Dashboard Designers: Dan Benevento, Katherine S. Rowell
Organization: HealthDataViz (http://www.healthdataviz.com)

Hospital Operating Room Utilization by Day
How efficiently and accurately are we scheduling and utilizing our OR resources?

September 2015	68%
October 2015	77%
November 2015	87%

Case Minutes Scheduled Accurately (click a day to filter)

50% ▬▬▬▬▬ 100%

September

Mon	Tue	Wed	Thu	Fri
			3 75% (27/36)	**4** 69% (33/48)
7 73% (24/33)	**8** 60% (18/30)	**9** 80% (12/15)	**10** 71% (15/21)	**11** 71% (15/21)
14 71% (15/21)	**15** 70% (21/30)	**16** 80% (12/15)	**17** 71% (15/21)	**18** 62% (24/39)
21 64% (21/33)	**22** 60% (15/25)	**23** 71% (15/21)	**24** 67% (18/27)	**25** 57% (17/30)
28 68% (19/28)	**29** 67% (24/36)	**30** 78% (21/27)		

October

Mon	Tue	Wed	Thu	Fri
			1 90% (27/30)	**2** 83% (15/18)
5 75% (27/36)	**6** 90% (27/30)	**7** 86% (18/21)	**8** 75% (18/24)	**9** 67% (24/36)
12 83% (30/36)	**13** 75% (27/36)	**14** 71% (15/21)	**15** 80% (24/30)	**16** 80% (12/15)
19 75% (18/24)	**20** 70% (21/30)	**21** 86% (18/21)	**22** 78% (21/27)	**23** 86% (18/21)
26 83% (30/36)	**27** 75% (27/36)	**28** 69% (27/39)	**29** 69% (27/39)	**30** 70% (21/30)

November

Mon	Tue	Wed	Thu	Fri
2 90% (27/30)	**3** 80% (24/30)	**4** 78% (21/27)	**5** 86% (18/21)	**6** 91% (30/33)
9 75% (9/12)	**10** 82% (27/33)	**11** 90% (27/30)	**12** 85% (33/39)	**13** 96% (26/27)
16 89% (24/27)	**17** 82% (27/33)	**18** 96% (27/28)	**19** 85% (33/39)	**20** 83% (30/36)
23 95% (20/21)	**24** 86% (36/42)	**25** 96% (22/23)	**26** 85% (33/39)	**27** 90% (27/30)

OR Utilization by Day: 25 September 2015

OR 1: 70 | 120 | 90 | 61 | 75
OR 2: 52 | 104 | 69
OR 3: 42 | 45 | 41 | 45 | 42 | 45
OR 4: 180
OR 5: 173 | 167 | 177
OR 6: 69 | 52
OR 7: 126 | 39
OR 8: 151 | 150 | 183
OR 9: 50 | 95 | 123
OR 10: 104 | 90

7:30am ... 3:30pm ... 5:00pm

07:00 08:00 09:00 10:00 11:00 12:00 13:00 14:00 15:00 16:00 17:00 18:00 19:00 20:00

▢ Scheduled Time ▢ Accurate Estimate ▢ Inaccurate Estimate

Details by OR: 25 September 2015

	Number of cases	% Cases Accurately Scheduled	Actual Case Minutes	Scheduled Case Minutes	Median Turnover Minutes
OR 1	5	60%	416	420	26
OR 2	3	33%	225	285	30
OR 3	6	100%	260	270	18
OR 4	1	100%	180	180	
OR 5	3	0%	517	360	30
OR 6	2	100%	121	120	30
OR 7	2	100%	165	165	30
OR 8	3	0%	484	300	30
OR 9	3	33%	268	270	27
OR 10	2	50%	194	210	30

Scenario

Big Picture

You manage a suite of hospital operating rooms (ORs) that are in high demand by surgeons and are costly to operate. In order to meet surgeon demand for OR time in a cost-effective manner and to ensure high-quality, safe patient care, you need a dashboard that makes it easy for you to examine how accurately procedures are scheduled and how efficiently OR resources are utilized.

This Hospital Operating Room Utilization dashboard displays surgical case and OR information in a clear and easy-to-understand way and helps OR managers, staff, surgeons, and anesthesiologists identify potential opportunities for improvement.

Specifics

The metrics included in this dashboard help viewers to compare the accuracy of the amount of time projected for an operation against the actual time it takes to perform. Inaccurately scheduled cases have a negative impact on metrics, such as:

- on-time case starts,
- resource utilization,
- operating room turnover times, and
- patient satisfaction.

Related Scenarios

- You need to visualize resource planning, such as scheduling of conference rooms.
- You need to visualize event planning, such as concert scheduling or maintenance of those venues, for example, which venues need to be cleaned, air conditioned, etc.
- You need to monitor scheduling of resources in health care.
- You need to visualize logistics, such as airline scheduling to ensure planes are in the right place at the right time or driver management for a transportation or logistics company.

How People Use the Dashboard

OR managers, surgical schedulers, surgeons, and clinical and technical teams may use this dashboard to:

- improve the accuracy of scheduled surgical case times;
- monitor and ensure the timely, efficient, and safe care of patients;
- monitor the time it takes to reset the operating room between cases and identify opportunities for improvement; and
- manage overall operating room utilization and efficiency, quantify resource requirements, and identify potential improvement opportunities.

The top section of this dashboard, shown in Figure 21.1, provides a three-month summary view of case scheduling accuracy.

At the top right, there's an overview of each month's overall scheduling accuracy encoded using different saturations of colors to show low and high percentages. For example, the viewer can quickly see that September OR cases were accurately scheduled only 68 percent of the time (displayed in orange), increasing to 77 percent in October (light blue) and 87 percent in November (dark blue).

Hospital Operating Room Utilization by Day
How efficiently and accurately are we scheduling and utilizing our OR resources?

September 2015	68%
October 2015	77%
November 2015	87%

HealthDataViz

Case Minutes Scheduled Accurately (click a day to filter)

50% ▬▬▬▬ 100%

September

Mon	Tue	Wed	Thu	Fri
			3 75% (27/36)	4 69% (33/48)
7 73% (24/33)	8 60% (18/30)	9 80% (12/15)	10 71% (15/21)	11 71% (15/21)
14 71% (15/21)	15 70% (21/30)	16 80% (12/15)	17 71% (15/21)	18 62% (24/39)
21 64% (21/33)	22 60% (15/25)	23 71% (15/21)	24 67% (18/27)	25 57% (17/30)
28 68% (19/28)	29 67% (24/36)	30 78% (21/27)		

October

Mon	Tue	Wed	Thu	Fri
			1 90% (27/30)	2 83% (15/18)
5 75% (27/36)	6 90% (27/30)	7 86% (18/21)	8 75% (18/24)	9 67% (24/36)
12 83% (30/36)	13 75% (27/36)	14 71% (15/21)	15 80% (24/30)	16 80% (12/15)
19 75% (18/24)	20 70% (21/30)	21 86% (18/21)	22 78% (21/27)	23 86% (18/21)
26 83% (30/36)	27 75% (27/36)	28 69% (27/39)	29 69% (27/39)	30 70% (21/30)

November

Mon	Tue	Wed	Thu	Fri
2 90% (27/30)	3 80% (24/30)	4 78% (21/27)	5 86% (18/21)	6 91% (30/33)
9 75% (9/12)	10 82% (27/33)	11 90% (27/30)	12 85% (33/39)	13 96% (26/27)
16 89% (24/27)	17 82% (27/33)	18 96% (27/28)	19 85% (33/39)	20 83% (30/36)
23 95% (20/21)	24 86% (36/42)	25 96% (22/23)	26 85% (33/39)	27 90% (27/30)

FIGURE 21.1 The top section shows an overview over time.

The calendar view displays the percentage of cases scheduled accurately for each day of the three months. This view uses the same orange/blue color scheme. The viewer can quickly see OR scheduling accuracy trends from low (orange) to high (blue). Detail is shown in Figure 21.2.

Two days are shown. On Thursday, 90 percent of cases were scheduled efficiently. There were 30 cases, of which 27 were accurately scheduled. The following day was less efficient, at 83 percent, with 15 out of 18 cases running to time. This detailed calendar view

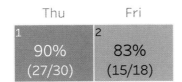

FIGURE 21.2 Two days of metrics.

is also interactive; users can click on any day to generate more details about specific cases and ORs in the lower half of the dashboard. In Figure 21.3, we show the detailed view that appears when a user clicks on a day. In this case, it's for September 25, 2015.

Each row (1) displays the name of each operating room; the x-axis displays hours (using a 24-hour clock). The shaded background of the chart reflects the start and end of the working day (2). The light-blue shading (3) begins at 3.30pm, which is when ORs should begin closing for the day. The area with white shading represents the regularly scheduled OR time. All scheduled cases should appear in the white space.

Gantt bars show the scheduled and actual times for each case. Light blue bars (4) show the scheduled time for a surgical case. Laid on top of those are the actual case time, in minutes. Accurately scheduled cases

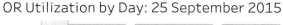

OR Utilization by Day: 25 September 2015

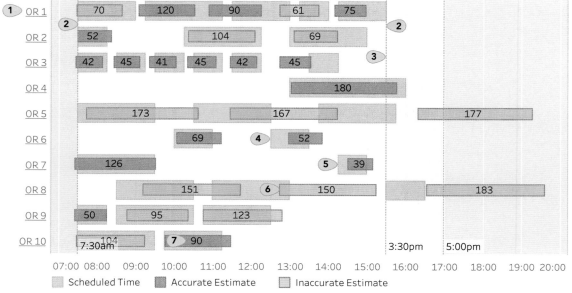

FIGURE 21.3   Utilization of ORs on September 25, 2015, shown in a modified Gantt chart.

are shown in darker blue (5), and inaccurately scheduled case are shown in orange (6). An accurate case is defined as one that is within 15 minutes of the estimate. The labels in the bars display the actual minutes the surgical case took to complete (7). The user can find out more via a tool tip that shows additional details of interest, such as the procedure performed, surgeon name, and the like. This is shown in Figure 21.4.

The OR scheduling Gantt chart allows viewers to examine and consider how well each OR was utilized on a specific date and to identify potential areas for additional analysis or improvement. (See Figure 21.5.)

Figure 21.5 shows that OR 3 was managed very efficiently on this day—there were six scheduled cases, and each

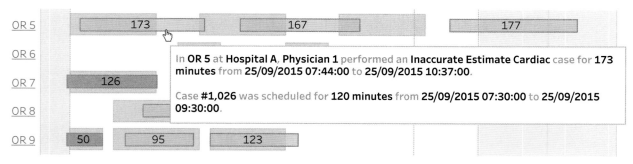

FIGURE 21.4   Tool tips add rich information.

OR 3 — 42 45 41 45 42 45

FIGURE 21.5 Detail for OR 3: a successful day of scheduling.

took somewhere between 41 and 45 minutes to complete. The first case of the day started on time, and subsequent cases all started a bit before their scheduled time. The last case of the day finished both before the scheduled time and before the scheduled OR closing time.

Figure 21.6 shows data for OR 5 on an inefficient day. All of the scheduled case times (light blue bars) were inaccurate, which we know because the actual case time bars are orange (i.e., inaccurately scheduled cases). We can also see that the first case of the day started late and overran, creating a domino effect of late starts for all subsequent cases.

Figure 21.7 shows that OR 8 has a similar experience to OR 5. The first procedure also started late, and the final procedure overran the time scheduled for it by a very significant margin, far past the end of the scheduled OR closing time.

The ability to view the available hours in each OR and the actual cases performed in them also helps viewers to understand overall OR utilization and to explore if there may be a need for more or less OR time. For example, consider ORs 6 and 7, shown in Figure 21.8. The case times never overlapped. It may have been possible to complete all of the cases in one OR instead of two.

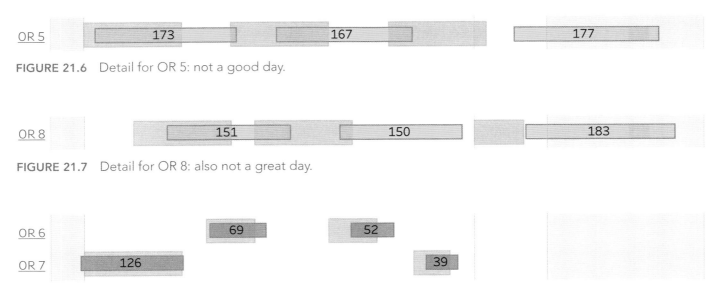

OR 5 — 173 167 177

FIGURE 21.6 Detail for OR 5: not a good day.

OR 8 — 151 150 183

FIGURE 21.7 Detail for OR 8: also not a great day.

OR 6 — 69 52

OR 7 — 126 39

FIGURE 21.8 ORs 6 and 7: Did both ORs need to be open this day?

OR Utilization by Day: 10 November 2015

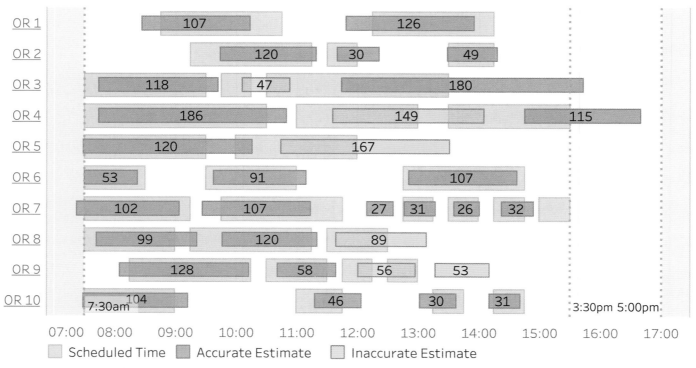

FIGURE 21.9   OR utilization on 10 November: a day of 82 percent efficiency.

Now contrast the efficiency in the first example in Figure 21.3 of September 25 (57 percent) with the example for Tuesday, November 10 (82 percent), shown in Figure 21.9.

Only six cases were scheduled inaccurately on November 10. The viewer can see that although several cases started late, overall the Gantt bars are densely packed and the OR utilization was high.

Why This Works

Calendar View Shows Exact Values

You might wonder why the calendar view is used instead of a line chart. A line chart does look good and provide insights. As you can see in Figure 21.10, the peaks and dips of efficiency are clear.

However, a calendar view and heat map works on this dashboard because of the design objectives. Most often, surgeons perform procedures in allocated time blocks or specifically assigned OR times and days each week. Therefore, it is useful to be able to identify and compare those days directly for several weeks and months and to consider any scheduling or utilization patterns and trends that may provide clues about opportunities to improve OR scheduling or the need for additional OR resources.

Hospital Operating Room Utilization by Day
How efficiently and accurately are we scheduling and utilizing our OR resources?

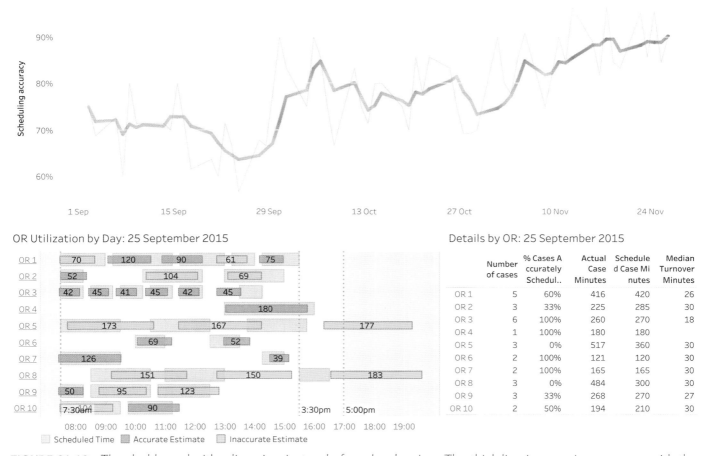

Case Minutes Scheduled Accurately   (click a day to filter)

FIGURE 21.10   The dashboard with a line view instead of a calendar view. The thick line is a moving average, with the actual daily values shown in a thinner line.

Although this dashboard is designed for online viewing and interaction, the reality is that often it will be printed and distributed on paper. And even though a printout shows only one day's detail in the Gantt chart, it allows exact details to seen for every day in the calendar. The line chart shows the trends but not the actual numbers.

Orange/Blue Color Palette Is Color-Blind Friendly

The use of orange and blue is a great choice to show good/bad without the risk of confusing people with color vision deficiency.

Color Palettes Are Consistent

As previously shown and discussed, calendar views at the top use a diverging orange/blue palette: bluer is better. (See Figure 21.11.) The Gantt chart also uses orange/blue, but in this case it is a discrete color palette: The orange shade shows inaccurate estimates and the blue shows accurate estimates.

Strictly, we could argue that the use of color on this dashboard is inaccurate because you could look at the Gantt bars and interpret them based on the diverging palette. The designers of this dashboard acknowledge that risk but wanted as few colors as possible. They decided that maintaining the general "blue = good" rule across both views was acceptable. With training and familiarity, users of this dashboard soon internalize this information to allow quick interpretation of the data.

All the Data Is Shown

In many situations, if you show only aggregated data, it's easy to justify reasons why numbers are below

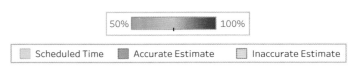

FIGURE 21.11 Both palettes use the same orange/blue theme. The diverging palette is used in the calendar view, and the categorical palette is used on the Gantt chart.

target. In this case, aggregated OR efficiency for each physician (i.e. just the calendar view in the top of the dashboard) could easily be dismissed as inaccurate data.

The ability to break down each OR by day (the Gantt bars in the lower section of the dashboard) shows the problems in detail. Prior to having a dashboard like this, physicians would have been able to access only overview data. If they saw they were scheduling cases correctly only 50 percent of the time, they could dismiss those results as inaccurate. Being able to see all the detailed data as well allows them to identify the problems and to identify opportunities to improve.

Author Commentary

JEFF: I really like the use of color on this dashboard for the Gantt chart. It is very easy to see the inaccurate estimates versus the scheduled times, and it is a color-blind-friendly palette. I also really like the use of the heat map on the calendar view. In the calendar view, we moved the day of the month up to the top left corner of each day and used a smaller font so that it wouldn't interfere with the data in each cell. However, I might have picked a different color to represent one or the other. Reiterating the concern that was addressed in the chapter, I would not reuse similar colors to encode data differently. Technically, the colors mean the same thing, but one color is measuring a different scale than the other. This was a design choice by the dashboard designer, but I think users could be confused by this.

ANDY: The dashboard answers many questions, but, like all dashboards, it can't answer them all. Consider the Gantt chart: Blue cases were accurately scheduled, and orange ones were inaccurate. In this dashboard, accuracy is defined as having an actual duration within 15 minutes of the actual duration.

However, consider what happened in OR 8. (See Figure 21.7.) The first case overran and is classed as inaccurate (because it overran). However, it started late. Why? In this dashboard, the answer to that question is not provided. This is an example of an unknown unknown question (see Chapter 36): Dashboards inspire new questions not thought of at the time of design. If that question of late-starting cases is important to many people, the dashboard should go through another iteration so that it can provide an answer.

Chapter 22

Showing Rank and Magnitude

Rank and magnitude sales dashboard.
Author: Steve Wexler
Organization: Data Revelations

Sales and Rank for Top 20 Products

Top 20 Overall

#	Product	Sales
1	GE Profile Refrigerator	$275,942
2	Samsung Smoothtop Range	$255,304
3	KitchenAid Wall Oven	$210,911
4	Whirlpool Upright Freezer	$206,494
5	Bosch Fully Integrated Dishwasher	$194,880
6	Frigidaire Fully Integrated Dishwasher	$147,395
7	Sharp AL-1530CS Digital Copier	$130,047
8	GE Profile Microwave	$128,100
9	Maytag Front Load Washer	$120,343
10	Maytag White Stackable Dryer	$114,173
11	Sony Playstation Deluxe	$112,759
12	Canon Personal Copier	$112,417
13	Microsoft Surface H3	$112,267
14	Epson R90 All-In-One	$111,221
15	Epson Ceiling Mounted Projector	$109,417
16	Panasonic OLED Television	$109,231
17	Fellowes Plastic Comb Binding Machine	$106,908
18	Brother PTouch Label Machine	$106,629
19	Fresno Karaoke Pro	$104,463
20	Hon Series Round Tables	$102,006

Rank by Region

#	Central	East	South	West
1		$77,683		
2				
3				
4			$67,595	
5				
6				
7				
8				
9				
10				
11				
12				
13				
14	$32,827			
15				
16				
17				
18				
19				
20				

Scenario

Big Picture

Imagine you are a sales director. You know which of your retail products are your top sellers but wish you had a better sense of how these products are performing in different market segments. For example, consider your best-selling refrigerator. Is it selling equally well in all regions, or is there one region where it's underperforming? Or think about your top computer tablet. It may be selling well overall, but are there market segments that avoid buying it?

You want to fashion an exploratory dashboard that lets you see both magnitude of sales and ranking for your top products broken down by virtually any demographic, revealing opportunities that you might otherwise miss.

Specifics

- You need to show the top 20 products sorted by sales.
- You want to see both the ranking and the magnitude of sales; that is, you need to be able to see easily just how much greater the sales are for one product than for another.
- You need to see how the rankings change when you look at sales across different dimensions—for example, region, customer segment, gender, and so on.

Related Scenarios

- You conduct a survey asking people a check-all-that-apply question and want to see which things are selected most often, ranked by different categories.
- You ask people to indicate their preference for political candidates and want to see how preferences differ by gender, age, and location.
- You want to compare the popularity of different music groups by country, age, and category.

How People Use the Dashboard

A user is first presented with a sorted list of the top 20 products by sales, as shown in Figure 22.1.

Selecting a product then shows how that product ranks within the selected category, in this case customer segment. (See Figure 22.2.)

In Figure 22.2, we can see that the Whirlpool Upright Freezer ranks fourth overall but is ranked seventh among consumers, first within corporate, and sixth within small office; it isn't in the top 20 in small business. The drop-down menu allows users to compare ranking among different dimensions.

Sales and Rank for Top 20 Products

Top 20 Overall

Rank by [Customer Segment ▼]

#	Product	Sales
1	GE Profile Refrigerator	$275,942
2	Samsung Smoothtop Range	$255,304
3	KitchenAid Wall Oven	$210,911
4	Whirlpool Upright Freezer	$206,494
5	Bosch Fully Integrated Dishwasher	$194,880
6	Frigidaire Fully Integrated Dishwasher	$147,395
7	Sharp AL-1530CS Digital Copier	$130,047
8	GE Profile Microwave	$128,100
9	Maytag Front Load Washer	$120,343
10	Maytag White Stackable Dryer	$114,173
11	Sony Playstation Deluxe	$112,759
12	Canon Personal Copier	$112,417
13	Microsoft Surface H3	$112,267
14	Epson R90 All-In-One	$111,221
15	Epson Ceiling Mounted Projector	$109,417
16	Panasonic OLED Television	$109,231
17	Fellowes Plastic Comb Binding Machine	$106,908
18	Brother PTouch Label Machine	$106,629
19	Fresno Karaoke Pro	$104,483
20	Hon Series Round Tables	$102,006

FIGURE 22.1 Top 20 products by sales overall.

Sales and Rank for Top 20 Products

Top 20 Overall

Rank by [Customer Segment ▼]

#	Product	Sales	Rank	Consumer	Corporate	Home Office	Small Business
1	GE Profile Refrigerator	$275,942	1		$107,312		
2	Samsung Smoothtop Range	$255,304	2				
3	KitchenAid Wall Oven	$210,911	3				
4	Whirlpool Upright Freezer	$206,494	4				
5	Bosch Fully Integrated Dishwasher	$194,880	5				
6	Frigidaire Fully Integrated Dishwasher	$147,395	6			$56,128	
7	Sharp AL-1530CS Digital Copier	$130,047	7	$43,054			
8	GE Profile Microwave	$128,100	8				
9	Maytag Front Load Washer	$120,343	9				
10	Maytag White Stackable Dryer	$114,173	10				
11	Sony Playstation Deluxe	$112,759	11				
12	Canon Personal Copier	$112,417	12				
13	Microsoft Surface H3	$112,267	13				
14	Epson R90 All-In-One	$111,221	14				
15	Epson Ceiling Mounted Projector	$109,417	15				
16	Panasonic OLED Television	$109,231	16				
17	Fellowes Plastic Comb Binding Machine	$106,908	17				
18	Brother PTouch Label Machine	$106,629	18				
19	Fresno Karaoke Pro	$104,483	19				
20	Hon Series Round Tables	$102,006	20				

FIGURE 22.2 Selecting the Whirlpool Upright Freezer shows its ranking and sales magnitude across four customer segments.

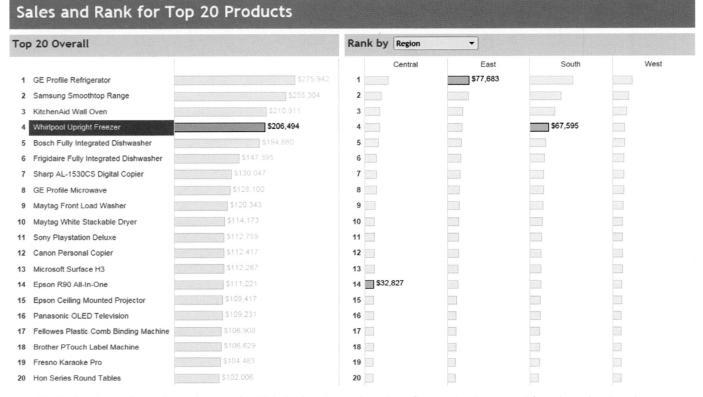

FIGURE 22.3   The selected product ranks 14th in the Central region, first in the East, and fourth in the South. It is not in the top 20 in the West.

In Figure 22.3, we see how the Whirlpool Upright Freezer ranks among different regions.

Why This Works

This Approach Is Very Versatile

This approach works for virtually anything that you want to rank. Consider how this approach works with

survey data. In Figure 22.4, we see the overall results to the survey question "As a doctor, indicate what health indicators you measure yourself; check all that apply," as well as the breakdown by generation for a selected response.

What do you measure?

Percentage of respondents that measure (Overall)

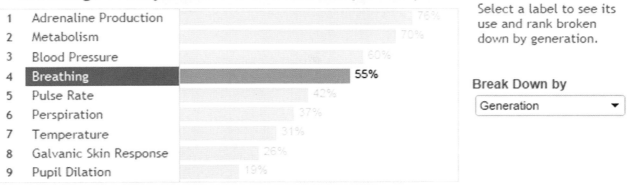

1	Adrenaline Production	76%
2	Metabolism	70%
3	Blood Pressure	60%
4	**Breathing**	**55%**
5	Pulse Rate	42%
6	Perspiration	37%
7	Temperature	31%
8	Galvanic Skin Response	26%
9	Pupil Dilation	19%

Select a label to see its use and rank broken down by generation.

Break Down by

Generation ▼

Percentage of respondents that measure by generation

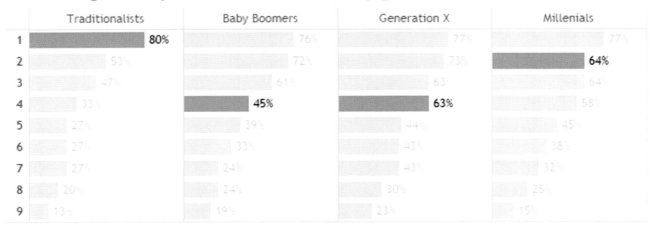

	Traditionalists	Baby Boomers	Generation X	Millenials
1	**80%**	76%	77%	77%
2	53%	72%	73%	**64%**
3	47%	61%	63%	64%
4	33%	**45%**	**63%**	58%
5	27%	39%	44%	45%
6	27%	33%	43%	38%
7	27%	24%	43%	32%
8	20%	24%	30%	25%
9	13%	19%	23%	15%

See http://www.datarevelations.com/visual-ranking-within-a-category.html

FIGURE 22.4   Breathing is ranked fourth overall with 55 percent but is ranked first with 80 percent among Traditionalists.

The differences really pop out when viewing by generation, as Traditionalists rank breathing first with 80 percent while Baby Boomers rank it fourth with only 45 percent.

Figure 22.5 shows another example where we rank employee performance overall and by six different attributes.

Here we see that Leonardo's overall ranking is sixth, but his rankings and scores vary widely among the different attributes.

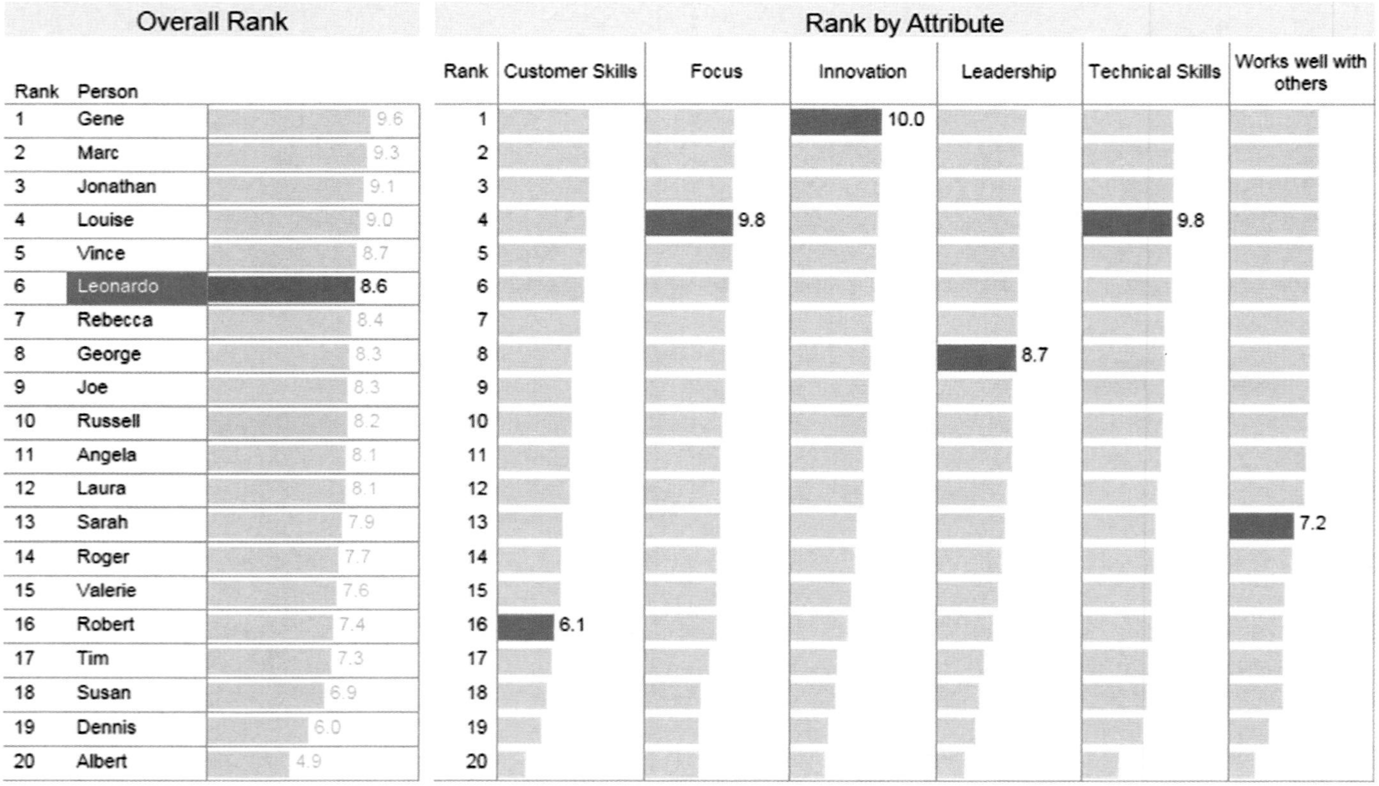

Overall Rank			Rank by Attribute						
Rank	Person		Rank	Customer Skills	Focus	Innovation	Leadership	Technical Skills	Works well with others
1	Gene	9.6	1			10.0			
2	Marc	9.3	2						
3	Jonathan	9.1	3						
4	Louise	9.0	4		9.8			9.8	
5	Vince	8.7	5						
6	Leonardo	8.6	6						
7	Rebecca	8.4	7						
8	George	8.3	8				8.7		
9	Joe	8.3	9						
10	Russell	8.2	10						
11	Angela	8.1	11						
12	Laura	8.1	12						
13	Sarah	7.9	13						7.2
14	Roger	7.7	14						
15	Valerie	7.6	15						
16	Robert	7.4	16	6.1					
17	Tim	7.3	17						
18	Susan	6.9	18						
19	Dennis	6.0	19						
20	Albert	4.9	20						

FIGURE 22.5   Overall employee ranking and ranking for particular attributes.

The Bars Show Magnitude

The bars make it easy to see just how much larger or smaller a particular product's sales are compared to another product. Indeed, even without showing mark labels (i.e., numbers next to the bars), in Figure 22.6, we can see that the sales for the top product is a little more than twice the sales for the seventh-ranked product.

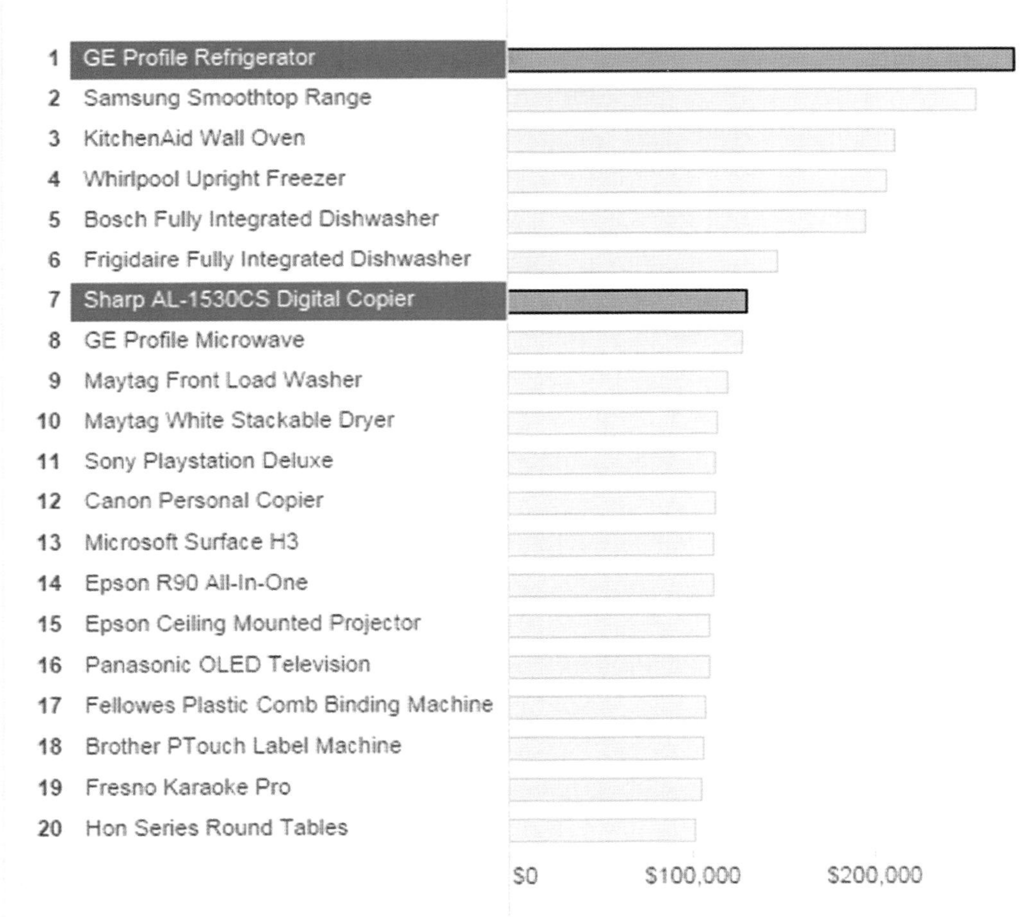

1	GE Profile Refrigerator
2	Samsung Smoothtop Range
3	KitchenAid Wall Oven
4	Whirlpool Upright Freezer
5	Bosch Fully Integrated Dishwasher
6	Frigidaire Fully Integrated Dishwasher
7	Sharp AL-1530CS Digital Copier
8	GE Profile Microwave
9	Maytag Front Load Washer
10	Maytag White Stackable Dryer
11	Sony Playstation Deluxe
12	Canon Personal Copier
13	Microsoft Surface H3
14	Epson R90 All-In-One
15	Epson Ceiling Mounted Projector
16	Panasonic OLED Television
17	Fellowes Plastic Comb Binding Machine
18	Brother PTouch Label Machine
19	Fresno Karaoke Pro
20	Hon Series Round Tables

$0 $100,000 $200,000

FIGURE 22.6   The bars make it easy to see just how much larger one product's sales are compared to another product's. Here we see that the GE Profile Refrigerator's sales are more than twice those of the Sharp AL-1530CS Digital Copier.

Another Approach: A Bump Chart

Another popular way to show ranking of individual products over time or across different dimensions is with a bump chart, as shown in Figure 22.7.

This is certainly a compelling visualization, but the ranking circles show us rank only, not magnitude. There's no way to tell just how much larger or smaller one product is than another.

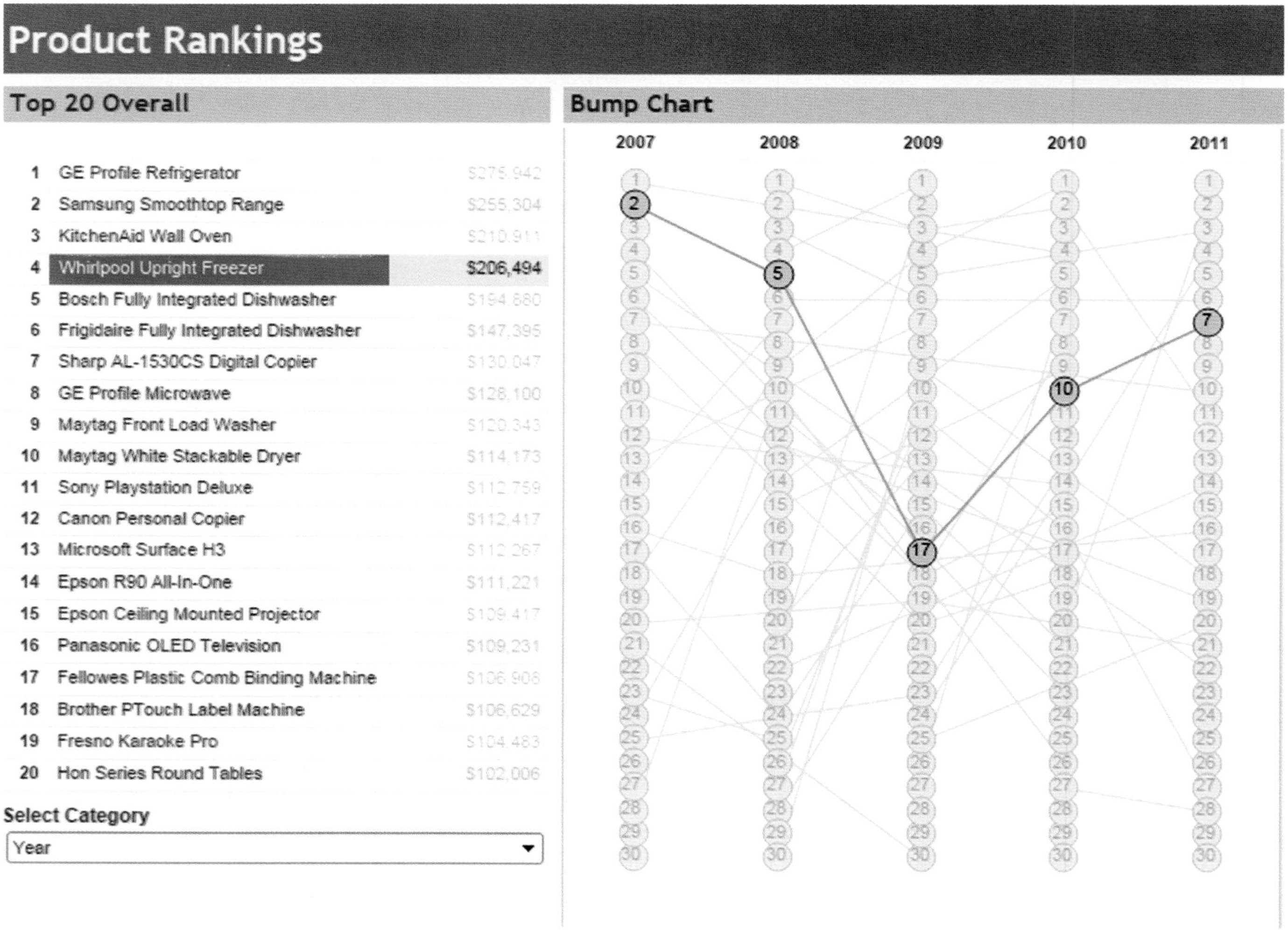

Product Rankings
Top 20 Overall
1 GE Profile Refrigerator $275,942
2 Samsung Smoothtop Range $255,304
3 KitchenAid Wall Oven $210,911
4 Whirlpool Upright Freezer $206,494
5 Bosch Fully Integrated Dishwasher $194,680
6 Frigidaire Fully Integrated Dishwasher $147,395
7 Sharp AL-1530CS Digital Copier $130,047
8 GE Profile Microwave $128,100
9 Maytag Front Load Washer $120,343
10 Maytag White Stackable Dryer $114,173
11 Sony Playstation Deluxe $112,759
12 Canon Personal Copier $112,417
13 Microsoft Surface H3 $112,267
14 Epson R90 All-In-One $111,221
15 Epson Ceiling Mounted Projector $109,417
16 Panasonic OLED Television $109,231
17 Fellowes Plastic Comb Binding Machine $106,906
18 Brother PTouch Label Machine $106,629
19 Fresno Karaoke Pro $104,483
20 Hon Series Round Tables $102,006
Select Category
Year
Bump Chart
2007
2008
2009
2010
2011

FIGURE 22.7 Bump chart showing the ranking of the selected product over time.

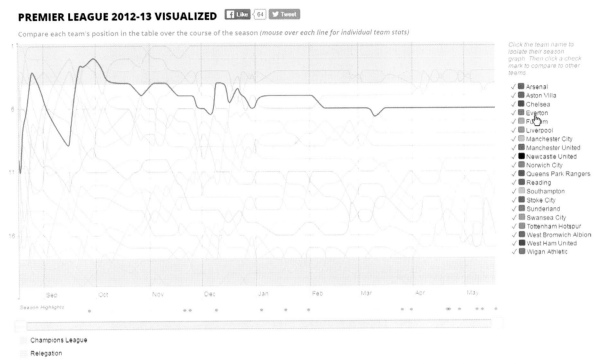

FIGURE 22.8 Highlighting a team in the legend, in this case Everton, shows that team's position over time.

Source: From kenandavis.com.

If magnitude isn't important, then a bump chart is an excellent choice. Consider Kenan Davis's terrific dashboard in Figure 22.8, which shows what place a team came in over time in the Premier League from 2012 to 2013.

To interact with the dashboard, see www.kenandavis.com/projects/a_season_visualized/ or http://tinyurl.com/gougppl.

One thing to note with both ranked bars and bump charts: You cannot show all the products, teams, issues,

and so on at the same time. Trying to do so would present users with an impossible-to-parse assortment of bars and lines. (See Figures 22.9 and 22.10.)

In both cases, to make the charts usable, you either need to select an item and take a screen capture of the state of the visualization or need to offer a dashboard that has the requisite interactivity.

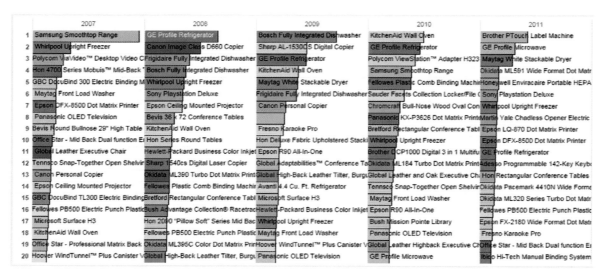

FIGURE 22.9   An impossible-to-parse collection of bars.

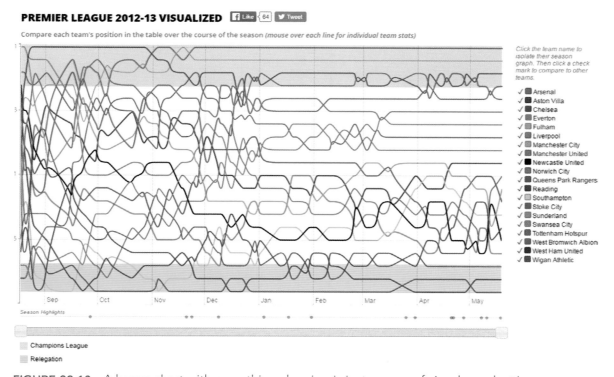

FIGURE 22.10   A bump chart with everything showing is just a mass of visual spaghetti.

Source: Statto.com

Author Commentary

ANDY: When I first saw this dashboard, I thought, Well, it doesn't do much, does it? Over time, however, I came to realize I'd fallen into a trap: expecting dashboards to do everything. This dashboard answers two questions: what's the overall rank of a product and how does that product rank in four regions. If that's all you need to know, then there's no need to add anything else.

After people explore this dashboard to find the product information they need, they might be left asking *why* a certain product is ranked high or low.

A poorly designed dashboard might try to provide answers to all potential questions on the one dashboard. The end result might be chaotic. Maybe the answers can be found in another dashboard. If not in another dashboard, the users should have access to the underlying data so they can find their own ad hoc answers to unanticipated questions. (See Chapter 36.)

Steve: I came up with what I think is a good addition to the dashboard. Because there's no common baseline it's hard to compare sales in Corporate ($107,312) with those of Consumer and Home Office ($43,054 and $56,126 respectively. See Figure 22.2.)

We can alleviate this difficulty by adding an additional chart that shows how sales for the selected product stacks up among the segments (See Figure 22.11.)

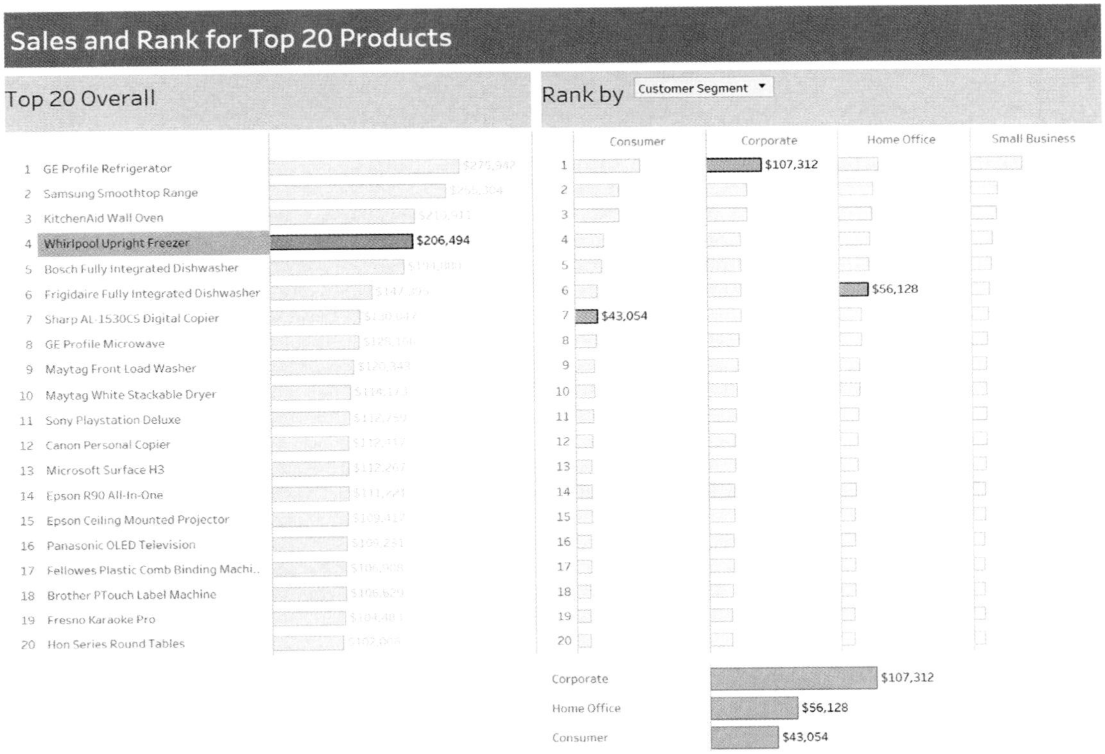

FIGURE 22.11   The additional chart allows us to easily compare sales across segments as it's easy to see that the bar for Corporate is about twice as long as the bar for Home Office.

Chapter 23

Measuring Claims across Multiple Measures and Dimensions

Workers' compensation dashboard.
Dashboard designer: Jonathan Effgen
Organization: CoEnterprise (http://www.coenterprise.com)

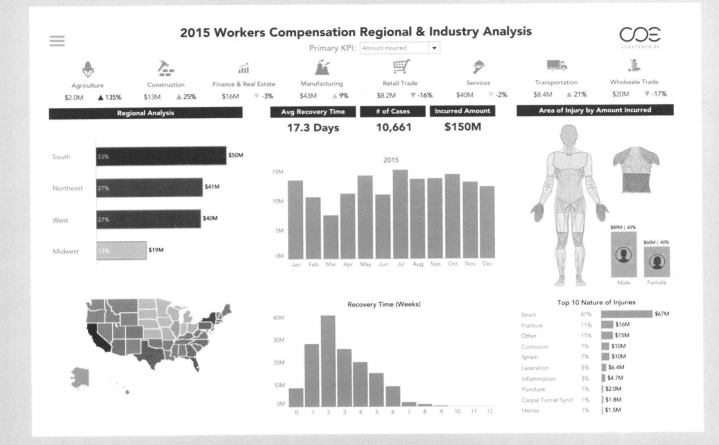

Scenario

Big Picture

You work for a very large multinational conglomerate and are tasked with understanding workers' compensation injury claims occurring in the United States. You need to grasp both safety and cost issues.

The data is overwhelming. Even a simple question, such as "Where do the most injury claims occur?," becomes two-pronged, as it can be answered by both *where in the country* and *where on the human body* most injuries occur.

There are four major metrics to understand—(1) number of cases, (2) claim amount, (3) the average claim amount, and (4) the average recovery time—and there are at least a half dozen ways you want to cut the data, including where on the body, where in the country, what type of injury (e.g., laceration versus strain), and when during the year the claims were filed. You decide to build a single, exploratory dashboard that helps you and others get a handle on the data.

Specifics

You need to:

- See and understand workers' compensation data by four key performance metrics:
  a. the total dollar amount incurred,
  b. the average dollar amount incurred,
  c. the number of cases, and
  d. the average recovery time (in weeks).
- Know when during the year these claims were filed.
- Know where on the body the injuries occurred.

- See how recovery times are bunched (i.e., for each key metric, you need to know how many claims and dollars involved a recovery time of one week, two weeks, three weeks, etc.).
- See how the charts change when you filter the data by a particular region of the country, region of the body, month of the year, and industry group.

Related Scenarios

You need to:

- Look further into the nature, cause, and severity of sports injuries and how long they keep athletes on the sidelines.
- Look into injuries and illnesses suffered by patients at a particular hospital or medical clinic.
- Analyze data on claims made by clients of an insurance company, which could, among other things, entail breaking data down by geographic region, type of claim, and amount claimed.
- Analyze maintenance and accident data for a rental car company that maintains a large fleet of cars.

How People Use the Dashboard

Change Key Performance Indicators on Demand

A drop-down menu at the top of the dashboard allows the user to select which of the four metrics to display. (See Figure 23.1.)

For example, instead of seeing amount incurred, the user may instead want to explore the number of cases. This will change all of the accompanying visualizations. Figure 23.2 shows the effect of changing the key performance indicator (KPI) from "Amount Incurred" to "# of Cases" on the region bar chart.

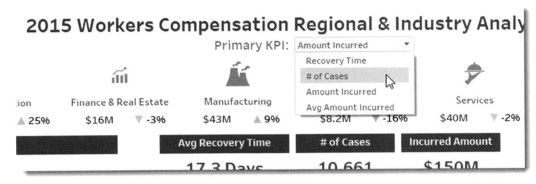

FIGURE 23.1 Drop-down menu allows you to select which metric to explore throughout the dashboard.

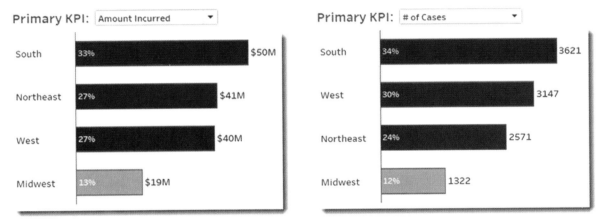

FIGURE 23.2 Amount incurred broken down by region compared with number of cases broken down by region.

FIGURE 23.3 The decorative KPI strip is also a filter. Selecting an industry group (e.g., agriculture, construction, etc.) will filter all of the charts on the dashboard by the selection.

Filter by Industry

The decorative KPI strip along the top of the dashboard is also a filter that allows the user to select an industry group. (See Figure 23.3.) Selecting an industry group will filter all of the charts on the dashboard to show results only for the selected group.

Everything Is a Filter

Clicking any part of any chart filters the other charts by whatever the user selects. This allows the user to freely explore the dashboard while looking for interesting patterns and relationships.

Consider the body map, gender, and injury bar charts. (See Figure 23.4.) On the left, you can see what they look like unclicked. On the right, is the effect of clicking the left hand.

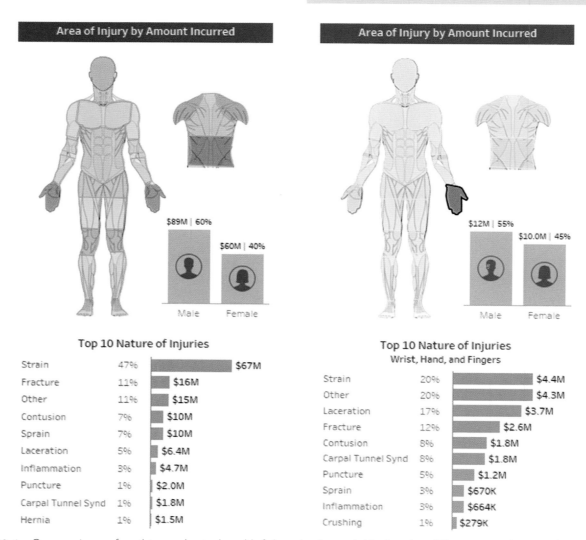

FIGURE 23.4 Comparison of nothing selected and left hand selected. Notice the difference in the gender and top-10 injuries charts.

Hovering over Marks Reveals More Information

Hovering over a mark shows details about a particular data point. Figure 23.5 shows a summary of all four KPIs for March.

Why This Works

Uncluttered Layout Despite Many Different Charts

There are eight different charts on this dashboard—nine if you count the industry group filter strip as a chart. (See Figure 23.6.)

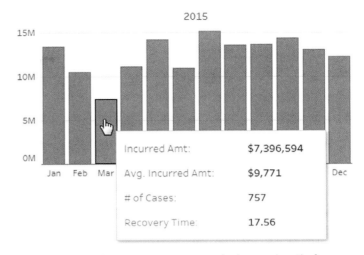

FIGURE 23.5   Hovering over a mark shows details for that mark, in this case all four KPIs for March.

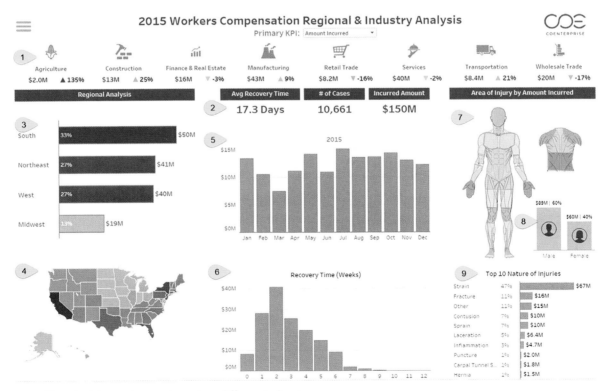

FIGURE 23.6   The dashboard contains nine different charts.

Finance & Real Estate	Manufacturing	Retail Trade
$16M ▼ -3%	$43M ▲ 9%	$8.2M ▼ -16%

FIGURE 23.7   Very light gray lines help separate the different industry groups without competing for attention.

The layout is relatively uncluttered (considering the dashboard displays nine distinct charts), and it is easy to see the different areas despite there being no line to separate them.

Shading and white space

Shading and white space, used subtly, create distinct zones on dashboards.

Indeed, the only lines are the faint gray rules separating the industry groups in the filter strip along the top. (See Figure 23.7.)

The Menu to Change the KPI Is Front and Center

The user doesn't need to hunt to find the control that changes the KPIs; it's directly below the title and functions as both a control and a label indicating what metric is being displayed. (See Figure 23.1.)

The Layout Is Easy to Explore and Discover Interesting Facts

This dashboard begs for exploration. There are so many different facets to explore, and users can see results instantly when they click on different marks. As we see in Figure 23.8, clicking Midwest on the Regional Analysis chart shows a radically different profile for when claims occurred (there was a big spike in February) and on what part of the body the injuries were located (the greatest percentage was on the head). The figure also shows a much larger percentage of women filing claims (48% for the Midwest versus 40% overall).

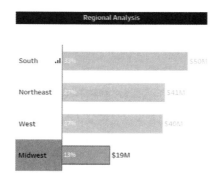
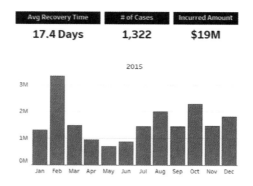
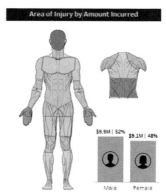

FIGURE 23.8   Selecting Midwest reveals very different results for incurred amounts by month, body location, and gender.

$89M | 60%

$60M | 40%

Male   Female

FIGURE 23.9 Gender icons placed atop a bar chart make the dashboard less stark but do not sacrifice the ease of comparison.

Color Is Used Sparingly and Intelligently

Besides the KPI indicators along the top, the dashboard designer uses colors only for the geographic regions and the body heat map. As there are so many charts competing for our attention, this sparing use of color is very welcome.

Nice Use of Gender Icons

The gender icons (see Figure 23.9) are clear and engaging without being distracting. Indeed, the designer eschewed making the icons themselves larger or smaller based on magnitude and instead placed them on an easy-to-compare bar chart.

Author Commentary

Steve: We refer to this as the kitchen sink dashboard as there are nine different charts and four different KPIs yielding 36 different combinations. I particularly like being able to change the KPI on the fly using the menu at the top of the screen. This dashboard also whetted my appetite to know even more (e.g., Why the drop in March? In what industries do women file more claims than men?, etc.), indicating the designers got me very engaged with the data.

My biggest concern is over the KPI strip along the top. When I asked the dashboard designer about this, he told me that this was essentially a requirement from the client. People using the dashboard already knew the industry group comparisons inside and out and wanted an icon-driven filter that, in their eyes, made the dashboard a little less sterile.

Sometimes there's nothing you can do when the client insists on having something a particular way. But I still worry that some important insights remain buried in the current rendering. Let me explain.

Figure 23.10 shows a segment of the KPI chart.

FIGURE 23.10 KPI strip makes it hard to compare values across industry groups.

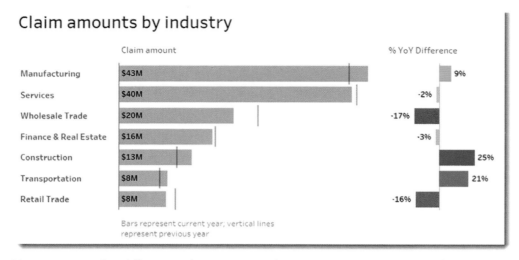

Claim amounts by industry

FIGURE 23.11   Claim amounts for different industry groups showing percentage change from the previous year.

Figure 23.11 shows the same information rendered as a bar chart.

Whoa! Now I can really see that claim amounts for manufacturing are more than twice as large as those for wholesale trade and that amounts for construction are way up compared with the previous year.

JEFF: We went through a number of iterations on this dashboard. We had several calls with the designers and, as a team, came up with a few suggestions that would improve the dashboard. As the weeks progressed, all three of us worked to improve it even more. As Steve mentioned, it was referred to as the kitchen sink dashboard, but as we worked through the process, we trimmed it down quite a bit. Even with a lot of pruning, the dashboard has lots of details with a number of charts, a geographic map, and a human body map as well as industry group icons. Yet the final design doesn't feel as cluttered as previous versions. As packed as this dashboard is, it still has some space to breathe.

As we discuss in this chapter, there are not many lines on this dashboard. This is particularly important because there are so many elements vying for attention. Borders and lines, especially vertical lines, can really create a feeling of clutter on dashboards.

Chapter 24

Showing Churn or Turnover

Subscriber churn analysis dashboard.
Dashboard designer: Steve Wexler
Organization: Data Revelations

Subscriber Churn Analysis

Subscriber activity - All

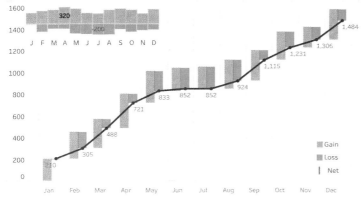

- Gain
- Loss
- Net

Net subscriber activity by division

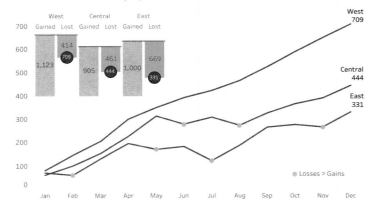

West 709
Central 444
East 331

Losses > Gains

Details

		Gained	Lost	Net	Running total
West	January	80	0	80	80
	February	80	-15	65	145
	March	90	-30	60	205
	April	120	-25	95	300
	May	100	-50	50	350
	June	119	-77	42	392
	July	75	-45	30	422
	August	119	-77	42	464
	September	90	-30	60	524
	October	80	-15	65	589
	November	80	-20	60	649
	December	90	-30	60	709
	Total	**1,123**	**-414**	**709**	
Central	January	60	0	60	60
	February	85	-45	40	100
	March	80	-27	53	153
	April	90	-17	73	226
	May	120	-33	87	313
	June	45	-80	-35	278
	July	75	-45	30	308
	August	45	-80	-35	273
	September	80	-27	53	326
	October	85	-45	40	366
	November	60	-35	25	391
	December	80	-27	53	444
	Total	**905**	**-461**	**444**	
East	January	70	0	70	70
	February	80	-90	-10	60
	March	100	-30	70	130
	April	110	-45	65	195
	May	70	-95	-25	170
	June	45	-33	12	182
	July	50	-110	-60	122
	August	99	-34	65	187
	September	112	-34	78	265
	October	99	-88	11	276
	November	55	-65	-10	266
	December	110	-45	65	331
	Total	**1,000**	**-669**	**331**	
Grand Total		**3,028**	**-1,544**	**1,484**	

Scenario

Big Picture

Your company has just launched a new monthly subscriber service. You need to get a handle on how subscriptions are growing over time, both overall and in different divisions. Subscribers can cancel at any time so you need to see for every month how many new subscribers you have gained and how many you have lost. You expect there to be some attrition, but you need to know when and where losses exceed gains as well as where gains occurred and when gains are particularly strong.

Specifics

- You need to be able to see fluctuations in subscriptions over time.
- You need to compare overall gains and losses for each division.
- You need to easily see for each division when losses exceed gains.
- You need to be able to see the details for each month.
- You need to see which months were worst and which were best, both overall and for a particular division.

Related Scenarios

- You manage human resources for a large company with offices in many countries and need to monitor employee churn by location and department.
- You manage a software development project and need to monitor assignments as they go through different stages of the process.

- You monitor unemployment statistics for the government and need to show employment churn by industry and state.

Understanding the Waterfall Chart

Before delving into the particulars of how a user would interact with the dashboard, let's first explore how the waterfall chart in Figure 24.1 works.

Table 24.1 presents the raw data that drives this particular visualization.

Here's how to interpret the numbers.

- In January, when the company opened its doors, it welcomed 210 subscribers.
- In February, the company gained 245 subscribers but lost 150 subscribers for a net of 95. Add that 95 to the previous month, and at the end of February we had a running total of 305 active subscribers.
- In March, the company added 270 subscribers and lost 87 for a net of 183 for the month. Adding that to the previous 305 yields a total of 488 by the end of March.
- The grand total at the bottom indicates that over the course of the entire year, the company gained 3,028 subscribers and lost 1,544 for a net of 1,484.

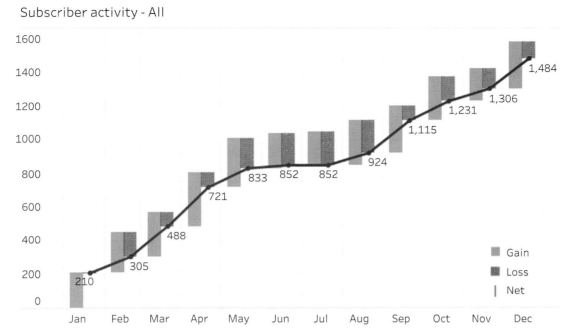

FIGURE 24.1 Waterfall chart portion of the churn dashboard showing activity for all divisions combined.

TABLE 24.1 Raw data for driving the subscriber churn dashboard.

	Gained	Lost	Net	Running Total
January	210	0	210	210
February	245	-150	95	305
March	270	-87	183	488
April	320	-87	233	721
May	290	-178	112	833
June	209	-190	19	852
July	200	-200	0	852
August	263	-191	72	924
September	282	-91	191	1,115
October	264	-148	116	1,231
November	195	-120	75	1,306
December	280	-102	178	1,484
Grand Total	**3,028**	**-1,544**	**1,484**	

With this in mind, let's see how to read first three months of the waterfall chart. In Figure 24.2, we see that we gained 210 subscribers and didn't lose anything, leaving us with a total of 210 at the end of the month.

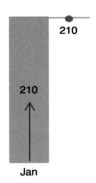

FIGURE 24.2   January portion of waterfall chart.

In Figure 24.3, we start at 210 (where we left off at the end of January) and gain 245 subscribers but lose 150, leaving us with a total of 305 at the end of February (210 from January and 95 from February).

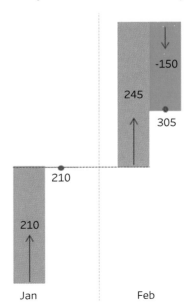

FIGURE 24.3   February picks up where January leaves off.

Figure 24.4 shows that in March, we start at 305, gain 270, but lose 87, leaving us with a total of 488 at the end of the month (305 + 270 – 87 = 488).

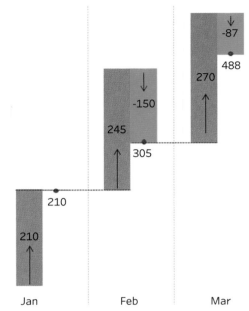

FIGURE 24.4   March picks up where February leaves off.

How People Use the Dashboard

Although there are neither controls to select nor sliders to move, clicking elements in one visualization on the dashboard will highlight and/or filter items in other portions of the dashboard. For example, in Figure 24.5, we see that selecting East from the summary bar chart filters and/or highlights the other charts on the dashboard to only show results from the East.

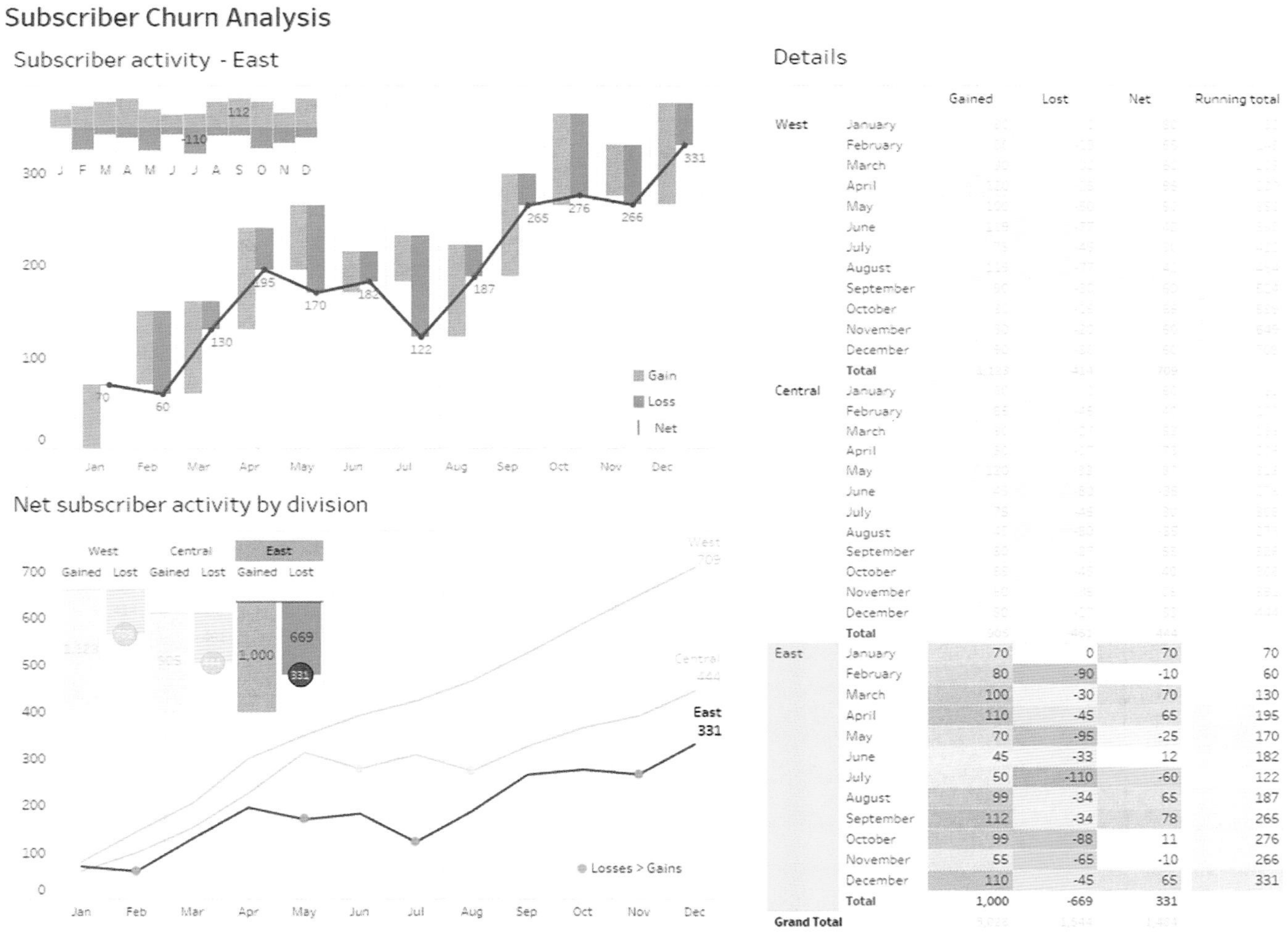
Subscriber Churn Analysis
Subscriber activity - East
J F M A M J J A S O N D
112
-110
300
200
100
0
70
60
130
195
170
182
122
187
265
276
266
331
Gain
Loss
Net
Jan Feb Mar Apr May Jun Jul Aug Sep Oct Nov Dec
Net subscriber activity by division
West
Central
East
Gained Lost Gained Lost Gained Lost
700
600
500
400
300
200
100
0
1,000
669
331
East
331
Losses > Gains
Jan Feb Mar Apr May Jun Jul Aug Sep Oct Nov Dec
Details
Gained Lost Net Running total
West
January February March April May June July August September October November December
Total
Central
January February March April May June July August September October November December
Total
East
January 70 0 70 70
February 80 -90 -10 60
March 100 -30 70 130
April 110 -45 65 195
May 70 -95 -25 170
June 45 -33 12 182
July 50 -110 -60 122
August 99 -34 65 187
September 112 -34 78 265
October 99 -88 11 276
November 55 -65 -10 266
December 110 -45 65 331
Total 1,000 -669 331
Grand Total

FIGURE 24.5 Selecting a division on one part of the dashboard filters and/or highlights that division in other parts of the dashboard.

Likewise, selecting a month highlights that month throughout the dashboard. (See Figure 24.6.)

Why This Works

Big Picture and Details

Three main chart areas present different levels of detail about the data.

Subscriber Churn Analysis

Subscriber activity - East, West, Central

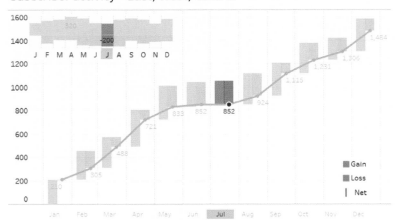

Net subscriber activity by division

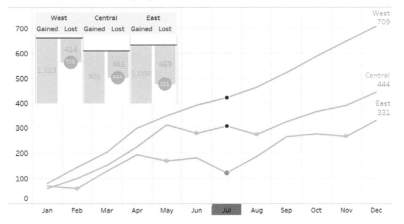

Details

		Gained	Lost	Net	Running total
West	January	80	0	80	80
	February	80	-15	65	145
	March	90	-30	60	205
	April	120	-25	95	300
	May	100	-50	50	350
	June	119	-77	42	392
	July	75	-45	30	422
	August	119	-77	42	464
	September	90	-30	60	524
	October	80	-15	65	589
	November	80	-20	60	649
	December	90	-30	60	709
	Total	**1,123**	**-414**	**709**	
Central	January	60	0	60	60
	February	85	-45	40	100
	March	80	-27	53	153
	April	90	-17	73	226
	May	120	-33	87	313
	June	45	-80	-35	278
	July	75	-45	30	308
	August	45	-80	-35	273
	September	80	-27	53	326
	October	85	-45	40	366
	November	60	-35	25	391
	December	80	-27	53	444
	Total	**905**	**-461**	**444**	
East	January	70	0	70	70
	February	80	-90	-10	60
	March	100	-30	70	130
	April	110	-45	65	195
	May	70	-95	-25	170
	June	45	-33	12	182
	July	50	-110	-60	122
	August	99	-34	65	187
	September	112	-34	78	265
	October	99	-88	11	276
	November	55	-65	-10	266
	December	110	-45	65	331
	Total	**1,000**	**-669**	**331**	
Grand Total		**3,028**	**-1,544**	**1,484**	

FIGURE 24.6   Selecting a month in one chart highlights that month in all the other charts on the dashboard.

The Big Picture

The top left area shows subscriber activity by month. In Figure 24.7, we can see that: (1) we had an overall net gain of 1,484 subscribers, (2) our best month for gains was April, (3) our worst month for losses was July, and (4) net growth was flat between June and July.

Easy Comparison of the Three Divisions

The Net Subscriber area in the bottom left allows for easy comparison among the three divisions (see Figure 24.8). It is easy to see that the East Division, despite gaining 1,000 subscribers for the year, also had by far the biggest loss (1). We can also see from the smooth trend line that the West division never had a month where losses exceeded gains (2).

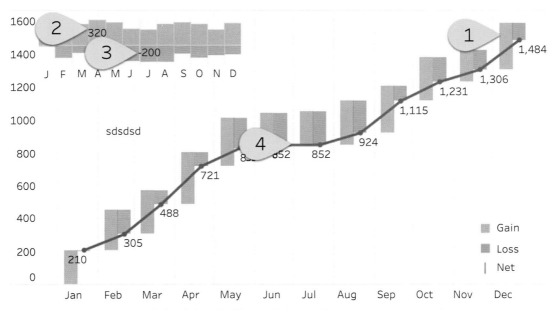

FIGURE 24.7   The chart in the upper left of the dashboard shows the big-picture trends.

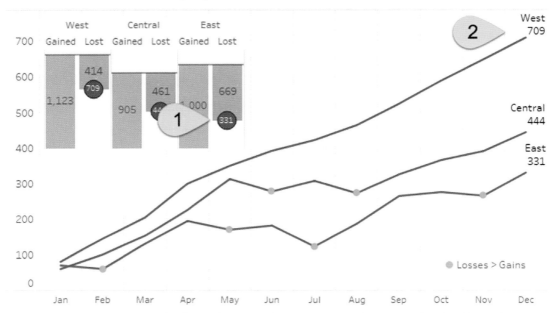

FIGURE 24.8   The chart on the lower left of the dashboard compares performance for the three divisions also note how the orange dots make it easy to see where losses were greater than gains.

Details

		Gained	Lost	Net	Running total
West	January	80	0	80	80
	February	80	-15	65	145
	March	90	-30	60	205
	April	120	-25	95	300
	May	100	-50	50	350
	June	119	-77	42	392
	July	75	-45	30	422
	August	119	-77	42	464
	September	90	-30	60	524
	October	80	-15	65	589
	November	80	-20	60	649
	December	90	-30	60	709
	Total	1,123	-414	709	
Central	January	60	0	60	60
	February	85	-45	40	100
	March	80	-27	53	153
	April	90	-17	73	226
	May	120	-33	87	313
	June	45	-80	-35	278
	July	75	-45	30	308
	August	45	-80	-35	273
	September	80	-27	53	326
	October	85	-45	40	366
	November	60	-35	25	391
	December	80	-27	53	444
	Total	905	-461	444	
East	January	70	0	70	70
	February	80	-90	-10	60
	March	100	-30	70	130
	April	110	-45	65	195
	May	70	-95	-25	170
	June	45	-33	12	182
	July	50	-110	-60	122
	August	99	-34	65	187
	September	112	-34	78	265
	October	99	-88	11	276
	November	55	-65	-10	266
	December	110	-45	65	331
	Total	1,000	-669	331	
Grand Total		3,028	-1,544	1,484	

FIGURE 24.9 Color-coded heat map makes it easy to see details and performance outliers. Note that the colors are based on the main color legend where gray represents gains, red represents losses, and the blue shows the running net.

Heat Map Shows Details

The heat map on the right of the dashboard (also called a "highlight table") makes it easy to see gains, losses, net, and running totals for each division and for every month. (See Figure 24.9.)

The Heat Maps Provide Richer Insights than Text Tables

Many people with a finance background often ask for a text table so they can "see the numbers." The heat map goes one better in that it provides the numeric details and accentuates the outliers, something that you can't see easily with a text table. (See Figure 24.10.)

The text table presents a sea of numbers, and the reader has to work hard to make comparisons. The heat map uses color coding to make that comparison much easier.

Cross tabs vs. highlight tables

When you need to provide a cross tab, consider using a highlight table instead of a text table: The color coding of the highlight table will make comparing numbers easier.

Dots Show Which Months Present Problems

The dots make it easy to see in which months and in which divisions losses exceeded gains. (See Figure 24.8.)

Central		Gained	Lost	Net	Running total
	January	60	0	60	80
	February	85	-45	40	145
	March	80	-27	53	205
	April	90	-17	73	300
	May	120	-33	87	350
	June	45	-80	-35	392
	July	75	-45	30	422
	August	45	-80	-35	464
	September	80	-27	53	524
	October	85	-45	40	589
	November	60	-35	25	649
	December	80	-27	53	709

Central		Gained	Lost	Net	Running total
	January	60	0	60	80
	February	85	-45	40	145
	March	80	-27	53	205
	April	90	-17	73	300
	May	120	-33	87	350
	June	45	-80	-35	392
	July	75	-45	30	422
	August	45	-80	-35	464
	September	80	-27	53	524
	October	85	-45	40	589
	November	60	-35	25	649
	December	80	-27	53	709

FIGURE 24.10 A text table (left) compared to a heat map (right). Note that the heat map makes problem areas pop out.

Sparkbars Allow Easy Comparison of Gains and Losses across Months

The sparkbar chart in the upper left corner of the dashboard makes it easy to compare gains and losses for each month and highlights the month with the greatest gain and the month with the greatest loss. (See Figure 24.11.)

Action Filters Make It Easy to Focus on One Division

Selecting a region in the Division chart or Details chart filters the waterfall and sparkbar so you can better understand churn within a particular division. Figure 24.12 shows what happens when a user selects the East Division.

The waterfall chart shows us just how volatile subscriber activity was in the East Division.

FIGURE 24.11 Even without a value axis, it's easy to see which months had big and small gains and which had big and small losses.

Other Use Cases and Approaches

With service subscribers, the goal is to gain and keep subscribers. Airport flow is another scenario that can be shown using similar techniques, but the goal is very different. You want the number of planes leaving the airport to equal the number of planes coming into the airport. Indeed, at any given hour, the goal is net zero.

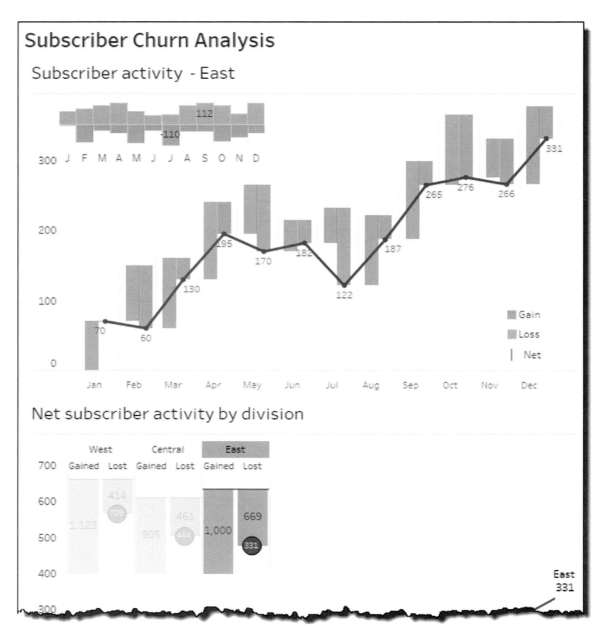

FIGURE 24.12 Selecting East in the bottom chart filters the other charts by that selection.

Given that this goal is very different from the goal for subscriber growth, the waterfall chart we presented in Figure 24.2 won't work well. One possible solution is shown in Figure 24.13.

Here we see the inbound and outbound flights presented in very muted colors, as it is the running net (the number of planes sitting on the tarmac), which

is most important. The goal is to make it so that as one plane lands, another takes off. We want the inner bars to be as close to zero as possible.

If the number of planes on the ground meets or exceeds 20, the bar color changes to orange. We can see that McGinty Airport was in an overflow state at 11 a.m., noon, 1 p.m., and 3 p.m.

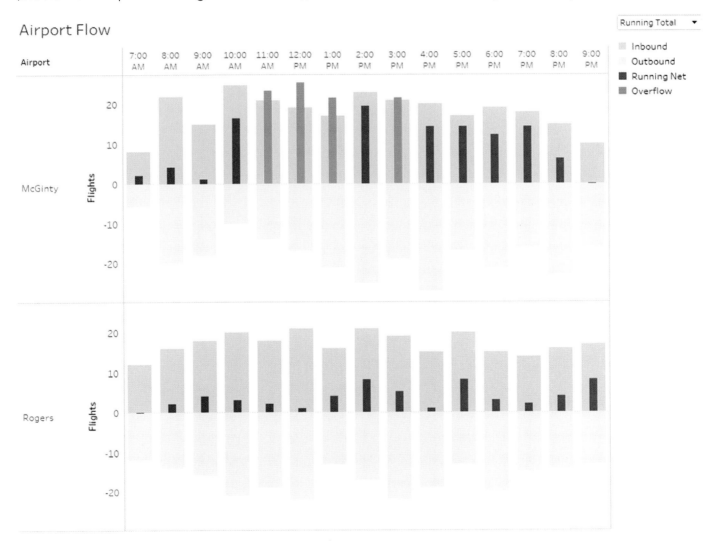

FIGURE 24.13   Inbound, outbound, and running net for two airports.

Author Commentary

Steve: I had no idea that visualizing turnover/churn would be so involved. The combination of different use cases and observers' preferences for different visualizations really surprised me. I went through at least 10 different approaches to the core waterfall chart and at least 30 different iterations of the dashboard as a whole.

One thing that surprised me was the popularity of a radical alternative to the waterfall chart, which I called the "mountain chart." (See Figure 24.14.)

A number of people took a shine to this chart, stating that it was particularly easy to see where both the bad things (red) and the good things (gray) peaked and where red exceeded gray. Yes, there was a little bit of a disconnect with the loss values showing as positive, but those who liked this chart were able to adjust to this quickly.

The biggest problem was that the area chart portion (the mountains) uses the axis values on the left and the line chart showing net subscribers uses the axis values on the right. Since a lot of people found using a dual axis confusing—and because a lot of people just didn't like the chart at all—I elected to go with the waterfall chart.

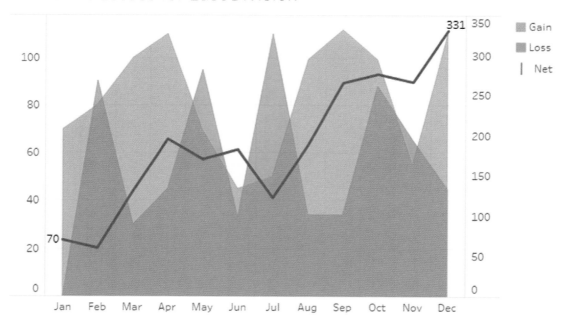

FIGURE 24.14 Mountain charts take a completely different approach to showing churn.

I also want to stress the importance of asking other people to review. Both Andy and Jeff gave me a lot of pushback on early prototypes. Jeff's recoiling at the Details text table was the catalyst for using a heat map instead.

Jeff: I much prefer the waterfall chart over other variations of this dashboard. It might be that people in banking and finance are more used to reading waterfall charts, but everyone I asked to review this chart also liked the waterfall chart the best. The alternative makes it difficult to see the area charts on top of each other, so it's really just the peaks that stand out. The waterfall fall chart better visualizes the ongoing increase and decrease over time.

The dots on the end of the division bars are also a little big to me. (See Figure 24.8.) Steve wanted to keep the labels in the circles, so it would be hard to make them too small. I would have made the dots smaller and moved the labels underneath the circles.

I really love the use of color throughout this dashboard. The color added to the text table really helps to highlight the data and provides additional context at-a-glance to the numbers.

ANDY: First appearances matter; they leave lasting impressions when you reflect on your experience of using things. In *The Design of Everyday Things,* Don Norman calls these the visceral responses. This applies to dashboards too. My first response when looking at this dashboard was very positive. The color, layout, and use of font make looking at this dashboard a pleasing experience. I don't feel like I am fighting to interpret any part of the dashboard.

It took me some time to get my head around this style of waterfall chart. However, the effort of understanding unfamiliar or complex charts is often time well spent. This chart contains a lot of detail, some of which is only apparent with familiarity.

Chapter 25

Showing Actual versus Potential Utilization

Utilization rollup dashboard.
Dashboard designer: Vanessa Edwards
Organization: Creative Performance Inc. (www.creativelyperform.com)

Agency Utilization Rollup

$3.8M Fees   **$3.4M** Potential   **$1.3M** New Biz + Opportunity   **$2.6M** Internal Projects   **+12.2** FTE Overstaffed

	Target vs Billable vs Non-Billable %		Non-Billable vs Billable Hours		Cost | Fees | Potential
Creative	99%	53% / 46%	5,749 / 6,743		$1,083K
Account Management	105%	47% / 58%	10,670 / 8,620		$1,159K / $795K
Project Management	104%	35% / 69%	8,396 / 4,274		$698K / $808K
Technology	102%	28% / 74%	14,454 / 5,468		$883K / $1,762K
Operations	4%		10 / 33		
Executive/Admin	57%	57%	2,179 / 16		
New Biz	106%	106% / 100%	2,350 / 1		Show Potential at 100% of Target ▼

New Biz + Opp

	hrs	%
Creative	1,456 hrs	12%
Account Management	4,524 hrs	25%
Project Management	1,455 hrs	12%
Technology	361 hrs	2%
Operations	6 hrs	0%
Executive/Admin	0 hrs	0%
New Biz	1,764 hrs	80%

Cost $533K

Internal Projects

	hrs	%
Creative	1,301 hrs	10%
Account Management	1,579 hrs	9%
Project Management	2,283 hrs	19%
Technology	9,608 hrs	49%
Operations	0 hrs	0%
Executive/Admin	4 hrs	0%
New Biz	40 hrs	2%

Cost $755K

Internal Admin

	hrs	%
Creative	2,992 hrs	24%
Account Management	4,567 hrs	25%
Project Management	4,659 hrs	38%
Technology	4,485 hrs	23%
Operations	5 hrs	0%
Executive/Admin	2,176 hrs	56%
New Biz	546 hrs	25%

Cost $1,163K

Utilization Trend

Billable vs Potential ▼

% Potential

% Billable

60% / 40% / 20% / 0%

J F M A M J J A S O N D
2015

Scenario

Big Picture

You are the principal, chief operating officer, chief financial officer, or director of client services for a marketing agency (advertising, integrated, digital, design, etc.), trying to understand your agency's current performance in billable hours and fee income.

Fee income (also known as labor income) is the main source of revenue for most agencies and is directly linked to billable hours. Understanding where time is being spent across the agency is critical to managing staffing and to overall agency profitability. As direct labor cost is often the largest expense agencies have, to manage profitability effectively, you must be able to monitor labor costs in relation to your fee income and fee targets.

Specifics

You need to:

- Understand how time entry is spent across the agency including:
    a. billable time on client projects,
    b. nonbillable time generating new business,
    c. nonbillable time spent on internal agency projects, and
    d. nonbillable time spent on internal agency administration.
- See how each department is performing in relation to its target utilization.
- See if a department costs you more than its potential fee income and what you could be making in additional fee income if that department hit its target utilization or a variation of that target.
- See the breakdown of nonbillable time in order to identify the potential cause of low utilization.

Related Scenarios

- You work in a law firm and need to compare billable hours and potential billable hours across departments and by individual attorneys and support staff. (Indeed, this would work for virtually any organization that bills on an hourly basis; e.g., software development, auto repairs, etc.)
- You work at a restaurant and need to track employee hours as well as monitor how resources (ovens, air conditioning) and food are utilized/underutilized.

How People Use the Dashboard

Key Performance Indicators

The numbers at the top of the dashboard represent the agency's current fees as well as the additional potential fees that could be made if the agency met its target. (See Figure 25.1.)

$3.8M   •$3.4M $1.3M $2.6M   •+12.2
Fees   Potential   New Biz + Opportunity   Internal Projects   FTE Overstaffed

36%   56%

FIGURE 25.1   Key metrics appear at the top of the dashboard along with a bullet chart.

KPIs as a color legend

Key performance indicators can be used as a color legend. Here blue indicates current fees and green indicates potential fees. This color scheme is used throughout the dashboard.

The numbers at the top of the dashboard represent the agency's current fees as well as the additional potential fees that could be made if the agency met its target. In addition, the numbers show how over-staffed an agency is based on its current workload as well as the amount of gross billable dollars or opportunity cost an agency is spending both on itself and on generating new business.

- Fees = Total amount of billable work that could be converted into labor income
- Potential = Additional labor income that could be generated if billable targets are met
- New Biz + Opportunity = Gross rates of billable employees spent generating new business
- Internal Projects = Gross rate of billable employees spent on internal agency projects
- FTE [Full-Time Equivalent] Overstaffed = How over-staffed (or "heavy") your team is

The utilization bullet chart is a visual quick reference that immediately informs the viewer how well the organization is doing toward achieving its utilization goals. The blue line represents current agency utilization, which is the total percentage of billable time logged across the agency, while the green vertical line represents the agency's utilization potential (or a variation of that potential, depending on the drop-down selection in Figure 25.5). The difference between these lines is the agency's utilization gap and corresponds to the $3.4M potential key performance indicator (KPI; the number in green at the top of the dashboard).

You might be wondering why the green bar isn't set to 100 percent. That is because no agency is going to be able to bill its workforce at 100 percent utilization, as it is simply impossible for every hour worked to be billable to a client.[1]

Target versus Billable versus Nonbillable Percentages

Figure 25.2 shows how each department is performing against utilization targets. It displays both the billable (blue) and nonbillable (gray) percentage of time for each department. Behind the stacked bars are wider, lightly colored target bars, which make it easy to see which blue bars are above or below target, and by how much. The red dots quickly identify the departments that are below their utilization targets. In the figure, you see that the Creative Department is above target while the next three departments are below target. Note that Operations, Executive/Admin, and New Biz do not have targets because they are considered "overhead departments" and often don't log all their time.

---

[1]The "magic number" is based on a labor budget per employee put together by the finance team. Finance sets the target for each employee and then applies a write-off factor to verify that the company can still meet its profitability goals, even considering an agency's overhead.

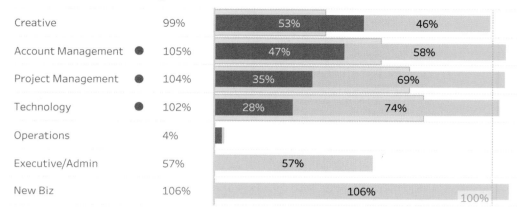

Target vs Billable vs Non-Billable %

Creative	99%	53% 46%
Account Management ●	105%	47% 58%
Project Management ●	104%	35% 69%
Technology ●	102%	28% 74%
Operations	4%	
Executive/Admin	57%	57%
New Biz	106%	106% 100%

FIGURE 25.2 Comparing billable percentages with a target and showing overall hours.

This utilization calculation is based on a 40-hour work-week, represented by the dotted vertical line, so it is possible for the billable and nonbillable percent-ages to be greater than 100 percent. We can see at a glance which departments are averaging more or less than a 40-hour workweek.

Nonbillable versus Billable Hours

Figure 25.3 shows the actual number of nonbillable versus billable hours for each department. The common baseline makes it easy to see which departments are performing the most and the least number of bill-able hours.

Non-Billable vs Billable Hours

Creative	5,749 6,743
Account Management	10,670 8,620
Project Management	8,396 4,274
Technology	14,454 5,468
Operations	10 33
Executive/Admin	2,179 16
New Biz	2,350 1

FIGURE 25.3 Nonbillable bars go to the left; billable hours go to the right, creating a common baseline for comparison.

FIGURE 25.4 Comparing costs, fees, and potential fees.

Cost, Fees, Potential

Figure 25.4 allows us to quickly see if the cost of labor is greater than or less than billable fees. Labor cost is represented by the lightly shaded bars, and the current utilization in fees is represented by the blue bars. The half-filled red dot shows which departments are producing fees that fall short of costs. The dashboard designer elected to use a half-filled dot to signify that costs were not being covered versus a full dot, which typically shouts "There's a problem here" but doesn't specify the exact nature of the problem.

The green bars represent this additional potential fee income that a department could be making. You can easily see the ratio of cost to revenue that you *could* have if the department's targets were met.

With the "Show Potential at" drop-down box in Figure 25.5, you can also see the ratio of labor cost to the total fees you *could be* producing if the department hit its utilization target or a variation of that target.

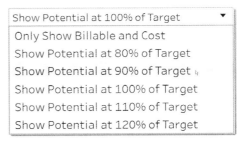

FIGURE 25.5 Drop-down menu allows you to see additional "what-if" revenue at different target rates.

Details

Figure 25.6 shows where all of the nonbillable time across the agency is being spent. Although this dashboard cannot tell you why this time is being spent here, it can point leadership teams in the right direction when they are trying to understand why billable targets are not being met. Maybe leadership has approved too many internal projects or the agency is working on too many new business proposals with

	New Biz + Opp		Internal Projects		Internal Admin	
Creative	1,456 hrs	12%	1,301 hrs	10%	2,992 hrs	24%
Account Management	4,524 hrs	25%	1,579 hrs	9%	4,567 hrs	25%
Project Management	1,455 hrs	12%	2,283 hrs	19%	4,659 hrs	38%
Technology	361 hrs	2%	9,608 hrs	49%	4,485 hrs	23%
Operations	6 hrs	0%	0 hrs	0%	5 hrs	0%
Executive/Admin	0 hrs	0%	4 hrs	0%	2,176 hrs	56%
New Biz	1,764 hrs	80%	40 hrs	2%	546 hrs	25%
	Cost $533K		Cost $755K		Cost $1,163K	

FIGURE 25.6   Details about each department allow leadership to see why goals are not being met.

a low win rate. It is also possible that the agency just has too many employees for the current amount of billable work. Below each of the reports, you can see the actual labor cost (i.e., what employees are being paid to perform this nonbillable work).

Utilization Trend

Utilization trend allows the dashboard user to compare actual versus potential billable percentage for the current year or to compare performance this year with the previous year. The default is to see how billable percentage is tracking against the target over time. (See Figure 25.7.)

Here we can see that the organization did much better in the second half of the year with respect to hitting its target. Note that in this example, we are showing a full year's worth of data. If we only had six weeks of data, the dashboard would show a weekly rather than a monthly view.

This Year versus Last Year

A question that often comes up when looking at any trend data is whether you are performing better this year than you did last year. The utilization trend chart contains a drop-down menu that allows you to switch between the current view and one that compares billable percentages for this year with the previous year. (See Figure 25.8.)

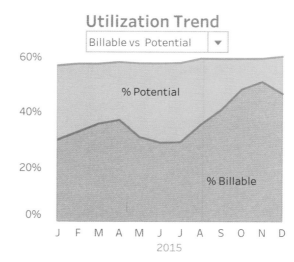

FIGURE 25.7   Comparing actual billable percentage versus goal over time.

Utilization Trend

Year-over-year ▼

2015

2014

22%

FIGURE 25.8 Comparing this year with last year.

Here we can see that billable percentage for the current year (the dark blue line) is up 22 percent overall for the entire year and performed better in every month except for March. We can also see that the peaks and valleys for 2015 parallel those for 2014, suggesting that metrics are cyclical, which should help predict trends for future years.

How Are Individual Departments Performing over Time?

By default, the numbers along the top of the dashboard and the utilization trend show results for the entire organization. You can also focus on individual departments, as shown in Figure 25.9.

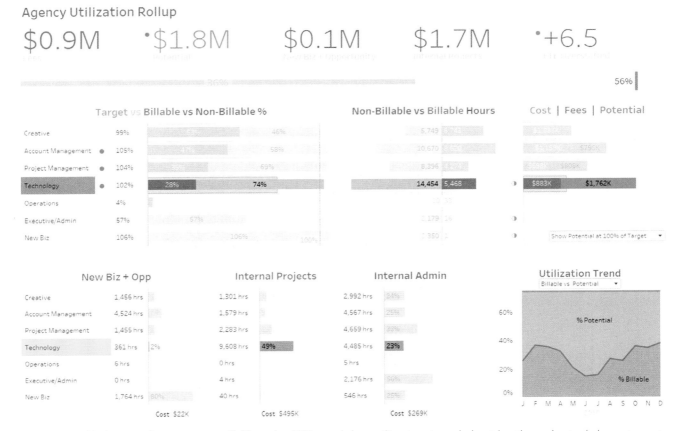

FIGURE 25.9 Clicking a department will filter the KPIs and the utilization trend chart by the selected department.

Why This Works

Problem Areas

The dashboard shows 50 different measures, but the KPI dots make it easy to focus on the areas that are performing poorly. (See Figure 25.10.)

Here we can immediately see that: (1) potential fees compared to actual fees is exceedingly high; (2) the organization is grossly overstaffed; (3) three departments are below target; and (4) three departments are not covering costs.

Big Picture and Color Legend

The numbers at the top of the screen in Figure 25.11 show the organization's performance along five key performance indicators and serve as a color legend.

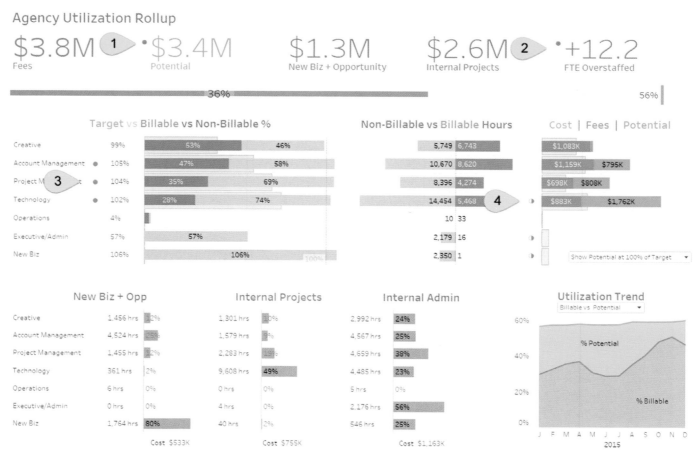

FIGURE 25.10   KPI dots make it easy to see which areas are performing poorly.

$3.8M   •$3.4M $1.3M $2.6M   •+12.2
Fees   Potential   New Biz + Opportunity   Internal Projects   FTE Overstaffed

36%   56%

FIGURE 25.11   Numbers at the top of the screen show key metrics and define color usage throughout the dashboard.

Sparing and Consistent Use of Color

The designer strove to keep the dashboard as uncluttered as possible and managed to avoid having a color legend altogether by using the color in chart titles. (See Figure 25.12.)

Bars Allow Easy Comparison

There's a lot of information encoded in Figure 25.13. Notice that we stack the blue and gray bars to see, overall, which departments are above or below the 100 percent mark, with account management being the highest at 105 percent and operations being the lowest at 4 percent.

The designer placed the blue bars along the baseline so we can easily sort and compare this metric. Even if we removed the numeric labels, it would be easy to see that the blue bar for Creative is roughly twice as long as the blue bar for Technology.

It's important to note that while the comparison of blue bars is easy (because of the common baseline), a comparison of the gray bars is not. Fortunately, comparing the blue bars is of much greater importance, hence its positioning along the baseline.

Behind the stacked bars are wider, lightly colored target bars, making it easy to see which blue bars are above or below target and by how much.

By arranging the bars intelligently and using color and a reference line, we can answer four questions in one compact chart:

1. Which department is working the most hours? (Account Management at 105 percent.)

2. Which department has the highest percentage of billable hours? (Creative with 53 percent.)

FIGURE 25.12   No need for a color legend as the colors are defined in the title.

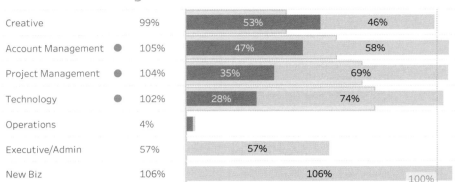

FIGURE 25.13   Lots of bars, intelligently arranged.

3. Which department is comfortably above target? (Creative.)

4. Which departments are considerably below target? (Project Management, which is at around 50 percent of target, and Technology, which is about one-third of the way to hitting its target).

If you need to know the exact numbers, you can hover over a mark, as shown in Figure 25.14.

You may not even need the hover functionality as people are very good at comparing the length of bars.

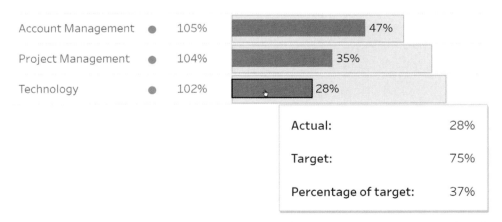

FIGURE 25.14   People really are good at comparing the length of bars using a common baseline, but you can provide details on demand with a pop-up.

Cost | Fees | Potential

FIGURE 25.15   Even at only 80 percent of the target, the organization is leaving a lot of fees on the table.

Trends and Year-over-Year Comparison

The utilization trends allow a quick toggle between showing actual versus target for this year and the actuals for this year when compared to the previous year. Both Figures 25.8 and 25.9 help users see if the organization is doing better or worse over time.

What's Being Left on the Table

The stacked bar chart and what-if drop-down menu really drive home just how much money is being left on the table when the organization isn't hitting its targets. (See Figure 25.15.)

The overarching goal of the dashboard is to change people's behavior. The green bars are a loud wake-up call that says "Look what you could be doing if you got your act together!"

Author Commentary

Steve: If we needed a case study to prove the utility of browsing through different scenarios on the book, this is it. This dashboard came into being after reviewing a half dozen dashboards already slated for the book, and we picked pieces from several of them to use here. For example, we borrowed the stacked bars from Chapter 20: Complaints Dashboard; the large numeric KPIs are from Chapter 2: Course Metrics Dashboard; the KPI dots are from the dashboard in Chapter 6: Ranking by Now, Comparing with Then; and the actuals versus year-over-year comparisons are from Chapter 10: Showing Year-to-Date and Year-over-Year at the Same Time.

I'm looking forward to seeing a new iteration of the dashboard that provides a way to compare one's performance with an industry average.

Jeff: As Steve mentioned, this dashboard represents how we hope people will use this book. As with most of the dashboards in this book, there were many iterations, and it was fun to see the progression. Notice the use of color throughout the dashboard. There are only three colors (blue, green, and gray), and they are used carefully and consistently.

Chapter 26

Health Care Provider Productivity Monitoring

The Provider Productivity report shows performance relative to key metrics.
Dashboard Designer: Jonathan Drummey, DataBlick
Organization: Southern Maine Health Care

Provider Productivity: Parkman, Dolly for FP Androscoggin

Current FTE	**0.75**	Scheduling Efficiency	**100%**	Hire Date 1/1/14	Data through Mar-16
	138 days				

wRVU per Month

Median = 293.4

Avg wRVU per Day
19.8
Median = 25.5

Encounters per Month

Median = 213

Avg Enc per Day
14.3
Median = 18.5

wRVUs/ Encounter

FP Avg = 1.47

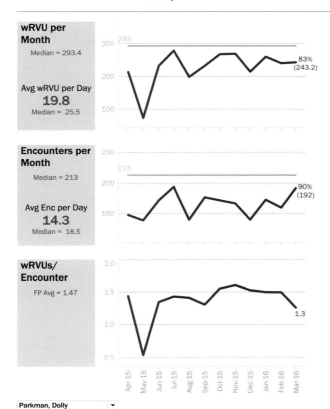

Panel Size

Median = 1,200

Ratio of Billed Level 4 to Level 3 Encounters

FP Avg = 0.93

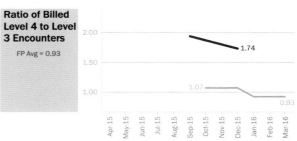

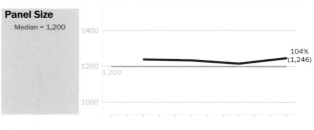

New vs. Established Billed

	Jun-15	Sep-15	Dec-15	Mar-16
New		4	4	
Established		468	424	
Ratio of New vs. Established		0.9%	0.9%	

Parkman, Dolly ▾

SMHC Confidential

Scenario

Big Picture

You are a primary care physician. Your prime role is to care for people, but you need to do it with the highest possible efficiency. When you work with your managers, dashboards like this one help to inform conversations about your efficiency levels. This is important for two reasons:

1. The organizational cost for a primary care physician is several hundred thousand dollars per year. This cost includes salaries for the provider and the necessary staff, office space, equipment, and so on. Southern Maine Health Care (SMHC) is a nonprofit organization with very tight margins in a state with one of the oldest populations in the United States. Therefore, it is necessary to monitor productivity and revenue closely.

2. Variation in practices leads to inefficient resource allocation. For example, you might not have enough patients. You might not be scheduling enough appointments. Each inefficiency increases cost.

Specifics

Factors for evaluating efficiencies include:

- How well are the health care providers performing?
- Are they scheduling appointments efficiently?
- Do they have the right number of patients?
- Are their appointments the right length?

Related Scenarios

This dashboard shows six key metrics and provides guidance in any scenario where you track metrics over time, such as:

- monitoring employee performance,
- assessing call center efficiency, and
- gauging sales targets.

How People Use the Dashboard

Although the dashboard only has five charts and two tables, the data and measures are complex for the common layperson. Let's break down each section and explain how we can identify areas in which Dr. Dolly Parkman[1] from the town of Androscoggin can improve. It turns out she is an established provider whose appointments are too long.

The top section of the dashboard (see Figure 26.1) provides vital contextual information needed to interpret the rest of the charts correctly.

- Current FTE (full-time equivalent) is the employment status, ranging from 0.5 FTE (half time) to 1.0 FTE (full time).
- Scheduling Efficiency shows how much of the provider's schedule is utilized. It excludes unavoidable cancellations and patients who don't show up. The target is 100 percent.
- Hire Date indicates when the provider started working at SMHC.

---

[1] Note: The names used in these dashboards are not the names of real people.

Provider Productivity: Parkman, Dolly for FP Androscoggin

Current FTE   **0.75**   Scheduling   **100%**   Hire Date   Data through Mar-16
                 138 days   Efficiency   1/1/14

FIGURE 26.1   Contextual metrics needed to interpret the charts.

Reading this, we can see that Parkman is a provider in the Androscoggin Family Practice with over two years of service at SMHC. She isn't full time; she is 75 percent of an FTE. Her scheduling efficiency is at 100 percent, meaning she's effectively fully booked each day.

The next chart, Work Relative Value Units (wRVU), shown in Figure 26.2 for Parkman, is a common metric in the United States that is applied to all health care providers. It standardizes the value of the appointments in that it allows the work of different physicians in different specialties (e.g., internal medicine, family practice, surgeons, etc.) to be aligned to the same scale based on a combination of time and acuity (severity).

On the dashboard, wRVU is displayed in two ways. The dark blue line shows monthly totals, and a single metric label in the shaded area shows overall daily average. The light blue line in this and other charts shows targets, which are based on the national

median of that measure. If the wRVU per month value is too far below target, then the health care system will be losing money.

In Parkman's case, the dark blue line shows that over the previous 12 months, she has improved but doesn't seem to be able to reach the median; each month is a little low. Her average wRVU per day is 19.8 and is red, indicating that it too is low.

The chart shows both the monthly wRVU and daily average because the monthly total is subject to fluctuation due to vacations, snow days, and so on. The daily average better reflects actual day-to-day work.

The next chart, Encounters per Month, shows the number of patient visits to the provider. (See Figure 26.3.) This is displayed as a monthly total (dark blue line) and daily average (label in the shaded area), again with a target (light blue line) based on the national median and FTE adjusted.

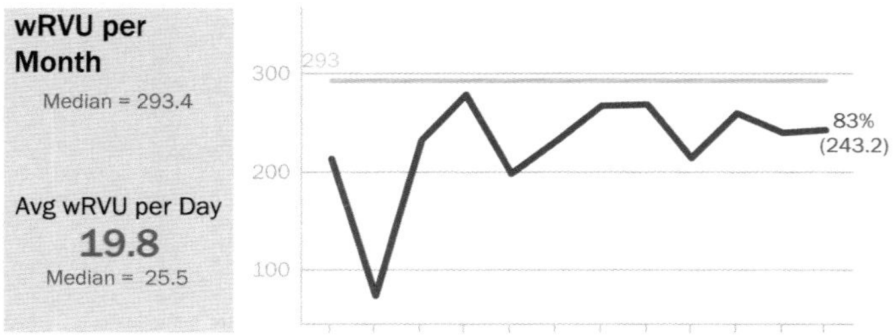

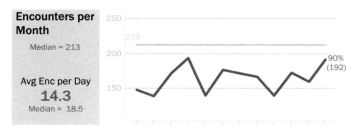

wRVU per Month
Median = 293.4

Avg wRVU per Day
19.8
Median = 25.5

300 — 293
200
100
83%
(243.2)

FIGURE 26.2   wRVU per month for Dolly Parkman.

Encounters per Month
Median = 213

Avg Enc per Day
14.3
Median = 18.5

250
213
200
150
90%
(192)

FIGURE 26.3   Encounters per month (i.e., how many patient visits there were).

Here we see that Parkman is also missing her appointment targets. Her average is only 14.3 a day compared to a national median of 18.5, and the line shows that she's been below target every month. Seeing too few patients directly affects revenue, so Parkman and her office staff need to work to increase appointments.

The next chart, wRVUs/Encounter (see Figure 26.4), shows the number of wRVUs divided by the number of encounters for each month. The average for the prior quarter (1.47) for the provider's specialty is displayed as a benchmark.

Unlike the other charts, there is no reference line for this measure. At the time of writing, this is a new measure for the providers, and a target has not been established.

For Parkman, we can see that while both the metrics are low, quality has been stable following a big dip in May 2015. The most recent month (March 2016) has seen a dip too, which is something to be monitored in future months.

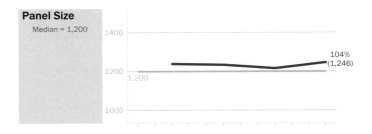

FIGURE 26.5   Panel size (i.e., the number of patients the practitioner has).

"Panel Size" (see Figure 26.5) is the number of patients associated with the primary care physician. The target (not shown on the dashboard) is 1,600 for a full-time provider and is adjusted based on the FTE.

Parkman is 0.75 FTE, so her panel size is lower (1,200). We can see that her panel is slightly over target, within acceptable range.

Figure 26.6, Ratio of Billed Level 4 to Level 3 Encounters, shows a key ratio. Patient visits (encounters) are coded according to the level of acuity, where Level 5 is most severe and Level 1 is least severe.

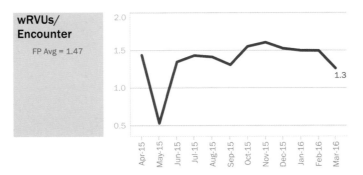

FIGURE 26.4   wRVUs per encounter is a measure of quantity and acuity.

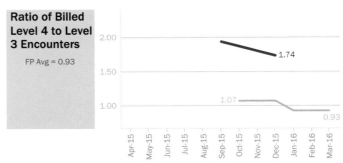

FIGURE 26.6   Ratio of Level 4 to Level 3 encounters. This chart helps users understand if charges are being correctly attributed.

The higher an encounter's level, the higher its reimbursement rate. If the ratio—the amount of Level 4 and Level 3 visits—is too low, then it could indicate that providers are not properly documenting the acuity of their patients. If it is too high, it could indicate *up-coding*, assigning a higher level than a patient's condition warrants, which is a form of medical fraud.

At the time the screenshots were taken, the data was available only quarterly and no targets were set, so the family practice (FP) average is shown on the left as a comparison (currently 0.93). This measure is an explanatory factor for wRVU totals and wRVU per encounter. Parkman's ratios were on the high side so even though her encounter totals were quite a bit below target in late 2015, her wRVU totals were close to target.

Figure 26.7, New vs. Established Billed, shows the number and ratio of new patients visiting the practice compared to the number of existing patients. The data ranges here can be quite large, ranging from a fraction of a percentage point for an established provider with a full practice to a percentage increase of tenfold or more for a brand-new provider.

New vs. Established Billed

	Jun-15	Sep-15	Dec-15	Mar-16
New		4	4	
Established		468	424	
Ratio of New vs. Established		0.9%	0.9%	

FIGURE 26.7   New versus Established Billed patients shows the numbers of new and existing patients.

Parkman's panel size is growing slowly. Since we know her panel size is a little above target anyway, there is no issue to track in this chart.

What have we learned about Parkman? She is an established provider who does not have enough patient appointments, leading to missing targets for wRVU.

This view makes it clear that the next step is to look at Parkman's schedule in more detail. Improving office workflow and office setup, shortening appointment times, or altering the provider's paperwork processes could address and help fix the problems shown in the dashboard.

Let's look at one more example to show how the dashboard can display other issues. (See Figure 26.8.) Harlan Palmyra is a provider in the Oxford Family Practice and an employee of SMHC since September 2014.

In this case, there are three areas of red on this dashboard where Palmyra misses targets: (1) scheduling efficiency is only 86 percent; (2) average wRVU per day is 11.6, against a median of 25.5; and (3) encounters per day is 7.2, compared to a median of 18.6.

On the wRVU per month and encounters per month line charts (4 and 5) we can see a rise a little over a year ago when Palmyra was in his first year. It's leveled off since then, remaining consistently below target.

The low scheduling efficiency of encounters per day might be the cause of Palmyra's missed targets, but the dashboard shows the problem goes a little deeper than that. The panel size is at 938, or 67 percent of target (6), and that's most likely why there's so much empty space in the schedule and not enough encounters.

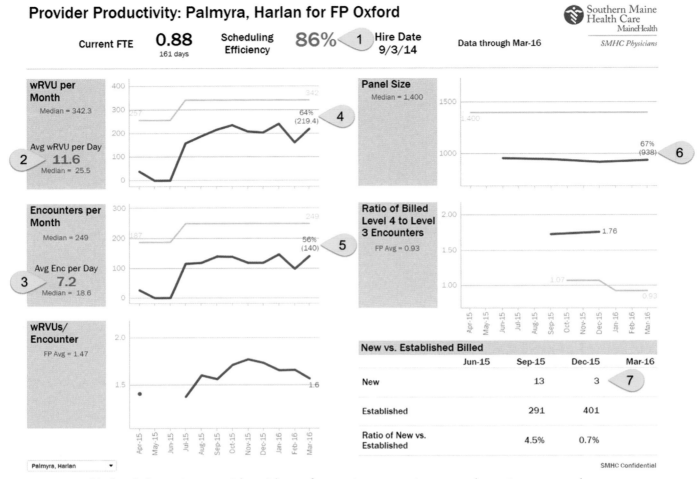

FIGURE 26.8   Harlan Palmyra is a provider with too few patients, causing several metrics to go red.

Even more worrisome in this case is the New vs. Established Billed chart. In the most recent quarter, with data ending December 2015, Palmyra had only three new patients (7). That number needs to grow to get more patients into his practice and fill out his schedule.

In conclusion, this provider has too few patients and is not attracting new ones. This situation would call for investigation of the provider's patient experience scores to see if there were any issues with regard to reputation. Also, increasing advertising to promote availability for new patients could help.

Why This Works

Print-Friendly Design

SMHC calls this a "report" rather than a dashboard because it has not been designed for interactivity. The report is formatted for a landscape display and often is printed. Although we may aspire to having fully interactive, paperless work environments, many times this is not achievable. In cases such as health care, design-for-print is still vital.

Appropriate Targets on Reference Lines

The term "median" is used instead of "target" on Figure 26.9 because the idea is to communicate that the goal is to be as good as the national median. The medians are adjusted according to each physician and his or her FTE level. Using the median allows providers to determine whether they are meeting national benchmarks or not.

KPIs Stand Out

You need to know if a metric is being missed. In this dashboard, the key KPIs are stated as numbers. If they are below target, they are red. This is

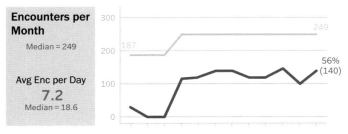

FIGURE 26.9 "Medians" are used rather than "targets."

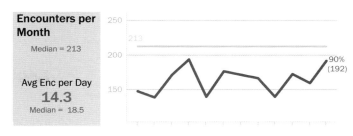

FIGURE 26.10 Shading and white space used to emphasize the data.

a simple and effective way to emphasize the numbers using preattentive attributes such as color. (See Figures 26.9 and 26.10)

White Space and Shading

The dashboard is designed so that there is adequate white space to allow the data to stand out and not be overwhelmed by complexity. (See Figure 26.10.) Borders, lines, and shading were removed wherever possible to allow lines and numbers to pop out.

The left-hand side of Figure 26.11 shows a section of the dashboard with no shading and with a y-axis that spreads to the full range of the measure. The right-hand side shows the shading used in the actual dashboard and the dynamically extended range. The shading provides a better visual indicator of the different sections of the dashboard, and the extended axis gives the data space "to breathe."

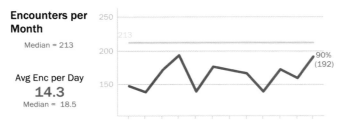
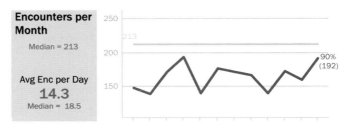

FIGURE 26.11   Two versions of the charts: with shading and dynamic axis on the right, without them on the left.

Shading and white space

Shading and white space, used subtly, create distinct zones on your dashboards.

Shading of the chart title areas uses the Gestalt principle of closure to create the region for each chart.

In the line charts, the y-axes automatically extend beyond the range of the data. This subtle approach ensures there is an amount of white space within the data area of the chart itself. It allows the data to sit more comfortably in its space.

Good Use of Tables

Why did the designers use a table in the bottom right of the dashboard rather than a visualization? Shouldn't we always visualize data when we can? In this case, there are three good reasons for using a table:

1. The possible data ranges are very large. In the example shown in Figure 26.12, the provider had four new patients in December 2015, adding to a panel of 424 existing patients (0.9 percent). Some providers might have a panel of 1,600+ patients and only a handful of new patients each month.

Others might have a small panel and many new patients.

2. The ratio of new to established patients is anywhere from a fraction of a percentage to over 10 percent. Drawing a chart that works for all these ranges is hard.

3. The data is available quarterly so there are really only eight data points, and there is not a need for trending view

---

When to use a table

A well-formatted table can be more useful than a chart when scales are varied or when there is a need to look up exact values of data.

New vs. Established Billed

	Jun-15	Sep-15	Dec-15	Mar-16
New		4	4	
Established		468	424	
Ratio of New vs. Established		0.9%	0.9%	

FIGURE 26.12   Sometimes a table is better than a chart.

Author Commentary

ANDY: The designer of this dashboard packed it full of subtle but important features to make it easy to understand. The gray shading and dynamically extended y-axes are two examples. Each one makes a small incremental improvement. However, make 10, or 20, small incremental changes, and the final impact is very large.

It is my experience over many years that the Pareto principle applies to effective dashboard design: 80 percent of the layout and design work will be done in 20 percent of the time. The remaining 80 percent of your time will be spent making small tweaks to formatting, layout, and annotation layers. This time should be spent in collaboration with the users of the dashboards.

Just because it's time consuming doesn't mean you should ignore it: You mustn't. Those final changes make the biggest difference to the successful adoption of a dashboard.

One thing I would change on this dashboard is to encode a missed target using more than just color. In this dashboard, missed targets are blue if met and red if missed. That's okay, but it might not be something that immediately pops out. There is also a chance some people with color vision deficiency might not be able to distinguish the red and blue correctly, especially when used for the targets on the gray-shaded areas. This could be fixed with a small dot, arrow, or other KPI indicator next to missed target numbers, as shown in Figure 26.13.

For other examples of dots or arrows used to highlight missed targets, see Chapter 6: Ranking by Now, Comparing with Then, and Chapter 8: Multiple Key Performance Metrics.

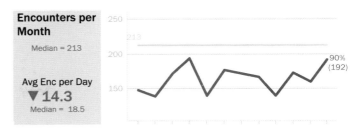

FIGURE 26.13   An arrow or similar indicator next to a missed target provides a clearer visual encoding than just using color.

JEFF: This dashboard designer applied the Gestalt principle well, but a bit too much for me. Sometimes in dashboard design, designers put borders around everything: every chart, every title, and the dashboard itself. I guess they think if they put their data in jail, we will feel safer about it all.

In this dashboard, the designer took great care to eliminate some of these borders. For example, there are no chart borders, just x- and y-axis lines. However, the gray boxes create additional separation that, in my opinion, is not needed. In addition, by putting the red KPI in a gray box, the red is muted when compared to what it would be on white.

Finally, I try to avoid rotated text whenever possible. In this dashboard, each month is labeled and the text is rotated 90 degrees. I would consider spacing those labels out and formatting in a way that I could avoid rotated text.

Figure 26.14 shows a version of the dashboard without the gray shading and with horizontal axis labels.

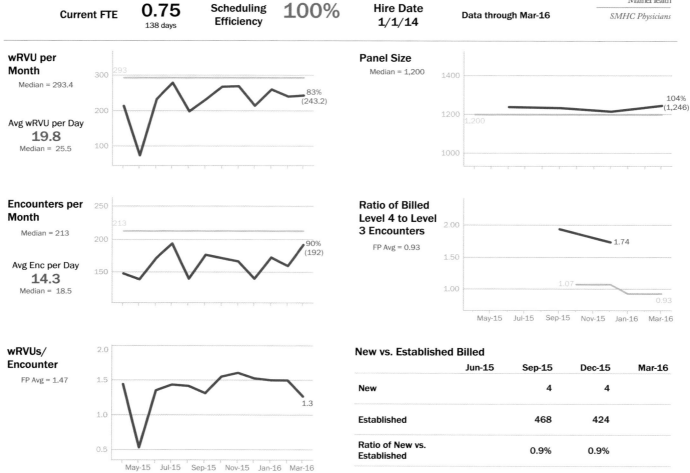

Provider Productivity: Parkman, Dolly for FP Androscoggin

Current FTE	**0.75** 138 days	Scheduling Efficiency	**100%**	Hire Date 1/1/14

Data through Mar-16

wRVU per Month
Median = 293.4

Avg wRVU per Day
19.8
Median = 25.5

300 — 293
200
100

83%
(243.2)

Panel Size
Median = 1,200

1400
1200 — 1,200
1000

104%
(1,246)

Encounters per Month
Median = 213

Avg Enc per Day
14.3
Median = 18.5

250
213
200
150

90%
(192)

Ratio of Billed Level 4 to Level 3 Encounters
FP Avg = 0.93

2.00
1.74
1.50
1.07
1.00
0.93

May-15 Jul-15 Sep-15 Nov-15 Jan-16 Mar-16

wRVUs/ Encounter
FP Avg = 1.47

2.0
1.5
1.0
0.5

1.3

May-15 Jul-15 Sep-15 Nov-15 Jan-16 Mar-16

New vs. Established Billed

	Jun-15	Sep-15	Dec-15	Mar-16
New		4	4	
Established		468	424	
Ratio of New vs. Established		0.9%	0.9%	

Parkman, Dolly ▾

SMHC Confidential

FIGURE 26.14   The dashboard with the shading removed and the axis labels horizontally laid out.

Chapter 27

Telecom Operator Executive Dashboard

Telecom operator executive dashboard.

Source: Images courtesy of Dundas Data Visualization, Inc. (www.dundas.com)

Dashboard Designer: Mark Wevers

Organization: Dundas Data Visualization

Source: https://samples.dundas.com/Dashboard/f78d570f-1896-441e-9b5e-90e0999db630?vo=viewonly

CTT Wireless
Created by Dundas Data Visualization Inc.

Goal 1: Reduce Subscriber Acquisition Cost

SAC **+4 YTD**

$16

PER MONTH OF CONTRACT

SAC by Contract Term
Monthly Average

- 1 yr
- 2 yr
- 3 yr

Devices Sourced from ODMs

Q1	80,900
Q2	80,700
Q3	101,000
Q4	114,100

Service Calls
During First 3 Months Svc

— FY 2014   FY 2015

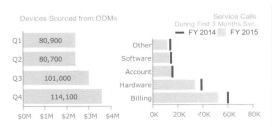

- Other
- Software
- Account
- Hardware
- Billing

Goal 2: Increase Average Revenue Per User

ARPU **+6 YTD**

$68

MONTHLY POSTPAID

ARPU by Plan Type

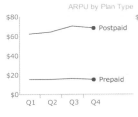

- Postpaid
- Prepaid

Voice, Data and Addons
Total Subscribers

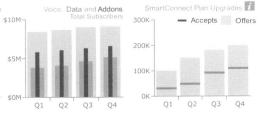

SmartConnect Plan Upgrades

— Accepts   Offers

Goal 3: Reduce Churn

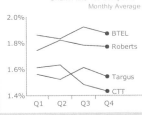

Churn **-0.18 YTD**

1.43 %

MONTHLY POSTPAID

Churn Rate vs. Competition
Monthly Average

- BTEL
- Roberts
- Targus
- CTT

Customer Support

Hold time	1st Call Res
80 s	**91** %

Call Length	Open Tickets
11 m	**8210**

Customer Satisfaction

— FY 2014   FY 2015

- Support
- Value
- Phones
- Network

Executive Summary

	FY 2014	FY 2015
Revenue:	$6.87B	$7.28B
OPEX:	$4.16B	$4.54B
EBITDA:	$2.71B	$2.74B

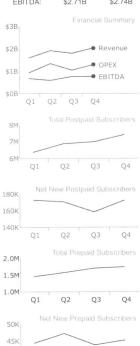

Financial Summary

- Revenue
- OPEX
- EBITDA

Total Postpaid Subscribers

Net New Postpaid Subscribers

Total Prepaid Subscribers

Net New Prepaid Subscribers

Scenario

Big Picture

You are an executive at a telecom company, and you need to know if you are on track to meet the strategic goals. Like many other businesses, you want to reduce the cost of acquiring new subscribers, increase the average revenue per user, and reduce churn. You need a dashboard to provide all these details to the executive level of the organization. The dashboard does not need to be interactive, but it needs to summarize all of the key information in a way that can be presented in a senior management/board of directors/stakeholders meeting.

Specifics

- You have three main goals to track: subscriber acquisition costs (SAC), average revenue per user (ARPU), and churn.

- You need to see the results of each goal over time, year to date (YTD). Then, next to it, you need to see the key risk indicators and key performance indicators that could be driving that goal.

- You need to see an executive summary of key financial information across revenue, operating expenses (OPEX), and earnings before interest, taxes, depreciation, and amortization (EBITDA) for the last four quarters and in comparison to the previous year's results.

- You need to see subscribers over the last four quarters across all key categories, such as total subscribers and net new subscribers for both prepaid and postpaid plans.

Related Scenarios

- You need to organize your dashboard by high-level goals and break down the drivers of those goals.
- You need a detailed summary, often a trend over time, of many metrics on a single view.
- You need to review SAC and/or churn. You need to compare the current period with a previous period.
- You need to review your call center metrics and their impact on your customers. This could include churn, likelihood to recommend, customer satisfaction surveys, or customer reviews.

How People Use the Dashboard

The dashboard is designed with four key areas: three goals and an executive summary. The three goals are laid out as rows, with four charts each (left to right). An executive summary is shown vertically on the right-hand side of the dashboard.

The first goal is to reduce SAC. (See Figure 27.1.) This metric is also called "cost per acquisition" and is a key metric used by many different types of businesses. In this scenario, the wireless company is measuring the cost to acquire a subscriber. The SAC has gone up, which is a bad thing, so it is shown in red along with a small red callout box that shows the cost has increased $4 year to date (YTD). A line chart shows the SAC is going up from Q1 to Q4 across all contract types but also shows the cost is higher for one-year contracts than for three-year contracts. The third chart shows devices from original design manufacturers (ODMs) by quarter, showing the dollars on the x-axis and number of devices as data labels. The last chart shows a bar for fiscal year 2015 against a target line of fiscal year 2014.

Goal 1: Reduce Subscriber Acquisition Cost

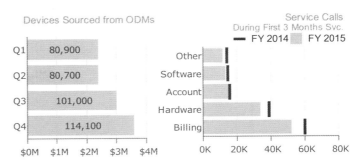

FIGURE 27.1   Four charts showing the key metrics for the first goal.

Be careful when using red and green

When using red and green together, consider an accommodation for people with color vision deficiency. In this case, the author uses a +/− indicator in the small box to indicate that costs are going up or going down.

The second goal is to increase the ARPU. (See Figure 27.2.) This has a very similar layout as the first goal. There are four charts from left to right showing the key metrics. The reader can quickly see the overall ARPU, the ARPU by plan type, total subscribers for three categories, and the number of offers for plan upgrades and how many subscribers accepted the offers. ARPU is going up, which is a good thing,

Goal 2: Increase Average Revenue Per User

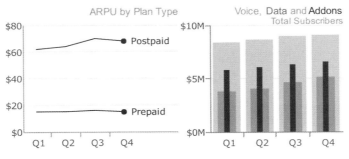
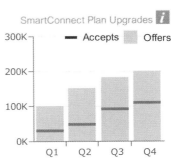

FIGURE 27.2   Four charts showing the key metrics for the second goal.

Goal 3: Reduce Churn

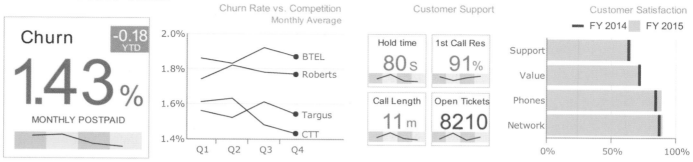

FIGURE 27.3   Four charts showing the key metrics for the third goal.

so it's shown in green with a callout box indicator showing a $6 increase YTD.

The third goal is to reduce churn. (See Figure 27.3.) Every business loses customers over time. As seen in Goal 1, it's expensive to get new customers, so keeping the current customers satisfied can be very important. As with the previous goals, there are four chart components in a row from left to right.

The first chart is the key metric with a sparkline showing the trend over the four quarters underneath. Churn is decreasing, which is a good thing, so this is shown in green, and the callout box indicates a decrease of 18 basis points YTD. The second chart is a line chart showing the monthly average churn rate over time for CTT Wireless and three of its competitors. The third chart has four small boxes showing four key metrics for the call center, and the last chart shows overall customer satisfaction for fiscal year 2015 (the bar) versus fiscal year 2014 (the target line).

The right-hand side of the dashboard has an executive summary showing a quick review of key financial metrics. (See Figure 27.4.) Revenue, operating expenses, and

EBITDA are shown at the top for fiscal years 2014 and 2015 and then graphed on a line chart for the last four quarters. Four line charts show the total customers and net new customers (i.e., new customers acquired in Goal 1 minus customers lost from churn in Goal 3). This is shown for both postpaid and prepaid plans.

Why This Works

Key Metrics Displayed without Clutter

This dashboard captures all the key data required to answer the business questions at an executive level without having to go very deep into other reports and the data. It's packed full of data but does not feel cluttered. This is accomplished by using small, well-designed visuals that employ different techniques to make it so compact.

For example, the line charts showing time-series data have trailing labels. (See Figure 27.5.) It's clear which line refers to which company without having to add a color or shape legend.

Color banding is used on the sparklines for the four quarters instead of additional labels. (See Figure 27.6.)

Executive Summary

	FY 2014	FY 2015
Revenue:	$6.87B	$7.28B
OPEX:	$4.16B	$4.54B
EBITDA:	$2.71B	$2.74B

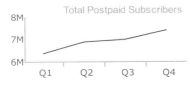

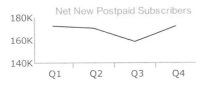

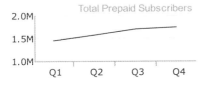

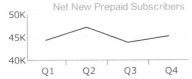

FIGURE 27.4 Executive summary showing the key financial metrics and number of customers.

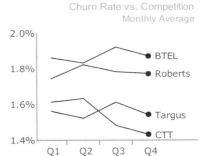

FIGURE 27.5 Line chart showing average monthly churn for last four quarters. Placing labels at the ends of the lines eliminates the need for color and a legend.

FIGURE 27.6 Four key metrics for call center performance. Sparklines and color bands for the four quarters allow these metrics to fit in a small space with a lot of information encoded.

Layout Supports Quick Reading

Using the Gestalt principals of design, such as proximity and closure, the dashboard provides insight into the four areas, each with the necessary detail, in an organized fashion. The key metrics are laid out in three rows and a single column, which makes them easy to group together and quickly scan. (See Figure 27.7.)

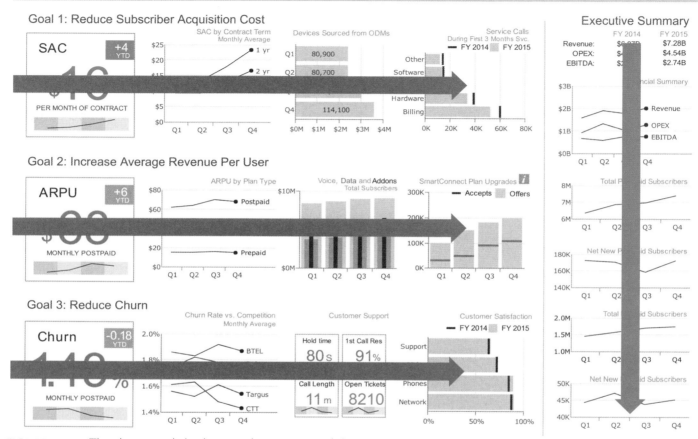

FIGURE 27.7 The three goals laid out in three rows and the executive summary in a column on the right allow for easy scanning of the information.

Good Chart Types for the Various Comparisons

Line charts are an excellent choice for showing a trend over time. They are used throughout this dashboard to show various metrics over the last four quarters. Sparklines are used to show the trends under the key metrics. Bar charts with target lines are used to show this period versus the previous period as a quick gauge of progress.

Starting the axis at zero

On graphs that use length, height, or area to encode the data for comparison from a common baseline (e.g., bar chart, bullet graph, lollipop chart, area chart), always start the axis at zero; otherwise, you will distort the comparison of the data. If encoding with position (e.g., dot plot, box plot, line chart), breaking the axis away from zero sometimes can be useful and will not distort the comparison of the data.

Author Commentary

JEFF: I really like the design and layout of this dashboard. I also like the minimal use of color. However, it's best to avoid red and green together (as discussed in Chapter 1: Data Visualization: A Primer). The little numbers, showing positive and negative, will help, but it still may not be clear to someone with color vision deficiency which numbers are good and which are bad. I would change this to blue for good and red or orange for bad. In addition, in Goal 1 on the third chart, Devices Sourced from ODMs, I would recommend flipping time to the x-axis. Every other time chart has the four quarters on the x-axis, and it would be best to do that for this chart as well. It could remain a bar chart or could be changed to a line chart like the others. This would help the reader see the trend over time better than what is shown here. Also, while the third chart in Goal 2 shows a good comparison of the subscribers, a line chart with three lines would be better.

ANDY: This is another dashboard where the design dial has been turned to 11, resulting in a dashboard that creates a sense of calm as you explore it. I especially like the simplified color palette across the dashboard.

It is possible to reduce colors too far. Consider Churn Rate vs. Competition on the bottom row. Do the lines for Targus and CTT cross, or do they merely converge before diverging again? Using the same color for all lines on a chart might cause confusion if they overlap. In Figure 27.8, you can see an example where this could be a problem. Look at sales in West and East regions: Can you tell where they overlap?

There are possible solutions, without reverting back to multiple colors. Figure 27.9 shows two examples. The one on the left puts the lines side by side in their own panes; the one on the right uses a palette of grays.

Note that both options work only with a small number of categories.

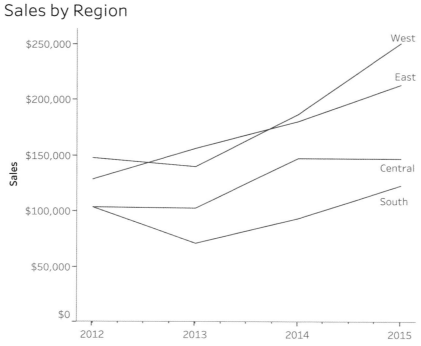

FIGURE 27.8 Which line is for the West region and which is for the East region?

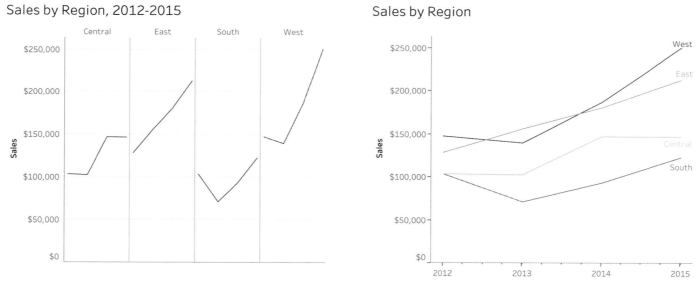

FIGURE 27.9 Two solutions to the problem of overlapping lines.

Chapter 28

Economy at a Glance

The U.S. economy at a glance.
Dashboard Designers: Sam Fleming, Emily Cadman, Steven Bernard, and Tom Pearson
Organization: *Financial Times*

Scenario

Big Picture

What are the states of the U.S., U.K., Japanese, and Chinese economies? Within each of those economies, which common economic indicators are rising and which are falling? What are the key takeaways for each? If you want more information, are there some key stories or source data to be looked at?

The economic snapshots from the *Financial Times* (*FT*) (a close up is shown in Figure 28.1) answer all of those questions for readers, researchers, economists, and journalists. This dashboard is a full snapshot of an economy. The *FT* has built the dashboards for the United States, the United Kingdom, Japan, and China.

Specifics

- You run an organization that is arranged into a number of discrete areas, each of which has two or three key metrics to track.

- You need to show actual and forecast values for all areas of a business with many ways of measuring performance.

- You need to add commentary at a macro and micro detail to explain the results.

- You need a dashboard that is mobile responsive.

FIGURE 28.1   Detail from the U.S. economy dashboard.

Related Scenarios

- You need a detailed executive dashboard that requires multiple metrics alongside brief commentary on each category of metrics.

How People Use the Dashboard

For economists, researchers, or journalists, it is useful to have a common reference for the state of a country's economy. The *FT* produces four dashboards, for the United Kingdom, United States, China, and Japan. Each dashboard brings together indicators that define an economy.

The data is updated once every 15 minutes. Text commentary and annotations are updated by journalists around once a week. These dashboards are reliable references for anyone seeking an economic profile of one of the four featured countries.

Each economy is broken down into major sections, such as gross domestic product (GDP), manufacturing, construction, and interest rates. Each section has up to four "cards." The U.S. labor market is shown in Figure 28.2. The first card, on the left, is a short commentary from a journalist that is updated weekly. To the right of the commentary card are up to three more cards, each with one metric relevant to that section.

The dashboard is designed to be responsive. On a desktop browser, the cards are stacked horizontally in each section. On a mobile device with a narrow

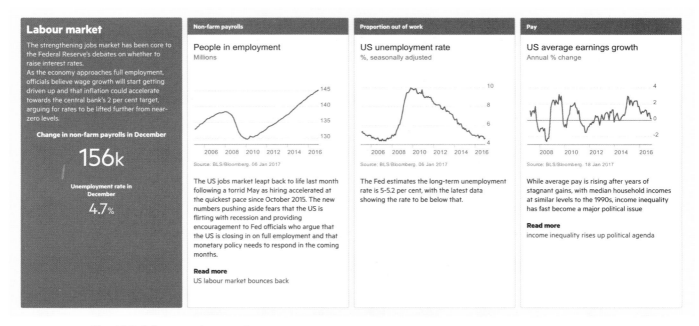

FIGURE 28.2 The U.S. labor market section.

screen, however, the cards are stacked vertically. Viewers are expected to scroll vertically through the metrics.

Why This Works

Links to Source Data

The dashboards are designed for economic experts and other users alike. In order to satisfy the various users, the charts themselves are kept as simple as possible so that all viewers can interpret them. Links to source data or relevant articles are added so that anyone may go find further details. (See Figure 28.3.)

The links are generally focused on the source data used to build the charts. The *FT* wishes to build trust in its journalism and its data. In the media and in politics, there is often a feeling that data is being manipulated to reinforce particular opinions. By crediting and linking to the source data, the *FT* is encouraging critics to visit the source data so they may check the *FT*'s interpretations.

Text Annotations and Commentary

Whether you are an economist by profession or an interested layperson, having commentary that frames the data and establishes a context will

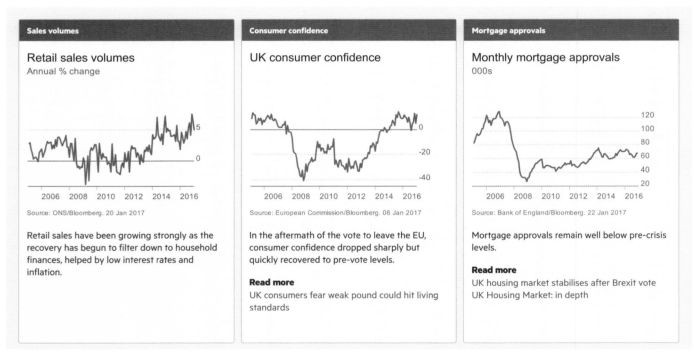

FIGURE 28.3   The UK consumer section shows data sources and links to new stories.

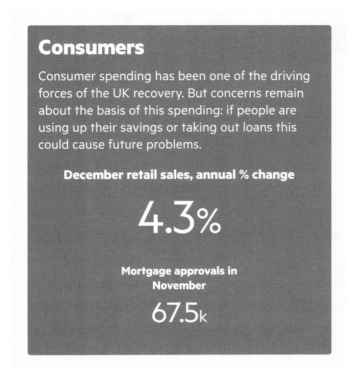

FIGURE 28.4 A picture may not always be worth 1,000 words: Journalists regularly update the commentary on each section.

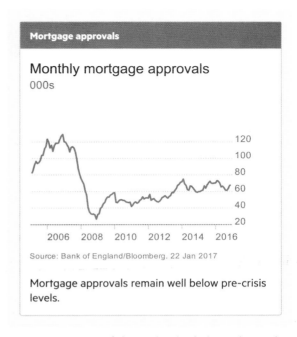

FIGURE 28.5 Many of the individual charts have their own short commentary.

help guide your understanding of the charts. (See Figure 28.4.)

On this dashboard, there is a main commentary card for each section with the headline story. If the section can be categorized with just one or two numbers, the numbers also will be shown. In the example for UK consumer charts, retail sales and mortgage approvals are highlighted as the key metrics. (See Figure 28.5.)

Commentary sections take up what can be valuable space on your dashboard. If your audience consists of people who know the data intimately,

you might not need the text. The audience for the *FT*'s economy dashboards range from amateur to expert. Therefore, the dashboards need to cater to all audiences, making the commentary a great addition.

Furthermore, because the dashboard adapts to mobile devices, it does not have a space restriction: People can keep scrolling down to find the information they need.

Formatting

There are many formatting choices in the dashboard in Figure 28.6, which make for a very easy-to-interpret and pleasing experience when consuming the data.

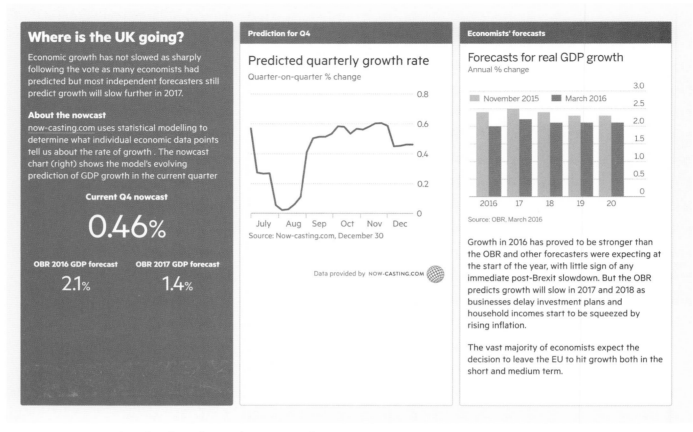

FIGURE 28.6   A multitude of intelligent formatting choices.

These decisions are consistent across all the charts. In fact, this chart style is consistent throughout the *FT*'s media.

- Gridlines are shown for the y-axis only (i.e., horizontal in Figure 28.6).

- Axes for bar charts always extend from zero. Axes for line charts always show the range from minimum to maximum.

- A white background is used to show forecasts which can be seen in Figure 28.7.

- Three shades of gray are used in the font as a hierarchy. The most important, the title, is darkest (and largest). Subtitles, axis labels, and legends are a little lighter. Finally, the data source text, the least important for understanding, is lightest. This hierarchy draws the eye to the most important aspects first.

Good formatting, applied across an organization, makes it easier for people to parse data they consume. As they become accustomed to the style, they can spend more time focusing on the data and less on understanding the layout, axis styles, tick marks, and so on.

Nowcasting

In many organizations, looking forward is more important than looking backward. Economics might be the field where forecasting is most important. In the case shown in Figure 28.7, the *FT* uses "nowcasting" data provided by Now-Casting Economics (https://www.now-casting.com). This example is from July 2016 when Nowcasting data was available.

Note

Nowcasting measures multiple other indicators to show the change in GDP in real time, ahead of the official GDP figure publication.

Nowcasting is a statistical method of calculating how a metric is evolving in real time before official figures are released. Data indicating how the economy is changed is released on an almost daily basis, but there is a considerable lag before official GDP figures are calculated. Nowcasting attempts to use all of these intermediate data releases to give a snapshot of how GDP looks at present. As a method, it is increasingly gaining credibility in economic circles as an alternative to more traditional, judgment-based forecasting methods.

Nowcasting has proven to have lower errors than traditional, judgmental methods of predicting low-frequency metrics such as GDP.

Prediction for Q2

Predicted quarterly growth rate

Quarter-on-quarter % change

Source: Now-casting.com, May 03

The now-cast of UK GDP growth in Q2 fell last week, from 0.52% to 0.40% quarter-on-quarter. This was partly due to the release of the first official estimate for Q1 GDP growth on Wednesday, which was slightly weaker than anticipated by the model (0.40% actual vs 0.56% anticipated). This was compounded by negative news from three surveys for April: the CBI's retail sales survey, the GfK consumer confidence survey, and the EU's Economic Sentiment Indicator, all of which showed weakening conditions.

Data provided by **NOW-CASTING.COM**

FIGURE 28.7   The UK economy on May 3, 2016. The Q2 GDP results are not due until after June 2016.

Responsive Card Design for Mobile

As we move away from our desktops and laptops to doing more and more of our daily work on mobile devices, dashboards are being built to work within these new paradigms. Traditional single-screen dashboards enable everything to be seen at once, but this is not always practical on smaller screens. We could show less information in order to pack it all onto one screen. Alternatively, since scrolling is the fast, universal way of moving through information on small screens, we could stack the information vertically. (See Figure 28.8.)

In the *FT*'s dashboard, this method works particularly well. Each card is distinct. This means that viewers don't need to see two views simultaneously in order to relate one chart to another.

FIGURE 28.8 The cards stack in different ways depending on the viewing device. Shown here are iPhone and iPad views.

Relevant Metrics

All economies are different, and attempting to use the same metrics for all of them will fail. Some metrics are common to all economies, such as GDP, employment, and inflation. Some metrics that well represent one economy might not work when applied to another. The *FT* dashboards recognize this by varying the metrics for each economy, showing the most relevant ones. For example, in the consumer sections, the U.S. dashboard uses sales of single-family homes. In the UK dashboard, mortgage approvals are shown; and in Japan dashboard, motor vehicle sales are shown (See Figure 28.9).

In each case, the *FT* has chosen a metric that is best suited to that scenario. This is undoubtedly harder work for the designers, but ultimately it shows the most relevant analysis for each individual economy.

This extra work for the designers is a real challenge in businesses. Often we build a single dashboard for all categories of business, even though a metric useful for one category might not be useful for another. It is important to track the most relevant data for each area of business, even if this means maintaining more dashboards and training users to use each one.

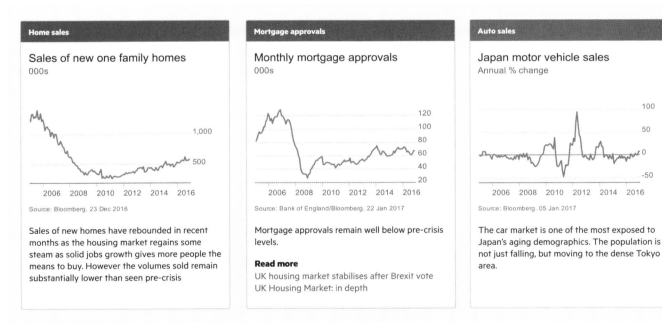

Home sales

Sales of new one family homes
000s

Source: Bloomberg. 23 Dec 2016

Sales of new homes have rebounded in recent months as the housing market regains some steam as solid jobs growth gives more people the means to buy. However the volumes sold remain substantially lower than seen pre-crisis

Mortgage approvals

Monthly mortgage approvals
000s

Source: Bank of England/Bloomberg. 22 Jan 2017

Mortgage approvals remain well below pre-crisis levels.

Read more
UK housing market stabilises after Brexit vote
UK Housing Market: in depth

Auto sales

Japan motor vehicle sales
Annual % change

Source: Bloomberg. 05 Jan 2017

The car market is one of the most exposed to Japan's aging demographics. The population is not just falling, but moving to the dense Tokyo area.

FIGURE 28.9   Three different ways of measuring consumer indicators. For the United States, the *FT* uses sales of new one-family homes. In the UK, it shows monthly mortgage approvals. In Japan, it shows motor vehicle sales.

No Arbitrary Interactivity

The economic dashboards have been designed with mobile viewing in mind. The designers chose not to add any interactivity. They felt that on a small screen, there was simply not enough to be gained from adding interactivity. Sure, they could have added tool tips to allow for lookup of exact figures, but they felt that it's not possible to point accurately using a finger-pressing gesture. Choosing instead to focus on a consistent, simple design, along with links to further details, lessens the need for interactivity.

When designing your own dashboards, do not add interactivity for the sake of doing so. Consider how and why you incorporate it into the dashboard. The following questions are helpful:

- Why does a viewer need to interact with the dashboard?
- What extra insight will be gained through the interactivity?

- Does the interactivity work correctly, whatever device the viewer is using?
- If users cannot interact with the dashboard, can they still get the insight they need?

Author Commentary

ANDY: "Great designers produce pleasurable experience," says Don Norman in *The Design of Everyday Things* (Basic Books, 2013). He goes on to describe three types of processing that control our reaction to things we interact with: visceral, behavioral, and reflective. The visceral response is about immediate perception. "This is where style matters," he says. Some people dismiss the visceral response, saying the purity of the functional design is the single most important thing. But functionality is of no use if people don't like your dashboard.

The formatting choices outlined in this chapter create a strong visceral response in me. Reading and interpreting these dashboards is a pleasure and makes me want to return to see updates.

Chapter 29

Call Center

Call center dashboard.

Source: Images courtesy of Dundas Data Visualization, Inc. (www.dundas.com)
Dashboard Designer: Jeff Hainsworth
Organization: Dundas Data Visualization
Source: https://samples.dundas.com/Dashboard/c397551a-e1f0-48e2-bb22-fa0def388063?vo=viewonly

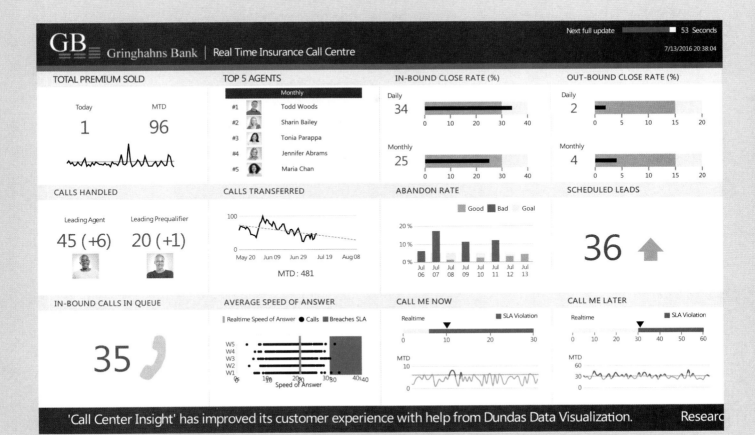

Scenario

Big Picture

You are the manager of a call center handling sales calls for an insurance company. You want real-time performance data for your group based on a number of key metrics. You want to see how many calls are being handled, both inbound and outbound calls, and you need to see the closure rate for the policies being sold and who the top agents are. Like most call centers, you need to monitor the abandoned call rate. Because of a service-level agreement (SLA), you also need to monitor the average speed of answer and the "call me now" and "call me later" outcomes, both in real time and month-to-date (MTD). This dashboard will run on a large wall-mounted display so that the manager and members of the call center can monitor it periodically throughout the day.

Note: Call centers often measure average hold time and average talk time (i.e., average length of the calls) by agent, but these metrics are not needed in this particular example.

Specifics

- You are tasked with showing the real-time performance of your call center by comparing it to SLAs and monthly results.
- You need to see how many calls are currently in the queue and how many are waiting for you to call now or later.
- You need access to the latest events that may affect your call center operations, such as phone service

downtime or other world events that may impact your calls.

- You need to compare the average speed of answer to the SLA but also see the distribution to understand how many calls are not meeting the SLA.
- You need to create a view that motivates agents by showing top agents and celebrates success by showing total premium offerings sold and how the call center is meeting the SLA. The goal is to drive change by reinforcing good behavior.
- You need to see the date and time of the last data update and when the next update will occur.

Related Scenarios

- You have a call center for customer service, sales, reservations, product/technical support, or credit or collections.
- You are a large retail store with a sizable number of checkout lines. You need to monitor the number of customers in the queue waiting for a register and the average checkout time.
- You need to communicate how your organization is meeting SLAs.

How People Use the Dashboard

Call center managers are focused on the metrics stipulated in an SLA. In addition to SLAs, management puts in place certain goals. One goal is to encourage current customers to upgrade to premium service. In the top left corner of the dashboard (see Figure 29.1), we see the number of premiums sold today, the premium services sold MTD, and a sparkline showing activity for the current month. This allows the reader to see key information at a quick glance.

TOTAL PREMIUM SOLD

Today   MTD

1   96

FIGURE 29.1 Total premium services sold today and MTD are displayed in the top left corner of the dashboard.

The close rates for inbound and outbound calls are shown with a bullet chart for both daily and monthly numbers. (See Figure 29.2.) The black bar shows the actual value (the closed percentage), and the gray performance bands show the target levels.

In Figure 29.2, the daily inbound close rate of 34 percent exceeds the target of 30 percent. The monthly inbound close rate of 25 percent is just below the 30 percent target. Those two metrics look pretty good overall. However, the outbound close rate is very poor. The daily outbound close rate is only 2 percent of a 15 percent target. This seems to be the trend for the month, with the monthly outbound close rate only achieving 4 percent of the 15 percent target.

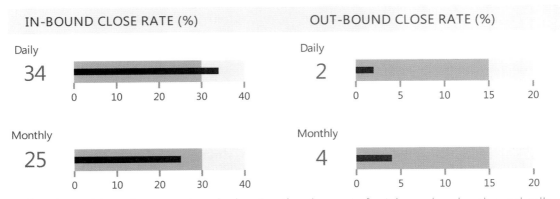

FIGURE 29.2 Bar chart with performance bands showing the close rate for inbound and outbound calls.

Alert indicators

Consider adding an alert indicator to highlight missed targets on key metrics. For example, a small red dot next to the bullet graph could be used to alert the reader that this goal is way off target.

Managers also use the dashboard to identify leading agents. (See Figure 29.3.) Doing this gives recognition to top agents and fosters healthy competition among the call center agents.

TOP 5 AGENTS

Monthly		
#1		Todd Woods
#2		Sharin Bailey
#3		Tonia Parappa
#4		Jennifer Abrams
#5		Maria Chan

FIGURE 29.3 Top five agents based on monthly performance are displayed in real time on the dashboard.

Agents in the call center use the dashboard to ensure they handle the volume of calls efficiently and to identify those areas that may require their attention. In Figure 29.4, the first chart shows the transferred calls as a line chart along with a trend line and a numeric key performance indicator (481 calls MTD). Transferred calls escalate in situations where the first line staff handles initial calls. New hires might escalate more calls as they do not have all the answers, but as staff members get more training, they should be escalating less. The line trending down indicates that fewer calls are escalated and transferred.

The next chart shows the daily abandon rate. The target goal is a gray bar. A red bar indicates that the abandoned rate for the call center was higher than goal for that day. (This is a bad thing.) A blue bar indicates that the abandoned rate was below the target goal. (This is a good thing.)

Agents will also get live updates using the scrolling marquee at the bottom of the dashboard. (See Figure 29.5.) This is a great spot for employee notifications, such as target goals being met, reminders for certain procedures, or notification of important upcoming events.

FIGURE 29.4 Key metrics are displayed for the manager and agents to monitor in real time.

'Call Center Insight' has improved its customer experience with help from Dundas Data Visualization.   Research

FIGURE 29.5   Scrolling banner across the bottom of the screen displays important information for the call center.

Why This Works

Personal Approach Uses Positive Reinforcement

People like to have feedback on their performance. They like recognition for success, and they like to know where they stand. This dashboard personalizes the data by listing the top agents (see Figure 29.3) and showing their pictures and ranks. In Figure 29.6, the leading agent and leading prequalifier are listed (the prequalifier is a person who handles qualifying the leads for the call center agents). By listing the top agents, the dashboard motivates people to do their best and stay focused on what matters. Everyone in the call center immediately knows who the top agents are and the key metrics for success.

FIGURE 29.6   Dashboard features the leading agent and leading prequalifier based on calls handled.

Automatic Updates

The dashboard updates every 60 seconds from the database, so it approaches a real-time measure. The fact that the dashboard is always up to date and features dynamic elements ensures that it always provides value and is engaging. Also, because the dashboard refreshes automatically, there is no need for a manual processes to update the data.

The date and time of the last update are displayed in the top right corner of the dashboard, along with an indicator displaying the time, in seconds, until the next update. (See Figure 29.7.)

FIGURE 29.7   Every 60 seconds, the dashboard refreshes with updated data and the date and time of the last refresh.

Details That Provide Clarification

The ability to see not only aggregated metrics results (such as real-time speed of answer) but also the distribution of calls provides great insight in a small amount of space. In Figure 29.8, it is easy to see the details for how many calls breach the SLA. Dots in the red area represent these calls. Only a few calls are in the red, breaching the SLA, so overall the calls are answered

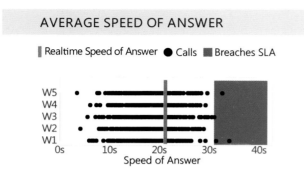

FIGURE 29.8   The distribution of the average speed of answering calls compared to the SLA (in red).

quickly and within the time specified by the SLA. W1 through W5 represent that data for the previous five weeks. The blue line shows how the group performs in real time, which represents the estimated time it would take to answer a call currently coming in.

Good Use of Color

Color is used very well in this dashboard. Blue and red are used to show good and bad. This palette is color-blind friendly, and red is a good choice to alert readers that things are not going well and need

attention. The color is also consistent throughout the dashboard. Red and blue are used on five different charts to encode the same information.

Good Chart Types for the Various Comparisons

The chart types are appropriate for the various comparisons. Sparklines show the trend of the data in small spaces on the dashboard. Bullet graphs show the actual values compared with progress toward a goal. (See Figure 29.2.) Where charts aren't needed, simple numbers give the reader the key indicator (see Figure 29.1)—for example, the number of scheduled leads and inbound calls in the queue.

In Figure 29.9, a slider indicator gives a clear indication on a scale coloring the SLA violation range in red. The black triangle moves in real time where the metric stands against the SLA thresholds. A sparkline underneath them shows the MTD range for the number. A target line is used; the line is red when it is over the threshold range and blue when it is under the threshold range. This is another example of consistent color use throughout the dashboard.

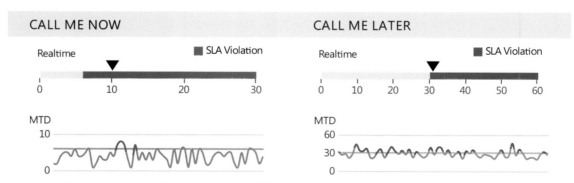

FIGURE 29.9   Example of the red and blue color used throughout the dashboard as well as good chart choices for the various comparisons.

Grid-Based Design

The charts are also well-organized, in a grid layout of four columns and three rows. Designing to a grid is a fundamental concept in graphic design. Strong horizontal lines are created across the dashboard using a gray header. Vertical lines, which can dominate a visualization, are very thin so they do not overpower the dashboard. This style creates a nice symmetry in the dashboard design and makes it easy to read, which is especially important as this dashboard will be displayed on a large-screen TV. People who use this dashboard need to know where each section is, and they need to be able to quickly identify the components of the dashboard from across a room.

Author Commentary

JEFF: The bar chart in the Abandon Rate section uses a gray bar for the target goal. (See Figure 29.10.) It's pretty clear on the good days where things stand. The blue bar is below the gray bar, and this allows us to see that things are good. However, there are a few issues with this method. Blue bars indicate abandon rates that are below SLA targets. Note that the higher the bar, the higher the abandon rates, so while it's below the target, all abandoned calls are a problem. In situations like this, it is worth noting the importance of correctly annotating dashboards. The legend says "Good," but a blue bar just below the gray target line isn't good, it's acceptable. In addition, having the gray bar as "Goal" implies that it is the target number to reach rather than a bottom threshold. We could change the legend to say "Within Target" to make this clearer. Also, in cases where things are bad, the red bar hides most of the gray bar for the goal.

In addition, the 36 leads is out of context. The arrow indicator is pointing up and is blue, which indicates a good thing, but it's not clear how good. Is it above target? And if so, by how much? Or is this just 36 higher than the previous period? When numbers are displayed out of context, it is hard to know what they mean.

Using a target line for the abandoned call rate, similar to what the author used in Figure 29.9, makes this figure easier to read, for both the good days

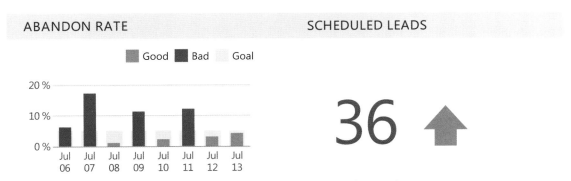

FIGURE 29.10　Abandoned call rate and scheduled leads from the dashboard.

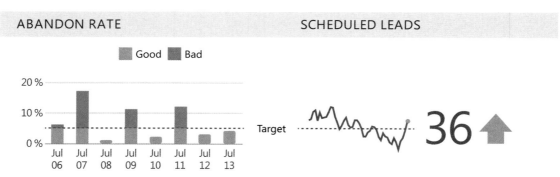

FIGURE 29.11   Using a target line and changing the color helps to identify the threshold for abandoned calls. Adding a sparkline to the leads provides needed context.

and the bad days. (See Figure 29.11.) In addition, coloring everything below the target line in blue emphasizes where the line is drawn between a bad number of abandoned calls and a good number and makes this chart more consistent with the rest of the dashboard. Adding a sparkline with a matching target band also gives context to the 36 leads. This shows how the metric is trending and where it is in relation to the target number.

Another option is adding color banding behind the bars to provide additional context. (See Figure 29.12.) This is similar to the technique used in Chapter 16.

ANDY: Call center dashboards are designed to go on large screens so that everybody can see them. This dashboard design facilitates large-screen presentation. The dashboard doesn't have a "flow" like many of the dashboards found in this book. Each section of the grid is a distinct chart, not directly linked to the others. There is no interactivity either: It's designed to show one set of metrics at a time. When shown on a large screen, this works really well. Over time, users come to know what question is answered in which section of the grid. As they look to the screens, they move their eyes directly to the necessary information.

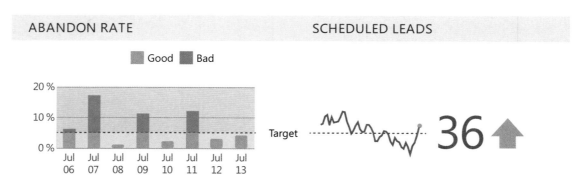

FIGURE 29.12   Color bands are used to show where the bars on the bar chart are in relation to the target threshold.

PART III

SUCCEEDING IN THE REAL WORLD

Chapter 30

Want to Engage People? Make Your Dashboards Personal

Here are some thoughts on making dashboards more engaging to the users. The answer isn't to resort to making things "flashy" or "beautiful" but to create a personal connection between the data and the user.

Overview

A few years ago, a client was updating a collection of survey data dashboards and wanted to revisit the way demographic data was presented. They thought that the collection of bar charts comprising the demographics dashboard was boring and wanted to replace them with something that was more visually arresting. In particular, they wanted to take something that looked like what is in Figure 30.1 and replace it with something flashy.

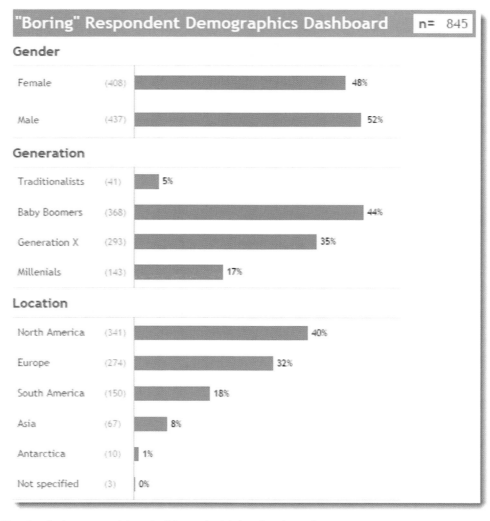

FIGURE 30.1 A "boring" demographics dashboard with boring bar charts.

Something with pizzazz! Something with treemaps and bubbles and pie charts! Something like what is in Figure 30.2.

Yikes. This is certainly a colorful montage, but it takes hard work to make sense of it. Instead of taking seconds to grasp, it will take several minutes to understand the demographics of the survey takers.

Avoid bubble charts

Bubble charts are not useful for precise quantitative comparisons, and treemaps are best used with hierarchical data or when there are too many categories to show in a bar chart.

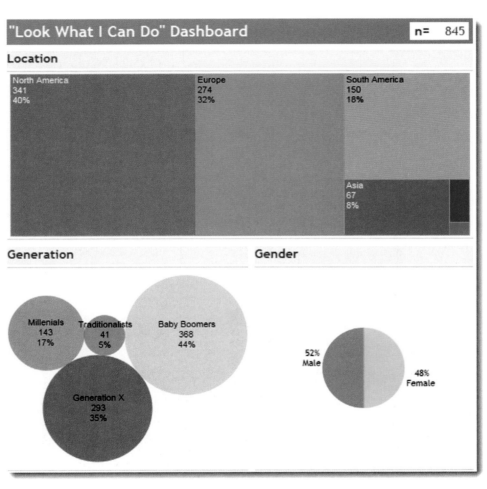

FIGURE 30.2   Flashy demographics dashboard.

When asked why they wanted something "flashier," they indicated a desire to draw the viewer into the dashboard, and they thought a dashboard with more than just bar charts would do the trick.

Why do they want to draw people into this dashboard? When pressed further, the client argued that because the data was boring, the dashboard needed to be cooler; otherwise people wouldn't engage with it.

But if the data is boring, why bother to visualize it? And why would you want users to spend time on this boring data when there was more important data to explore and understand?

There was, in fact, a very good reason to show the demographics of people who took the survey: to let interested parties see for themselves if there was enough overlap between the survey participants and the interested party. That is, the key to getting an individual involved with this dashboard and all the related dashboards was to *show that individual how the data pertained to him or her*.

So, how can we do that?

Personalized Dashboards

At the 2015 Tapestry conference on data storytelling, Chad Skelton, then of the *Vancouver Sun*, presented a great session making the case that people are ravenous for data about themselves.

Chad created an interactive dashboard that allows Canadians to see how much older or younger they are than other Canadians. Below is a similar dashboard using United States census data.

Figure 30.3 presents a histogram showing the distribution between age and U.S. population.

Not exactly thrilling stuff.

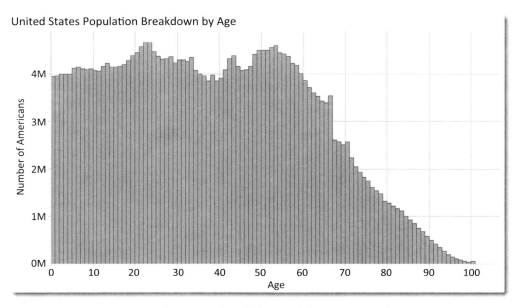

FIGURE 30.3   Histogram showing a breakdown of the U.S. population by age.

Are you over the hill?

See how many Americans are older and younger than you

Move slider to select your age

40

You are older than 53.0% of All Americans

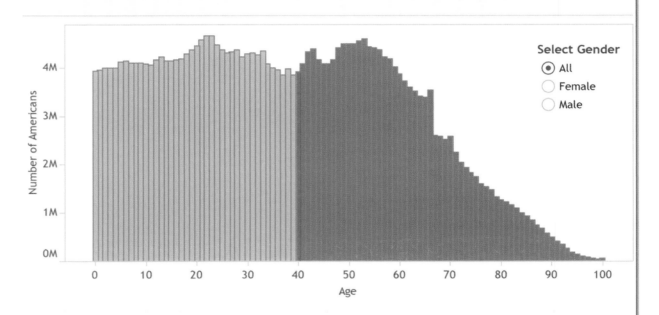

Select Gender
- ● All
- ○ Female
- ○ Male

Americans younger than you	167,491,882
Americans the same age as you	3,904,767
Americans older than you	144,732,190

Population estimates as of 2013. Source: United States Census Bureau https://www.census.gov/popest/data/. Special thanks to Chad Skelton at http://blogs.vancouversun.com/author/chadskeltonvansun/.

FIGURE 30.4 Personalized U.S. Census Bureau dashboard with slider and filters.

Now let's contrast the general-purpose graphic in Figure 30.3 with the personalized dashboard shown in Figure 30.4.

> ### Note
>
> You can try this for yourself at http://www.datarevelations.com/are-you-over-the-hill-in-the-usa.

Every person seen using this dashboard immediately moves the slider left and right and applies the filters—first to compare his or her own age and gender, then to compare the age and gender of a spouse, friend, or child. Users find the allure of the dashboard changing based on an individual's input irresistible.

Indeed, data is much more interesting when it is about you. So, how can we apply this concept to our "boring" demographics dashboard?

Make the Demographics Dashboard Personal

With the goal of personalization in mind, let's see how we can make the dashboard in Figure 30.1 more interesting.

Let's start by gathering some information about the person viewing the dashboard; that is, let's present some parameters from which the viewer can apply personalized settings. (See Figure 30.5.)

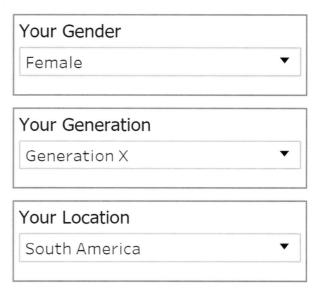

FIGURE 30.5   Get users to tell you something about themselves.

Now we can take these parameter settings and highlight them in the dashboard (and all of the other dashboards, for that matter, see Figure 30.6).

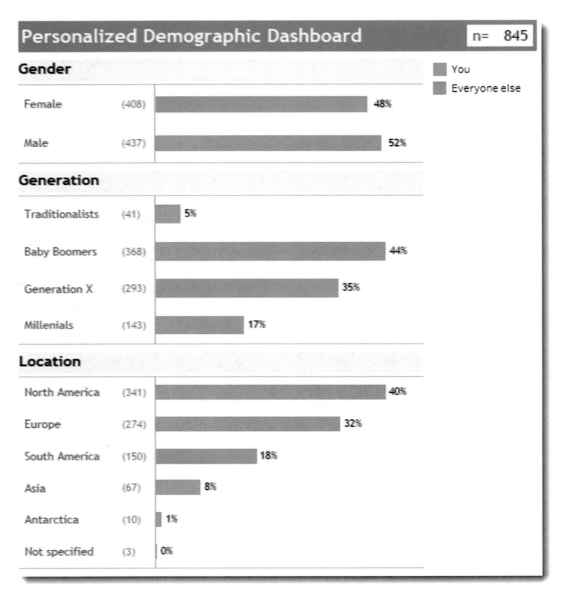

FIGURE 30.6   A personalized demographics dashboard.

We can then go one step further and invite the viewer to select the colored bars to see exactly how many people who took the survey have the same demographic background as him or her. That is, have viewers click to select their gender, their generation, and their location. (See Figure 30.7.)

Twenty-seven people fall into the identical demographic pool as the person viewing the dashboard.

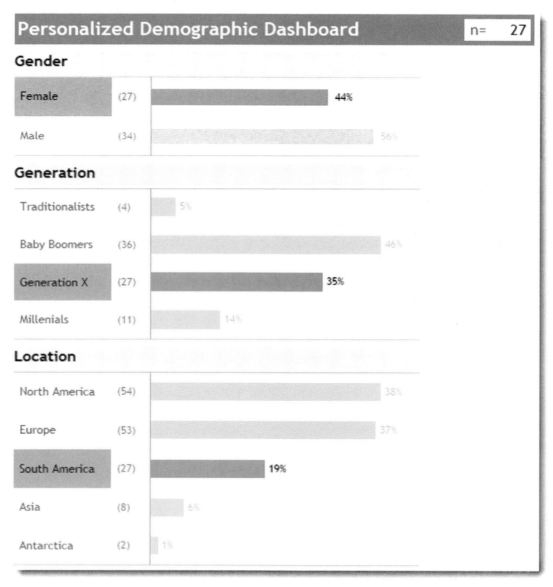

FIGURE 30.7   A personalized dashboard with selections.

But What If You Still Want to Make Something Beautiful?

There may be times when you feel the inexorable pull to make your dashboards more beautiful. You see stunning visualizations like the ones in Figures 30.8 through 30.10 and wonder, "Why can't I make something like that?"

Realize that these data visualizations were built for public consumption, not internal use. They compete with other visuals for readers' attention. They virtually scream "Look at me! Look at me!" Indeed, the treemap, pie chart, and bubble chart demographics

dashboard in Figure 30.2 was from a client who was building a *public-facing* dashboard.

Personally, I think the bar charts in Figure 30.7 are beautiful, but I get the point. You see these come-hither dashboards and wonder if maybe you can borrow some design elements from them.

If you're the only person looking at the dashboard, I suppose you can do anything you want. Sure, go ahead and replace those bar charts with donut charts if you like. As long as doing so doesn't impede your understanding of the data, then what's the harm?

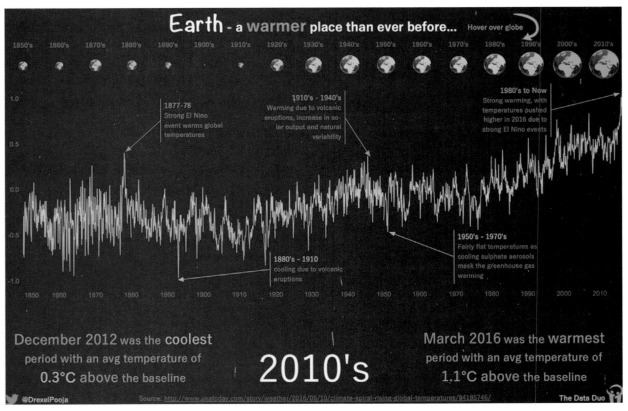

FIGURE 30.8   Global warming dashboard published on Tableau Public.

Source: Used with permission of Pooja Gandhi

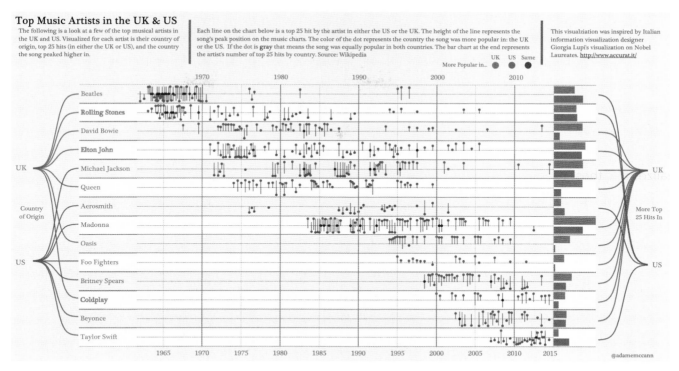

FIGURE 30.9   Dashboard on Tableau Public comparing top music artists in the U.K. and the U.S.

Source: Used with permission of Adam E. McCann

But if others need to understand the data, you should proceed with caution. Your goal is to make something that is accurate, informative, and enlightening. You need to make sure whatever you add does not compromise that goal.

And how do you do that? Ours is not a book about graphic design and we do not attempt to tackle issues related to sophisticated use of typography, layout, and shapes here. But I want to show you a chart type that combines the analytic integrity of a bar chart with the "ooh, circles" of a bubble chart.

FIGURE 30.10 New York City rat sightings dashboard on Tableau Public.

Source: Used with permission of Adam Crahen

An Alternative to the Bar Chart: The Lollipop

A *lollipop chart* is simply a dot plot chart superimposed on top of a bar chart that has very thin bars. Figure 30.11 shows an example using sales data.

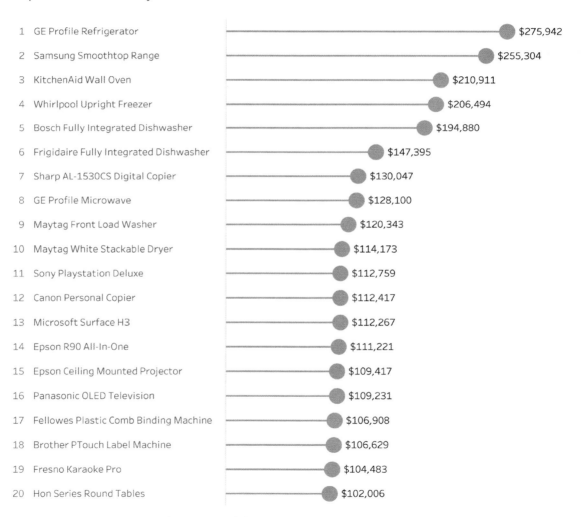

Top 20 Products by Sales

1	GE Profile Refrigerator	$275,942
2	Samsung Smoothtop Range	$255,304
3	KitchenAid Wall Oven	$210,911
4	Whirlpool Upright Freezer	$206,494
5	Bosch Fully Integrated Dishwasher	$194,880
6	Frigidaire Fully Integrated Dishwasher	$147,395
7	Sharp AL-1530CS Digital Copier	$130,047
8	GE Profile Microwave	$128,100
9	Maytag Front Load Washer	$120,343
10	Maytag White Stackable Dryer	$114,173
11	Sony Playstation Deluxe	$112,759
12	Canon Personal Copier	$112,417
13	Microsoft Surface H3	$112,267
14	Epson R90 All-In-One	$111,221
15	Epson Ceiling Mounted Projector	$109,417
16	Panasonic OLED Television	$109,231
17	Fellowes Plastic Comb Binding Machine	$106,908
18	Brother PTouch Label Machine	$106,629
19	Fresno Karaoke Pro	$104,483
20	Hon Series Round Tables	$102,006

FIGURE 30.11   Top 20 products by sales using a lollipop chart.

Figure 30.12 presents the demographic dashboard from earlier, rendered using a lollipop chart.

I personally prefer the bar chart but would not protest if a client wanted to use the lollipop version instead.

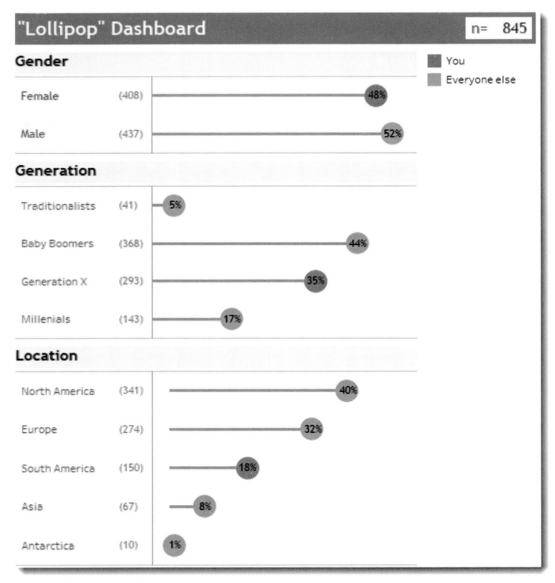

FIGURE 30.12   Demographics dashboard rendered as a lollipop chart.

Conclusion

If people aren't using your dashboards, it's because the information isn't meaningful to them, not because the dashboards aren't cool. Adding packed bubbles and pictograms in the hope of getting people engaged may attract attention at first but likely will hinder people's ability to understand the data. Then they will abandon the dashboards.

Although a lollipop chart might add some visual variety without sacrificing analytical clarity, if you really want to engage people, *make the data meaningful*. One of the best ways to do that is to *make it personal*.

For the record, I think personalized bar charts beat packed bubbles any day of the week.

Note

Be sure to read Chapter 32: Beware the Dead-End Dashboard.

Chapter 31

Visualizing Time

Introduction

Of all the dashboards in this book, how many contain a chart showing time? 23 of the 28 scenarios. There are many ways to visualize time, beyond the basic timeline. The method you choose will change the kind of insights that can be found on your dashboards.

Visualizing time correctly is vital to a successful dashboard, and it is the reason why we devote an entire chapter to the topic.

The timeline is an amazing invention. Figure 31.1 shows William Playfair's line chart from 1786. Being amazing doesn't mean it is always the best way to show time on your dashboards. There are many scenarios, discussed in this chapter, where a standard time series actually *hides* important stories in your data.

In this chapter, we look at seven different time-based questions and explore the best chart for each one:

1. How does today compare with the start of a time period?

2. Are there cyclical patterns in my data?

3. How can I look up trends across two time dimensions?

4. How can I look at rank, not value, over time?

5. How can I compare values of things that did not happen at the same time?

6. How can I show the duration of an event?

7. How can I focus on bottlenecks in a process?

How Much Time Do You Want to See?

What type of data is time?

Most commonly it is treated as continuous, with one instant following another. In such cases, time is shown on the x-axis, flowing from left to right, with the quantitative measures on the y-axis.

1786: William Playfair

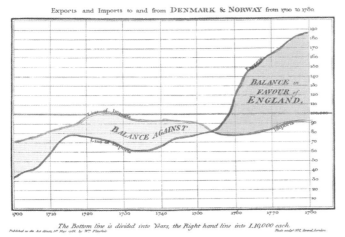

2015: Financial Times

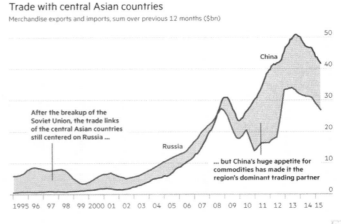

FIGURE 31.1   The first statistical timeline was drawn in 1786. Over 200 years later, we still use similar techniques.

But time can also be ordinal: Days of the week are discrete, but they have an order (Monday, Tuesday, Wednesday, etc). You can group together all the Mondays and Tuesdays and Wednesdays to look for trends. If you put that into a sorted bar chart, the days of the week wouldn't necessarily be in the Sunday-Saturday order. Let's see four simple examples using data from Citi Bike, the New York cycle hire scheme operated by Motivate. Figure 31.2 displays four different ways to show the number of journeys in the Citi Bike share program.

The view you choose depends on your objective. Let's look at the examples in Figure 31.2. Charts A and B represent continuous time. Chart A shows the macro trend over one year of bike journeys, with one mark

for each month. Chart B shows the number of journeys by day. You can still see the seasonal trend, but you can also see which days were outliers; it's easy to spot which are the highest-use and lowest-use days, for example. However, Chart B is noisy and might have too much detail.

Charts C and D use time as an ordinal number. Chart C shows journeys by day of the week. You can see that the most and least popular days are Wednesday and Sunday, respectively. Chart D shows journeys by hour of day. You can clearly see the two commuter peaks around 9 a.m. and 5 p.m.

Whichever level of detail you choose for your time series, you will show one thing at the expense of

Journeys on Citi Bike share program, New York

A: Monthly

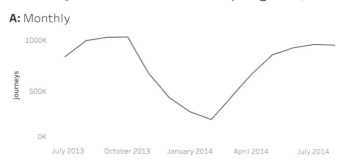

B: Daily

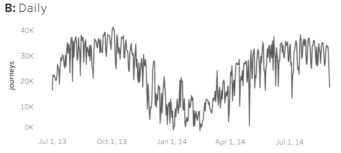

C: By day of week

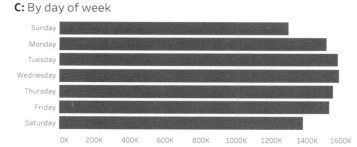

D: By hour of day

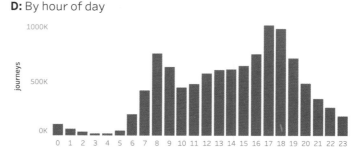

FIGURE 31.2   Four ways of showing Citi Bike journeys.

another. The right choice? We can't tell you: It depends on your objective. This chapter explores different questions you might ask of your time data and various charts you can use to answer those questions.

How Does Today Compare with the Start of a Time Period?

Imagine you are interested only in the values at the start and end of your time series. If that is the case, is it important to know what happened in between?

Let's look at an example using data from Citi Bike. Figure 31.3 shows the number of journeys between July 2013 and August 2014 at the eight most popular stations in the network. The station names have been replaced with numbers.

This makes for a fine line chart. The seasonality in usage is clear: Fewer journeys are made in the depth of winter.

You can see that, overall, each of these stations has a very similar pattern. You can also see which station had the highest and lowest overall journey count.

But what if your business question is to compare the most recent data with the earliest data? Which stations have changed in popularity since the start of the time period? Can you see an answer to that question in the standard time series? To answer this question, we can use a slope chart, as in Figure 31.4. We remove all the data points except for the first and last in the series.

Suddenly we see something the standard line chart did not show. All stations saw a growth in numbers except for Station 8. In fact, Station 8 went from being the most popular station to the least popular station in this time period. Since there are only two data points for each station, it is very easy to see which categories are rising or falling between the two endpoints.

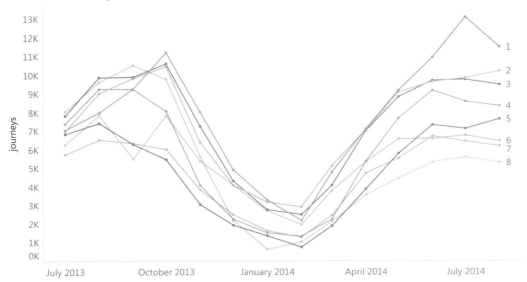

The Top 8 Citi Bike Stations: Which stations have seen the biggest change in use since July 2013?

FIGURE 31.3   Line chart showing journeys at the top eight Citi Bike stations in New York.

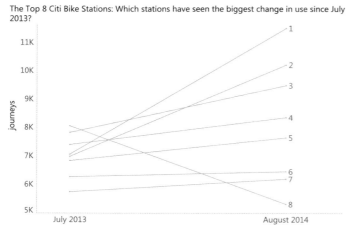

The Top 8 Citi Bike Stations: Which stations have seen the biggest change in use since July 2013?

FIGURE 31.4   Slope chart showing top eight Citi Bike stations.

The insight about Station 8 is clear in the slope chart but hidden by the standard trend line in Figure 31.3.

The slope chart in Figure 31.4 shows all the stations in one pane: There are eight lines, one for each docking station.

Sometimes it can be hard to distinguish one line from another, especially if they are labelled. For example, look at Figure 31.5, which is a slope chart showing the results of a survey on people's intentions to buy consumer gadgets between 2015 and 2016.

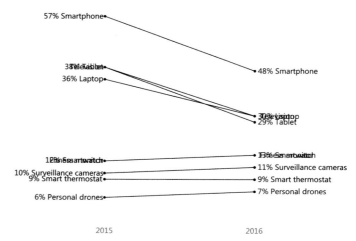

People are getting tired of buying new devices — and this chart proves it

What percentage of consumers are planning to purchase the following devices in 2016?

FIGURE 31.5   Slope chart showing intent to purchase gadgets in 2015 and 2016.

Source: Accenture

Design: Andy Cotgreave (@acotgreave)

In this case, some of the lines are very close together. Some labels overlap, and others are too close together to read easily. How can you solve the labeling issue? You could break each line into its own pane, as shown in Figure 31.6.

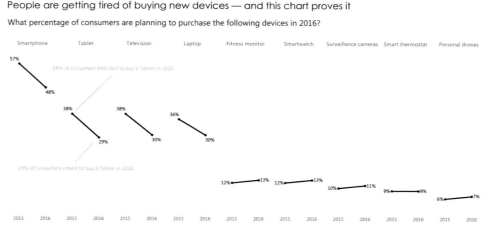

People are getting tired of buying new devices — and this chart proves it

What percentage of consumers are planning to purchase the following devices in 2016?

FIGURE 31.6   Multipanel slope chart showing intent to purchase.

Are There Cyclical Patterns in My Data?

There are many ways to show cyclical patterns. Here we look again at Citi Bike data. Imagine you need to know which stations get most or least crowded at different hours of the day. This is important so you can ensure that bikes are correctly distributed across the network so that customers can hire or dock a bike when necessary. A valid question is: For any hour of the day, which days are most and least busy? For example, is 8 a.m. a really busy hour on a Monday or a Sunday? On which day is it most busy at 12 p.m.? Figure 31.7 shows a standard timeline of total journeys on Citi Bike throughout a week.

Is it easy to find and compare 8 a.m. and 12 p.m. on each day of the week? No. It's possible, but you need to search along every point on the timeline.

Our first solution would be to just show total journeys for each hour of the day. You can see that in Figure 31.8.

Citi Bike in New York: What do the hours of 8 to 9 a.m. and 12 to 1 p.m. look like?

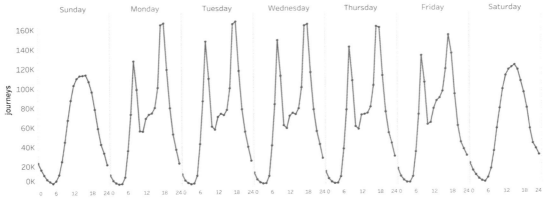

FIGURE 31.7   Line chart showing Citi Bike journeys throughout the week. Which day has the most journeys at 8 a.m. and 12 p.m.?

Citi Bike in New York: What do the hours of 8 to 9 a.m. and 12 to 1 p.m. look like?

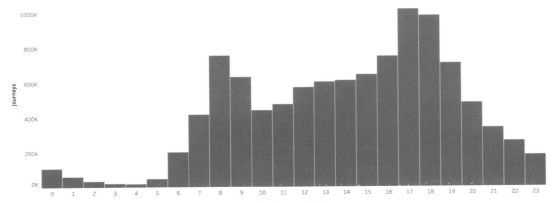

FIGURE 31.8   Bar chart showing journeys by hour of day.

Citi Bike in New York: What do the hours of 8 to 9 a.m. and 12 to 1 p.m. look like?

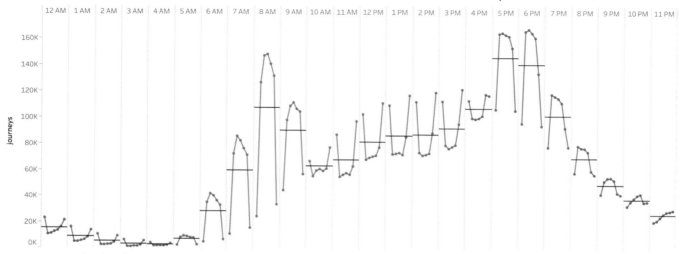

FIGURE 31.9   Cycle plot showing weekly trends within each hour.

Aggregating all the journeys by hour of day seems to answer the question: 8 a.m. is a morning commuter peak, and 12 p.m. is kind of quiet. This is a great way to summarize and view data for one time period. There's a problem, though: Each bar in the chart is the total for *all* days of the week. We're missing important extra details of the story.

Figure 31.9 is a cycle plot version of this data. In a cycle plot, each hour contains two lines. The red line shows journeys *at that hour on* each day of the week. The horizontal line represents the average for the seven days. Within the pane, the line shows the values for the larger time period (days).

What a difference! This view is very powerful and reveals many details not visible in the standard timeline or the bar chart of just the days.

Figure 31.10 shows the details for just the two periods that interest us (8 a.m. and 12 p.m.).

Each line has seven dots, one for each day of the week. The first dot is Sunday, and the last dot is Saturday.

Citi Bike in New York: What do the hours of 8 to 9 a.m. and 12 to 1 p.m. look like?

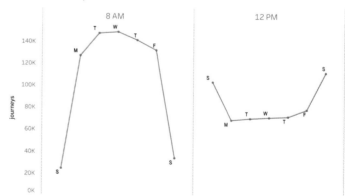

FIGURE 31.10   Cycle plot showing journeys at 8 a.m. and 12 p.m. Each dot represents one day of the week. (Sunday is the first dot.)

Now you can see how different these hours are. On a Saturday or Sunday (presumably New Yorkers are sleeping in on those days), 8 a.m. doesn't see many riders. But 8 a.m. is very busy during the weekdays. It's busiest on Tuesday and Wednesday. However, 12 p.m. is the opposite. It's a popular hour on weekends but not so busy during weekdays, when most New Yorkers are at work.

Now go back to the full cycle plot in Figure 31.9 and look at each hour of the day: You can see the different shapes very clearly. It's easy to identify which hours of the day are busy on workdays and on weekends.

The cycle plot, then, is very powerful. Imagine being a planner at Citi Bike. You could build a dashboard comparing usage at different stations and discover many different patterns. For example,

Figure 31.11 shows cycle plots for two very different Citi Bike stations: Eighth Avenue and West 31st Street (next to Penn Station, a busy commuter stop) and Central Park South and Sixth Avenue (next to Central Park).

The differences pop out. The black horizontal reference line is the average journey count for that hour. You can see that both stations have a peak from 5 to 7 p.m. Other than that they have very different patterns. Eighth Avenue is very busy during the morning commute (but strangely not as busy in the evenings). Central Park is busiest in the afternoon and evening. The cycle plot lines show a clear "n" shape during the morning for Eighth Avenue, revealing the dominance of the weekdays. All hours in Central Park are "u" shaped, showing that journeys there happen mostly on the weekends.

Citi Bike: A tale of two docking stations

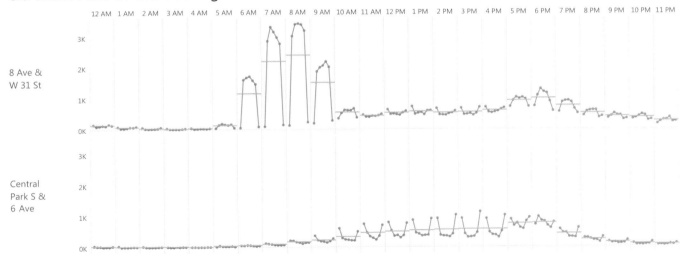

FIGURE 31.11   Cycle plot showing two stations in New York.

A cycle plot needs to be quite wide and can take up a lot of real estate on your dashboard. If that is a problem, you can plot the hours of the day along the x-axis and draw a separate line for each day of the week in one pane. An example is shown in Figure 31.12.

In this example, we can see the same trends as the cycle plot. The advantage of drawing the lines on top of each other is that the chart can be made much narrower, which is useful if you need to save space on your dashboard. The difference between weekend days and weekdays is strikingly clear. Plotting each day as a separate line within the same pane in this way also allows

you to compare the actual differences between the days at any given hour more easily. The trade-off is that it's harder to see which day is which; this is a problem that is easily solvable if the dashboard is interactive.

Our Citi Bike example looked at weekly trends for any given hour of day, but you can create a cycle plot for any two time periods. For example, in a sales organization, you might want to look at the yearly trends for any quarter.

As the next section shows, you can also look at the yearly trends for any given month.

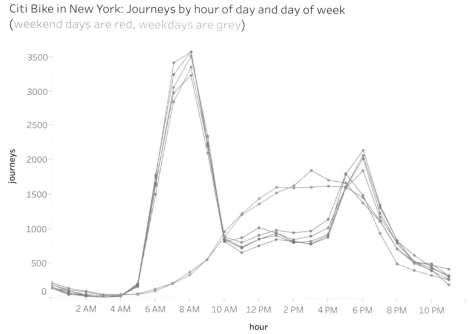

FIGURE 31.12   Line chart alternative to a cycle plot that uses less width.

Number of live births per day in England and Wales, 2013

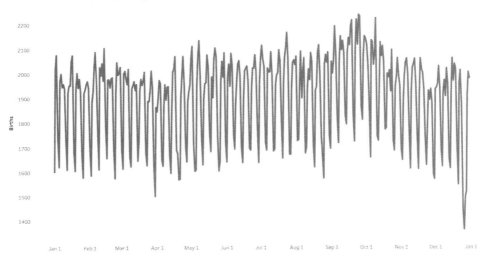

FIGURE 31.13   Line chart showing the number of live births in England and Wales, 2013.

Data source: Office for National Statistics

How Can I Look Up Trends Across Two Time Dimensions?

What are the most popular birthdays in England and Wales? Figure 31.13 is a line chart showing the number of live births in England and Wales for each day in 2014.

It's very hard to make out much detail on the figure. You can see many spikes, but they hide the trends. The spikes actually show that there are fewer births on the weekends in England and Wales. You can see this fact much more clearly in Figure 31.14.

Isn't it amazing to see the drop in births on the weekends? Figure 31.14 uses day of week as an ordinal measure to reveal something the line chart conceals.

Back to the spikey line chart in Figure 31.13. You can see which is the lowest day of all (December 26) and

that the most popular days are in September. Beyond that, the line chart is very hard to read and hides many great insights.

Number of live births by day of week in England and Wales, 2013

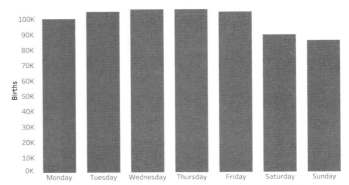

FIGURE 31.14   Bar chart showing the number of live births in England and Wales, 2013.

Data source: Office for National Statistics

Like cycle plots discussed earlier, highlight tables/ heat maps are great ways to show seasonality. Figure 31.15 is a highlight table showing the most and least popular days for birthdays in the United States and in England and Wales.

This is an entire calendar year in a table. Each column is a month, and each row is a day. There's one table for the United States and one for England and Wales. The darker the color, the more people are born on that day.

Digest the highlight table for a few moments: What can you see that you couldn't in the line chart? Which

days of the month are not popular? What is the effect of Christmas in the different countries? What about national holidays, such as Independence Day (July 4 in the United States)? Which months are most popular?

You can see a clear light stripe across the thirteenth day of each month. In both countries, there are fewer births on the thirteenth day. Did you realize we are that superstitious? There are other striking gaps. Check out New Year's Day: There are plenty of births at the end of the year in each country but very few in the first few days in January. In the United States, fewer children are born on Thanksgiving and on July 4. Over

How common is your birthday?

Two charts showing the most and least popular birthdays in the USA and England/Wales. The darker the colour, the more common that birthday is.

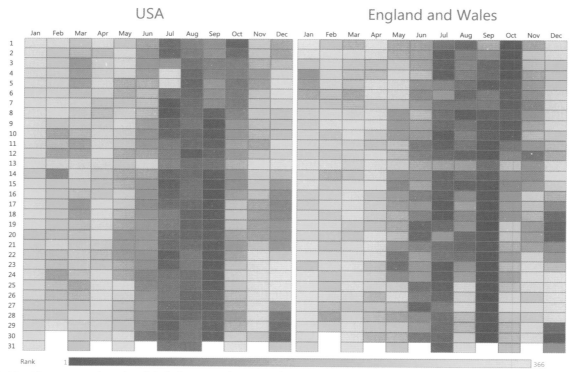

FIGURE 31.15   Heat map showing birthday popularity in the United States and in England and Wales.

Christmas, especially in the United States, there are few births. In England and Wales, there are few births at the end of August. There is even a visible bump in births on February 14, Valentine's Day.

The highlight table of births shows the level to which childbirth is a planned and managed process. Consider the line chart in Figure 31.13. How many of these insights would you have spotted had you used a line chart?

How can we apply this learning to business data? In another example, we can use a more somber dataset, the number of fatalities on U.S. roads over 36 years. Figure 31.16 shows fatalities, by year, from 1975 to 2011. The line chart provides some great insight.

You can see the peak of deaths in 1982 followed by a significant drop. There is another significant drop in the late 1980s. It's important to remember that correlation does not necessarily mean there is a direct link, but related trends can guide our understanding of events and help us to think about them in new ways. For example, notice the big drop in road deaths

in 2009. The timing could lead a person to wonder whether this drop was somehow connected to the financial crash.

Should axes start at zero?

The y-axis in Figure 31.16 does not start at zero. The goal of this chart is to show relative change rather than absolute change. Truncating an axis is acceptable in cases where position is used to encode data—for example, a line chart or dot plot—and where the goal is to show the difference between data points, not their actual size.

However, dashboard users might be more interested in more detailed seasonal trends. Which months or days see the most deaths? Let's break the line chart into months in Figure 31.17. Can you see the seasonal trend?

Once again, it's too hard to see the seasonal trend because the spikes generate too much noise. Figure 31.18 shows the same data in a highlight table.

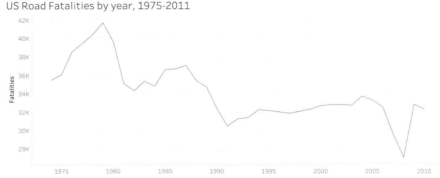

US Road Fatalities by year, 1975-2011

FIGURE 31.16   Line chart showing fatalities on roads in the United States, 1975–2011.

US Road Fatalities by month, 1975-2011

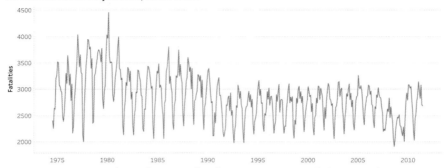

FIGURE 31.17   Line chart showing fatalities on U.S. roads by month, 1975–2011.

US Road Fatalities by month and year, 1975-2011

Fatalities
1,900 ▭▭▭▭▭ 4,500

	Jan	Feb	Mar	Apr	May	Jun	Jul	Aug	Sep	Oct	Nov	Dec	
1975													35,504
1976													36,102
1977													38,564
1978													39,482
1979													40,430
1980													41,762
1981													39,670
1982													35,141
1983													34,359
1984													35,390
1985													34,846
1986													36,655
1987													36,731
1988													37,101
1989													35,460
1990													34,748
1991													32,413
1992													30,540
1993													31,328
1994													31,468
1995													32,311
1996													32,220
1997													32,072
1998													31,913
1999													32,143
2000													32,361
2001													32,746
2002													32,850
2003													32,844
2004													32,802
2005													33,771
2006													33,368
2007													32,586
2008													29,640
2009													27,097
2010													32,885
2011													32,367
	87,799	81,356	94,439	98,615	109,060	112,068	120,164	121,517	111,238	114,346	106,399	106,669	

FIGURE 31.18   Heat map showing U.S. road fatalities by month and year, 1975–2011.

This view, unlike the others, reveals some very powerful insights. Looking at the months (columns in Figure 31.18), we can quickly scan down and see how many more fatalities happen in August than in any other month. Looking across at the year (rows), we can quickly identify that 1980 saw the most deaths and 2009 the fewest. The "island" of red in the top center shows that the summer months in the late 1970s and 1980s were periods of high fatality numbers.

With seasonality charts, you can choose the two time aggregations that are most relevant to your needs. For instance, we can change our table to show month and day instead of year to find trends within each year, as shown in Figure 31.19.

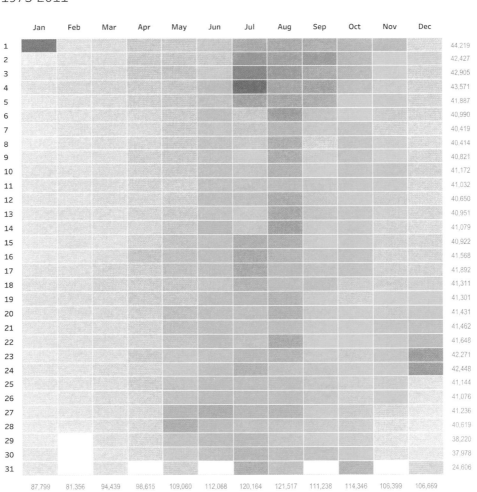

US Road Fatalities by month and day, 1975-2011

FIGURE 31.19 Heat map showing U.S. road fatalities by month and day, 1975–2011.

The most fatalities have occurred on roads in the United States during holiday periods: January 1, July 4, and Christmas Eve. This data doesn't include number of journeys made, so we cannot conclude that there are more deaths per journey on those days, but we do see the impact on fatalities extremely clearly. It would be great to find the data on number of car journeys on each day and normalize the fatalities to find out which are the most and least dangerous days to drive in the United States.

When building your dashboards, you should choose the time aggregation levels that are appropriate for your business needs. If you are a transport planner managing congestion at a train station, for example, choosing weekday and hour of day might be appropriate to allow you to see when your stations are most busy.

A final advantage of highlight tables is their tabular structure. It's easy to look horizontally and vertically to cross-reference specific information. This tabular structure can also help you convince people of the value of visualization. We've all experienced working with people who insist on just having the table of numbers. So give them the numbers, but as a highlight table. Simply add the labels to each cell, and you have a labeled highlight table, shown in Figure 31.20.

Changing hearts and minds

Labeled highlight tables are a great way to get people to move from tables toward visualizations.

US Road Fatalities by month and day, 1975-2011

Fatalities 810 ▭ 5,189

	Jan	Feb	Mar	Apr	May	Jun	Jul	Aug	Sep	Oct	Nov	Dec	Total
1	4,654	2,914	3,115	3,405	3,459	3,560	3,981	3,993	4,003	3,923	3,884	3,328	44,219
2	2,575	2,920	3,102	3,415	3,459	3,495	4,217	4,074	4,173	3,891	3,596	3,510	42,427
3	2,781	2,927	3,092	3,383	3,525	3,599	4,613	4,135	3,974	3,880	3,616	3,380	42,905
4	2,779	3,012	3,136	3,313	3,458	3,759	5,189	3,969	4,095	3,849	3,561	3,451	43,571
5	2,685	2,936	3,030	3,314	3,427	3,684	4,062	4,043	3,954	3,637	3,679	3,436	41,887
6	2,783	2,851	3,073	3,173	3,395	3,775	3,520	4,188	3,735	3,599	3,532	3,366	40,990
7	2,660	2,923	3,014	3,148	3,405	3,672	3,540	3,889	3,659	3,765	3,461	3,283	40,419
8	2,594	2,845	3,048	3,223	3,429	3,714	3,558	3,984	3,341	3,786	3,560	3,332	40,414
9	2,752	2,724	2,900	3,318	3,461	3,702	3,604	4,028	3,567	3,817	3,579	3,369	40,821
10	2,780	2,782	2,998	3,256	3,451	3,746	3,680	3,913	3,599	3,785	3,744	3,438	41,172
11	2,768	2,905	2,995	3,306	3,324	3,728	3,713	3,862	3,683	3,741	3,660	3,347	41,032
12	2,791	2,753	3,075	3,182	3,350	3,748	3,746	3,965	3,550	3,651	3,534	3,305	40,650
13	2,807	2,872	2,942	3,226	3,371	3,667	3,620	4,059	3,696	3,741	3,526	3,424	40,951
14	2,787	2,914	2,998	3,187	3,457	3,853	3,645	4,137	3,624	3,687	3,450	3,340	41,079
15	2,684	2,883	2,867	3,248	3,522	3,694	3,919	3,932	3,592	3,661	3,499	3,421	40,922
16	2,752	2,722	3,097	3,488	3,547	3,738	3,978	3,887	3,683	3,808	3,431	3,437	41,568
17	2,954	2,874	3,175	3,330	3,550	3,738	3,991	3,863	3,714	3,776	3,484	3,443	41,892
18	2,861	2,890	3,211	3,332	3,439	3,649	3,885	3,779	3,779	3,526	3,445	3,515	41,311
19	2,868	2,927	3,009	3,329	3,431	3,740	3,846	3,894	3,629	3,463	3,568	3,597	41,301
20	2,833	2,923	3,022	3,265	3,540	3,733	3,703	3,904	3,646	3,630	3,544	3,688	41,431
21	2,760	2,897	2,956	3,249	3,555	3,740	3,691	3,819	3,636	3,606	3,718	3,835	41,462
22	2,723	2,933	3,034	3,208	3,515	3,800	3,684	3,982	3,597	3,582	3,681	3,909	41,648
23	2,667	2,835	2,954	3,373	3,628	3,690	3,870	3,898	3,655	3,539	3,784	4,378	42,271
24	2,825	2,789	3,086	3,275	3,596	3,769	3,910	3,746	3,737	3,643	3,667	4,405	42,448
25	2,902	2,880	3,043	3,357	3,641	3,812	3,804	3,814	3,680	3,523	3,547	3,141	41,144
26	2,727	2,904	3,126	3,259	3,649	3,831	3,824	3,787	3,684	3,514	3,652	3,119	41,076
27	2,771	2,950	3,110	3,235	3,866	3,929	3,877	3,887	3,643	3,544	3,394	3,030	41,236
28	2,783	2,861	3,111	3,247	3,921	3,837	3,726	3,718	3,539	3,551	3,306	3,019	40,619
29	2,744	810	3,111	3,280	3,683	3,852	3,874	3,682	3,569	3,554	3,145	2,916	38,220
30	2,865		2,960	3,291	3,582	3,814	3,908	3,855	3,802	3,697	3,152	3,052	37,978
31	2,884		3,049		3,424		3,986	3,831		3,977		3,455	24,606
Total	87,799	81,356	94,439	98,615	109,060	112,068	120,164	121,517	111,238	114,346	106,399	106,669	

FIGURE 31.20 Highlight table of U.S. road fatalities by month and day, 1975–2011: the gateway to visualization?

How Can I Look at Rank, Not Value, Over Time?

Sometimes the rank of things over time is more important than actual value. Take the Billboard Top 40. We only want to know who is number one. It doesn't matter to us how much more the number-one artists sold, it just matters that they sold the most.

The same is true in sports. In the English Premier League, for example, we don't remember exact points each season for teams, but we do remember where they finished and what kind of roller-coaster ride they had throughout the season. Figure 31.21 shows the bump chart for the 2014–2015 season, with two teams, Leicester and Newcastle, highlighted.

English Premier League 2014/2015: How did Leicester and Newcastle perform?

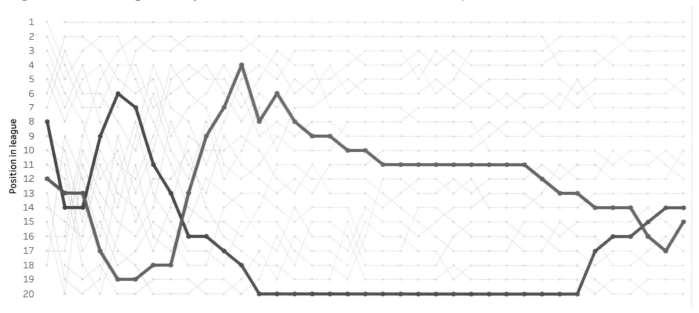

FIGURE 31.21   Bump chart showing two teams' roller-coaster rides during the English Premier League of 2014–2015.

Let's go back and look at our Citi Bike data. In our slope chart example in Figure 31.4, we saw that there was a big change in the most popular stations over time: Station 8 went from being the most popular station at the start of the scheme to the eighth most popular 13 months later.

We might be interested in the rise and fall of popularity of stations. The standard line chart showing number of journeys by month doesn't make the ranks obvious, even when one station is highlighted. (See Figure 31.22.)

What if we change this to a bump chart instead? In a bump chart, the x-axis continues to show time. In this case, we're showing months. For the y-axis, instead of showing journeys, we show the rank of each station, based on journeys, for each month. We can see this in Figure 31.23.

Citi Bike's Top 8 stations: How did W 20 St & 11 Ave change in rank over time?

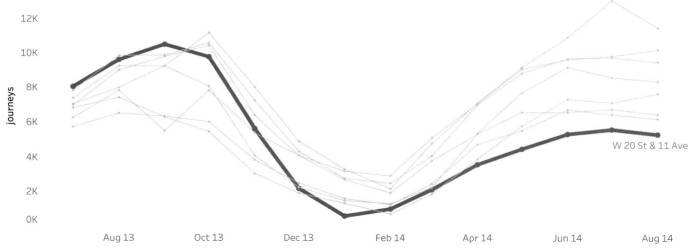

FIGURE 31.22   Line chart showing journeys at the top eight Citi Bike stations. It is not easy to see how the rank changes over time. One station has been highlighted.

Citi Bike's Top 8 stations: How did W 20 St & 11 Ave change in rank over time?

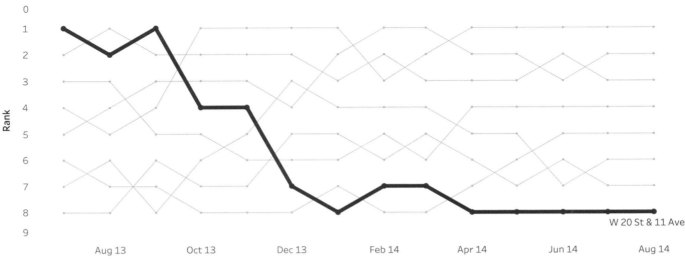

FIGURE 31.23   Bump chart showing changing rank in top eight Citi Bike stations. One station has been highlighted.

Bump charts

Bump charts make rank very clear, but they conceal the actual values.

Compare the bump chart with the line chart. If your scenario requires you think about changes in rank over time, a bump chart is much clearer than a regular line chart.

Bump charts do present a couple of challenges that must be overcome. In Figure 31.23 one Citi Bike station is red and the others are all gray. If all the lines were gray, it would be next to impossible to discern one line from another. If you make them all different colors, the chart can be overwhelming to look at. In Figure 31.24, one color is used for each of the eight stations.

Eight colors is on the limit of what is comprehensible for a user. If your dashboard is interactive, you can use highlighting and tool tips to make each station clearer.

Another issue with bump charts is that by showing rank, you've hidden the actual values. Can you have your cake and eat it, and show both rank and numbers in a bump chart? One way would be to label each point on the line, as shown in Figure 31.25. Also see Chapter 22: Showing Rank and Magnitude which shows several ways of approaching this challenge.

This chart solves the problem only partially: The size of the numbers is not represented visually. You can only look up the value of each number. Bump charts work when you are interested *only* in rank.

Citi Bike's Top 8 stations: How did the top 8 stations change in rank over time?

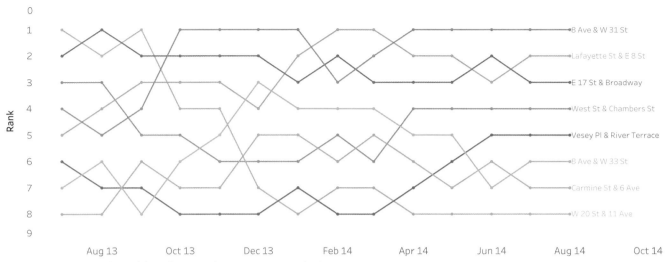

FIGURE 31.24   Colored-line bump charts are overwhelming.

Citi Bike's Top 8 stations: How did W 20 St & 11 Ave change in rank over time?
Labels: journeys, 000s

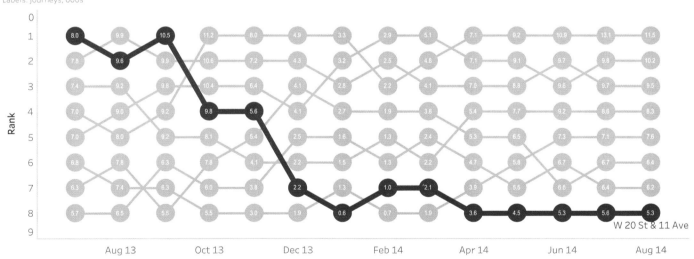

FIGURE 31.25   Labeled bump chart.

The Brill School Pub Quiz: Positions after round 16, "The last round"

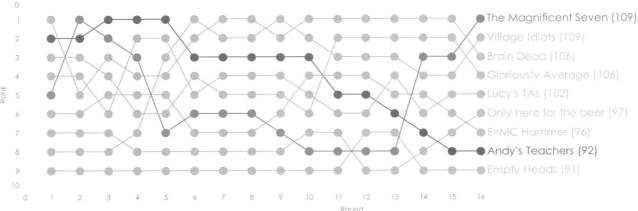

FIGURE 31.26   Bump chart showing progress through a pub quiz/trivia night.

If you are incentivizing a sales team, measuring each member against each other could be more successful than just focusing on the raw numbers. If you are tracking popularity of products, say in a bookstore, rank is very important.

For one final example, Andy keeps score at local trivia nights (pub quizzes). As well as reading out the scores after each round, he shows a bump chart on a big projector. Teams get excited seeing their own trajectory through the duration of the quiz. Have a look at the example in Figure 31.26. Imagine how everyone felt when they saw that the Magnificent Seven came from behind at the end to win the quiz. Also, imagine how Andy's Teachers' team felt to have gone the other way.[1] Only a bump chart shows this information so well.

---

[1] Andy (the author) would like to point out that "Andy's Teachers" was not his team. Andy is also the name of his school principal.

How Can I Compare Growth Rates of Things That Happen at Different Times?

Let's imagine you produce music videos, really popular ones for the global pop superstars. In the modern age, success is made in the first few days after a new release. You want to know total views and compare growth rates of your content over time.

For example, Figure 31.27 lists the top-viewed YouTube videos of all time (as of September 2016).

Instead of just seeing which video is most popular, what if the goal is to measure which ones went viral the quickest? The bar chart clearly shows that Psy's "Gangnam Style" leads the pack, but did it reach 1 billion views more quickly than any other video?

The Top 10 most viewed videos on YouTube
Highlighted: **Hello by Adele** and **Gangnam Style by PSY**

			Views (billions)
1	Gangnam Style	PSY	2.64
2	See You Again	Wiz Khalifa	2.00
3	Uptown Funk	Mark Ronson ft. Bruno Mars	1.82
4	Sorry	Justin Bieber	1.78
5	Blank Space	Taylor Swift	1.74
6	Hello	Adele	1.70
7	Shake It Off	Taylor Swift	1.62
8	Lean On	Major Lazer & DJ Snake	1.60
9	Recipe for Disaster	Masha and The Bear	1.58
10	Bailando	Enrique Iglesias	1.58

FIGURE 31.27   Bar chart showing views of the top YouTube videos of all time.

First, let's look at the standard timeline, shown in Figure 31.28. Two videos are highlighted: "Gangnam Style" by PSY and "Hello" by Adele.

The line chart is great. You can see how "Gangnam Style" was such a trendsetter; it reached its peak view

count long before the more recent megahits. "Hello" jumps out with the astonishingly high weekly view count, which peaked at 129 million views in its second week of release.

Views per week of the 10 most popular YouTube videos.
Highlighted: **Hello by Adele** and Gangnam Style by PSY

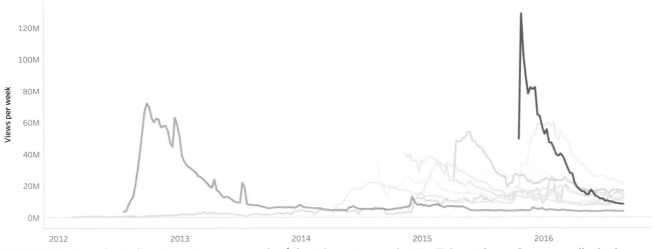

FIGURE 31.28   Line chart showing views per week of the 10 most popular YouTube videos. Can you tell which grew the fastest?

But the chart doesn't show us which video reached a certain threshold the most quickly. We could show the data as a running total over time, as shown in Figure 31.29.

In Figure 31.29, you can see the cumulative total views for each video very clearly, but which one hit the billion-view mark fastest? Was it Adele or Psy? You can't tell because, although we are good at reading slopes, we cannot easily compare them when they start at different points.

Cumulative daily views of the 10 most popular YouTube videos.
Highlighted: **Hello by Adele** and **Gangnam Style by PSY**

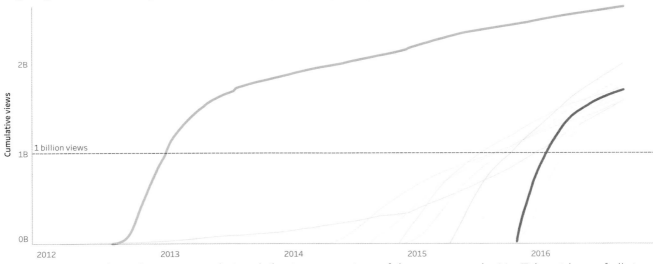

FIGURE 31.29   Line chart showing cumulative daily views over time of the most popular YouTube videos of all time.

We can solve all these problems by using an index chart. An index chart changes the x-axis. Instead of the actual date, it is an index representing units of time since an anchor point. In this case, the x-axis shows number of days since the video was released. The chart is shown in Figure 31.30.

Finally, this chart makes it easy to see which video was the fastest growing. Not only did "Hello" reach 1 billion views, putting Adele in an exclusive club on YouTube; the video did it more quickly than any video in the history of YouTube (88 days, to be precise).

As we scan the lines, we can see different shapes of growth. Most videos see the fastest growth soon after their release. However, there's one video that has grown very slowly: a "Masha and the Bear" cartoon, a Russian animated series.

Index chart are useful when you want to compare growth of events that happened at different times, such as:

- comparing ticket sales for events run over different periods;
- looking at progress of different cohorts of students;
- purchasing behavior of cohorts of customers; and
- A/B testing different types of marketing campaigns.

Cumulative daily views of the 10 most popular YouTube videos.
Highlighted: **Hello by Adele** and **Gangnam Style by PSY**

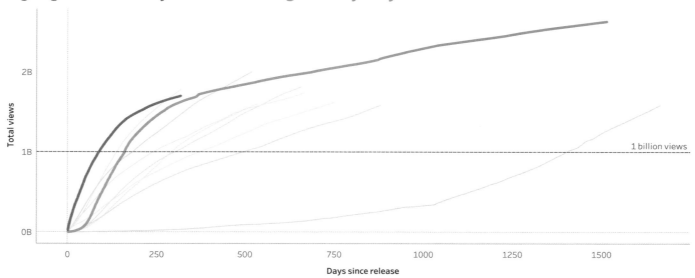

FIGURE 31.30   Index chart of cumulative daily views over time of the most popular YouTube videos of all time. "Hello" by Adele was the fastest video ever to reach 1 billion views on YouTube.

How Can I Show the Duration of Events?

All the charts we've looked at so far involved displaying one measure at various points in time. What if you want to examine *durations* of time of different events? In this situation, a Gantt chart is a great solution. (See Figure 31.31.)

Gantt charts are used most commonly in project planning. A project is made up of many discrete tasks, each of which has a start time, a duration, and a planned end time. Some projects can run concurrently. Some can begin only once another project has completed. Each task has an estimated and actual duration. With a Gantt chart, it is possible to line all these items together using bars to work out the total duration of a project.

Gantt charts allow you to see progress toward a goal. As events unfold, you can replace estimated duration with actual duration. Doing this enables you to see if your project is ahead of or behind schedule.

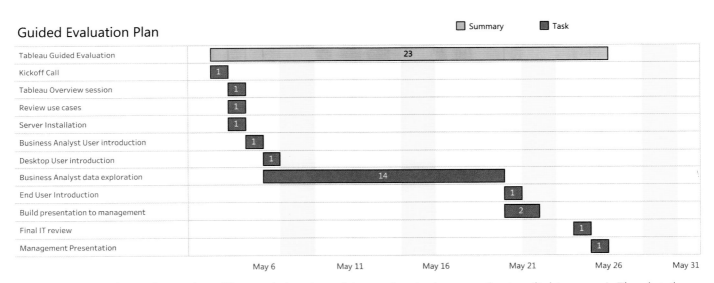

FIGURE 31.31 A basic Gantt chart. The total duration of the project is shown at the top (light orange). The detail tasks are shown in dark brown.

How Can I Focus on Bottlenecks in a Process?

By guest author Chris DeMartini

The jump plot, invented by Tom VanBuskirk, is a chart type specifically designed to analyze event sequences and identify bottlenecks and outliers within them. The chart can accommodate data in aggregation as well as scale to distribution views. Unique to the jump plot is its ability to visualize event sequences where some events may be optional. For example, when looking at a contract approval workflow, the second or third approval step may be required only if the contract exceeds certain amount-based thresholds.

The jump plot displays linear event sequences moving left to right on the x-axis in the form of checkpoints, defined as notable events in your sequence between which time will be measured. To a user's eye, the x-axis therefore represents sequential events over time. The duration of time elapsed between two checkpoints (referred to as a "hop") is represented on the y-axis by the height of the hop. In this example, the hops are drawn between checkpoints using Bézier curves. See Figure 31.32 for the basic layout of the chart.

The x-axis shows the discrete steps in the process. The elapsed time of hops is shown on the y-axis. The total duration is 10.81 seconds. There were six hops (a–f). The longest hop, the bottleneck, was the hop between step b and c, which took 5.43 seconds. You might wonder why this figure isn't shown as a bar chart; we'll look at that in a moment.

Another useful layout for jump plot is one where hops are measured against an expectation or threshold, referred to as a threshold-based jump plot. Each hop can be compared with its own threshold, or a single threshold can be applied across the sequence. If the hop was below the threshold, it is shown below the x-axis. If it was above the threshold, it is shown above the x-axis. (See Figure 31.33.)

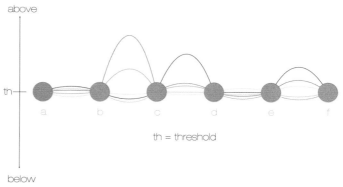

FIGURE 31.33 Threshold-based jump plot layout.

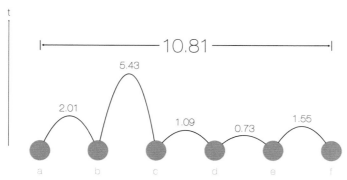

FIGURE 31.32 Jump plot layout.

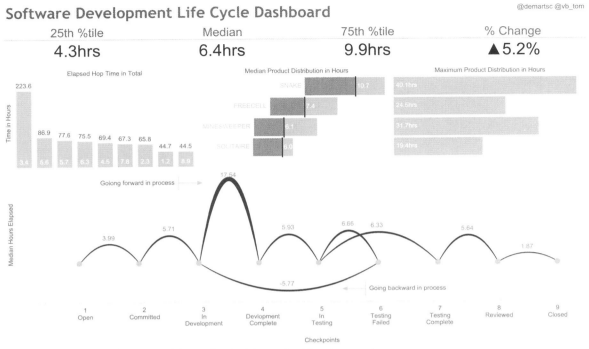

FIGURE 31.34 System development life cycle dashboard with a jump plot.

You can see why a bar wouldn't be a good way to represent the data: The curves allow multiple sequences to be shown.

The jump plot is designed to identify outliers and bottlenecks in a sequence of events. Figure 31.34 shows a top-down analysis of a software development life cycle workflow consisting of nine checkpoints: open, committed, in development, development complete, in testing, testing failed, testing complete, reviewed, and closed.

The jump plot at the bottom of the dashboard shows elapsed time between the hops in the development life cycle. The biggest hop is between jump 3 and 4: that's the development step. Note the jumps after step 5. The quicker jump, 6.33 hours, jumps directly to step 7 (testing complete). This is a successful test. The other jump from step 5 goes to step 6 (testing failed). It then has to go *back* to step 3 to be redeveloped, which is shown beneath the dots.

Read more about jump plots at www.jumpplot.com.

Which Time Chart Should I Use on My Dashboard?

As we've seen, there are many different ways to show time. Which is the right one? It depends. This answer doesn't just apply to timelines; it applies to every chart.

When building dashboards, you need to choose the chart that best addresses your scenario. A bump chart is no use if you want to see actual sales or cumulative sales, but it is great for looking at a change of rank over time. A highlight table can't show you trends over time for multiple categories, but it can show you seasonal trends for one measure. Don't forget that a standard trend line will work perfectly in many scenarios.

We recommend you consider the different ways time has been visualized in the scenarios throughout this book. Each chart shows the data in a different way to achieve a different goal.

Chapter 32

Beware the Dead-End Dashboard

You've considered the purpose of your dashboard. You've worked with colleagues to ensure the questions being answered are the correct ones. You've considered layout and design and made something beautifully functional. In fact, you've made a successful dashboard that helps people answer the questions they are asking.

Congratulations! Building an effective dashboard is a difficult thing to do, and you've done it.

But if you think your work is done, think again; you're just getting started.

Dashboard projects do not have endings. Your business evolves over time, and your dashboards should do the same. If not, they run the risk of becoming dead-end dashboards.

A couple of years ago, I (Andy) purchased a Fitbit. The wearable device tracks your daily activity, focusing on how many steps you walk each day, with a default 10,000-step target. For the first few months, this device and its online dashboard were hugely motivating. (See Figure 32.1.)

Fitbit took something that was difficult to record, step count, and made it easy to track. The dashboard didn't just reveal my daily walking patterns; it motivated me to change my behavior and walk more. The dashboard showed me which days I was failing (mostly on workdays) and allowed me to make strategies to

FIGURE 32.1   Fitbit dashboard.

walk more by, for example, taking morning strolls before my commute. The dashboard answered my questions and allowed me to take action.

After a while, I came to know everything the dashboard was going to tell me. I no longer needed to look at the dashboard to know how many steps I'd taken. The dashboard had educated me to make a good estimate without needing to look at it. Step count had, in other words, become a commodity fact. I'd changed my lifestyle, and the dashboard became redundant.

Now my questions were changing: What were my best and worst days ever? How did my daily activity change according to weather, mood, work commitments, and so on? Fitbit's dashboard didn't answer those questions. It was telling the same story it had been telling on the first day I used it, instead of offering new insights. My goals and related questions were changing, but Fitbit's dashboard didn't.

After a year, my Fitbit strap broke, and I decided not to buy a replacement. Why? Because the dashboard had become a dead end. It hadn't changed in line with my needs.

This happens in business scenarios too. Dashboards that don't evolve at the same pace as your questions don't get used. They become zombie dashboards, updating daily, shuffling along like the living dead. How many organizations have dashboards that perhaps were useful once upon a time but outlived their usefulness and were never replaced or updated?

How exactly do you avoid a Fitbit fate for the dashboards in your business or organization and ensure you have an evolving, thriving dashboard culture? We recommend taking four steps, discussed next.

1. Review Your KPIs

Every dashboard you build answers questions that are current at the time of the design. Consider the key performance indicator (KPI) dashboard featured in Chapter 8, shown again in Figure 32.2.

Look at the reliability rate. It's been hitting target for a considerable time. There might come a time when the business should ensure it is still measuring the right thing. If that KPI *never* fails, why measure it? In this case, there is only one year of data so it is probably too early to be sure this KPI is fixed, but after another year?

2. Track Usage with Data

Do people use the dashboards you've designed for them? If a dashboard was intended to be looked at by, say, 20 senior managers once a week, are you achieving that? Maybe the dashboard's never been used, or maybe its usage is waning.

Identifying a dashboard that's becoming less popular is a great way to identify a potential dead-end dashboard. Maybe the business question it asked is now solved. In that case, it might be time to remove the dashboard from your servers.

"Low dashboard usage typically signals a need for change," says Matt Francis, who is responsible for analytics at the Wellcome Trust Sanger Institute. "Sometimes they are for projects that are wound up. Other times requirements have changed so we work with people to refresh them. This way we ensure dashboards on our systems are giving users answers they need."

KPI Executive Overview

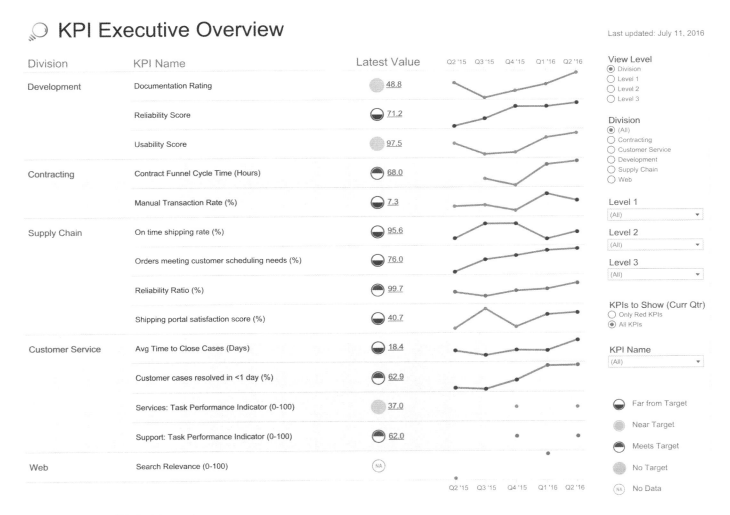

FIGURE 32.2 KPI dashboard.

Here are a few specific questions to begin your review:

- Which dashboards are most and least popular?
- Which dashboards *were* popular but aren't anymore? These dashboards might cover a problem that the business has now solved.
- Which dashboards are used by only a small section of the intended audience? Low usage might

indicate that some users haven't been trained properly in using the dashboard. It could mean that some users have different questions that the dashboard does not answer.

These questions can be answered by using data. Get the metrics on the number of times a dashboard has been looked at, over time.

Mark Jackson, the author of the Tableau Server dashboard in Chapter 18, also has multiple dashboards looking at how people use analytics across the organization.

In Figure 32.3, you can see how Mark looks out for dashboards that aren't reaching the right size of audience. Look at two workbooks around the center: User Audit and Core Staffing (labeled 1 and 2).

User Audit has around 30 views with an audience of approximately 15 people. Core Staffing has well over 100 views for the same audience size. Mark should investigate why the User Audit workbook is not receiving as many views as it should be by consulting the users. It might be that these particular dashboards need to be looked at only a few times a year. The data helps Mark, but he needs to talk with his audience to get the complete picture.

Another innovative way Mark tracks dashboards is to look specifically at his organization's executives and how often they look at the dashboards. How many business endeavors fail because they don't have committed executive support? If the people at the top don't support use of your organization's dashboards, there's a high chance adoption will fail. As shown in Figure 32.4, Mark specifically tracks executive usage

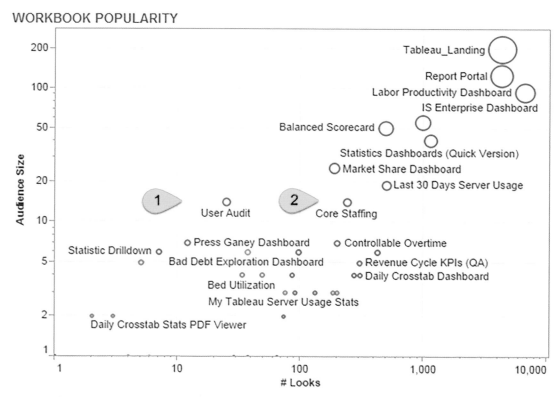

FIGURE 32.3   View of all dashboards on a server, showing number of views (Looks) and size of audience.

Source: Mark Jackson (http://ugamarkj.blogspot.com), Piedmont Healthcare

Executive History - Live Views (Last 14 Days)

friendly_name	hist_workbooks_name	hist_views_name			
Charles Scott	Statistics Dashboards (Quick Version)	Enterprise Revenue Dashboard	● Mon		
		FTE / Man Hours Variance Das..	● Mon		
		Key Hospital Statistics Dashbo..	● Mon		
Edward Lovern	Balanced Scorecard	Balanced Scorecard		● Wed	● Sun
	Statistics Dashboards (Quick Version)	Enterprise Revenue Dashboard	● Mon		
		Key Hospital Statistics Dashbo..	● Mon		
	Tableau_Landing	Dashboard_Tableau_Landing_..		● Wed	● Sun
Frank R. Powell	Tableau_Landing	Dashboard_Tableau_Landing_..		● Thu Mon ●	
Jyoti Rajagopal	Controllable Overtime	Controllable OT - Paid	● Tue		
		Controllable OT - Productive	● Tue		
	Tableau_Landing	Dashboard_Tableau_Landing_..	● Tue		
Leigh S. Hamby	Aug '14 Peer Review Scorecard	Specialties			Mon ●
	Clinical Cost Dashboard	Clinical Support Area			Mon ●
		CPT Codes			Mon ●
		Physician Activity			Mon ●
		Primary ICD-9 Dx			Mon ●
	First Case Delays	First Case Delays	● Thu		
	Infection Dashboard	Infection Dashboard			Mon ●
	OR Turnover Time	OR Turnover Time Dashboard	● Thu		
		Physician Turnaround	● Thu		
		Physician Turnover Time	● Thu		
	OR Utilization Dashboard	OR Utilization Dashboard	● Thu		
		OR Utilization Dashboard (30 ..	● Thu		
Mark Cohen	Aug '14 Peer Review Scorecard	Physician Scorecard		● Thu	
		Specialties		● Thu	
Michael Burnett	Imaging Services Productivity	Imaging Services Productivity ..	● Mon		
Sherry Henderson	POS	POS Collections by Day			Mon ●
		POS Collections by Pt Type an..			Mon ●
		POS Collections Trending			Mon ●
	Statistics Dashboards (Quick V..	LOS Dashboard	● Fri		

Aug 4   Aug 9

FIGURE 32.4   Mark tracks how often his executives look at the dashboards.

Source: Mark Jackson (http://ugamarkj.blogspot.com), Piedmont Healthcare

with their consent. If executive use dwindles, he knows he has to address the issue.

Find out more about Mark's administrator dashboards here: http://ugamarkj.blogspot.co.uk/2014/08/custom-tableau-server-admin-views.html.

3. Speak to Your Users

If you're designing dashboards for other people in your organization, when was the last time you asked them what they think of the dashboards? In fact, have you ever actually sat down, in a room, in front of the dashboard, and talked through how it is used? My hunch is that many people don't speak to the intended audience enough.

Why do I have that hunch? I was guilty of this in my early days as an analyst. I would publish what I thought were beautiful, insightful dashboards, then proudly send an email to everyone proclaiming something as grand as "It's here! The dashboard you've all been waiting for. Click this link and insight will follow!" In the following weeks, I would become frustrated as I looked at the data on who was using the dashboards, wondering why my work was being ignored.

What I hadn't done was enough consultation with the users at the end stages of the project. I hadn't sat down and watched them use the dashboard I'd created. As you build and fine-tune a dashboard, you are acutely aware of what every pixel means. You know where the color legend is because you put it on the dashboard. You know what to click to make the interaction work because you coded those interactions. You know what the scatterplot means because you chose the variables.

Sitting down behind someone and asking them to use your dashboard can be a very humbling experience. ("Oh no, they can't answer their questions and I thought I'd made it easy.") It can also be frustrating. ("How can you not see that there's a filter on the lower right? All you have to do is click it!") However, it's the best way to spot the mistakes in your dashboard and fix them before sending something to your organization that people won't be able to use.

4. Build Starter Dashboards

We like to personalize our possessions. We all buy the same smartphone but then accessorize it with a case in order to make it our own. What if you gave all users a basic dashboard and allowed them to personalize it for their own needs? Doing this acknowledges that fact that everybody wants to tailor data in their own way.

I work at Tableau. We do have core sales dashboards, but when we hire new salespeople, instead of pointing them to a set of dashboards that they need, we point them to a very basic dashboard, showing very basic sales information: sales over time and by geography.

They tailor the dashboard over time, as they get used to their part of the sales organization, so that it answers the questions they need for their jobs. Not only do they build something relevant to their needs, they also have a better sense of pride and ownership because it's their own toy.

What does become critical in this situation is that there is consensus around the goal. Not only must everybody be using a well-governed data source, it's also important that each employee is well aware of the strategic goal.

Although we have many, many dashboards in our organization, they all use the same governed data sources. We can be confident that we have a sales team proud of their own individual dashboards, making conclusions from the same single source of the data.

Summary

The real world is not a static place. To avoid dead-end tools, you should regularly review your dashboards using data and conversation. As you remove old ones, publish new ones, and adapt existing ones, you need to work closely with all stakeholders to make sure they are supportive and aware of the changes.

Chapter 33

The Allure of Red and Green

With 8 percent of men and nearly 1 percent of women suffering from color vision deficiency (CVD), using red and green together is a common problem when creating visualizations. People with strong CVD ("strong" meaning a more severe CVD) see both red and green as brown. People with weak CVD see bold red and green colors as different colors but still may have trouble distinguishing them if the red isn't red enough and the green isn't green enough.

This chapter provides different approaches for creating color-blind-friendly visualizations (even ones that use red and green).

Designing Color-Blind-Friendly Visualizations

Use a Color-Blind-Friendly Palette When Appropriate

One color used together in combination with another color is generally fine when one of them is not associated with CVD. For example, blue/orange is a common color-blind-friendly combination. Blue/red or blue/brown would also work. For the most common conditions of CVD, all of these work well, since blue would generally look blue to someone with CVD.

Figure 33.1 shows the Tableau color-blind–friendly palette designed by Maureen Stone. This palette works very well for the common cases of CVD. Notice how well this color palette works for the various comparisons of color under both protanopia and deuteranopia simulations.

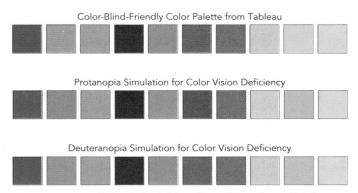

FIGURE 33.1 Color-blind-friendly palette from Tableau designed by Maureen Stone shown with protanopia and deuteranopia simulation.

What to Do If the Client/Boss Requires the Use of the Stoplight Color Palette

You understand that using red and green together (and other color combinations discussed in Chapter 1) can be very problematic. However, the boss/client has given a strict requirement that you use red and green together. It might be part of the company colors or the corporate style guide, or maybe you are working on a project for the country of Mali. (See Figure 33.2.) Now what can you do?

FIGURE 33.2 Flag of the Republic of Mali

Traffic Light Colors   Deuteranopia
                            Simulation

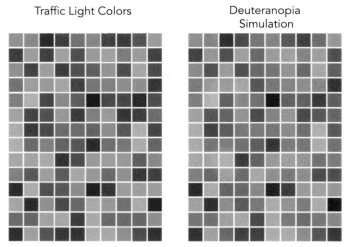

FIGURE 33.3   Heat map (highlight table) using red and green and a color-blind simulation of that same table. Red and green won't work in this case for someone with CVD.

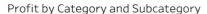
Profit by Category and Subcategory

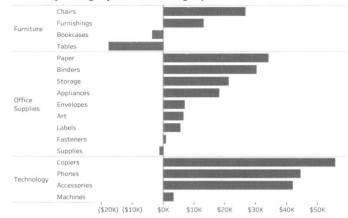

FIGURE 33.4   Diverging bar chart showing positive and negative values.

The first thing to consider is that being able to tell these colors apart in a visualization is *an issue only if color is the only method to make a distinct comparison*, for example, a good number versus a bad number in a heat map or one line versus another line in the same line chart. In Figure 33.3, color is needed to tell a good square (green) from a bad square (red). Using the deuteranopia CVD simulation we can see that this would be an impossible task for someone with CVD.

Alternatively, if red and green are not the only method of encoding the data, it might be fine to use them side by side. For example, if the length of bars in a bar chart is encoding the same data—and if those bars are labeled or marked in a way that you could tell them apart—then it may not be an issue at all if they both appear brown in color.

Figure 33.4 shows one example where it's easy to see from the axis line that most numbers are positive and three are negative. Color is a secondary feature simply encoding positive versus negative. Although this may not be the best choice of colors, someone with CVD still can interpret this chart correctly without the use of color.

Offer Alternate Methods of Distinguishing Data

If you do use red and green to encode your data, you can help people with CVD distinguish good (green) and bad (red) by using other indicators such as icons, directional arrows or labels. Figure 33.5 shows sign-up rates at 3 percent lower than the prior year, which is bad and indicated in red, but they are 2.8 percent higher during 2015, which is good and shown in green. Someone with CVD could have tremendous difficulty knowing that one is bad and the other is good. Adding the small arrow indicators makes it clear to anyone that one number is down and the other is up.

FIGURE 33.5   Arrows used as indicators when using red and green together.

Profit by State

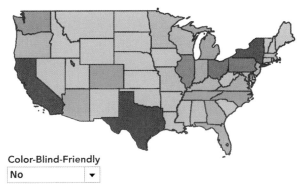

Color-Blind-Friendly

| No | ▼ |

FIGURE 33.6 Map showing a color-blind-friendly drop-down box that adjusts the color of the map.

Profit by State

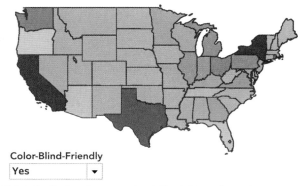

Color-Blind-Friendly

| Yes | ▼ |

FIGURE 33.7 Selecting a color-blind-friendly palette changes the map colors away from red and green.

Provide an Option to Swap the Colors

Another option might be checkboxes or drop-down selections for a user to switch the color palette for the entire visualization to a color-blind-friendly palette. This method allows for the red/green pairing for the majority of the audience and can be the default color scheme, but it allows someone with CVD to change the color palette to a color-blind-friendly one. (See Figures 33.6 and 33.7.)

Use Light and Dark Colors to Create Good Contrast between Red and Green

For someone with CVD, the problem is primarily with color *hue*—for example, the color of red versus green—and not with the color *value* (light versus dark). Almost anyone can tell the difference between a very light color and a very dark color, so another option when using red and green together is to use a really light green, a medium yellow, and a very dark red. This would appear to be more of a sequential color scheme to someone who has strong CVD, but at least the person would be able to distinguish red from green based on light versus dark.

This technique will work only if using the stoplight colors in a categorical color scheme. It will not work when using a diverging color scheme, because a diverging color palette requires the use of light to dark colors to encode data, and that will cause problems if using a light green to distinguish from a dark red.

Figure 33.8 shows a standard stoplight color palette with the hex color codes listed. Notice that

Traffic Light Color Palette

#E22049   #FFF200   #0D9E49

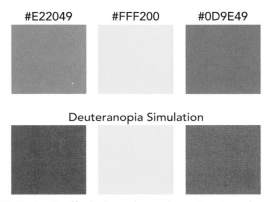

Deuteranopia Simulation

FIGURE 33.8 Traffic light color palette (top) and deuteranopia color-blind simulation (bottom).

under the deuteranopia simulation, the green and the red are very close in hue. It would be very hard for someone with CVD to distinguish between these two colors.

Alternate Traffic Light Color Palette

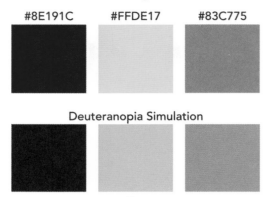

FIGURE 33.9 Alternate traffic light color palette that is more color-blind-friendly (top) and deuteranopia color-blind simulation (bottom).

Figure 33.9 shows an alternate stoplight color palette, this time leveraging color hue to make a better distinction between colors. The green is a light green and the red is very dark. Notice that under the color-blind simulation, the red and green are easy to distinguish from each other.

Leverage Blue in the Green Color

We discussed using blue and red as an alternative color palette because blue is a color-blind-friendly color. Along those same lines, we can use a version of green that has more blue in it, creating a bluish green. Doing this will create more contrast for people with CVD. Using a light bluish green versus a dark red creates even more contrast.

Figure 33.10 shows a very similar color palette as Figure 33.9, but this time the green has more blue. Under the deuteranopia simulation, there is more contrast between the dark red and light green (with blue).

Alternate Traffic Light Color Palette

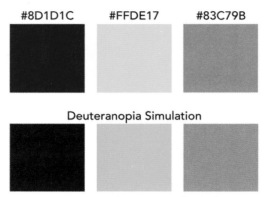

FIGURE 33.10 Another alternate traffic light color palette using bluish green (top) and deuteranopia color-blind simulation (bottom).

Browser add-in simulates CVD

In addition to a number of online color-blind simulators, a plug-in available for Chrome called "NoCoffee" simulates all types of color vision deficiency right in your browser. See Chapter 1 for more details.

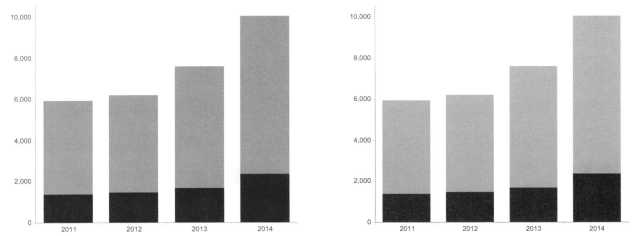

FIGURE 33.11 Stacked bar chart showing the color-blind-friendly palette shown in Figure 33.10.

Figure 33.11 shows a stacked bar chart using the color palette that was used in Figure 33.10 (left) and deuteranopia simulation (right).

Conclusion

This chapter has offered a number of alternatives for creating visualizations that can include red and green (or other non-color-blind-friendly color combinations). You don't have to avoid red and green; you can use them in conjunction with other accommodations or find shades of red and green that work for almost anyone reading the visualization, including those with CVD.

Chapter 34

The Allure of Pies and Donuts

It's easy for us as teachers, writers, or speakers to discuss data visualization best practices, but we also realize there will be times when you will not have complete control over design decisions. There may be situations where you cannot avoid using pie and donut charts. A client request or a demand from the Director of All Things Circular may force decisions to be made about a visualization that are not best practice. It is our hope that this chapter will help you in these situations.

Background

As discussed in Chapter 1, the two best encoding methods for making precise quantitative comparisons are (1) using length or height from a common baseline for the comparison (e.g., a bar chart) and (2) using position to make the comparison (e.g., a dot plot).

When trying to show precise quantitative comparisons, using angles, arcs, area, or size of circles is not as good as using length or position to encode data.

For this reason, pie charts, donut charts, and bubble charts typically are not good choices for visualizing data. There are the occasional exceptions, but be very cautious in your use of these charts. Some examples follow.

Pie charts may be useful on a map to show a part-to-whole relationship within a geographic region. (See Figure 34.1.) This is because there is no easy way to present multiple bar charts on a map where there is no common baseline for making comparisons.

Using size of a circle for precise comparisons can be especially difficult, but using size as secondary encoding in a scatterplot to show additional context to the data might be useful. For example, Figure 34.2 visualizes the comparison of fertility rate versus life expectancy at birth by country as a scatterplot. The size of a circle encodes population by country, a secondary metric that is not critical to the analysis (and color encodes the continent).

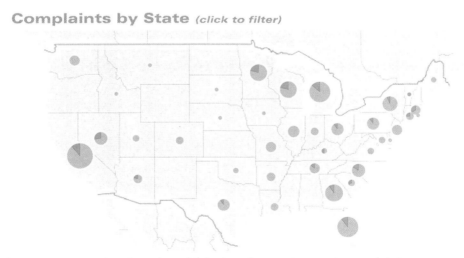

FIGURE 34.1 Pie charts on a map showing closed (blue) and open (orange) complaints.

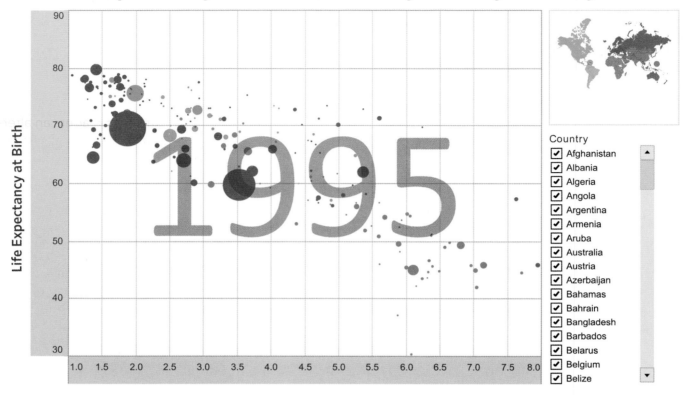

FIGURE 34.2   Scatterplot showing life expectancy at birth versus fertility rate by country.

Source: A re-creation of Hans Rosling's Gapminder. Free material from www.gapminder.org adapted by Jeffrey Shaffer using Tableau.

The primary purpose of this visualization is to compare fertility rate and life expectancy, not to show population. This secondary metric is less important. It is not critical to the analysis to make a precise comparison of the population among countries, yet it provides additional context to the overall story. It's also easy to see the most populated countries in the world (China and India, which are the large red circles).

The Client or Boss Requires a Pie Chart

Say the boss/client wants a pie chart and the data has lots of categories. The first thing to consider is the type of data that is being displayed. The purpose of a pie chart is to show a part-to-whole relationship. The primary problem when reading a pie chart is comparing slices to one another. Try to minimize this in the design. Avoid dividing the pie or donut chart into many slices. As the slices in the chart increase, the data becomes more difficult to interpret.

Consider the example in Figure 34.3, which shows a pie chart with too many slices. There are 17 categories showing a percentage of total sales. Each category is a slice representing a different color. Even though the pie chart is ordered, making comparisons among the categories is very difficult and requires our eyes to go back and forth from the legend to the chart.

Now consider Figure 34.4. The same data is visualized in a pie chart but with a few major changes. First, there is only a single slice with a label, the category that is highlighted (phones). Instead of

17 categorical colors, there are only two, the highlighted category in blue and all of the others in gray. A bar chart has been added in place of the color legend. Now users can make a precise comparison using the bar chart and, if interactive, the user can select a bar to highlight any category in the pie chart.

Figure 34.4 meets the requirement of using a pie chart, but at the same time, it offers readers an alternative that utilizes the strength of the visual system: the precision that the bar chart offers. Notice that this solution provides an additional piece of information that was not immediately present in the other charts: the comparison of 85.6 percent versus 14.4 percent, which is now clearly indicated and is not easily seen in Figure 34.3.

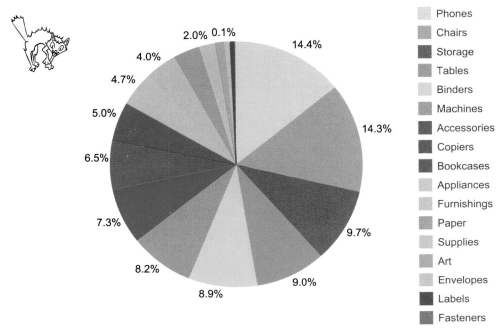

FIGURE 34.3 Pie chart with 17 categories.

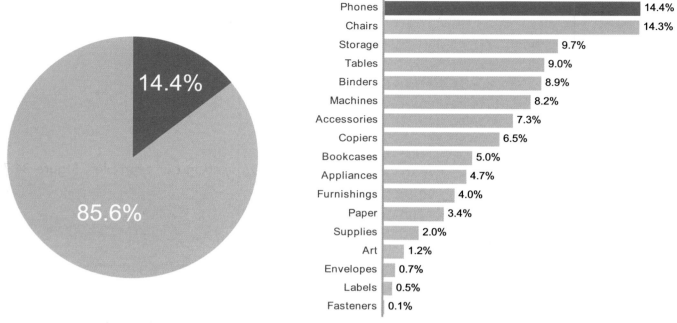

Phones	14.4%
Chairs	14.3%
Storage	9.7%
Tables	9.0%
Binders	8.9%
Machines	8.2%
Accessories	7.3%
Copiers	6.5%
Bookcases	5.0%
Appliances	4.7%
Furnishings	4.0%
Paper	3.4%
Supplies	2.0%
Art	1.2%
Envelopes	0.7%
Labels	0.5%
Fasteners	0.1%

FIGURE 34.4 Pie chart with a single category highlighted and a companion bar chart.

The Client or Boss Requires a Donut Chart

Donut charts often are used as alternatives to pie charts to show a part-to-whole relationship. They also are used frequently as a key performance indicator (KPI); for example, Figure 34.5 shows that the North sales region has reached 64 percent of the target goal.

FIGURE 34.5 Donut chart showing a KPI that has reached 64 percent of goal.

As a single KPI indicator, this donut chart certainly is easier to understand than the pie chart example with 17 categories in Figure 34.3. The reason is that this donut chart does not require the reader to compare one category to another. It's simply an actual value coming full circle back to 100 percent of target.

However, although a single value is easy enough to see, consider what happens when four regions are being compared, as in Figure 34.6.

Try comparing the North versus East regions and then the South versus West regions. This comparison is much harder than interpreting a single KPI donut chart, and we think users will find themselves relying on the labels inside of the donuts.

FIGURE 34.6 KPI donut chart showing four regions.

Also, it's important to note that this type of KPI visualization is useful only when the goal has an upper bound of 100 percent, as, for example, the number of seats in a sports arena, the capacity of a storage facility, or the number of cars on a lot. These things have an upper bound limit, which makes the goal fixed at 100 percent. A sales target, however, might not have an upper bound limit. It's possible that the sales team could sell at a higher price than expected, regardless of quantity, and achieve 106 percent of goal. A KPI donut is difficult to use if it is important to show that performance over the goal.

Throughout the book, we've discussed better chart types for this type of comparison—for example, a bullet chart with a bar chart showing the actual result and a target line showing the goal. These chart types don't have the same limitation as donut charts, and it will be easier to compare 106 percent of goal to 110 percent of goal.

Another alternative is a progress bar. Progress bars are very common, and often you probably don't even realize when they are being used. For example, Time Warner Cable uses a beautifully designed progress bar to show what time a TV show starts, when it ends, and how far into the show it is at any particular moment. The design also features a blue

and gray color scheme, very similar to the color scheme being used in our examples. Figure 34.7 shows the data from the KPI donut chart as a progress bar.

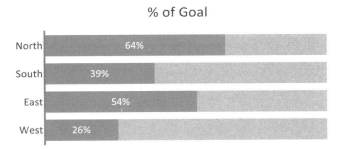

FIGURE 34.7 Progress bars showing the KPI for four regions. Notice how easy it is to compare one region to another region.

Where's My Donut?

Despite your efforts to present the data in the best way, you've hit a roadblock with a boss/client. Although the boss/client agrees that a bar chart with a target line or a progress bar might make the comparison easier, too many bar charts are "boring." The boss/client says something like "It needs more visual impact" or "Make it pop more." The person probably can't define this in any further detail either but insists on donut charts.

Defect Rate

FIGURE 34.8 Series of donut charts showing defect rates for different categories or time periods.

If you find yourself in this situation, try:

1. Taking a deep breath.

2. Doing a quick YouTube search for "needs more cowbell."

3. Read on.

The next examples propose alternatives that may help you in these situations.

Note that we are not recommending these charts as best practice data visualization methods. We assume that if you have read this far, you have no choice but to give in to the requirements of the client/boss. We propose that you accommodate the poor choice by redundantly encoding the information in a better way.

May I Have a Dozen Donuts?

Figure 34.8 shows an example where multiple donut charts are used for a comparison of defects. (It's not actually a full dozen.) As discussed previously, a series of donut charts makes it really hard to compare one chart to the next. This specific example is also problematic because all of the values are very low, so seeing the differences in the data is very difficult.

By adding a bar chart, the small differences in the defect rate can be seen. (See Figure 34.9.) This is because the bar chart uses length from a common baseline, which allows for a very precise comparison that donut charts do not.

In Figure 34.10, the defect rate is plotted underneath the donut chart. This technique is similar to the one used in Figure 34.9, but a dot is used to represent each defect. Notice how easy it is to see the difference between 2 percent and 3 percent in both Figures 34.9 and 34.10. It's much easier to see this small difference using the bar chart or dots than trying to decipher and compare tiny segments of donut charts.

Defect Rate

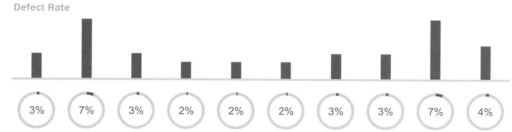

FIGURE 34.9 The same series of donut charts but with a bar chart on top.

FIGURE 34.10 The same series of donut charts plotted with individual dots showing the defects.

Conclusion

It is our hope that showing a few of these examples illustrates how accommodations can be made. Yes, there may be instances where you are forced to make bad design decisions; the boss/client just wants a dozen donuts. By offering small accommodations for these choices, you can help readers better understand the data and still meet the boss/client's demands.

And maybe if you are lucky, after a month or so, the boss/client will see that it is the bars or dots that are making the comparison easy, and you will get the all-clear to delete the donuts.

Chapter 35

Clouds and Bubbles

The Allure of Word Clouds and Bubble Charts

As you know from reviewing the scenarios and reading about the problems with pies, circles, and donuts, word clouds and bubble charts may look great, but they are analytically impoverished.

So what do you do if somebody shows you an infographic that has a word cloud or a bubble chart, or both, and asks you why your dashboard—which they think is boring because it has a lot of bar charts—doesn't have either?

We thought it would be useful to share a case study about an organization that grappled with this very issue.

Marist Poll and Views of the 2016 Presidential Election

The Marist Poll, a survey research center at Marist College, partners with media organizations including NBC News, *The Wall Street Journal*, and McClatchy to provide publicly available poll results on elections and issues. In November 2015, the Marist Poll asked Americans to describe in one word the tone of the 2016 presidential election. Figure 35.1 shows the results.

Attempt 1: Word Cloud

The results from the poll are very compelling, but the results as depicted in the text table don't exactly pop. Marist first tried a word cloud, shown in Figure 35.2.

Although the graphic has more visual interest, it's hard to make sense of the six terms, let alone discern that the results for "crazy" were almost three times greater than the results for the next most popular term.

Crazy	40%
Mean-spirited	14%
Passionate	13%
Traditional	13%
Informative	9%
Principled	9%
Unsure	2%

FIGURE 35.1   Marist Poll results in tabular form.

Source: The Marist Poll, Marist College

TraditionalMean-spirited

Unsure Crazy

InformativePassionate

Principled

FIGURE 35.2   Marist Poll results using a word cloud.

Attempt 2: Bubble Charts (aka Packed Bubbles)

Not happy with the word cloud, Marist next tried a bubble chart. People love circles, and the chart in Figure 35.3 certainly looks cool, but what does it reveal other than that the "crazy" circle is larger than the other circles?

Although the bubbles may grab the reader's attention, they do little to facilitate a fast understanding of the data.

Sure, we could add numbers to the bubbles, but why not use a simple bar chart?

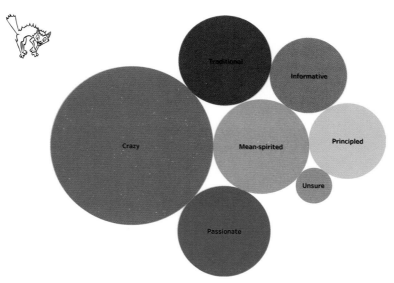

FIGURE 35.3   Marist Poll results with packed bubbles.

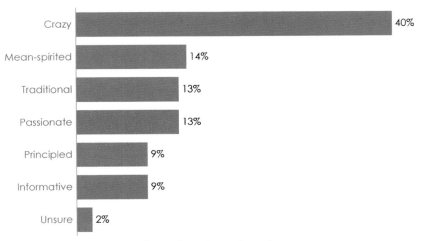

FIGURE 35.4   Marist Poll results using a bar chart.

Attempt 3: A Simple Bar Chart

Figure 35.4 presents the same data rendered using the tried-and-true bar chart.

This is a big improvement over the word cloud and bubble chart with respect to clarity. People can easily sort the responses and see how much larger the "crazy" response is than the other responses.

But for that boss, client, or stakeholder who pines for bubbles, the bar chart is a bit sterile. What can we do to make the "crazy" pop out without dumbing down the analysis?

Attempt 4: Colored Bar Chart

The major takeaway from the poll is that 40 percent of respondents characterized the election as "crazy." We can make that pop by making that bar a bold color and all the other bars muted, as shown in Figure 35.5.

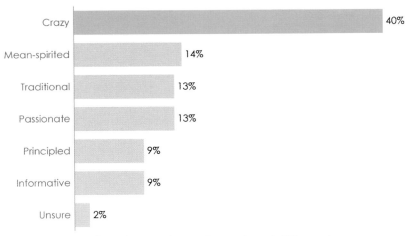

FIGURE 35.5   Marist Poll results using a bar chart with one bar colored differently.

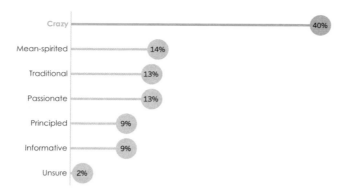

FIGURE 35.6   Marist Poll results as a lollipop chart.

Attempt 5: Lollipop Chart

If Marist was tasked with building a dashboard for internal use, then the colored bar chart absolutely does the job and does it well. But Marist has to produce things that are public facing and wanted something that was both beyond reproach analytically and had more aesthetic allure. A lollipop chart is simply thin bars with circles at the end. (See Figure 35.6.)

The lollipop is an excellent compromise between the analytical integrity of the bar chart and the "ooh . . . circles" appeal of the packed bubbles.

Final Attempt: Adding a Compelling Title

There's still one critical piece of information missing, and that's the title. That is, in the chart, we have "the answer," but without a title or some other form of description, we don't know what the question is. A concise, descriptive title can make a huge difference in garnering attention and making a chart more memorable. (See Figure 35.7.)

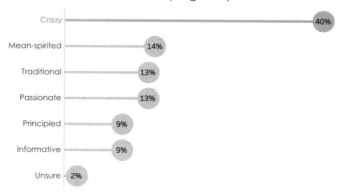

FIGURE 35.7   Marist Poll results as a lollipop chart with descriptive headline.

> **Note**
>
> The descriptive title works here because this is a one-off graphic that will appear on a website or in a magazine. You probably would not see a title like this on a day-to-day business dashboard.

Conclusion

We're confident many readers of this book will be asked to create a dashboard that incorporates word clouds and bubble charts. In this section we've provided some workarounds that will placate the bubble lovers without compromising the analytic integrity of your dashboard.

Chapter 36

A Journey into the Unknown

Reports that say that something hasn't happened are always interesting to me, because as we know, there are known knowns; there are things we know we know. We also know there are known unknowns; that is to say we know there are some things we do not know. But there are also unknown unknowns—the ones we don't know we don't know. And if one looks throughout the history of our country and other free countries, it is the latter category that tend[s] to be the difficult ones.

—Donald Rumsfeld, February 2002

We hope the dashboards and real-world advice in this book leave you feeling inspired. We also hope you use the content here to make amazing dashboards that reveal great insights to you and your colleagues.

Now, in this final chapter, we bring you a shocking message: *All dashboards are incomplete.*

What? How can that be?

Consider all the scenarios in this book. Each one has been designed to answer a specific set of questions. Not only a specific set of questions, but a specific set of questions that were decided when the dashboard was conceived. These are the *known unknowns*. You know the questions you need to ask (e.g., How many patients were admitted to the hospital yesterday?) but you don't know the answer.

In itself, this isn't the end of the world. By using your dashboard, you can see your data and get answers to those anticipated questions. Most businesses have a core set of questions that need to be monitored. However, a dashboard presents a fixed perspective on your data. The filters and interactivity limit the questions you can answer. Where is the space for exploration and serendipitous discoveries? Where is the space to freely explore your data?

What happens if looking at your dashboard raises new questions? "Hospital admissions went up," you might see. Next, you're likely to ask "*Why?*" At some point you have a new question that the dashboard can't answer. There is a famous mantra in data visualization, coined by computer scientist Ben Shneiderman: "Overview first, zoom and filter, then details-on-demand."[1] Lots of the dashboards in this book allow that, but even the best can take you down to only a narrow set of predefined details.

Well, what next? What happens when your dashboard provokes an unexpected question or, as Rumsfeld called it, an *unknown unknown*? There's a more fundamental assumption that should be challenged: Are dashboards the right way to look at your data?

Let's look at two ways visual analytics can help you add extra value on top of your dashboarding strategies.

Keep Asking Questions

Sakichi Toyoda, born in Japan in 1867, was a formidable engineer. He invented looms that transformed the textile industry, and his company, Toyoda Automatic Loom Works, went on to become Toyota Motor Corporation.

---

[1] Ben Shneiderman, "The Eyes Have It: A Task by Data Type Taxonomy for Information Visualizations," *Proceedings, IEEE Symposium on Visual Languages*, 1996.

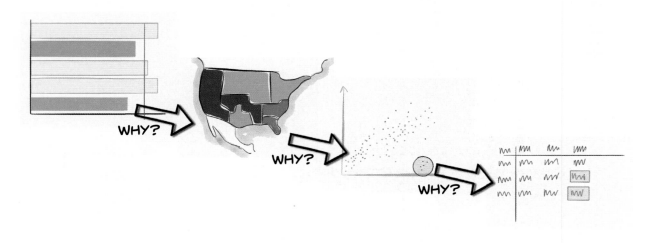

FIGURE 36.1   Ask your data: "Why?"

Toyoda also came up with many ideas about how to run business efficiently. One of these was the Five Whys technique, a simple way to get to the root cause of a problem and take action. (See Figure 36.1.) The premise is simple: When you come across a problem, ask why again and again until you get to the root cause. Once that root cause is discovered, you can put a new process in place to prevent the problem from recurring.

Another effective approach is to proceed through different levels of questions, starting with straightforward ones about what the data says (e.g., "How much?" or "How many?"). The next questions are the why questions, which can explain why the data says what it does. Finally, there are questions about making actual changes at the root-cause level.

No matter which method of analysis you prefer, the important thing is to keep asking questions.

What does this have to do with dashboards? Most dashboards have limited analytical paths built into them. Even if they allow you to jump to another dashboard or report, you'll be stuck on the path someone else anticipated. Exploring the data behind the dashboard directly, beyond the limits of the filters and interactions enables you to understand the unknown unknowns.

Let's look at an example. Figure 36.2 shows a dashboard displaying sales and profit in a fictional superstore.

What pops out? Furniture is miles away from its profit targets. (Note the red dot to draw attention to the

SALES METRICS ANALYSIS AND KPIS

Region
All

How are **sales** and profit in our main categories? *(most recent period)*

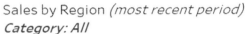

Sales by Region *(most recent period)*
Category: All

Profit over time by Ship Mode
Category: All

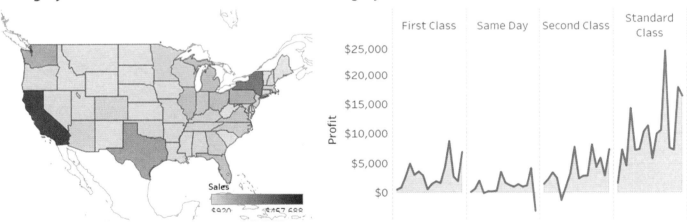

FIGURE 36.2 Sales and profit in a fictional U.S. superstore.

problematic area.) The dashboard has a filter for region, but it's unlikely that's going to show the root cause of the problem. In fact, we reach a dead end quickly.

It might take a few steps to find the root cause by looking at the underlying data. In this case, you might ask questions about furniture sales, including manufacturers, individual orders, and discounts. To do this, we disaggregate this data from the overall sales and profit key performance indicators (KPIs). A KPI is by definition a single number representing some aggregation of multiple values. The aggregation is great

Sales and Profit for all Tables, and Orders. Color shows Discount.

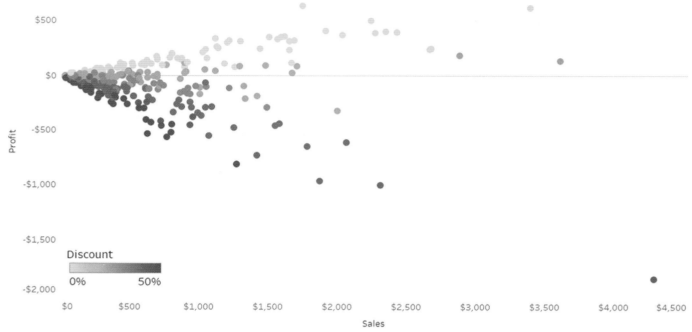

FIGURE 36.3   Each dot represents a single order for a table in our superstore. The discount is causing us to lose money.

for an overview, but each individual data point might tell its own story, as in the patient-tracking dashboard from Chapter 14.

After just a few questions, you might end up with a totally new chart, such as the scatterplot in Figure 36.3.

Just look at that. The darker the orange, the bigger the discount—and the bigger the discount, the bigger the loss. You can see that most orders below 0 on the y-axis were discounted. Barely any profitable orders had a discount applied. We have found the root cause of the profitability problem: The discounts are too generous. Now it's possible to take action and fix the problem.

Dashboards get you a long way to insight, but you need to be able to go beyond the farthest questions your dashboards reach to answer the unanticipated questions they provoke.

The Squiggle of Visual Exploration

What if we didn't even start with a dashboard? What if people could explore data freely in order to make accidental discoveries that could revolutionize their businesses?

Dmitri Mendeleev, a Russian chemist, created the Periodic Table of Elements in 1869 while writing volume two of *The Principles of Chemistry*. He was struggling to find a way to represent the known elements in a logical way. He'd developed some insights by sketching ideas on the back of an invitation to visit a local cheese co-operative but these hadn't given him the satisfaction of a complete solution.

His flash of inspiration came while playing with a special set of cards with the elements drawn on them. Free of the restrictions of pen and paper, he could rearrange the cards freely on a table, perhaps by atomic weight or other properties. He rearranged his data until a spark of insight lit in his mind, leading to the periodic table of elements. The rearrangement, exploration, and freedom of movement led to the insight.

Dashboards don't let you move the data around. If you want to make your own perspective-shifting discoveries, you need to be able to explore data in the same way Mendeleev did.

Figure 36.4 shows how this process could work. Yes, that squiggle represents a path to insight using data. Instead of beginning with a fixed, rigid view of your data via a dashboard, you start with just a connection to your data and a blank canvas. Quickly, you throw data around, and charts appear, one after another. Focusing initially on ad-hoc exploration, you can try lots of different approaches letting the data reveal its own stories. You improvise and change direction. You chase hunches and shift perspectives, like Mendeleev did, until a spark of insight reveals something new.

That example shows how one person can explore data to find new insights, but what if you could scale that up within your organization?

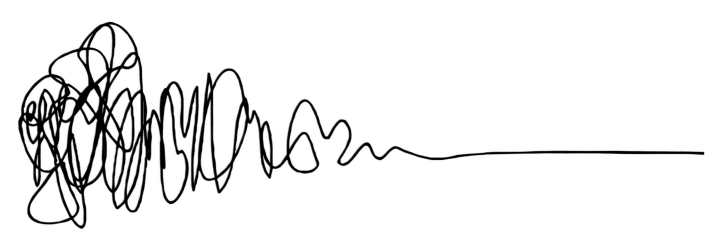

FIGURE 36.4 Complete Squiggle of Visual Analysis.

Source: Diagram based on "The Design Process Squiggle" by Damien Newman. http://cargocollective.com/central/The-Design-Squiggle.

In 2016, along with Andy Kriebel, Head Coach at the UK's Data School, I ran a project called Makeover Monday (http://tabsoft.co/MakeoverMonday). Each week we would find a chart somewhere on the web. Often it was one which was poorly designed, or told its story weakly. We shared the data to the wider data visualization community and asked people to remake the chart. Could they find a new angle on the story? Or a better way of presenting it?

What happened was astonishing: Over 52 weeks, we had more than 3000 makeovers submitted by over 500 contributors (some are shown in Figure 36.5). Just think: For every person who opened and played with the data, they went on their own unique, squiggly path to their own discoveries. Each person honed in on a different articulation of the data. Each week the same data revealed scores of insights hidden in the original

chart. What if people in your organization were free to explore their data freely?

For many organizations, starting from scratch and following a squiggle is a new paradigm. However, this is the only way to discover the answers to the unknown unknown questions. A successful data strategy needs to tackle these too.

We hope our scenarios have inspired you to try new ways to show the answers to the questions you know your organization has to answer. We have also shown that even the known questions themselves evolve. Because of this, so should your work.

A finished dashboard is not the end of the process of analyzing your data: It is just the beginning.

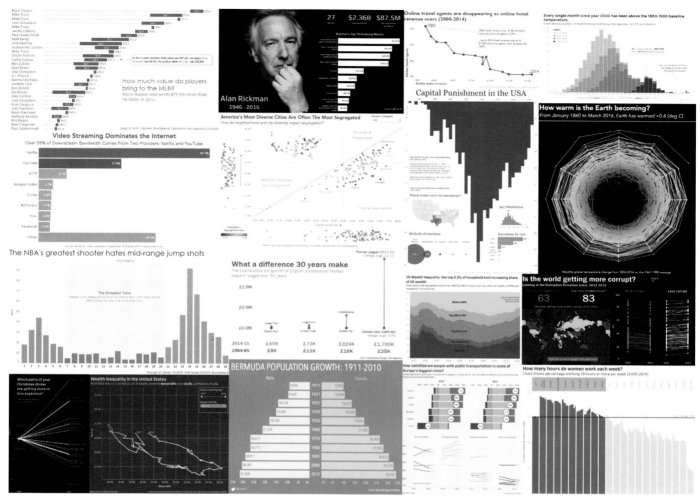

FIGURE 36.5 Selection of the 3,000+ makeovers from Makeover Monday.

Glossary of Chart Types

Area Chart

encodes data using position and height and shows trend/volume over time.

Bar Chart

encodes data using height/length of bar and shows categorical comparisons.

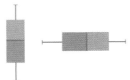

Box Plot

encodes data using position and height/length to show the distribution of the data.

Bullet Graph

encodes data using length/height, position, and color to show actual compared to target and performance bands.

Choropleth Map (Shaded Map)

encodes data using color and position to show data geographically.

Diverging Bar Chart

encodes data using height/length of bar diverging from a midpoint to show categorical comparisons.

Dot Plot

encodes data using position to show the comparisons.

Dot Plot with Jitter (Jitterplot)

encodes data using position to show comparisons but offsets points randomly to reduce overlap of dots.

Gantt Chart

encodes data using length and position to show amount of work completed in segments of time.

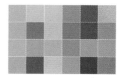

Heat Map

encodes a data table using color to highlight the differences in the table without numbers.

Highlight Table

encodes a data table using color to highlight the differences in the table numbers.

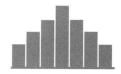

Histogram

encodes data using height and shows a distribution.

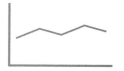

Line Chart

encodes data using position and often shows trend over time.

Lollipop Chart

encodes data using height/length of bar and shows categorical comparisons.

SCATTER PLOT

encodes data using position to show the relationship between two variables. Size can also be used to show a secondary comparison.

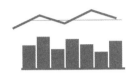

SLOPEGRAPH

encodes data using position to show quantitative comparison or rank, typically between two time periods.

SPARKLINE/SPARKBAR

encodes data using position (line) or height/length (bar) in a small, word-sized graphic.

STACKED BAR CHART *

encodes data using height/length of bar and color by segment and shows categorical and part-to-whole comparisons.

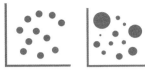

SYMBOL MAP (DOT MAP)

encodes data using position to show data geographically and can also use size to show quantitative data.

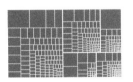

TREEMAP

encodes data using size and color and is useful for hierarchical data or when there is a very large number of categories to compare.

WATERFALL CHART

encodes data using height and often color to show increase and decrease between time periods or categories.

* CAUTION

Be careful not to slice stacked charts into too many segments.

Bubble Chart

encodes data using size of circle to show comparisons, which is difficult for making precise quantitative comparisons.

Concentric Circles (Radial Bar Chart)

encodes data using arc and area to show comparisons but problematic for many reasons.

Donut Chart

encodes data using arc and area to show a part-to-whole comparison but problematic for many reasons.

Pie Chart

encodes data using angle, area, and arc to show a part-to-whole comparison but problematic for many reasons.

Word Cloud

encodes data using size of word to show comparisons, which is difficult for making precise quantitative comparisons.

Caution

These chart types are not recommended.

Bibliography

Anscombe, Francis. *Graphs in Statistical Analysis*. The American Statistician, Vol. 27, No. 1., 1973.

Bertin, Jacques. *Semiology of Graphics*. Redlands, CA: Esri Press, 1983.

Birch, Jennifer. *Diagnosis of Defective Colour Vision*. Oxford, UK: Oxford University Press, 1993.

Cairo, Alberto. *The Functional Art: An Introduction to Information Graphics and Visualization*. Berkeley, CA: New Riders, 2013.

Cleveland, William. *The Elements of Graphing Data*. Summit, NJ: Hobart Press, 1994.

Cleveland, William. *Visualization Data*. Summit, NJ: Hobart Press, 1993.

Craig, James, and Irene Korol Scala. *Designing with Type: The Essential Guide to Typography*, 5th ed. New York, NY: Watson-Guptill Publications, 2006.

Duarte, Nancy. *Resonate: Present Visual Stories that Transform Audiences*. Hoboken, NJ: John Wiley and Sons, 2010.

Duarte, Nancy. *Slide:ology: The Art and Science of Creating Great Presentations*. Sebastopol, CA: O'Reilly, 2008.

Few, Stephen. *Information Dashboard Design: Displaying Data for At-a-Glance Monitoring*, 2nd ed. Oakland, CA: Analytics Press, 2013.

Few, Stephen. *Now You See It: Simple Visualization Techniques for Quantitative Analysis*. Oakland, CA: Analytics Press, 2009.

Few, Stephen. *Show Me the Numbers: Designing Tables and Graphs to Enlighten*. Oakland, CA: Analytics Press, 2012.

Norman, Donald A. *The Design of Everyday Things*. New York, NY: Basic Books, 1988.

Nussbaumer Knaflic, Cole. *Storytelling with Data: A Data Visualization Guide for Business Professionals*. Hoboken, NJ: John Wiley and Sons, 2015.

Shneiderman, Ben. *The Eyes Have It: A Task by Data Type Taxonomy for Information Visualizations*. VL '96 Proceedings of the 1996 IEEE Symposium on Visual Languages, 1996.

Snowden, Robert, Peter Thompson, and Tom Troscianko. *Basic Vision: An Introduction to Visual Perception*, 2nd ed. Oxford, UK: Oxford University Press, 2012.

Stone, Maureen. *A Field Guide to Digital Color*. Natick, MA: A K Peters, LTD, 2003.

Tufte, Edward. *Beautiful Evidence*. Cheshire, CT: Graphics Press, 2006.

Tufte, Edward. *Envisioning Information*. Cheshire, CT: Graphics Press, 1990.

Tufte, Edward. *The Visual Display of Quantitative Information*. Cheshire, CT: Graphics Press, 2001.

Tukey, John. *Exploratory Data Analysis*. Reading, MA: Addison-Wesley, 1977.

Ware, Colin. *Information Visualization: Perception for Design*. San Francisco, CA: Morgan Kaufman, 2004.

Ware, Colin. *Visual Thinking for Design*. Burlington, MA: Morgan Kaufman, 2008.

Index